THE LEGS MURDER SCANDAL

THE LEGS MURDER SCANDAL

...

HUNTER COLE

University Press of Mississippi / Jackson

www.upress.state.ms.us

The University Press of Mississippi is a member of
the Association of American University Presses.

Page ii: The Confederate monument,
north side of the Jones County courthouse, 1930s.
(Collection of Hunter Cole)

First printing 2010

∞

Library of Congress Cataloging-in-Publication Data

Cole, Hunter.
The legs murder scandal / Hunter Cole.
p. cm.
ISBN 978-1-60473-722-6 (cloth : alk. paper) —
ISBN 978-1-60473-723-3 (ebook : alk. paper) 1. Keeton,
Ouida, 1899–1973. 2. Carter, W. M. (William Madison),
d. 1949. 3. Murder—Mississippi—Laurel—Case studies.
4. Trials (Murder)—Mississippi—Case studies. I. Title.
HV6534.L38C65 2010
364.152'3092—dc22   2010003211

British Library Cataloging-in-Publication Data available

For Joan Husband Sentilles

Lizzie Borden with an ax
Gave her mother forty whacks.

The spirit of my mother seems to descend, and
smile upon me, and bid me live to enjoy the
life and reason which the Almighty has given
me—I shall see her again in heaven. She will then
understand me better.

—MARY LAMB

We are not safe. Terrible things can happen to
anybody.

—WILLIAM MAXWELL

Powers quite beyond our reach . . . may change in
a moment all the conditions of our life.

—J. H. THOM

THE LEGS MURDER SCANDAL

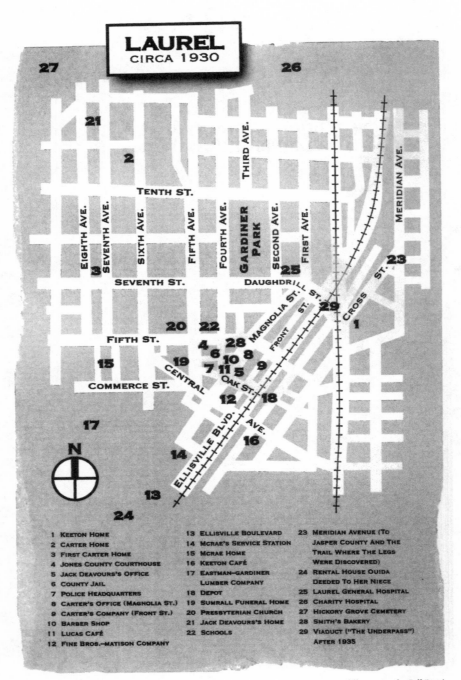

LAUREL
CIRCA 1930

27

26

21

2

THIRD AVE.

MERIDIAN AVE.

TENTH ST.

EIGHTH AVE.

SEVENTH AVE.

SIXTH AVE.

FIFTH AVE.

FOURTH AVE.

GARDINER PARK

SECOND AVE.

FIRST AVE.

3

25

SEVENTH ST.

DAUGHDRILL ST.

23

CROSS ST.

29

1

MAGNOLIA ST.

20   22

FIFTH ST.

4   28

6   10   8

FRONT ST.

19

15

7   11   5   9

CENTRAL

COMMERCE ST.

OAK ST.

12   18

17

16

N

14

13

24

1   KEETON HOME
2   CARTER HOME
3   FIRST CARTER HOME
4   JONES COUNTY COURTHOUSE
5   JACK DEAVOURS'S OFFICE
6   COUNTY JAIL
7   POLICE HEADQUARTERS
8   CARTER'S OFFICE (MAGNOLIA ST.)
9   CARTER'S COMPANY (FRONT ST.)
10 BARBER SHOP
11 LUCAS CAFÉ
12 FINE BROS.–MATISON COMPANY

13 ELLISVILLE BOULEVARD
14 MCRAE'S SERVICE STATION
15 MCRAE HOME
16 KEETON CAFÉ
17 EASTMAN–GARDINER LUMBER COMPANY
18 DEPOT
19 SUMRALL FUNERAL HOME
20 PRESBYTERIAN CHURCH
21 JACK DEAVOURS'S HOME
22 SCHOOLS

23 MERIDIAN AVENUE (TO JASPER COUNTY AND THE TRAIL WHERE THE LEGS WERE DISCOVERED)
24 RENTAL HOUSE OUIDA DEEDED TO HER NIECE
25 LAUREL GENERAL HOSPITAL
26 CHARITY HOSPITAL
27 HICKORY GROVE CEMETERY
28 SMITH'S BAKERY
29 VIADUCT ("THE UNDERPASS") AFTER 1935

(Illustration by Bill Pitts)

■ ■ ■

W ho now could make her out, this home-loving girl devoted to her vigilant mother? One was seldom seen without the other. Yet the daughter had secrets, and she carried them closely and never uttered a word about them.

The full moon of Saturday had begun its wane. On Monday night, howling winds diffused murky clouds of chimney smoke over the neighborhood and across the moon's beaming face, and before daybreak the frightening bluster was pounding on the windows and doors as though her mother were on the porch, demanding to be let in. The dying gusts blew up a misty rain.

Through the night she had no sleep.

She backed the car from the garage, headed toward the street, and then looked cautiously in both directions. As she left the driveway beside the hedge, the glow of headlights cut through raindrops and early-morning darkness. She was muffled in a mink jacket. Her bruised legs were bare and cold. Her soggy stockings she had stripped off and left wadded beside the bedroom chair.

An instant of trauma changed everything. Nothing thereafter could be the same. A seismic divide obstructed past from present. She was now on its new side. It would determine everything that was to come, even a lifetime.

Her nervous fingers gripped the steering wheel, and she headed north to the intersection where Cross Street merged with Meridian Avenue and Highway 11. There was little traffic at this hour, only an occasional car or truck coming south into Laurel. It was nearly eight o'clock in the morning, January 21, 1935, a day past the full moon. Most workers driving into town had passed along this route already.

Beside the driver lay a large bundle wrapped in white. It took up half of the front seat. Sheets of the *New York Times* had been placed over the upholstery and on the floor in case of leakage.

At the edge of town, as she approached the concrete bridge at Tallahala Creek, she slowed down. In the middle she stopped and gave darting glances before and behind. An urgent compulsion to be rid of the bundle made her pause. Below, the creek was swollen, a convenient place to drop it. Suddenly a car came into view, then another. She shifted the gear and headed on.

A few miles north of Laurel she considered a second stop. Over the black fenders of her maroon sedan she peered toward the trees with intense concentration. Quickly she turned at a lonely side road, and her eyes searched the scrappy woodland. She was looking for an old plum thicket she had visited with her mother. The amorphous load swaddled in scraps of one hundred–pound sugar sacks loomed large, about the size of a sleeping toddler. Though time was passing, the cloth remained unstained. There was no noticeable odor.

To her dismay, this slippery dirt lane was a wrong turn. It was a private road trailing closely past a farmhouse. When a man in overalls appeared on the porch and looked at the sky, apparently to assess the strange weather, she raised her shoulders to hide her face in her fur collar. For an instant their eyes locked. At the farmyard fence she backed the car around, quickly retraced her way, and sensed that the man was watching the taillights as far as the main road. She observed him in the rearview mirror. A woman had joined him. The driver felt the sting of rising fear that took her close to panic.

Her mother's family, the McKinstrys, once lived north of here, near old Corinth Church, and her grandparents and aunt were buried in the graveyard there. She pointed the car in that direction, not sure where to turn. She was so disoriented and drained that she was not thinking clearly. Between Sandersville and the road to Heidelberg she chose a little-used trail on the right. While chugging up the low rise, she realized she had taken another wrong turn. Was this the place she and her mother came to pick wild plums? It was hard to tell in winter. Most of the leaves had fallen and left only switches. It was a wagon road, only one lane.

Not far from the highway she eased the car to a stop, her eyes panning the landscape. Seeing no one near, she made her decision. She would leave it here. Her hands were icy.

She did not kill the engine, since she planned a quick disposal. With caution she opened the door and hurried around to the other side. Rain was more steady now, and the world was in full daylight. Anyone in a passing car or truck could see her. She was as nervous as in a nightmare, one in which she was dashing naked down Cross Street with the hope of getting safely through her bedroom window before anyone could see her. While opening the right-hand door as if to assist a passenger, she was enveloped in a fine rain that was turning into sleet. Her fur coat sparkled with tiny droplets catching the light.

It was not easy for a frail, exhausted woman to manage so hefty a load. An hour earlier, halfway across the backyard, she had dropped it in the dirt when struggling to reach the garage. She had looked up to see Clayton Therrell next door, waiting by the hedge for her husband to get the car out of their garage and take her to work. Clayton waved and asked if she was not chilly there in that sleeveless dress. Then, for some reason, Clayton asked if her mother was sick.

"Sick? No, Mother's not sick," was the reply.

Now, only half an hour later, she heaved the quivery load and staggered across the stubble. Her chronic backache was killing her. Wisps of wet broom sage caught her coattails and swept across the bruises on her legs. She squeezed her burden too tightly, and a dribble of juice trickled down her bluish shin, mixing with rainwater and splotching her suede shoes. She could go no farther. She set it down. If she had the strength, she could seclude it in the woods, but she feared that if she attempted to lift it again she would faint.

So she left it, exposed and starkly white against the sandy soil, and hurried toward the comforting purr of her automobile, and inside she felt safe. A thrill rushed over her when she had pulled the doors closed. The seat beside her was empty. She swiped the moist newspapers to the floor. And now the escape, and it would be finished. But she was wrong. Truly, it was only the beginning, for she had crossed to the other side of the divide.

She shifted the gear into reverse, intending to back around and head directly toward the highway. But the lane was too narrow, confined by winter sprigs scratching the doors and by young trees and underbrush attempting to make a thicket. She struggled to turn the steering wheel. For a moment there was an ominous sound, a scraping against the undercarriage. The car would not move. She tried again, gunning the accelerator and jerking her foot off the clutch. The sound stopped, but the car would not budge. Her hand trembled as she shifted. There was a grinding of gears. The back tires spun, but the car went nowhere.

The rain, steady now, blurred the view from the windshield. The car would not move. Through the wriggles of water flowing over the passenger's window, she could see the white bundle, saturated and mocking her. She tried to remain calm, but Ouida Keeton was a picture of panic.

At the best of times Ouida was praised for her appreciable charms. She had a curvaceous figure, deep-brown eyes, and bobbed brunette tresses that with secret applications from her dye bottle verged on black. She was among those special few who know the joy of being gazed upon and who understand the power of beauty. Her only physical flaws were a cicatrix from a childhood inoculation, which her sleeve covered, and nail-bitten fingers, which she redeemed with diamond-and-sapphire rings. Even though it was the Depression, Ouida had sufficient money for both necessities and extras—jewels, cosmetics, perfumes, frills, fashionable frocks, and such. Well into her thirties, she was not married, and many in Laurel wondered why such a pretty young woman remained single. For several years she held a good job working for a middle-age employer who took an unusual interest in her. Two years earlier she spent a few months in Washington, D.C., but returned home to her mother. Afterward, she became ill off and on.

Nearly everybody in Laurel knew the Keetons. They had been embroiled in lawsuits and trials that drew considerable notice. Daisy Keeton was perceived as rich and bossy. Of her four children, Ouida was the one she always could count on. The two shared an illusion of homey devotion. The others—a wild son, Earl, and two headstrong daughters, Maude and Eloise—were less bound to Daisy's needs and went their own ways.

In 1913, as a thirty-four-year-old widow, Sarah Daisy McKinstry Keeton had moved to Laurel with her children and her bulging bank account. Her late husband, high-tempered John Monroe Keeton, had owned a store and run a sawmill in the tiny town of McNeill, Mississippi, until he was killed in a railway accident. The details of his death were puzzling. For his widow, it was one of those fortuitous evils that strike when least expected. Because his life was so exceptionally well insured, some speculated that he had committed suicide, that he had thrown himself under the train. Indeed, his six policies indemnified him in the base amount of $30,000. On most he had paid only the first year's premium. Since some carried double indemnification, the full payout, by monetary standards of the late twentieth century, made his widow, at the age of twenty-nine, a millionaire. When one

Photo of Ouida Keeton circulated by
the Associated Press. (Permission of the
Laurel Leader-Call)

company refused to pay, Daisy sued. Establishing a pattern of tenacity, a
passion for money, and shrewd management that would continue throughout her life, she persisted aggressively through the courts until she received
every penny that was due her. In addition, she inherited her husband's business, his rental properties, their home, and land across the Pearl River, in
Louisiana. A portion of the insurance was allotted to each of her children,
with Daisy as trustee.

For six years after John's death she lingered in McNeill amid sad memories and tried to manage her four children, but in 1913 she counted her
money and moved on. Her children were ages sixteen, fourteen, eleven, and
seven. In Laurel, she bought a house at 539 Cross Street near the home of her
parents, George and Laura McKinstry, and the grandfather was named the
children's legal guardian. Before the move, Maude, the eldest, had been living with the McKinstrys and attending the Laurel schools. Two grown McK-
instry daughters, the children's aunts, lived with them as well. The home
of another of Daisy's sisters, Stella (Mrs. M. A. Sherrill), was close by. The
McKinstrys were considered clannish and odd.

By 1913 the Keetons' new hometown in Jones County, deep in the piney
woods of south Mississippi, was gaining a look of prosperity, a benefit of the
astoundingly rich traffic in yellow pine. The October 8 issue of the *Laurel
Daily Argus* optimistically claimed Laurel to be "probably the largest lumber

producing center in the world, and will certainly enjoy that distinction when another large mill is erected." Two major railroads served the town—the Gulf Mobile & Northern (GM&N) and the Illinois Central—and a spur line of the Gulf and Ship Island as well.

Established only thirty years earlier, Laurel had grown to a population of about thirteen thousand when the Keetons arrived. It was one of the fastest-growing towns in Mississippi, a state consisting mainly of small communities and farmsteads. The largest city, Meridian, in fact, had only twenty-three thousand people, and Jackson, the state capital, had fewer than twenty-one thousand. Close families, pleasant neighborhoods, and good schools made Laurel a felicitous place to bring up children. Unlike the older towns and those along the Mississippi River, Laurel had no entrenched antebellum tradition of old families, old money, and faded grandeur for newcomers to contend with. Nor was it like the towns in the Delta, the other developing region of the state, where large landowners were re-creating Old South cotton-plantation ways. Laurel was New South. Jones County had a history of backwoods lawlessness, but its new county seat embraced a more civilized culture. Many of its settlers were wealthy lumber families from the North. They brought a sophistication and outlook that was unusual in post-Reconstruction Mississippi, and they generously used their wealth to benefit the town.

Prospects for downtown construction were bright. A new Methodist church graced Fifth Avenue, and plans were under way for a new city hall, a fire station, an opera house, a Young Men's Christian Association (YMCA), new downtown office buildings, and the $80,000 Pinehurst Hotel, to be erected on one of the most valuable and beautiful lots in the city. Heralded as the best of all the improvements of the past year were the streetcar system and the interurban line between Laurel and Ellisville, the two courthouse towns of Jones County. Laurel was no cosmopolitan city like New Orleans. Neither was it a backwoods village when Daisy and the children moved into their new home.

Daisy Keeton's residence on Cross Street was ideal for a household compressed by motherly control. It was a conventional middle-class dwelling with a nice front porch, big rooms, young oaks at the curb, and a location with easy access to downtown. Set on the hillside curve just beyond the railroad tracks, it faced southwest. The road passing in front took traffic north to Meridian and south to Hattiesburg and New Orleans. Though only a city block from the tracks, the neighborhood was honorable, and Daisy, rich and respectable, could easily afford to buy property there.

One of the givens of living close to the railroad was the harmonizing of the human life cycle with the rail traffic's tick-tock regularity. Meals, meetings, bedtimes, risings, and even deaths were synchronized with the passing of trains. Most residents became inured to the billowing soot, the clicking of iron wheels on iron rails, and the hooting whistles. There was no need to consult the mantel clock to know the hour was after midnight. The roar of the GM&N served as a reliable chronometer, and, from the 1920s, its companion in the heart of Laurel, a cast-iron sentinel that hung on the southwestern corner of Commercial Bank, rang quarter hours. Its four moon faces and Gothic numerals beamed up to office windows and down to passersby. On a still day the sweet tones of its Westminster chimes wafted in many directions, all the way to a Cross Street porch, where a mother and a daughter sat side by side in their rockers.

Ouida, whose real name was Juanita, was Daisy's second child, born on March 26, 1899. The year, however, remains in dispute, for Keeton women fibbed about their ages, and there were no official birth certificates in Mississippi until 1912. Maude was the eldest, born in 1897, and the third child, Earl Cotton Keeton, who assumed the name of John Earl after his little brother John died, was born in 1902. From adolescence Earl was a hothead, a rakehell always deep in trouble or chicanery. Eloise was the youngest, born around the time of her father's death.

The Keeton children were strikingly handsome. Depending on how one considers their fates, Ouida and Eloise were blessed, or cursed, with beauty. Eloise was a naughty girl after a good time, but the home-loving Ouida was inordinately shy, reclusive, and afraid of the dark. Rather than enjoying play with other children, she fled to her mother for fellowship. From early childhood she engaged in fearful temper tantrums and long spells of pouting. She took sides with her brother and with Eloise rather than with Maud.

At twenty, in 1917, Maude married David F. McRae before he left to serve in World War I and thereby removed herself from her mother's control. After he was discharged, they bought a bungalow on Short Seventh Avenue, across town from Daisy and almost next door to David's widowed mother and her houseful of unmarried children. He worked as a timekeeper at Eastman-Gardiner Lumber Company, the sprawling giant among Laurel's sawmills, and operated a shoe-repair shop and a gas station. Maude and David's only child, Maude Louise, was a student at Laurel High School during the 1930s and a favorite of her aunt Ouida. A family tiff kept Maude and her mother apart, but Ouida was not drawn into the squabble. Keeping their distances, mother and daughter held to an edgy truce. From 1932 to 1935 Maude and David did not enter her house.

Daisy Keeton's maternal chord was so firmly tied to Ouida, however, that the mother trailed after her wherever Ouida might go. Cammie Cook, the observant widow next door, surmised that years of love and devotion were reflected in the relationship. Ouida and Daisy spent long hours together rocking on the porch. In summer the two drove up to Jasper County to pick plums along old trails near Daisy's girlhood home. They prowled the Mc-Kinstry graveyard, reminiscing about deceased kin. They admired each other's handsome wardrobes. "Mother was beautiful in gray," Ouida would recall. They took trips together, three times to Hot Springs for treatments at the spas. Ouida needed a masseuse's attention for an obstinate back problem. In 1932 they made plans for a joint business venture.

This mother-daughter bond developed in Ouida's early childhood and before the Keetons moved to Laurel. In McNeill, Ouida had taken a hard fall that injured her spine, and the accident made her dreamy and sensitive. A bout with the mumps cost her most of the hearing in one ear, and as she was nursed and petted, possibly she lost one or two years of school. As Daisy babied her and showered her with attention, the two became ever more inseparable.

When the Keetons moved to Laurel and the children enrolled in school, Ouida, about fourteen, registered as being eleven or twelve because she was behind in her regular class. Shaving off a few years during the painful time of adolescence would make Ouida feel more comfortable among younger students and give her an advantage in Laurel classrooms, where standards were higher than in the county. All the Keeton children survived the Spanish flu in 1918, and Ouida sailed through school without missing a grade, graduating at midyear 1920 with grades ranging from 77 to 86. Her social life, however, was undeveloped. She was bashful, quiet, aloof, emitting mystery and keeping her distance from boys. Though she was a beautiful girl, she did not date or attend parties. Instead, she retreated to her mother.

After graduating, Ouida enrolled for just over three months of study at Soule Business College in New Orleans. It was advertised in the Laurel newspaper as "the South's Greatest School of Business . . . recognized everywhere as Wide Awake, Practical, Popular, and Successful." Daisy's sister Paula was living in New Orleans at the time, and a direct train from Laurel made for easy visits.

After finishing her business courses, Ouida hoped by midsummer to find a job in Laurel so that she could be near her mother. Since Daisy Keeton's assets gave them comparative ease, the loyal daughter could have remained idle at home. As a mama's girl, Ouida seemed destined to be Daisy's lifelong companion.

One of Ouida's letters of job application altered her fate. It went to the owner of the W. M. Carter Lumber Company, one of Laurel's many sawmills, and prosperous W. M. Carter, a civic-minded, churchgoing businessman, considered her for employment. He asked his son-in-law, P. H. Decker, then principal of the high school, to give his evaluation. Decker recommended Ouida, and Carter hired her as his secretary. His offices in the Carter Building on North Magnolia were near the mainstream of downtown commerce and a few streets west of the Keeton residence. Instead of having to take a streetcar to work, Ouida could walk up the hill just as she had walked to the high school. Her new boss, having passed fifty, had not lost his manly vim. Soon the plump and pretty Ouida Keeton proved herself to be not only a willing workhorse but also an eye-catching ornament.

When Carter moved his business a block east, to Front Street, Ouida was even closer to home. If the double railroad trestles had not been so high, the Keeton house on the rise would have been visible from an upstairs window in the rear of Carter's new building. It was so close that each day Ouida walked the few blocks to have lunch with her mother.

W. M. Carter had gentlemanly manners and a businesslike command of thorny exchanges. He appreciated the genteel traits in his young secretary. She spoke articulately, and except in rattling moments when she was stricken by great stress, she was impressively ladylike. Rising from secretary to confidential secretary and office manager, she administered collections and demonstrated a natural aptitude for business. With professional dignity she met the customers, kept the company books, engaged in sales, and coordinated the activities of the office. Carter's son Newton served as his young partner, but the father began to rely more and more upon Ouida. She was so charming, endearing, and physically appealing that Carter protected his interest in her, warding off any other male's advances.

Her efficiency nonetheless gained the notice of other businessmen. Impressed by her aplomb and ability, Dr. R. H. Cranford, chief physician of Laurel General Hospital, attempted to lure her away to run his business office, but Carter countered and raised her salary. She would remain with him for twelve years.

Besotted with her youth and beauty, he complimented her with many little attentions and inviting smiles, and Ouida blossomed under his special treatment. Enveloping himself in the Keetons, he found any pretext to be around the entrancing creature throughout the workday and in the evenings. For privacy, he had the window of his office door painted opaque white. After rising from the supper table, he sometimes left his wife and children and began a habit of dropping by the Keeton home. It was not uncommon in a small town for thoughtful married gentlemen to keep watch on women who lived alone and to offer assistance. Carter did not perceive the dire consequences of his stepping into this circle of fire, and on several evenings each month he appeared at Daisy Keeton's threshold in a nice and friendly way. His car would pull up to the curb, and he would hurry to the porch and give a tap at the front door. Ouida, as though expecting him, would delight him with an invitation to come in. Daisy Keeton, always the reigning presence in her home, rose to greet him.

These ingratiating social calls fell into routine. After Carter began advising the rich widow on property, investments, and bonds, Daisy invited him to join them in her bedroom so that the three could warm themselves before the fire and converse more intimately. Their association ripened into friendship. Absorbing the overdone splendor of her decor, Carter felt free to stretch his legs, rest his feet on a small rug, and exude fiscal know-how. Feeling mellow and welcome, he would cast fresh wood on the grate when the fire died down.

Sometimes they discussed the news, sometimes their families, and sometimes Daisy's investments. A recurring theme of their talks was Ouida's devotion to home. Carter made light of it, but he perceived the smothering restraint with which Daisy held her child. Though most young women of Ouida's age had broken free of maternal watch, the matriarchal Daisy Keeton's penetrating gaze missed little. She was displeased when Carter suggested that Ouida should be independent. Spreading her bonds and bank statements for him to examine, she changed the subject to finance. Whenever Daisy had spare money to invest, she solicited his astute advice.

Whatever the subject of conversation, Carter was ever aware of the lovely Ouida—the way her voluptuous body curled into her armchair, the allure of her downcast eyes reflecting the dancing flames, and her seductive glances at him as her mother babbled on and on. In these circumstances it was a challenge for Carter to be amiable, and the moment that Daisy swept away for sweets and brandy, he would sneak a touch or a kiss. If the flighty Eloise or one of Daisy's sisters from across the street fluttered through the room, their intrusion ruffled the instant of ease. When the hour grew late, the gracious guest went home to his family, ecstatic with anticipation of future encounters.

In the next stage of romancing Ouida, Carter began dropping secret notes on Daisy Keeton's living-room sofa. The billet-doux was ready in his pocket as Ouida welcomed him. She would see it flutter to the cushion and be tucked away for later. They did not dally but went directly to Daisy's room and settled yet again into the routine of after-supper chat and cookies. Through the evening Carter's thoughts were neither on Daisy's finances nor on her palaver. They flickered on Ouida and on the delight his notes would bring as she read each adoring word later in bed. Desire made him as foolish as a smitten schoolboy. When Ouida was seeing him to the door, she would retrieve the latest of his love-struck expressions, according to their plan.

For Ouida, it was first love, and she did nothing to thwart Carter's florid expressions. She told her mother nothing about his attentions. Carter grew blind to the real risks, and in this romance he was also very foolish. In a later year, his words of endearment would be haunting, ludicrous, and shaming.

Presently his fingers ventured to give Ouida a chuck that brought a dimple to her pretty chin. His touches advanced to a quick goodnight kiss at the door and in due time a fondle. Once or twice he claimed to have forgotten his hat and returned to retrieve it and gain a second kiss. Whispering goodnight, with just the screened door between them, they looked like conspirators. Afterward, Ouida would switch on the porch light so that Carter could see his way down the front steps without stumbling over one of her mother's potted ferns.

It was the age-old farce about the married boss canoodling with his pretty secretary under everybody's noses but behind everybody's backs. In the embarrassing denouement the frisky couple always gets exposed in flagrante delicto.

The neighbors on Cross and Daughdrill streets noticed Carter's comings and goings. They knew that he visited the Keetons regularly but that his car never remained past a respectable hour. A few times he brought his wife along for the evening visits. He did so presumably to ward off suspicion and gossip. Also, he called on the Cook family next door. Phil Cook, a carpenter, was terminally ill, and his widow, Cammie, would recall Carter's kindness in looking in on her husband.

Mrs. Keeton, Ouida, and the sweet-talking boss with adulterous cravings passed many pleasant evenings chatting before the cozy embers in Daisy's room. It was a curious trio—a senescent, lovesick man; an imperious widow; and a coy beauty not averse to the overtures of a married man more than thirty years older than she. He brought them ice cream, sweetmeats, and surprises. Perhaps at first Daisy thought his interest was in her. She was on the heavy side, with graying hair and modish dresses. But in the presence of this handsome man, only twelve years older than she, she prattled and sashayed flirtatiously as the perfect hostess. Like many widows dreaming of recovering lost hopes, surely Daisy looked forward to his calls, although she knew very well that he was prominently married. So she regarded him as a devoted family friend and counselor. In the Keeton family debacles Earl and Eloise touched off during the 1920s, Carter was indispensable. Along with David McRae, he was Daisy's anchor and a mainstay, but his ulterior motive for helping Daisy is easy to deduce.

Earl Keeton was a heavy drinker who often brought his mother grief. From the late 1920s he was employed as a baker at Smith's Bakery. In 1930 he and his young wife, the former Jewel Anderson, and their little daughter were living in a rented apartment at the intersection of Daughdrill and Cross streets, his mother's and his grandparents' neighborhood.

In 1921, at the age of nineteen, Earl had his first serious brush with the law. One morning he was hanging around the tables in a downtown pool hall with Eugene Evans, a swaggering tough, also nineteen. Evans had been sentenced to the state penitentiary after a conviction of car robbery, but because of his youth, he had been released early. Burns Deavours, a prominent young attorney and the father of two children, had argued with Evans a few days earlier, and he summoned Evans to come outside for a confrontation. As Evans laid down his pool cue, Earl foolishly joked that Deavours was about to be killed. Evans was carrying a pistol. They rushed outside, and Evans shot Deavours in the head. He died three hours later. Earl was charged with being an accessory to murder. With Evans, he was hauled into Jones County court to be indicted. To his mother's relief, the nasty case against him fell apart, and he was never prosecuted.

When this happened, Ouida had been working for Carter for no more than six months. Earl's notorious deportment drove her into retreat. She shied away from the public and stayed close to her mother. With conduct that ranged from horseplay and waggery to deviltry and crime, Earl was daring and reckless, an uncontrollable bad boy blessed with good looks and good fortune. His long streak of luck would not run out until 1941.

In 1922 Earl's misconduct took him back to the courtroom. He and two pals, Lafayette Holifield and Will Davis, enticed a divorced cotton-mill worker into their car. They claimed she was a known prostitute. After they drove to a back road south of Laurel, two held her down as each raped her in turn, threatening her if she told on them. As they were driving her back to town, she cried out to a passerby for help and later charged them with rape. Earl and his two friends were arrested and jailed.

For two days as news spread, a tumultuous lynch mob threatened to drag the accused men from jail. The mixed population of Laurel comprised elites, good country people, farsighted businessmen, and ragtags from the mills and scrappy farms. Such occasional mobbings of the jail had given Jones County a regrettable notoriety. On the front steps of the courthouse, Ouida's boss was among the prominent citizens appealing to the angry rabble for calm as the accused men were sneaked away to safety. By the time the riffraff broke down the jailhouse doors, the three had been incarcerated elsewhere.

They were indicted a week later. In the malignant atmosphere, their attorneys petitioned for a change of venue, claiming the impossibility of seating an unbiased jury and holding a fair trial in Jones County. The motion was denied, and Earl and the others were tried in Laurel, convicted, and sentenced to life imprisonment. On appeal their convictions were reversed and remanded. The appeal judges ruled that the lower court had erred in not allowing a change of venue. The victim did not renew her suit, and there was no retrial. For a second time Earl was exonerated by blessed good luck.

While the family was in such a spotlight, the shy Ouida, age twenty-three or so, again retreated to her mother. Her embarrassment was so keen that she withdrew within herself and again refused invitations to parties. In an outburst of narcissism she focused on her appearance and began passing hours before her mirror, painting her lips and arranging her hair. Her aunts joked about her primping, perhaps hoping to provoke Ouida into being more sociable.

Earl was not the only Keeton to cast shame upon the family. His youngest sister, Eloise, the family coquette, did her part as well in making them uncomfortably notable. When Eloise was thirteen, Daisy petitioned the court to remove her daughter's status as a minor. The motive remains a mystery. The court acceded and granted Eloise full access to her inheritance and the right to make all decisions concerning her life. In 1925 this callow girl asserted her independence and eloped with Rayburn Robinson, a Chicago man she had met at a street show. When Daisy found out, she was distraught. No matter that her daughter had been granted the rights of an adult, the irate mother demanded her return. Again, Carter and her son-in-law David McRae answered Daisy's plea, and from their investigation she learned that the couple had been married in nearby Ellisville and had left immediately on a train for Chicago via Birmingham and Chattanooga. Daisy solicited Police Chief Jim Brown's help, and Brown notified lawmen in both cities and authorized them to intercept the runaways. Robinson had signed his name on the marriage application (September 28, 1925), testifying "that the parties applying for license to marry [had] arrived at the statutory ages prescribed by law, 21 and 18 years, respectively, and that there [was] no legal cause to obstruct the marriage." Unless the bride was a posthumous child, she had been born before her father's death in 1907, making her at least eighteen in 1925. Yet the sheriff demanded Robinson's arrest for perjury, claiming he had eloped with a girl who officially was underage.

Just before midnight Daisy learned that the Chattanooga police had apprehended the newlyweds. She caught the next train, and when she arrived the following day, she rushed to police headquarters and confronted Robinson and Eloise, berating the bridegroom for abducting her precious daughter, for his duplicity in courting her, and for never once having had the decency to come to their home. Then Daisy conferred privately with her hysterical daughter and, overwhelming her with the force of her maternal power, persuaded her to return home. After they had boarded the train, the police released the angry husband from custody. Robinson went on to Chicago, and mother and daughter hastened to Laurel to arrange an annulment.

But the calm was transitory. In less than a week an enraged Robinson returned to Laurel and claimed a right to see his wife. When he was rebuffed, he instituted habeas corpus proceedings to possess her and then legal action for alienation of affection. To their astonishment, Robinson not only sued Daisy but also all who had assisted her—Earl, Ouida, the McRaes, and Carter.

In the November 1925 term of the Jones County circuit court the case was brought before a jury. Robinson asked $100,000 in damages. With this news Daisy fell ill and petitioned for a continuance. The court refused, and the trial proceeded on schedule. In disbelief the defendants received the verdict. Though the jury sided for Ouida, Carter, and Maude McRae, they upheld Robinson's charge against Daisy, Earl, and David McRae and awarded Robinson the sum of $9,500. The firm of Welch & Cooper, attorneys for the defense, petitioned for retrial, and when their motion was denied, there was an appeal. In the interim Robinson filed writs of garnishment on Laurel's two banks, where Daisy maintained accounts; on Eastman-Gardiner Lumber Company (David McRae's employer); and on Pollman's [Smith's] Bakery (Earl's employer).

A year of anxiety passed, and when the appeal court announced its decision, it was a mixed blessing. It held that Robinson was not entitled to any judgment and annulled the $9,500 award. This was welcome news, but not for Daisy. The court announced further that only she should have been charged in Robinson's suit and that her action against him was taken not in malice but in maternal love for the safety of her young daughter. Removing all except Daisy from prosecution, the court remanded the case to Jones County for possible retrial. A statute of limitations awarded Robinson seven years to renew his suit. Although Ouida, Maude, and Carter had been exonerated, Robinson's garnishment of David McRae's wages continued. Robinson had named Eastman-Gardiner, McRae's employer, as garnishee and "debtor" in the amount of $546. The firm's denial of any indebtedness was the basis of an appeal arguing that since the case against McRae in the alienation-of-affection suit had been nullified, this suit had no merit.

The appeals court sided with Eastman-Gardiner and reversed the judgment. The decision was a triumph, but in deepest anxiety Daisy awaited Rayburn Robinson's next move. His loss of both his lawsuits could fuel his aggression against her. Could she endure the emotionally punishing suspense of seven years?

With a bossy, money-mad matron; an audacious teenager; a Yankee outsider; a rapist son; a beautiful, unmarried sister; a wary brother-in-law; and a family friend with an eye for the family beauty, this rocky escapade of flight, recovery, and lawsuits includes madcap scenes and sharply drawn characters that are stock material for comedy or melodrama. However, the case had more sobering and long-lasting effects. Eloise's foolish marriage and its repercussions can be regarded as the real turning point in the Keeton family story. The outcome of the lawsuit struck Daisy at her most vulnerable point. Her cash, her bonds, her property—all were in perilous balance. What must she do? For the answer, perhaps she relied on the advice of W. M. Carter, perhaps on her lawyers Welch & Cooper, or perhaps even Ouida. Daisy's obsession with wealth and her ploy for protecting it would explode in doom and tragedy.

■ ■ ■

Frantic, Ouida shifted into reverse again and floored the accelerator. The back tires continued to spin. She tried again and again, but the car stalled and did not move, like a chase in a nightmare. On the verge of hysteria, she got out and made an inspection. The wheels were sunk in soft mire. A small pine tree was bent beneath the back bumper, preventing the car from moving forward or backward. If she continued the struggle, the wheels would sink deeper. The rain was pelting the car with a steady patter. Her clothes were clinging to her body, and she pulled the collar of the fur coat over her wet hair for protection. Thoroughly drenched, she was so near exhaustion that she relied on her feet for a decision. They tramped down the trail to the gravel highway and took her south, back toward home.

She may have walked as far as half a mile when a car approached. She waved her arms, and it stopped. The smiling driver leaned over and rolled the glass down.

"What in the world are you doing out on a day like this, lady!" he exclaimed, cracking the mood in a joking way.

Through her daze she answered.

"My car got stuck back there," she said, pointing. She found her voice. It sounded high, like a child's speaking in apology. With a shiver she got inside.

He introduced himself as W. E. Kennedy. Since an explanation seemed expected, she told him a lie about how she came to be rambling down the highway.

"I drove out this way to pick up an old woman to stay with me while my mother's out of town, and my car got stuck."

She asked if he would be passing through Sandersville so that she could get help. She knew she must hurry, for her car could be examined, and anybody with the least bit of curiosity could spot the bundle.

Kennedy nodded as though her story was plausible. He said he was heading to Jackson, and Sandersville was on the way.

The Keeton home at 539 Cross Street. (Permission of the *Laurel Leader-Call*)

As they approached the town, she asked if he would be passing through Laurel. If so, he could drop her there instead. She kept her face turned away and her soaked collar pushed up around her ears. She was so sopping wet that he could not tell whether she was pretty or not. They were silent most of the way. From the highway they moved over the smooth concrete bridge and approached Laurel. As Meridian Avenue became Cross Street, Ouida took note of her two aunts' house on the far right-hand side. On the left and at the end of the street she noted her mother's brown house. They splashed through the wet thoroughfare full of traffic, for Laurel had come to life.

"You can let me out at the Lorimar gas station on the corner. I can get home from there."

The station was across from where she lived, but she did not tell the driver.

The rain was falling when Kennedy's car pulled to a stop. He said he was sorry she would get drenched again. She muttered her thank-you and waved good-bye, then waited until he had passed the new road construction site, turning right at Daughdrill, and jouncing over the railroad tracks. If he was going to Jackson, she knew the route he would take. At the station, Mr. Sims, the owner, was inside. There was no business yet.

She darted across the rain-pattered pavement, over the curb, and to the shelter of the front porch. In summer, shaded by the oaks out front, this was where she and her mother sat in the late afternoon, seeing and being seen. Two empty rocking chairs had been pushed to the side in winter. She stamped her wet feet on the mat so that she wouldn't track up her mother's floors. Then she shook the raindrops from her coat and turned to face whatever awaited inside.

Her mother hated to be alone.

Sensing a creeping dread, she turned the brass doorknob. The day that began unseasonably mild with windy skies now promised a long, cold night that would allow her no time for sleep. It was the kind of weather that foreboded sickness. As the door swung open, she felt the reign of quietness. The plush sofa, the formal chairs, the cherished bric-a-brac placed about the tables and on the mantelpiece, the Heatrola heating unit, the gorgeous draperies—all were familiar yet alien, too. A hanging pungency of ashes made her nostrils flare. But she could not dwell on odors now. She must recover her car. It must not be found. Besides, there was even more to be done.

The house was in disorder, and her mother's sisters could come in without notice, and Earl lived nearby. However, her sister Maude would not intrude. Their mother's long-lingering fuss with her would prevent that.

Despite being wet and exhausted, she did not rest or dawdle but went directly to the telephone. This time there was no sound of her mother's footsteps trailing behind her, no imperious voice giving orders. Dripping a pool of rainwater on the polished floor, she told the operator the number of her mechanic, and when friendly W. P. Duckworth, easily charmed, came on the line, she explained her problem. It was urgent. She told him to please come quickly and take her north of Sandersville and pull her stalled car out of a muddy rut.

Before he arrived, she made her plans and decided what else she could tell him. She flitted to her bedroom, took a towel to her wet hair, and gave her locks a few strokes with a hairbrush, patting moist waves into place around her ears. All the while, she was focusing her thoughts on the story she would tell. Since the mirror revealed that she looked a fright, she powdered her nose and covered her mouth with lipstick. As she whisked away some of the moisture from her fur coat and hung it up to dry, she decided she wouldn't stay at home for the next few nights but would sleep over at her aunts'. They wouldn't want her to be alone in an empty house if her mother was away in New Orleans.

Hurrying, she grabbed her silvery raincoat from the chifforobe, thrust her arms into the sleeves, and went to the front porch to wait.

W. P. Duckworth arrived by 9:30. He stopped at the curb under the oaks and honked loudly.

She was astonished that he had arrived in a wrecker. Its high crane looked like a gallows, with a rusty hook instead of a noose. It must be attracting everyone's notice. She rushed out into the rain, her purse held over her hair. When he leaned toward her and opened the door, she wondered why he had not come in a pickup. She had never ridden in a tow truck, and as she strained to put her foot on the high running board and heave herself onto the seat, she realized how spent she was.

They headed north along the very same route she had taken earlier. On the outskirts of Laurel they passed over the concrete bridge. Rain was falling on the water.

"My car stalled while I was out in the country picking up a woman who was to stay with me while my mother is in New Orleans."

Duckworth later would recall she didn't say much else.

It was getting close to ten.

She pointed to the side road. Her car was still parked there, apparently unmolested. It looked shiny in the dismal rain. She took a mental picture of the setting—a maroon Willis Knight sedan with a metal trunk rack on the rear, parked off on the edge of a little trail. It was wedged against two little sticks of plum bushes and a pine sapling.

Duckworth figured he simply would drive the car up a piece and turn around on the high place, but she sternly objected and ordered him to connect the hook of his wrecker to the bumper and pull the car backward toward the highway. He preferred to do things his way, and as he inspected the rut, he remarked that the tire was not sunk deeply. She could have extracted the car herself. Awake to the consequences if he spotted the gleaming white bundle, she refused to let him drive the car forward and then back it into the thicket.

So he did expressly as instructed. In no time at all her car was parked beside the highway. When he stepped out of the wrecker to see if all was OK, she asked how much she owed him, and she paid him then and there. She took her seat at the wheel and drove directly home to begin cleaning the house.

The gloomy Monday morning progressed rapidly into afternoon. To some dilatory salesclerk a few blocks away from Cross Street the town clock may have seemed to lag, but in the house on the knoll the hours vanished as though blown away by a heavy wind. A frantic figure moved from room to room, cleaning the house. Meanwhile, stinking smoke rising from the brick chimney dipped and dissipated in the soft drizzle.

■　■　■

In 1931 five years had passed since the appeals court's decision, and Rayburn Robinson had not renewed his lawsuit. In the meantime Daisy had taken several precautions against any threat. However, her solution for protecting her assets would bring unanticipated turmoil.

The 1930 federal census of Laurel presented a striking revelation at the listing of 539 Cross Street. The head of household was enumerated as Ouida Keeton, not Daisy Keeton. The mother had divested herself of her wealth, and Ouida was now the homeowner, not Maude, not Earl, not Eloise, but Ouida, the good child. The others were disloyal or unstable. On November 25, 1925, Daisy had transferred the Cross Street deed to Ouida, and, as would be tirelessly reported, legally explored, and publicly discussed ten years later, she had warded off the threat of Rayburn Robinson's litigation by shielding her money from him. She put all her cash, investments, and property in Ouida's name. If Robinson should renew and win his lawsuit, Daisy would have no discernible assets for him to tap. All was entrusted to Ouida, and legally for seven years everything Daisy owned was in Ouida's trust. If the mother so much as offered money to Earl or Eloise during this period, she had to defer to her empowered daughter for funds. Robinson's statute of limitations would expire in 1932.

When the years clicked past the deadline and he had made no threatening move, Daisy was freed from her onerous worry. However, three years later, 1935, Ouida still maintained her hold on her mother's estate. Daisy, fifty-six, was ready to reclaim and control it. She told Ouida the time had come for the transfer.

What was the extent of this fortune in the depths of the Depression? The census states the approximate value of the Keeton house to be $3,000, a figure that is appropriate according to this time and in the Cross Street neighborhood. The appraised amount of other Keeton assets is not known, but cash in Ouida's bank accounts totaled some $20,000. Gossips speculated that Daisy, whose fancy home furnishings imparted an aura of luxury, was a woman of large wealth. Sparkling diamonds adorned her fingers, and she wore pretty clothes and carried herself haughtily with an air of prosperity.

She was a stylish stout of about 180 pounds, big-hipped, and of imposing height at five feet eight inches. Tittle-tattlers broadcast the word that with Carter coaching her, she had made a killing when selling the government a parcel of her Cross Street land for the construction of the viaduct to be dug beneath the railroad tracks. A rental house she owned just south of hers had been demolished to make way for the road expansion reconfiguring the intersection of Cross and Daughdrill streets.

Although a mama's girl, Ouida was neither a freeloader nor a drudge. Besides the windfall of her mother's assets, she had rental property and income of her own, as well as what remained in the legacy from her father. Even though these were the Depression years, it was reported that she never dipped heavily into her savings and was stingy about dispensing moneys from her mother's accounts. She was seen wearing a diamond brooch set in platinum, her so-called thousand-dollar pin. She enjoyed her rings studded with diamonds and sapphires, and she owned stylish frocks, the mink coat, and the rather new Willis Knight sedan. If money equaled social superiority, the Keeton women were financial stand-outs amid their neighbors—a carpenter, a locomotive engineer, a garage mechanic, a lumberyard laborer, a construction foreman, a railroad flagman, a laborer in a wagon factory, a lineman, a telephone operator, a sales clerk, and a schoolteacher.

In the 1930 census Ouida's age is listed as twenty-four, which, by a reliable estimate, is seven years under the true mark. Her occupation is stated as "office manager, lumber office." Reflecting Daisy's demotion in proprietary status is her enumeration as "mother" and "widow." She seems in this dry report to be a mere dependent rather than the breadwinner. Her listed age, fifty-one, is close to the target. Two others are residing with Ouida and Daisy: Eloise Daniels ("sister"), and James B. Daniels ("brother-in-law"), age twenty-five and a "machinist in a machine shop." Eloise had recovered from the debacle of her flawed elopement and married again. The marriage would be the second in Eloise's rich matrimonial history. Surrounded by the demanding, strong-willed Keeton women, James Daniels no doubt felt trapped. With this stranger in their midst, the household routine was disrupted. Ouida, always moody, kept her thoughts private and retreated to her room. Eloise was her opposite—high-spirited, difficult to manage, and disposed at will to give vent to her passionate tempers. Her marriage was not a happy one, and it quickly ended. By 1935 Eloise was living in New Orleans.

Earl and his wife, Jewel, were renting a house on First Avenue. Earl, like Ouida and Eloise, seldom resided far from his mother's beck and call.

Intelligent and quick, Earl set few if any goals to advance himself. His bad reputation hung over him, but he held on to his job at the bakery. He lived hard from paycheck to paycheck and found wild pleasure in a honky-tonk life. Carter considered him to be fearsomely dangerous.

In 1932, when the Depression battered Carter's firm and Ouida left his employ, it was the first time since graduation from Soule's that she was jobless. She was past thirty and verging on the unfortunate status of "old maid." She had begun to show pronounced idiosyncrasies. She occasionally lost her cool reserve and prattled aimlessly. Her intrusive aunts continued to comment on her primping. They were aghast at her impractical purchases, such as baby clothes. They remarked that her face was hardened by a fixated stare. These, her mother surmised, were not exclusively the symptoms of advancing spinsterhood but were also signs of the unhappiness and dejection that take over when one loses one's job. There were no desirable openings for Ouida in Laurel.

When Daisy suggested that they explore the idea of renting or purchasing a hotel they could operate together, Ouida agreed, and they took the train to New Orleans, consulted a real-estate agent, and found the prospects in New Orleans promising. Realizing they needed professional training to undertake so risky a venture, they decided on a management course in Washington, D.C. Daisy was possessive of her daughter and disliked being at home alone at night, yet she agreed that Ouida should enroll. While she was away, Daisy would remain in Laurel, relying on her sisters across the street, her two daughters, and a fierce backyard dog to protect her. She asked Earl and his wife to move in with her.

Ouida completed the registration forms by mail. Daisy and Eloise put her on the train, waved good-bye, and began counting the days till she would come home for Christmas vacation.

When she had completed her course and had returned to Cross Street, she made a startling announcement. She was engaged. The prospective bridegroom was a stranger she had met in Washington. Since no wedding date was set, she would remain in Laurel until plans were made final. Still she had no secure job, but in the interim she found stenographic work at the Railway Express office.

A whole year passed, and in 1934 she and Eloise, divorced from James Daniels, took a getaway trip to Washington. Since Eloise had made plans to enroll in a business course in New Orleans, she limited her vacation to two weeks, and in August Ouida sent her back to Laurel alone and extended her own stay in the capital. By September Daisy summoned her home.

Ouida confided little information about her future husband, moped in her room, and had no appetite. Nearly everyone was dispirited. Neither Ouida nor Eloise had jobs, and the country was sinking deeper into economic chaos.

After Eloise had departed for New Orleans, Daisy and Ouida were the sole occupants at 539 Cross Street. Back under Daisy's roof Ouida was irritable, bored, and ill. To help her escape her doldrums, her imperturbable brother-in-law, the peacemaker, hired her part-time as cashier at his filling station. She was employed there at the time Daisy Keeton vanished.

■　■　■

Ouida's mysterious bundle lay in the rain for no more than four hours. Around noon, during a lull between showers and just before a cold front caused the temperature to plummet well below the norm, two dogs belonging to Dan Evans Jr., a black farmer hunting rabbits, came upon it.

Evans shushed their howls and drove them back so that he could take a look. After resting his shotgun, he picked up a stick and warily lifted the edge of the wet rags, then shrank back in revulsion and fear. His startled eyes saw fresh meat, but it was neither beef nor pork. It was pale flesh and a pudendum, pieces of a white woman.

Frightened, he replaced the cloth and fled home. He told his wife and brother of his discovery and then summoned a white man, who notified the constable. Deputy Sheriff G. E. Cook of Heidelberg, Laurel Chief of Police J. E. (Jim) Brown, and Jones County Chief Deputy Sheriff J. C. Hamilton were called to conduct the investigation until the arrival of J. C. Bassett, sheriff of Jasper County, in whose jurisdiction the body parts had been found.

As the temperature plunged during the afternoon, law officers, led by Sheriff Bassett, staked out the crime scene, and the lonely trail teemed with life as never before. In the weeds searchers found paper litter and a ragged scrap of female underwear. Also picked up was a magazine subscription form torn from a salesman's tablet. Both items seemed possible clues.

The men summoned as a coroner's jury shivered in the biting cold as they hunched around the bundle for three hours and eyed each and every part. E. S. Conliff of Laurel would recall his experience of examining the grisly pieces of flesh and bone.

> Well, I looked at them and seen what was there. They were a set of limbs that were cut off at the knee and cut off about the waist and split in two practically in the center. . . . They was lying with the hips pulled close together, practically closed together and the knees placed even. Evened up pretty well with the knees of the limbs at the bottom and covered up. . . . They were practically seventy-five or eighty yards from the highway off on a little road, lying over a mound, practically a small

knoll in an open space. . . . The Negro had undertaken to take a stick
and lift the cloth up, and I went on the side where he was and took
the stick from the Negro and held the cloth up and made sure it was a
female and then handed him the stick and he covered it back up. . . . It
was pretty flabby . . . the part that I handled with the stick . . . not damaged or discolored at all . . . there was no blood running out, just water,
you know. It was rained on at that time. It was raining at the time,
about 2:15 on Monday.

Griffin Cook, constable of Beat Five of Jasper County, also recalled the
investigation. He

got a bunch of men for a jury and come about two or three miles this
side of Heidelberg and found the part of the body, human body, about
two-and-a-half miles west of Corinth Church. . . . It was about ninety
steps from the road, and on the right-hand side of the path was an opening, just a small opening, just some sage there, and the part of the body
was laying on the right-hand side of the path going from the highway, in
the opening. There wasn't any road there. It was a path, and the path had
been used for one rut and there was another car track over there. There
wasn't any road there much, and it was laying right side of the rut, the
right-hand car track. . . . The weather was raining and freezing.

Just before dark the dismembered limbs, beginning to reek with an awful
odor, were placed in Constable Cook's car and driven to the Sumrall Funeral
Home in Laurel for preservation.

On Monday night after rain turned to sleet, a heavy snow fell over Mississippi. If Evans's dogs had not chanced upon them, the body parts would
have frozen and been cloaked beneath the snow until the thaw.

As far south as New Orleans the freezing weather caught southerners by
surprise. Such a snowfall, rare in the Southland, covered the landscape from
Memphis to the Gulf. In the Mississippi Delta snow was a foot deep. At West
Point the thermometer read nine degrees. Down in Hazlehurst a coating
of ice silenced the town's fire whistle, and in its failure to alert firefighters a
residence burned to the ground. In Laurel, out in the Keetons' garage, the
radiator of the Willis Knight froze up, and a water pipe between the back
porch and the washhouse froze solid. Inside the Keeton home Ouida stoked

the fireplace in her mother's room and maintained a roaring blaze through-out the afternoon and until evening. Neighbors took note of a putrid stink. It reminded them, as best as they could describe it, of burning hair, parching deer horn, or scorching rubber.

Ouida left the smoldering fire and went across the street to spend the cold night with her aunts, as she had planned. She told them her mother had taken the train to New Orleans for a visit with Eloise. On Tuesday morning Ouida went back home and throughout the day kept the fire going.

By word of mouth the rumor of the ghastly find spread quickly. The next day press reports from Jackson, Hattiesburg, New Orleans, Mobile, Memphis, and the Associated Press spread the story across the nation. The Tuesday afternoon edition of the *Leader-Call*, the Laurel newspaper, fed pieces of news to the hungry public. The banner headline announced "Severed Legs of Woman Found in Woods," followed by two subheads: "Parts of Dismembered Corpse Wrapped in Sugar Sack Found Off Road Near Sandersville" and "Negro Rabbit Hunter Discovers Human Legs as Dogs Run Ahead; Officers Without Clue." The report imparted the grisly detail that the legs had been severed at the knees and at the hips and then riven apart. A portion of the torso below the umbilicus remained attached to one of the limbs. Surgeons who examined the remains had declared that the victim evidently was a woman between thirty-five and forty years old who weighed about 190 pounds. She had blondish hair streaked with brown and had borne children. There was reason to believe that she had been killed elsewhere, and it was presumed that piece by piece other body parts would be found. Possibly, at the hour her remains were discovered, she had been dead between twelve and fourteen hours. "One of the hip bones was severed with the thigh, while the other was cut in two, apparently having been struck a blow with the blade of the axe. . . . One thigh bore a severe bruise as though struck with a heavy instrument."

Dan Evans Jr., the story reported, was "horrified at his discovery." His dogs "running ahead of him had nosed out the legs and were pulling at them."

This news account whetted the public thirst for full information, but Chief Brown's announcement of the medical findings did not slake it. He told that the body parts were found in a perfect state of preservation. In all likelihood the murder had been committed on Sunday night or early Monday, and the victim was estimated to have been five feet eight inches tall and was of a light complexion.

Dan Evans Jr. posing with his dogs at the place he discovered the mysterious bundle. (Permission of the *Laurel Leader-Call*)

Whoever could this be? A country girl? Someone known about Laurel?

Then the chief supplied other facts gained from his detective work at the scene: the legs were wrapped in two pieces of cloth. One of these was a striped sack, split open. Originally it had contained a hundred pounds of sugar. The other was a piece of white fabric. Because there were only slight traces of blood on the cloths and no blood on the ground, Chief Brown believed the crime had not occurred at the site. Tire tracks within some twenty steps of the corpse were impressed in the mud, and wheels had spun as the vehicle was attempting to leave. He surmised that the bundle had been thrown away hurriedly. He suggested that bootleggers may have been involved, for use of large quantities of sugar was characteristic of their trade.

What a story! Everyone was wild to know what homicidal maniac could have committed this monstrous deed. The Jasper County sheriff speculated that probably it had been perpetrated locally, for only a local person would have known how to find the obscure trail. Flocks of sightseers rushed to the isolated crime scene to explore. As soon as the snow let up, car upon car filled with thrill-seeking gapers lined the highway. Instead of the grisly gloom they had hoped would greet them, they found a blank landscape of frozen weeds and gray, scrappy undergrowth, no different from the rest of the winter scene. As they trampled the sagebrush and plundered the ground for souvenirs, their foot tracks obliterated the muddy ruts left by car tires. Having made contact, they turned around and went home to share reports.

Before the sightseers had ransacked the spot, two photographers hurried there to snap pictures. In the darkroom one of their negatives disclosed an astonishing phenomenon. The camera had caught an eerie face peeking toward them through the wintry leaves. On that cold morning only they were present, but in the photo this mysterious stranger was staring down at the trail where the legs had been found. In reporting the "queer story," the *Leader-Call* did not reveal the photographers' names or joke that perhaps the ghost of the murdered woman was haunting the site. The reporter supposed the face was merely a trick of lighting.

After the thaw L. M. Jones, a Laurel photographer, enticed Evans to pose there with a mock-up of the cloth-bound bundle. The photo, headlined "Negro Rabbit Hunter Who Found Legs and His Dogs," was published on the front page of the Laurel newspaper.

Jack Deavours, the elected attorney of Jones County and a younger brother of the murdered Burns Deavours, joined Chief Brown and Sheriff Jordan in supervising the investigation. Long ago, the pronunciation of the family's Huguenot surname had been Americanized to "Devvers," and no one in Laurel knew it any other way. Jack had graduated from Laurel High School in 1921, a year behind Ouida, and then studied at Johns Hopkins University and the law school of the University of Texas. Having been elected without opposition, he had served Jones County since 1932. In investigating this case that the public was terming "the Legs Murder," Deavours was careful to be commanding and impressive, for he was honing his candidacy (yet unannounced) for district attorney. The election was seven months away.

He believed there might be a Jones County connection to the crime. If so, then he, the police chief, and the sheriff would be working conjointly in solving it. Fishing for uncovered information, he questioned both Dan Evans and the white man Evans had notified of his find, though both lived across the line in Jasper County. Deavours learned from Evans that the desolate trail was frequented by lovers as a place for roadside romance. From inspection of the muddy tracks, he concluded that a small automobile had brought the legs to the site.

On Wednesday public speculation was rampant. Feelers were extended into all parts of Jones and Jasper counties for the names of missing persons. One of these was a woman from Vossburg, in Sheriff Bassett's district. She had not been seen since the Thursday before the legs were discovered. Her name was being withheld, and there was a strong possibility that she was the unfortunate whose pieces of flesh had been left on the wooded hillside. The investigation already was producing results. The source of the magazine subscription form found near the crime scene had been traced. Its serial number identified the periodical as the *Southern Agriculturalist*, published in Nashville. The form was one of several issued to an employee, H. S. Holman of Carrollton, Mississippi.

On Thursday Holman telephoned Laurel about having seen in the paper that he was wanted for questioning. He claimed to have been at home since December 28 and was willing to drive down to Laurel if he could assist in the investigation. He could arrive on Saturday if the icy roads were clear.

In addition to these leads, Will S. Saul, a farmer in Jasper County, drove into town to volunteer a report. He, like nearly everyone else in the county, was eager to share in the notoriety of the developing case. On Monday about eight o'clock in the morning, "on a dim local road not far from the scene of the ghastly discovery," Saul had witnessed "a lone woman . . . driving a maroon-colored small car with a bundle beside her." He had "remarked to his wife that the way the woman drove was so mysterious it caused them to notice the car particularly." The driver had sped along the road, but when the farmhouse came into view, she had turned around and hurried back to the highway. He said she headed north, the direction of the crime scene.

Deavours, as though polishing his image for advancement, kept himself out front with the police chief. At a press conference he stepped forward to offer newsmen his views and to calm the hurly-burly. Having toured the site again, he announced being perplexed that the bundle had been abandoned on wide-open land so easily visible. The highway was only seventy-five yards away. In his opinion, it was likely that a woman was at the center of this criminal business. He agreed with other officers "that a woman might have been in such haste and fright that her common sense would have left her and she would have hastily deposited the limbs in the open and rushed away." Only a woman would have wrapped the thighs in so careful a manner.

"They talk about the butcher murder in this case," Deavours remarked, "but I'll tell you, it was one of the cleanest cutting jobs I ever saw. The limbs were cut evenly at the joints and the flesh was not hacked. It seems that whoever did this horrible job knew something about how to un-joint a body."

When Deavours finished, Chief Brown, though feeling a bit under the weather, took his turn before the newsmen. He told of receiving mail about another missing woman who might connect to the Legs Murder case. She was from north Mississippi. The chief mentioned that her anxious husband relayed word that she weighed only 125 pounds but said she did have legs that were "rather large." Then the chief allayed concern about the missing Vossburg wife. She had been located. She was surprised, he said, that her worried family thought she had been murdered by the human butcher.

When two more witnesses came forward with startling information, the case blew wide open. The Laurel police were not ready to issue an official announcement, but hanging around the station a dogged *Leader-Call* newsman sniffed out the scuttlebutt. Reported on the same page with news about the Vossburg woman was this teasing statement: "Much official activity was noted this afternoon in the 'legs murder' investigation. It was indicated in official quarters that 'we know who did it and who the victim was' but nothing was available for publication pending further investigation. The *Leader-Call* will issue an extra if developments warrant."

■ ■ ■

On Friday morning, January 25, some time around eight o'clock, Chief Brown's car pulled up at the curb of 539 Cross Street. He had a sinus infection and felt really miserable, but as a duty-proud public servant he did not flag. With him was Jack Deavours. Arriving in a separate car was J. C. Hamilton, the deputy sheriff who had assisted the chief at the crime scene. Earlier this morning the police chief and Deavours had stopped by David McRae's filling station to look for Ouida but learned that she worked only in the afternoon.

Deavours and Hamilton waited in the car while Chief Brown walked to the porch and knocked on the Keetons' front door. They saw him remove his hat when Ouida appeared. After a pause, the chief went inside. It was not the first time he had entered this home.

Ouida and her aunt Paula's daughter Jean Richeimer were there. Ouida had spent Thursday night with the Richeimers and had come home to scrub the floor in her mother's room. For five days she had been without restful sleep.

The chief, a wise owl who knew how to temper urgency with courtesy, asked Ouida if she would answer a few questions.

She nodded, and after she sat down, he sank heavily into the luxurious sofa.

The fancy decor of the room expressed Daisy Keeton's concept of home. He could feel her presence. Sensing that the house had a story to tell, he intended to draw it out. Although he had a sore throat, responsibility to duty eclipsed his pain. He excelled in moving from assumptions to conclusions, and in his three decades as a lawman he had soaked up an ocean of human variety and moods. He sat stiffly and locked his gaze on Ouida's. There was electricity in the air. The unnerving feature about the young woman sitting across from him was her blank, empty gaze. She appeared high-strung but calm. It was strange behavior. Both Ouida and Chief Brown were fairly well acquainted. He had known the Keetons for about twenty years, mainly because of Earl's and Eloise's escapades. In passing, he had observed Ouida many times downtown.

"May I see your mother, Miss Ouida?"

He had addressed her with the respectful familiarity accorded southern women of her station when they have reached a certain age, yet he continued to peer at her intently, as if to discover deep secrets.

Dark crescents marred her wide eyes. He recalled her days as rosy and plump, a strapping, voluptuous girl. She had taken off a great deal of her weight. She was gaunt, not the buxom lass he remembered as young and alluring. He thought there was a crazed glimmer in her glance.

"My mother is not home at present," she replied. "She is visiting my sister in New Orleans." She spoke politely, in the defensive tone of a child who could expect a berating if discourteous.

"In New Orleans?"

This answer sounded like a complete invention. Neither of them blinked, and Chief Brown, raising his eyebrows to cast a ray of doubt on her assertion, showed no trace of impatience or frustration. The protocol of courtesy did not lapse.

"Yes, I have just had a letter from her," she replied as though to offer proof and to kill silence.

"May I see it, Miss Ouida?"

"I don't know where it is. I could not find it just now."

He was a little put out by her evasion but was unruffled.

Her hands were rough and red, and deep scratches had gouged her wrists. He realized he had interrupted her while she was housecleaning. Possibly she had no maid to take care of such tasks.

She must have understood the purpose of his encroaching questions. In silence they looked at each other for a long, uncomfortable moment. It allowed the chief time to tighten his grip. He liked to sniff around and get a feel of a place. In the overstuffed luxury of the rather chilly room he noted Daisy Keeton's pretty whatnots. Ouida's eyes, he would remember, never lost "a staring look."

Jean Richeimer sat quietly. Chief Brown knew she was wondering why the police chief was calling, but he offered no explanation. He asked if she would excuse herself, and Jean went home with the puzzling news that the police were interviewing Ouida.

Jim Brown had a big, intimidating face, a grim mouth, and slicked dark hair parted off-center in country-boy style. His piercing black eyes didn't blink, and they could strike fear in the lawless. During the Spanish-American War he had been stationed in the Philippines and in Puerto Rico. In a second

J. E. (Jim) Brown, chief of the Laurel police
department (Permission of the *Laurel
Leader-Call*)

enlistment he acted as a bodyguard for President Theodore Roosevelt. He
had served his town in law enforcement for thirty years and as police chief
for twenty. In 1935 he was supervising a force of fourteen lawmen, surround-
ing himself with young deputies and jailers, several from the Valentine family, whom he was training to follow in his footsteps. He and his wife, Miss
Lily, had five children and five grandchildren.

He continued the interrogation in customary procedure.

"Do you have a car, Miss Ouida?"

She replied that she did.

"May I take a look, Miss Ouida?"

Ouida politely gave him full permission. She rose from her chair to
accompany him in the inspection. Chief Brown leaned out the front door
to summon Deavours and Hamilton. They hastened to the porch and came
politely inside.

"Hello, Ouida," Deavours said.

"Hello, Jack," she replied.

Ouida led the chief through the dining room and into the kitchen. From
somewhere Chief Brown could hear the gush of running water. The bathroom must be nearby. He followed the sound, and Ouida came along behind
him. He saw that the tap of the bathtub was wide open, and when he reached
to turn it off, he noted there was no stopper in the drain.

Ouida did not explain.

"Is the next room a bedroom?" he asked.

"Eloise's."

He peeked in but did not enter. Instead, they passed back through the kitchen. On a shelf behind the door he noted a neat collection of cloth sacks. Some of them were green-striped. As Chief Brown reached to open the back door, he glanced toward the sink. Three large carving knives, all of them encrusted, lay on the counter.

"I was cutting the fern," Ouida remembered, as though she had used the knives long ago. "It had frozen during the cold," she explained.

He looked into her eyes, and she returned his gaze. It was like a staring contest, except she seemed not to be seeing anything.

She did not appear to be a violent woman. If she wanted to fly at his throat or scratch his eyes out for bullying her, she was holding back. Could it be that in the presence of fatherly authority she was like a child who preferred to resist in silence? Was her behavior her instinctive respect for elders?

As they started down the porch steps, a vicious German police dog rushed across the yard. Chief Brown backed against door.

"Can you tie up your dog, Miss Ouida?"

Her angry pet was barking ferociously, its tail ducked, its ears cocked back, and its angry eyes fixed on the chief. As she held on to the collar and reached for a rope, the dog jerked violently in trying to attack the stranger. A deep bark answered beyond the hedge bordering the driveway. Chief Brown concluded that both the Keetons and the neighbor next door had watchdogs.

The chief stopped her.

"I can go through the house and come down the driveway and meet you at the car shed, Miss Ouida."

Near the back of the residence was a washhouse and clotheslines. The alley between the Keeton property and Cammie Cook's served as a shared driveway. At the end and on the right was the Keetons' garage, on the left Mrs. Cook's. When the chief had circled round the house, Ouida was waiting for him, standing beside her car. It was, as the chief expected, maroon with black fenders. His eagle eye saw what he needed to know.

"What is this on the fender, Miss Ouida?"

He watched as she slid her fingers over a greasy smear. The rains had not removed it. Then he took a look inside and examined the floor and the front seat. Their eyes met again, and Ouida offered no comment. But the chief had seen enough to make a decision.

"Miss Ouida, I want you to come downtown with me. Will you do that?"

"I will," she replied without a pause. "But, first, I must change my dress."

Their encounter, lasting about half an hour, had not become confrontational. Neither had lost composure. Ouida crossed the yard and went indoors. Chief Brown joined Deavours and Hamilton on the front porch. When Ouida was ready, she emerged from her bedroom. With Chief Brown guiding at her elbow, she walked down the steps to the car as though in a daze. Perhaps thinking she would be detained for only a short while, she did not take her purse. Jack Deavours followed, opened the door for her to get into the backseat, and then slid in beside her. Across the street Jean and her mother were watching, unsure why the police were taking Ouida away.

After a muttered conversation with Hamilton, Chief Brown took the wheel. Hamilton tipped his hat, and they left him there to guard the premises. Brown turned into the driveway, then backed into Cross Street. He went right at Daughdrill. The car rumbled over the train tracks and headed to town. There was no chitchat. After taking a left at Front Street, they passed the Carter Building and Supply Company. At the end of the block the car turned right onto Oak Street and proceeded one block to the Commercial National Bank building. Deavours's office in the Deavours & Hilburn law firm was upstairs. Deavours preferred to question Ouida there rather than at police headquarters or at the courthouse. They led her up the steps and shut themselves inside a private room at the back of the building, then began their interrogation.

Chief Brown felt so wretched that he could not stay. He left for an hour or two to doctor his bad throat, but, fine lawman that he was, planned to return and take command. For as long as it took, Deavours, Van Valentine, and Sheriff Jordan planned to grill Ouida. Relentless battering often brought positive results in police interrogations. In many cases the accused eventually gave up and confessed.

By the time the Friday afternoon newspaper came out, Ouida Keeton was already in police custody. As local eyes scanned the tiny space given the big news item that an arrest was imminent, Jack Deavours was bombarding Ouida with questions.

On Wednesday the two men who helped her had identified her. Ouida had been careless. If she hadn't been so weary that morning, she might have escaped the turmoil. Her trail to the woods and back was easily traced. The newspaper had fired up the heat of local curiosity, and then, almost with no great effort at detection, the police had found her. Claiming evidence, Farmer Saul and a number of volunteers had popped up.

Among these were the two witnesses with conclusive information. W. P. Duckworth and W. E. Kennedy, the men who had encounters with Ouida on Monday morning, had come forward to offer their statements. Their testimonies focused on the Keeton house and clinched Chief Brown's decision to bring Ouida in for questioning. After reading about the severed limbs near the spot where her car had stalled, Duckworth told the police Ouida had phoned him. At his home in Port Gibson Kennedy read the sensational news reports. He put the facts together and realized that the crime site was near the place he had met the drenched hitchhiker. In a letter to Sheriff Bassett of Jasper County, he wrote of having given a woman a ride as he was driving from Quitman via Laurel en route to Jackson.

She got out as if she lived in the large brown house just across the street from the service station. I did not notice to see where she went. She might have been going on further or she might have stopped there. She first told me that she wanted to go to Cross Street. I do not know whether the place is called Cross Street or not where she got out. The lady did not have on any stockings, a light short coat, no hat. When she flagged me to stop she had the short coat over her head and was walking down the road toward Laurel. I would say she was 27 or 28. Her hair was bobbed but had not been cut for some time. Black hair. Due to the fact that she kept her back turned on me most of the way I am unable to give you a good description of her. She stated to me that she was going for an old lady to stay with her while her mother was out of town and that she lived down this road referred to above and that she got stuck and had to leave her car. I thought that she was telling the truth. I was driving a 1934 Chevrolet, dove-color coupe with red wheels and unloaded the lady around nine o'clock Monday at the service station.

Rumors were flying. Word of Ouida's questioning in Deavours's office quickly circulated. Earl got wind of it at the bakery, a stone's throw away. He charged up the stairs and demanded access, his boss trailing close behind him.

Chief Brown, feeling better late Friday afternoon, had come back to relieve Deavours and was present when Earl was admitted. Brown announced that he wanted to make a thorough inspection of the Keeton house. Even though Ouida had been housecleaning and tidying up, he sensed that incriminating evidence had not been obliterated. Getting a search warrant would delay the investigation for maybe a day or two, and, restless to get started, he put his request to Ouida. Sleepless and tense, she was on the edge of hysteria. She had chewed her fingernails to the quick, but she agreed. However, she stipulated that during any search Earl must be present. She wanted her purse, and she asked the chief to bring it to her. As he looked for it, she explained, he likely would find a pistol. Evidently she thought it a good idea to mention that a gun was on the premises.

Snoops hanging around on the street saw officers get into a car with Earl Keeton and speed away. Wanting instant news and possibly a glimpse of the human butcher, a small crowd had assembled outside the bank building at the corner of Oak and Magnolia streets. Aimless bystanders with nothing better to do killed time in anticipation of some big break. They had seen officers escorting Farmer Saul up the steps to Deavours's office. Later they heard he had said, "Yes, she's the lady who drove past my house." He also had identified Ouida's car.

The assortment of curious Laurelites included courthouse idlers, residents from Cross and Daughdrill streets, rubes from the country, two reporters representing the local paper, and a staff writer for the Associated Press. Above the inquisitive heads the ponderous cast-iron clock ticked away the minutes, then the hours. Yet the crowd lingered in the cold, ready to snatch any report of news. By ten o'clock the evening had become too chilly, and most had drifted homeward. Only a few hung on. They could not know that already Ouida had made an incriminating statement. She had opened up by afternoon after enduring over five hours of questioning and was on the verge of collapse. Deavours, the Jasper County sheriff, Constable Cook, and Wayne Valentine absorbed her story with full attention. No one uttered a peep as she began to recount it.

She told them that while she and her mother were taking a drive to the north of Sandersville the car broke down. Mrs. Keeton agreed to remain and guard it while Ouida hitchhiked to town for help. But Mrs. Keeton had grown tired of waiting and hailed a ride herself. She and Ouida met at home. Then Mrs. Keeton decided to visit Eloise in New Orleans, and Ouida told of putting her mother on the train.

She tried to satisfy the lawmen with rambling explanations and hoped to convince them that she was mystified herself. She held to this story, though Deavours tested it repeatedly for details and clarifications about her stalled car and about hitchhiking home with Kennedy's help. Cornered and weak,

Ouida began to waver. In the late afternoon she dramatically altered her tale. Lelia Mae Martin, a deputy circuit clerk, was called in to take it down in shorthand.

The sky grew increasingly black, and the men on the street knew lawmen still were interrogating Ouida Keeton upstairs. Long after night had fallen and the air had grown very cold, newcomers continued to drift to the stretch of pavement outside the bank. They muttered their comments in the darkness, and until a smoker's struck match revealed a face that was familiar, the crowd was a only collection of black silhouettes and restive shadows under the streetlight. Ouida was aware neither of this congregation nor of the claim some would make that mob power was stirring again in the streets of Laurel. That evening, even though she had not been charged, indicted, or given a fair day in court, the moral shock of her accused crime established an enduring taint. How could a daughter, a beautiful woman who walked among the people of Laurel, commit this unspeakable crime against her own mother?

Ouida had been permitted to phone her sister in New Orleans, and Eloise rushed to Laurel, arriving around midnight. Earl picked her up at the depot, at the foot of Oak Street, and together they hurried one block to Deavours's office. The sheriff's men let them through the cordon, and they raced upstairs.

With ears pricked for a revealing outburst, newsmen from the *Leader-Call* monitored the murmurous sounds coming from Deavours's inner sanctum and settled into the monotony of waiting in the reception room. Goode Montgomery Jr., a young reporter for the newspaper, sneaked out back, scaled a gas pipe, and leaped to the roof. Through the window he witnessed Eloise's arrival. Ouida fell into her sister's arms, and from his perch Montgomery heard her exclaim, "They are trying to say that I killed our mother, and you know I didn't do such a thing!"

He observed a small room crowded with a rotating team of interrogators. They passed in and out the door in progression, and only Ouida—frail, vulnerable, and restrained—never left. During the barbarously long sessions Eloise and Earl were excluded from the inner room, and neither tried to shield their sister or volunteered to summon the family lawyer. Earl sauntered off to fetch a snack for Ouida. In a quiet corner flirtatious Eloise was having a tête-à-tête with Jack Anderson. She was too distracted by the handsome twenty-two-year-old Laurel policeman to give full sisterly attention to Ouida's legal rights and needs.

The continuing interrogation trespassed on privacies too painful for Ouida to endure. She drooped in the chair, a frail woman surrounded by burly men. With every sensitive nerve abused, she was on the edge of physical and emotional collapse. Her chronic back ailment was shooting pain through her body. For five days she had hardly slept or rested. The faded, apathetic beauty, once so attractive to all eyes, was unappealing and lifeless. She sat like a staring mannequin.

Earl brought in the sandwiches, but through the tiring ordeal Ouida was able to take only a few sips of Coca-Cola. She turned away, revolted by food, and thought she might vomit. After the interrogations her brother recalled that, if she ate anything, she only nibbled at a sandwich.

Some crimes stir up a public sensation. This case was one of them. The next day headline writers rose to their top form with shocking facts. The Saturday edition of the *Leader-Call* reported what everyone knew already, that Ouida Keeton had been arrested. However, the banner headline and the meaty story that followed unveiled new information that held readers spellbound: "Woman Questioned All Night in Legs Case." The subhead continued: "Farmer Says He Recognizes Miss Keeton as Woman He Saw in Car in Woods Last Monday Morning."

The boldly displayed report extending across two columns presented a hectic tale of kidnapping, extortion, and greed for Daisy Keeton's money. It was a variation of Ouida's earlier statement. Some speculated that Ouida had been devious only because she feared the abductors would take her mother's life when they learned she'd divulged the truth. In this latest version of Daisy Keeton's disappearance, Ouida

told the officers she and her mother were driving north of Sandersville when they met an elderly woman wearing a bonnet, walking along the highway. They picked her up and, at the point the dim trail leaves Highway 11 toward the scene of the gruesome find, were forced to drive into the woods, the woman remarking to Mrs. Keeton, "You're the woman that has all that money, aren't you?"

A blindfold was placed over her eyes, Miss Keeton related, but she said she heard the voices of two men who approached, and she and her mother were forced at the point of a gun to get out of the car. She said the men informed her then that her mother was being kidnapped but if she brought them $5,000 in bonds Mrs. Keeton would be released.

Miss Keeton, it was learned, said that they refused to allow her to drive her own car back to Laurel, but compelled her to go back to the main highway and hail a ride into town. She did so, according to the story, obtained the bonds, returned to the woods and delivered them.

Instead of releasing her mother, however, Miss Keeton said, the kidnappers then decided to take their victim to New Orleans and to set her free there after they had realized cash for the bonds. The men disappeared with her mother, it was not exactly clear how, and Miss Keeton said she had not seen or heard from her mother since that time.

After Ouida had given this astonishing statement, her volatile brother, bristling with anger, burst into the room, exclaiming, "Why didn't you notify some of us about Mother's disappearance?"

But this account was only one of several far-fetched narratives Ouida related during the nineteen hours she was grilled. Mrs. Martin dutifully took down every word, and someone in the room let the testimony seep to the press.

Later Ouida recounted still another fantastical tale. A man, she said, had come to the Keeton home about two in the morning. He struck and killed her mother and then locked Ouida in a closet. Ouida's latest bore the gist of the confession that would serve to charge her and an accomplice with murder.

Defiant, she remained limp in the office chair, awaiting the next session of Deavours's constant grilling. Her former schoolmate was in no way softened by their old-school association. He was brutal and unrelenting, doing his job.

She had been under fire throughout the day. The chiming clock on the wall outside kept reminding them. Deavours began again, intensifying the plan of maneuvering Ouida into a vulnerable position and pinning her down. Part of his duty was to make people talk, and if she had not been so whipped by fatigue, maybe she could have held out longer. His piercing eyes and his incessant questions were unrelieved punishment.

Ouida become limp. Against him, she was no match. She repudiated the fantastical story of kidnapping.

Mrs. Martin sat quietly in the shadows with her stenographic pad.

"It was you that took those legs to the woods, wasn't it, Ouida?" Deavours pressed.

"I have no memory of it."

"Were they your mother's?"

She would not reply.

"Why did you take them there, Ouida?"

She didn't answer. So he continued to plague her.

"Did you kill your mother, Ouida?"

"I did not!" she cried.

"Who was it, Ouida?"

"Mother was standing beside the fireplace," she muttered, and a new story began to ravel. "And he struck her down with the iron poker."

"Who did this awful thing to your mother, Ouida?"

Instead of answering, she told that the corpse had been dismembered and, except for the legs, which wouldn't fit, packed into a box.

This lurid particular caused agitation in the room, but every listener held still so that the interrogation could continue.

Mrs. Martin was poised and ready.

Deavours turned the screw even tighter.

"Tell us who did it, Ouida."

She gave up, and the name tumbled out. W. M. Carter, her former employer. After it was spoken, the rest poured forth as though unstoppable.

"Now I am going to tell you the truth this time," she said.

Ouida's previous admissions of kidnapping and extortion were wildly improbable. This one rang true.

Mrs. Martin was getting it all down, the first of Ouida's statements to afford valid substance for a murder charge. How and when the *Leader-Call's* sleuths obtained this version from Friday is unknown, but an extra edition on Monday fed it to excited readers:

Mamma was killed by Mr. W. M. Carter on Saturday night when
he struck her over the head with a poker as she stood at the mantel.
Mamma fell to the floor, and he hit her on the head with the poker
six times more. Mr. Carter took [her] away with him in his car. It was
parked at the back of the house, and he loaded the body in the rear and
drove away. In just a few minutes he returned and said he had forgotten his hat. He put it on and left again. Later that night he came back
and brought the two legs. He said he had packed everything else in a
box but there wasn't room enough for the legs and that I'd have to dispose of them. His car was parked again at the rear of the house and we

carried the legs inside, he taking the heavy one and I the lighter one. We wrapped them in sugar sacks and then put them on the front seat of my car. He said I was to drive out Highway 11 and drop them into Tallahala Creek from the bridge. He told me the rest of her body was on the Ovett road. When I got to the creek bridge, the legs were too heavy - for me to lift out of the car and over the bridge rail, so I kept on driving toward Sandersville. I remembered a plum orchard a neighbor had once directed me to, and I decided to go there. I got on the wrong road leaving the highway and saw a house. I returned to the highway as quickly as possible and drove to the other road. I dragged the legs out of the car and the bundle fell to the ground about seventy-five yards from the highway. Then I started to back my car out and got stuck. I heard a car coming and decided to try for a ride back home.

Even with this new information Deavours was not satisfied. It opened yet another door on mystery. The violent act showed no motive. While Ouida was still in his grip, he asked another wrenching question.

"And why would he kill your mother, Ouida?"

She was reluctant to say.

"Why was it, Ouida?"

He kept pressing her. As their eyes met, he broke through her barrier, and the words spilled out.

"So that I would have more privileges."

Deavours turned loose and let Ouida relax. Her haywire narratives seemed to be connected. She vowed that this was the full story. It was authentic enough for Deavours and Chief Brown. They put her under arrest.

Next, the lawmen must direct their questions to Carter. Some around town had joked about his having taken a shine to Ouida. He was known through the years and via the city grapevine as Ouida's overattentive boss. He had squired his pretty secretary around in his car, and on many evenings his Pontiac was parked at the curb on Cross Street. Mostly this was substance for gossip. No one could verify actual mischief.

While Ouida was held in Deavours's office, Chief Brown gave his men the signal to pick up Carter and deliver him to the courthouse rather than to bring him through the crowd loitering outside the bank.

Ouida sat like a dead doll on the hard chair and stared at nothing. Her eyes remained wide open but empty. Although her gaze was lackluster, she did not appear sleepy, only exhausted. Deavours was not sure he had the full story yet. Peppering her with further questions, he kept her in his office until a time that was neither night nor day. Fatigued himself, he decided he had wrung about all the information he was going to gain from her. The iron clock outside told that it was Saturday morning. In the hours they had bombarded her, Ouida never rebuked them or called for the family lawyer.

Deavours turned her over to jailer Van Valentine, a former schoolmate of theirs. Valentine trooped the frail prisoner to the Jones County jail, a second-story wing on the back of the courthouse, and sent her through the routine of processing. She came to life and fell into weeping.

The horror of confinement in a concrete cell, in sordid communion with frowsy women drunks and petty criminals, and in smelly, far-from-sanitary conditions, gave Ouida extreme fright. Her eyes roved over the walls specked with cigarette burns and obscene sentiments. The filthy toilet had no seat. It was in plain view to one and all. The iron bars on the door were flaking shards of old paint. Her jailer expected her to lie on the low cot, cover herself with an itchy blanket, and place her head on a sour pillow encased in grimy ticking. The cell was cold, and the light was poor, a single bulb outside that seemed to be left on all night and all day.

Ouida was stricken by panic. It became hysteria. This was the new side of the divide, and she was a genteel young woman terrified of prisons. Such conditions could drive sensitive people mad. She had a frenzied breakdown and kept calling for Mrs. Keeton, but there was no mother to console her.

Through the night the jailer witnessed a continuing fit that was charged more by emotion than by fearsome violence. Because the untouchably pretty girl he had gazed upon in school days was now his prisoner, her incessant wailing and drenching tears gave him an unnerving peek at intimacy that was strange and dazzling.

■ ■ ■

W. M. Carter, like the rest of Laurel, had been following news stories of the Legs Murder case. His rendezvous with Ouida at David McRae's filling station on the afternoon of January 19 came to light. Gossips shared their speculations about a sinister purpose, the planning for Daisy Keeton's death on that very night.

Three years had passed since Ouida had worked for Carter, but her old boss couldn't get her out of his system. When she came home from Washington making an out-of-the-blue announcement that she was engaged to marry a man she spoke of as "Mr. Grace," Carter was stung by disbelief. He still yearned to be close to her. It was inconceivable that she had taken up with a stranger. Carter kept dreaming of cozy times and of out-of-town trips he and Ouida might take together, and he renewed his visits to the Keeton home. He held hopes that they could fall back into the groove of their former pleasures. When Ouida took the job at her brother-in-law's, Carter began buying gasoline there. On two separate visits on the nineteenth he gassed up his Buick sedan and then his Pontiac coupe, and each time he had a short conversation with Ouida. It was difficult for her to give him a snub even though she was wearing Mr. Grace's engagement ring. Carter told her his plans to drive the Pontiac to Alabama the next day.

The Carters were even better known around town than the Keetons. At sixty-seven, W. M. Carter remained a striking figure. He was favorably regarded in banking circles as a savvy businessman and in the general population as a devout leader in his church, a devoted family man, and a doting grandfather. Among the well-to-do, the Carters ranked high. His wife, Nettie, was a lovely woman blessed with refined Alabama manners. The Carter daughters likewise were polished with appropriate graces and in girlhood were featured in piano recitals and at the better social functions. Like their brother, the Carter girls in adolescence were popular in church and school. The three were an impressive contrast to Ouida's brother and little sister.

William Madison Carter, called Matt, had risen to become one of Laurel's worthies by amassing wealth and taking a place in the mid-tier of Laurel's lumber businessmen. In the competitive marketplace, his enterprises were unquestionably successful. In the lumber boom that began in 1891, Carter's mills competed in a crowded industry that included the largest—Eastman-Gardiner (1891), Gilchrist-Fordney (1906), Wausau Southern (1911), and Marathon (1914)—as well as Cohay, Lindsey, and others. The Carters came to Mississippi in 1893 when the town of Laurel was ten years old and when the piney woods region was still dense with stands of virgin timber. The W. M. Carter Lumber Company originated north of town in sawmills around the Jasper County community of Haney and on a creek beside the GM&N railroad. Even in these early years Carter was cutting six to eight thousand feet of lumber a day.

In 1911 he incorporated the W. M. Carter Planing Mill with his brother C. H. Carter and E. T. Williams, both of Laurel, and P. J. Toomer of Hattiesburg. The amount of its capital stock was $45,000, and each share was valued at $100. The papers of incorporation stated their plan: to dress, buy, and sell lumber wholesale and retail; to buy timber land; to buy and sell sawmills; and to own and operate the same. Also in 1911 Carter and his brother joined with P. J. Toomer and Ashton Toomer to incorporate a second business, Carter-Toomer Lumber Company, with capital stock of $20,000. The value of its shares and its purpose were identical to those of the planing mill.

In 1912 Carter was buying and selling land for home building. The W. M. Carter Lumber Company also was supplying construction materials to the city government. In 1914 the company owned a Shay steam locomotive for its Laurel operation and a similar engine for W. M. Carter & Bro. in Sandersville. By the 1920s W. M. Carter had expanded his business into building contracting and sales of real estate. In July 1928 his advertisement in the Laurel newspaper stated, "Let me erect that new home for you" and "Choice Homes For Sale in Nearly All Parts of the City." In the 1930s, by a feat of Babbittry, he cornered local sales of Masonite fiberboard, invented and manufactured in Laurel, and became the city's exclusive retailer. He was a director of Commercial National Bank & Trust Company and among the proven business leaders reelected to its board each year.

The Carters lived at 706 Seventh Avenue, an imposing residence at the intersection of Seventh Street. Facing the white two-story home was the columned mansion of Dr. J. B. Jarvis, one of Laurel's most well regarded physicians, specializing in gynecology. For medical opinion he would be a significant figure himself in the Legs Murder case. The vicinity in which they lived, comprising a quarter-square mile of residential blocks, was an enclave of Laurel's well-to-do. In the hierarchy of locations it was the best.

Photo of W. M. Carter circulated by the Associated Press. (Permission of the *Laurel Leader-Call*)

Many residents were descended from ancestors long native to the South, like the Carters, but the richest had migrated from Iowa and Wisconsin or were first-generation southerners. In the 1880s, when logging slowed down in the North, northern lumbermen had looked to the South for the next boom in the timber industry. Around a community ten miles north of the county seat at Ellisville, moneyed speculators established their base and bought up huge tracts of forests and mineral rights, built their sawmills, and created a town called Laurel—named, it is presumed, for the copious *Kalmia latifolia* (mountain laurel) in the rustic landscape. After amassing their great fortunes, the most elite of these northern families clustered in a small but formidable coterie. Its members belonged in a world of their own. Its Episcopalian and Presbyterian reserve, its patrician refinement, and its lofty cultural standards influenced Laurel's public institutions and architecture. The lavish homes the lumber barons erected north of town nestled along brick pavements and amid parks, private gardens, and in time scenic oak avenues. At its core Laurel was northern but in a southern setting.

The respectable Carters, southern gentry, were on the select fringe of this genteel caste of northern lumbermen. W. M. Carter maintained a financial prominence in the upper crust until the Great Depression. Leaving Alabama, he and his wife, the former Nettie Newcomb of Belleville, Alabama, had come to the lumber region of Mississippi with their first child, Mary Lou, born in 1890. Carter was descended from colonial forebears in the Old Dominion. In the seventeenth century his earliest American ancestors settled in Lancaster County, Virginia. Later generations of this Carter line migrated through North Carolina, then to Laurens County, South Carolina, and to Bartow County, Georgia, where W. M. Carter was born in 1867. His close-knit brothers and sisters—Charles, Eugene, Ida, and Rosa—settled in Laurel too, and he, the eldest, was the presiding figure.

Besides Mary Lou, W. M. and Nettie Carter had three children born in Mississippi—Pauline, Charles Newton, and Helen. Paul H. Decker, a northerner, a schoolteacher, and afterward the principal of the high school, fell in love with Pauline. They married and had one son. W. M. and Nettie's only son, Charles, called Newton, would marry Carolyn Sharborough. He joined his father in business and was father of a son and a daughter. Helen, the youngest of the Carter children, would marry into another of Laurel's lumber families, the Baileys, and would be the mother of three sons. In its own way the household of W. M. Carter was happy. His affectionate children called him "Papa," and the family was loving, well liked, well-off, comfortable, educated, respected, and blessed. But in the early years there had been sadness. Daughter Mary Lou was not well. Because Mary Lou required medical care, a private nurse was hired to attend her. She died at the age of twenty in 1910, when Carter was forty- three. To lose a precious daughter was a grief almost too painful to bear. The death of one's child may have seemed the darkest hour through which this father could pass, but it would not be so. A drearier cloud was destined to hang above him.

None of the Carters knew there was a dark and secret need in the husband, father, and brother's heart or realized he was one of those publicly respectable citizens who derive clandestine gratification from a double life. He was a philanderer, and among his conquests Ouida Keeton was not the first.

In the year of Mary Lou's death three unmarried schoolteachers were boarding in the big Carter house on Seventh Avenue, but Carter was a discreet and very selective skirt chaser, and Nurse Harriet Adams, of Mobile, fell into his arms. By 1920, when Ouida Keeton caught his eye and he became foolishly fond of her, his secret romance with Harriet Adams had continued for just over a decade. In public, he was a wealthy, respectable gentleman who always spoke politely of "Miss Adams" and "Miss Keeton," but in private he became a passionate man with masculine cravings for appealing young women.

In 1922 he sold the house on Seventh Avenue, and the family moved three blocks north to a fine new residence Carter had built on Sixth Avenue. This was his home in the year Daisy Keeton went missing. The setting was a haven of new mansions and affluent lumbermen. The Masons lived next door, and the Joneses, the Gilchrists, and the Kressmans a block beyond. The married Carter children and W. M. Carter's brothers and sisters owned homes nearby, on Fifth, Sixth, and Seventh avenues. Most members of the family were Presbyterian churchgoers, and in the 1930s the Deckers lived next door to the Presbyterian minister.

■ ■ ■

After Ouida had been taken into custody, the Keeton property was placed under heavy guard. On Friday afternoon, while lawmen combed the premises for additional clues, Earl, as Ouida had demanded, was present to monitor them. They found dried blood on the seat and floor of Ouida's car. The fireplace in Daisy Keeton's room, streaked with blood not entirely cleansed away, bore the heavy smell of recent burning. From the ashes Deputy Sheriff Hamilton extracted hair, finger joints, and bits of fingernails. A substance like melted lard had dripped through the flooring around the hearth and collected on the earth under the house. Chief Brown discovered a pair of rolled-up women's stockings in Ouida's cold fireplace. They reeked of gastric juices. In her room he came upon a pair of brown suede shoes stained by splotches that bore a similar odor. Brown's team inspected the blood-smeared woodwork around the bathroom door and a slab of joist beneath the fireplace.

As Chief Brown concentrated on Ouida's room, he was inclined to expect other telltale traces of horror than the suede shoes and the foul stockings. He felt beneath Ouida's pillows and mattress and looked behind the furniture and under the bed. As he crouched, his flashlight exposed only a few puffs of dust that rolled away as his breath stirred them. From the kitchen and hallway came low-volumed conversation of his officers, also groping for clues. Earl meandered back and forth, keeping watch, but the chief was not deterred.

Ouida's bedroom had three windows, two facing west and one facing south and within the screened portion of the front porch. The head of her bed was catercorner between the windows. Opposite its foot was her fireplace. The chief stood still for a moment as his eyes swept over the room, taking note of the contents.

Then he moved through the transomed door connecting with a middle bedroom, Mrs. Keeton's. The pillowless bed was at the far side, the foot toward Ouida's door. The other furnishings were placed in a bed-sitting room arrangement, with cozy chairs in front of the mantelpiece. The bricks inside the sooty fireplace, splashed with blood drops, retained the slightest trace of heat. The hearth and the brick fascia had been freshly painted and the floor in front of the hearth aggressively scrubbed. All the varnish had been scoured away. Beneath a throw rug Chief Brown drew his finger across white powder. It was Old Dutch Cleanser.

He examined Mrs. Keeton's bed. When he threw back the coverlet, he exposed an ugly blotch, a circular bloodstain toward the middle of the mattress. A trail of blood had been dribbled from the bed toward the bathroom. He called in Hamilton and Valentine to take charge.

The chief was drawn back to Ouida's room. Earl came in to watch. Brown's manner remained professional as he probed into personal nooks and crannies. As he moved forward to inspect the dresser, its mirror simultaneously caught the reflection of the pistol on his hip and of Ouida's dainty vanity set spread haphazardly as she had left it before he took her away. The comb, the brush with stained bristles, and the hand mirror lay on the somewhat soiled doily in the dust of pinkish face powder. He did not handle these, but he could not help noticing such delicately personal intimacies as stray dark hairs in the brush and a human smear on the powder puff.

But the chief was not searching for the ordinary. Among Ouida's personal effects this room must conceal some secret. Where was the gun she had mentioned? Where would she hide it? He proceeded to the drawers of the dresser. Nothing exceptional there, only knickknacks, hair curlers, Kotex, and a bottle of hair dye. He eased past Earl and turned to the chifforobe for a clue. In the section for frocks, his hands examined pockets. A mink coat. Nothing there. He shook slippers for hidden notes. Next he rifled the first of the drawers. A woman's handbag. This was what she had asked him to deliver to her. Inside, a tube of lipstick, a comb, a tin of aspirin, a wadded handkerchief, and a coin purse containing a fold of cash and loose change. But there was no gun. In the next drawer, here was a mystery! He was surprised to behold brand-new baby clothing carefully folded within tissue paper. But there was no infant child in the household. Of what use would these little dresses and booties be to Ouida?

In the next drawer, his instinct was proved true. His fingers stirred through soft, pink things. Beneath veils and delicate garments smelling of powder, lotions, and perfume, he touched cold metal. He drew out a black revolver. It had a rubberized handgrip and a foreign look.

He clicked it open. The cylinder held six cartridges, three of them spent and blunted. He took a whiff of the black powder left on the chambers. The gun had been fired three times with the point of the barrel against some firm object. Otherwise, the spent shells would not be blunted. The chief surmised that this alien revolver, rather than the poker, may be the real murder weapon.

When the inspection of the premises was concluded and Earl had been sent on his way, the chief's men gathered crime evidence, drove back to town, and secured it at Deavours's office. Chief Brown then went over to the jail to deliver Ouida's purse. The black pistol was in his pocket.

Valentine unlocked the cell, and the chief removed his hat and gently took a seat. Smells of dried blood and sour gastric juices were still in his nostrils.

Ouida was huddled in a corner, and his shadow fell over her. Wiping her tears, she thanked him for the purse, opened it, handled the fold of currency, and told him she liked to have a little money handy.

When he shifted his position, his shadow lifted, and he saw the shivering prisoner in full light. He asked her to tell him the story of the gun. Wise from long experience rather than from books, Chief Brown could read motive and character from a person's conduct. The jail, the crime scene, and the interrogation room, for him, were the repositories of knowledge.

Ouida appeared weak, still upset and fearful in her cold, dismal surroundings, but she replied readily, as though she had expected the gun would stir his interest. Yes, she knew it was in her room and wasn't the least bit surprised that he'd found it. No, she had not hidden it. She had merely placed it in her drawer for safekeeping. No, she didn't know where it came from. In fact, she had been rather shaken on discovering it.

With fixed eyes attached to her stare, the chief was reading her. She mirrored his study and saw a fatherly face round as a pie and tight lips like the slot in a child's bank.

When he asked where, her wondrous strange answer gave him good reason to suspect that her mind was addled.

"Where did you say you found it, Miss Ouida?" he asked a second time.

"On a hen's nest in the backyard."

■ ■ ■

On Friday evening, soon after Ouida incriminated Carter, Chief Brown had issued an order that he be brought in for questioning. When officers knocked at his door and asked him to come downtown, Carter felt the earth heave and sway. He could not believe this was happening to him. Instinctively, he began to plan how to vindicate himself from what he exclaimed to his astonished family was a blatant lie. This setback dealt a smarting blow to his self-confidence. It was an appalling situation, the kind of thing that could be a disaster for business.

Newsmen and idlers hanging around in hope of pecking the latest tidbits in the case were rewarded. Two lawmen were seen shouldering Carter up the steps of the courthouse. Ouida was still in Deavours's office a block away. Well known and easily recognized, Carter was a figure of evident dignity, just under six feet tall, with white-streaked hair. In his gray suit and hat, he did not look like a murderer.

They seated him and began their interrogation. When Chief Brown confronted him with the accusation, Carter expressed amazement. Like the rest of Laurel he'd heard news that Ouida was in police custody, but he claimed to have absolutely no knowledge of Daisy Keeton's disappearance. On learning of her probable death and of Ouida's arrest, why then had he, a friend of influence and position, not come forth to inquire?

"I have nothing to tell," he said.

His whereabouts on the night of the murder?

Warily he told that he had been at home that Saturday evening, and on Sunday he had driven to Alabama on business. He had returned to Laurel on Wednesday afternoon along the snowy highway. He divulged no more.

Because he was a family man and a church leader, his particular affairs in Mobile were closely under wraps. At this time he neither offered the name Harriet Adams in support of an alibi nor revealed that he had gone to Mobile, as on so many other occasions, solely to share Miss Adams's warm company. Unknown to his children and friends, Carter's philandering with her had flickered and fluttered over the years. In 1935 he had visited her once each month. He cherished the fact of having a lady love to lure him away and another to draw him back home again. Careful not to mention Mobile, he had told his family the purpose of his Alabama traveling was to check on oil drilling close by his late wife's land near Evergreen.

Despite all his scrupulous calculations, the sneaky escapade was nearly wrecked. On Sunday, January 20, as he and Miss Adams were taking a chilly afternoon stroll around the city park, whom, to his disgust, should he chance to meet there but Mrs. Lewis Winn of Laurel? She and her husband, whose place of business was next to Carter's on Front Street, were in town on a Sunday holiday. Mrs. Winn was sure to tell Mr. Winn and a friend or two of the encounter, and word could circulate to Carter's children. The furtive romance was his and Miss Adams's business alone and certainly not that of the Winns or the Laurel police. Carter didn't want it splattered over the front pages to cause a scandal.

As he responded to questioning, he held back a second secret. In returning to Laurel, he had stopped to see Ouida. Thus his homecoming had been by way of Waynesboro rather than by Richton, the more direct route. When passing through Citronelle, Alabama, he had stopped to sell a customer a load of Masonite. The Waynesboro road connected with Highway 11 just north of the Keeton house. He had pulled his Pontiac coupe across the lane and parked with the driver's side of the car against the curb. Filled with romantic notions, he had rushed to the porch and rapped on the front door. There was no answer. He rapped again. Still no one answered.

Carter took no notice of two or three men at the Lorimar station across the street warming themselves by a fire. They watched him coming down the steps to his car. As he was about to crank the engine, they saw him brighten when he spotted Ouida emerging along the driveway. She was carrying a milk bottle. Carter sprang from behind the steering wheel, scooped up a handful of snow, and playfully tossed a snowball at her. They saw him coax her into the car and kept watch as the two sat together talking for nearly an hour. Ouida was seated behind the steering wheel. What could they be discussing for so long in a cold automobile? They could not know that he was telling her of his hours with Harriet Adams and was conveying Miss Adams's best regards to Ouida, or that Ouida was complaining that her car radiator and a water pipe had frozen. Nor could Carter know what the men around the fire would be concluding after he was arrested—that he and Ouida had sat intimately in the Pontiac, probably scheming about a cover-up. During the time Carter and Ouida were conversing near the driveway, Cammie Cook, the neighbor, had come out her front door with a broom and had begun to sweep snow off her porch. The men observed that she, too, took note of Carter and Ouida and watched them get into his car.

Carter was not aware of the eyes scrutinizing him. The men around the fire watched Ouida get out and Carter drive away. But he returned soon afterward, bringing Earl McLeod, his hired man. The two went around to the back of the Keeton house and remained for half an hour. At that time no one connected the Keetons with the mystery legs, but when news of Ouida's arrest broke, the men drew their own conclusion and shared it freely with eager listeners.

It was close to midnight when Chief Brown allowed Carter to return to his residence. But he could not have rested. In the early hours of Saturday morning he was roused and taken back to town. Between three and four o'clock that morning, in the custody of J. C. Hamilton and Jack Anderson, he was on the highway to Mobile so that they could check out his alibi at the hotel. During the ride Carter began mulling thoughts about the best lawyers for his defense. He knew how to reach them.

When the *Leader-Call* published Ouida's accusation, opinionated readers pictured how pieces of the murder puzzle were beginning to interlock. Nearly everyone expressed a bias, as varied reactions to the scandal piqued debate in homes and workplaces. Such a model citizen's disgrace was considered a betrayal of the public trust. This revelation of the real self was an astonishing letdown of correctness and decency, as though Carter were a popular preacher engaged in bootlegging and Ouida a favorite schoolteacher hiring herself out as a nude model or a prostitute. For some, the account in the newspaper confirmed long-held suspicions that Old Man Carter was sweet on the Keeton girl. His exposure was deserved justice and evidence of the great brought down. Others were aghast: "Not the irreproachable, civic-minded Mr. Carter! The fine Presbyterian churchman!" While acknowledging that a notable Laurelite had been discredited, the broadminded only raised eyebrows and acceded to a different reality, of a good man cheating on his good wife. So what if he ran around a little. Such misbehavior didn't make him a murderer. Besides, this Ouida Keeton, impressed by his status and influence, was a perverse little schemer who had whipped her smitten boss into submission. Still others simply did not believe Ouida's accusation. She had always been strange, they said, and her mother, too. On the other side, a part of Laurel was certain that Carter was entirely to blame. This Svengali had manipulated a helpless girl to do his will.

Fate played despicable tricks. Out of nowhere a catastrophic blow had changed the order of things—for Ouida Keeton, for Carter, and for the town. Staggered by the dark reality of Daisy Keeton's violent death, citizens of Laurel contemplated the savage cruelty and the bloody specifics of what had happened to someone they knew. The mutilated victim was a familiar figure, the proud rich woman they so often saw shopping at R. C. Gaddis Department Store and the Fine Bros.-Matison Company and riding around with her daughter. Her sudden absence and the bewildering disorder caused by the ghastly crime demanded that things be set aright, that some skillful hand reconfigure the community picture. Jack Deavours stepped forward.

■ ■ ■

After passing a second chilling night in the jailhouse, Ouida was an emotional and physical wreck. She was too fearful to sleep, and whenever she ate, she vomited. On Sunday afternoon, January 27, a visitor broke her scary solitude. Van Valentine opened the iron-barred door to admit the newcomer, and Chief Brown introduced him.

He was Alexander Currie, the district attorney elected to serve the counties of Forrest, Jones, and Perry. He was at forty a vigorous prosecutor, a veteran of the war, and a resident of Hattiesburg. For this official first encounter with the assumed perpetrator of the crime, he had driven the thirty miles north to Laurel. Mainly his purpose in this meeting, he advised her, was to announce that, with Jack Deavours assisting, he would be leading the prosecution if the case were brought to trial. He advised further that Ouida's family had retained the firm of Welch & Cooper to represent her. A grand jury would weigh the facts of her mother's death and determine whether to issue an indictment.

On hearing that she faced terrifying legal procedures, she broke down in sobs. She repeatedly had told officers that she was the helpless victim, manipulated to do the will of the murderer or be killed herself. She displayed bruises on her shins where she claimed he had kicked her. Hadn't anyone been listening? Could she make Currie understand? She told him she would like to make a new statement to augment the admissions she had made in Jack Deavours's office. Currie said he would permit this, though whatever she said might be used against her. Yet Ouida proceeded, and again she told that W. M. Carter had come to her house and murdered her mother and then threatened to kill her if she did not follow his directions. This time, since Mrs. Martin was not present with her stenographic pad, there was no written record.

When Ouida had finished, she was distraught. Currie remained professionally objective and stepped away from her. She collapsed in a fainting fit, and her sisters and Dr. T. R. Beech, the county physician who attended patients in the jail, were summoned to help bring calm. Van Valentine was standing outside the bars, absorbing the exciting drama. This was but one

Alexander Currie, district attorney for Jones, Forrest, and Perry counties and the chief prosecutor during the Legs Murder case trials. (Permission of the *Hattiesburg American*)

of Ouida's many teary outbursts the jailer would witness during the next three days.

Meanwhile, Carter was frightened. After Hamilton and Anderson had brought him home from Mobile, he figured correctly that he remained under Deavours's cloud of suspicion and anticipated being arrested should Deavours believe Ouida's testimony. Though Carter was fearful of Deavours, he was more dreadfully afraid of Earl Keeton. He had witnessed explosions of Earl's temper. If drunk or if riled by Ouida's charges, Earl could raise a mob to maim or even kill him. He had no doubt that Earl would believe his sister.

Not yet under a summons of arrest, Carter left Laurel. The threat of bodily harm drove him back to Mobile. He needed a quieter place to ponder his defense. He confided with his son and his son-in-law, and on Saturday, January 26, Sid McLeod, the brother of his employee who had made the repairs at Ouida's house, accompanied him in the Pontiac, serving as bodyguard. They checked into Carter's old haunt, the St. Andrew's Hotel, and, for Carter's safety, shared a room.

He had the frightened look of an anxious man who knows that something unsavory awaits him. Out of harm's way, he hoped to regain his balance. He telephoned Miss Adams. He continued to speak of her as "Miss Adams" out of respect. Such little courtesies softened the seamy edge of their affair. This time, however, he had not arrived in Mobile for dalliance but for making a plan to save his skin. He, McLeod, and Miss Adams drove to the park, and to his horrified listener Carter poured out details of the story breaking in Laurel. She might be called to testify as an alibi witness.

Back at the hotel, he faced the pain of his dilemma. To save himself from a murder charge he must expose the secret liaison. But how could he substantiate his alibi without losing the trust and confidence of his family? They knew nothing of his romantic adventures. He had to confront his own guilt. The hotel registry, which Hamilton and Anderson had examined, proved the hours of his stay in Mobile, but his children would demand to know why he had not told them of the side trip, the true purpose of his travels. Newton, Pauline, and Helen had no inkling that he had dallied in Mobile both before and after going to Evergreen.

The dreaded time had come. He would have to whisk the dark cloak off his shameful romance with Miss Adams. It was better that he do this himself. They would be astounded, and he feared they'd never forgive him for this, a love affair with their late sister's nurse, of all people.

He had many burdens to weigh. The best legal counsel was essential. He calculated the monetary sacrifice he would lay out for his defense. It probably would consume the suffering residue of what once was his fortune. The enterprising business leader was in inescapable distress. He wondered what people back home were saying.

After collecting his thoughts, Carter took sheets of hotel writing paper from the drawer and wrote two letters. He addressed one to his attorney, Walter S. Welch, who also served the Keetons from time to time. He did not know that they also were consulting Welch and his partner about Ouida's defense. The other was to his son Newton. It included instruction on what to do in case of mob violence. These writings, it must be assumed, also spoke to the matter of his legal counsel, should he be arrested. He was hesitant to depend on the public mails. The letters would be hand delivered.

By Sunday morning he had prepared himself to confront the inevitable. Facing personal and professional humiliation, he would put his faith in parental love to carry him through this test with his family. He would rely on the law to shield him from Earl and any mob. Realizing that arrest was probable, he told McLeod they were returning to Laurel.

During the drive home, they stopped, by prearrangement, in Richton to meet with Carter's son and his son-in-law Paul Decker, who brought a report of public feelings in Laurel. As Carter feared, the townspeople were against him.

On Monday, eight days after the murder, he was arrested. Deavours deemed the weight of Ouida's accusation sufficient. Immediately, as instructed, Carter's family retained the eminent Jackson attorney William H. Watkins to represent him, since Welch was representing Ouida.

Carter continued to deny he had any connection with the crime, but the Alabama part of his alibi covered only Sunday and the days thereafter and not the late night of Saturday, January 19, the time Ouida would claim her mother was slain. Carter was processed at the jail, but instead of incarceration in Jones County, he would be locked up in Jackson, ninety miles away. Relocating him to the Hinds County jail was an unusual move. Hotheads had given Jones County its infamous history of violence and occasional mobbings of the jailhouse. Being in Jackson, Carter would have protection from Earl or an unruly mob, but Sheriff Leon Jordan claimed a different reason. The cells in Jones county were overcrowded.

Details of the developing case were still far from clear. To solidify the conflicting facts given in Ouida's varying testimonies, Deavours conceived a ploy of arranging a face-to-face confrontation of the two presumed murderers: let Carter defy his accuser.

Why in Hinds County?

"I thought that would be a good place," Deavours advised, dodging reporters' questions about specifics.

Perhaps the pressure of being confined together in a small interrogation room would bring Ouida and Carter to the breaking point. Maybe both would make outright confessions of what really had happened. As Deavours and Chief Brown collaborated on this phase of the investigation, Brown held to his theory that Mrs. Keeton's body had been chopped up, put in sacks, and dispersed throughout the county. If Carter and Ouida should fall into an angry dispute, perhaps the concealed locations would be revealed.

In separate automobiles the two prisoners were transported to Jackson. By the time Deavours arrived with Ouida, Carter already had been locked up. With no other available space, he had been assigned a cell on death row. Across from him was Alonzo Robinson, also known as James H. Coyner, a prisoner from the Delta put forward as "the Negro ghoul." A gigantic man

Jack Deavours, former schoolmate of Ouida's and prosecuting attorney in the Legs Murder case investigation and trials, 1940s. (Courtesy of Bill Deavours)

convicted of murdering two people, of grave robbery, and of cannibalism, he was in protective custody at Jackson, awaiting execution in Boliver County on March 5.

Carter did not lose his composure. He was still dressed in his business suit when he and Will Watkins were directed to a private room where Ouida, her attorney Walter Welch, David McRae, and the Jones County lawmen were waiting. Some who witnessed Carter's quiet demeanor and distinguished appearance that day thought he looked out of character with the crime with which he was charged. He was offered a chair, and in the prickly atmosphere of facing his accuser he remained dignified and quiet. In this intense ordeal he was a gentleman, a picture of calm. Ouida fidgeted and trembled. Her anxious hands continued flexing, as though she were eager to get to work at an unseen task. Her eyes flared wide in a stony stare.

In another part of the jail, Carter's apprehensive family was waiting. They bravely faced the intolerable embarrassment his folly imposed upon them. They had driven over from Laurel, his son, both daughters, and their husbands, to stand beside him and to understand his needs.

In the examining room Deavours put harsh questions to Ouida and challenged her to recount again, this time for Carter's ears, her story of the murder. In her flash of anger the county attorney and the police chief witnessed a new stage in Ouida's behavior. She spurned Carter and for the first time expressed blatant disdain for this man who had showered her with gifts and affection. With a quavering voice she repeated her accusation of how Carter, whom she had believed to be her friend, came to her home and killed her mother. She told that he took the body away in his sedan and returned with only the thighs, which they put into her car and which he instructed Ouida to throw into Tallahala Creek from the bridge. If she did not follow his directions, he would do to her what he had done to her mother.

The woman's stark naked corpse being run through sawmill blades was the inescapable image that rushed to mind. Claiming that on other occasions Carter had spoken about killing Mrs. Keeton, Ouida whimpered that she had no idea that he planned the murder for the night he killed her. She pointed her finger and cried out for him to "tell all."

Carter winced at her plaintive sob, but for the most part he showed no sign of emotion except for a slight flush of color.

"Tell what you did with the rest of Mother's body," she wailed, "so we can give her a decent burial!"

When Deavours turned to him for a reply, Carter denied her charge.

"I have nothing to tell. I have complete ignorance of the crime."

He spoke with quiet dignity. Will Watkins nodded in approval of his response.

Carter was the soul of politeness. The face-to-face confrontation had not fulfilled Deavours's and Brown's hopes.

As the jailer led Carter from the room to meet with his family before the lockup, a few newsmen trailed after him with a barrage of questions. Watkins gave him a signal for caution.

He answered with courtesy.

"I haven't anything to give you."

They pressed him for answers, and he replied jokingly.

"I can give you no more than if I gave you a glass of water."

He sat with his son and daughters for about two hours. They had brought him a suitcase of fresh clothes.

After her exhausting journey to confront Carter in Jackson, Ouida was taken back to Laurel and locked again in her icy cell. She would remain there for two nights, until January 30. Under the strain she suffered a nervous collapse, and the county physician called for Dr. Thomas R. Ramsay Sr., for a second opinion. He examined her and agreed that Ouida required hospitalization.

He summoned Eloise, and though disrupting her date with Jack Anderson, she rushed to her sister's side, bringing with her Lettie Laurendine, a tall, attractive nurse about Ouida's age. There is reason to suspect that she

South Mississippi State Hospital (Charity Hospital), where Jack Deavours interrogated Ouida a second time, now in ruins. (Photo by Hunter Cole)

was an old friend. Miss Laurendine's family lived nearby in Richton, and she had been professionally trained at Morten Sanitarium in McNeill, the Keetons' former hometown.

Horrified that the jail was frigid, they found Ouida in a stupor. She could not stand or walk. Her face was pallid, her hands trembled, and her eyes were sunken. On Dr. Ramsay's instruction, J. C. Hamilton carried Ouida out to a car. Reporters waylaid them long enough for Hamilton to give a quick statement. Breathing hard beneath the limp burden in his arms, he hastily explained. "We are moving her to the hospital on the advice of her physician. The jail cannot be heated properly. Steel and concrete walls."

At 2:45 p.m. Hamilton, his charge, her sister, and her nurse were speeding toward the South Mississippi State Hospital, on the outskirts of town two miles north of the courthouse. Locally it was called the Charity Hospital because most patients there were indigent and could not pay for care. At the hospital, nurses loaded the flaccid body onto a stretcher and took Ouida inside for treatment.

"The pretty brunette," the *Leader-Call* reported, could not eat and after her harrowing week in jail had suffered an "almost complete nervous breakdown."

When Jack Deavours was told of Ouida's sudden transfer, he was furious. He sputtered that she must be returned to jail at once. Moving her had been illegal incursion, since no habeas corpus had been mandated. His officers defended their action on the grounds of medical urgency. Despite this requirement, no red-tape transaction had delayed Ouida's immediate hospitalization. That could be prepared after the fact. The next morning Eloise responded to inquisitive newsmen's queries. The crisis had passed, she said, and Ouida was "doing nicely." Deavours relented and announced that she could remain hospitalized until her health improved.

Although badly shaken by the marathon interrogation, by her lack of sleep, and by her weeklong confinement, Ouida was not the utterly broken waif the press was depicting. Her iron will power and cunning mind were continuously in play. As she lay on her hospital bed, her thoughts focused on defeating Carter and her persecutors, on justifying herself, and on making authorities understand that she was the victim of the abusive, powerful man she accused of killing and butchering her mother.

Jack Deavours was no less astute. On February 2 he went to Ouida's bedside. His presence there seemed to her a cordial inquiry about her health and progress. Actually he came with a devious plan. He was building a case for her prosecution, should the grand jury bring an indictment. He was accompanied by Wayne Valentine of the police department and by Mrs. Martin, who was prepared to take notes. Deavours signaled for Miss Laurendine to step outside and then came to the point.

He asked Ouida if she felt like making a final statement for the record. He was solicitous and easy and appeared earnestly gracious when he told Ouida he did not want to distress her. Since only two days had passed since her breakdown, he would not insist if she did not feel up to a long interview. He did not advise her that she might summon her attorney. Nor did he divulge a legal error he had made in processing the admissions she made in his office. Even with Ouida's signature, they lacked a notary's seal and the oath of witnesses. The new interview, secured with these iron-clad safeguards, would be evidence for the prosecution.

Ouida, persuaded by his pleasant overtures, replied that in the spirit of calm around her, she wanted to clarify her earlier remarks. She displayed no surliness or ill will toward him for the past Friday's punishing interrogation. Yes, she would give him a new statement. Perhaps she could ease her burdens and tribulations.

The curtainless charity room was severely plain and almost as severe as her jail cell. Outside the high windows the bare branches of old oaks swayed in the winter wind. Ouida lay on a paint-chipped iron bed, her dark hair spreading over a clean white pillow.

Efficient Mrs. Martin dragged a side chair close and rested her pad on her lap, waiting for the session to begin.

"Miss Ouida, do you feel like making this statement?"

"Yes, sir."

"You really do? Because if you don't, we don't want to take it. Do you feel all right?"

"Yes, sir."

And so he began.

"How old are you?"

"To be plain about that, I really don't know because I thought I was twenty-eight or twenty-nine." Ouida spoke in a voice of childlike innocence, as though making apology for not being precise. "We haven't a family Bible, and the whole family has put their ages back so that I really don't know."

As former schoolmates they evidently were contemporaries, but Ouida, actually about three years older, was not truthful.

Deavours eased her into speaking about her association with W. M. Carter and about the history of her employment. She replied with a succinct résumé. Next, he gently probed for facts about Carter's behavior after she returned from Washington.

"I saw him each month for my rent money. He didn't start coming over to the house regularly until something over a year ago," she answered, downplaying the fifteen years of Carter's furtive attentions. He had sold Ouida a house on the south side of town, rented by Mr. and Mrs. W. O. Hedgepath, and as a courtesy continued with collections. They next spoke about Carter's involvement in the Rayburn Robinson lawsuit and about the balance in her mother's bank account.

"During the time you worked for W. M. Carter, did you ever lend him money?"

"I let him have part of the money on the Hedgepath house I owned on the Boulevard."

This loan, she advised, was her personal money and not her mother's, and besides an accumulation of family money, as Ouida continued to explain, bonds and jewelry were kept in a lockbox at the bank.

"Now, getting back toward Saturday night. When was the first time that Mr. Carter suggested this crime to you?"

"He didn't suggest the crime to me."

"What did he do?"

"He told me that if I didn't comply with his every wish that he would place me so that nothing would mean anything to me."

She told that Carter had urged her repeatedly to take trips with him to Mobile and New Orleans, but she had refused to go. He had made improper advances, but she did not tell her mother.

"And it was the result of those suggestions and your refusals that he threatened to kill your mother?"

"Yes."

Ouida exposed further intimate facts about her former boss. She told that for several years he had been having a love affair with Harriet Adams of Mobile. They had involved her in their devious plans as the two were arranging for a surreptitious visit Harriet was to make to Laurel. Carter asked Ouida and Mrs. Keeton to be her hosts. They agreed, but Ouida explained that her mother knew nothing of Carter's love affair then. It came to light about two months before the murder. She also told that a few years back while Miss Adams was riding around Laurel with Carter, there was a car wreck, and the guest was injured. Carter sneaked her to Hattiesburg for treatment. To their surprise, Mrs. Carter found out, and the lovers pressed Ouida for further help. Carter told her to write his wife a letter explaining that Miss Adams was the Keetons' houseguest and that he was assisting them in entertaining her. She declared also that she herself once had accepted Miss Adams's invitation to spend a few days in Mobile.

As Ouida continued, Deavours and Mrs. Martin were absorbed by the stirring report. She divulged that Carter harbored another deep secret. As his personal secretary, she had been privy to one matter he wanted kept strictly confidential, a downtown mailbox for intimate correspondence. She gave Deavours the details but denied having written to this box herself while she was in Washington.

Deavours then asked her for an account of Carter's coming to the gas station on January 19. Ouida traced his purchases of gas for each of his vehicles. Later that night her mother would be murdered, but Deavours did not ask Ouida whether Carter had whispered any plans to her. Most of his questions flowed in soothing tones, and in the ease of the exchange Ouida continued to speak with apparent candor. She remained calm, showing little stress as she recounted events of Saturday. No legal or family adviser was present to warn her to curtail her discussions. Mostly, she focused on timetables and occurrences. She told that after returning home from work on Saturday, she and Mrs. Keeton went for a thirty-minute car ride, and soon after they came back, Carter briefly dropped by with a gift of ice cream. Her mother answered his knock. Ouida herself was planning to pass the rest of Saturday evening across the street at Mrs. Richeimer's, but she remained at home. Then around eight o'clock Carter returned to the Keetons', his purpose in this second visit that evening, Ouida said, being to hand her the rent on the Hedgepath house. He took a seat beside her and her mother in Mrs. Keeton's bedroom. As they chatted, a discussion of the difference in the rearing of the Carter children and the Keeton children turned into a mild argument. Mrs. Keeton rose from her chair and went to the kitchen for refreshments, brandy and cookies.

"Did the argument get heated?"

"Not too much."

"Did it get loud?"

"Their voices were raised above the average speaking voice."

"Did you anticipate any actual conflict between them?"

"No."

"Did your mother know he had tried to get you a job in New Orleans?"

"She had heard him talking about it."

"Did you join in the argument?"

"I asked them not to discuss it."

"Did you see Mr. Carter when he picked the poker up?"

"I saw him when he picked it up and turned the wood over in the fireplace. Next thing I knew, I heard Mother's head hit the mantelpiece."

"Were you looking?"

"Not right at that exact minute."

"What side of the head hit the mantel?"

"Right."

"Was her back to him or her face?"

"She was pouring the brandy from the mantel."

"Then did she fall to the floor?"

"As she went to fall, that's when I dropped to the floor with her."

"Did you catch her before she struck the floor?"

"I can't remember that. All I can remember is I was on the floor with her."

"Is that the only lick that was struck?"

"No, he struck her several more times after she fell."

"While you were down there with her?"

"Yes, sir."

"Did he strike you?"

"No, he pushed me back."

"At the time your mother fell, did you say anything?"

"No, except started crying."

"Did you call?"

"I called to her."

"That was about what time?"

"It was early in the night."

"Before 9:00 o'clock?"

"I don't know whether it was before or after 9:00 o'clock."

"You say you gathered her head up in your arms there on the floor?"

"Yes."

"The blood from her head, did it get on the floor and the hearth?"

"Most of it was on my clothes."

"But there was some on the hearth?"

"Yes."

"Some on the floor?"

"Yes."

"When Mr. Carter came the second time, how was he dressed?"

"In a gray-looking suit."

"After your mother was knocked to the floor, how long did she stay there?"

"I don't know, Jack."

"Now, Ouida, do you know that your mother was killed there in front of that fireplace?"

"That's what I think. I couldn't feel her pulse. And she didn't speak to me."

"What did he say after it was done?"

"Told me to get up."

"What did you do then?"

"I was there crying, and he told me I had to help him."

"And what did you help him do?"

"Take her body out to his car."

"Was his car in the driveway then?"

"Yes."

"What kind of car was it he had at the back gate?"

"A large car."

"Was it the Buick or Lincoln?"

"I don't know."

"Was it a four-door car?"

"Yes."

"Where did you put her body?"

"In the back."

"When you picked your mother's body up, did you pick up the head or the feet?"

"Where the head was."

He asked if she changed her clothes. Ouida replied she had removed her red pajamas and robe and later burned them. Carter returned before daybreak, parking in the back. He was in his Pontiac. The watchdog began barking, and she told that Carter ordered her to go to the front.

"What happened then?"

"He told me that he couldn't destroy all of Mother in that box."

"What box?"

"I don't know."

"What else did he say?"

"That I had to help him."

"And his car was in the driveway?"

"Yes, and I went back to the back and put the dog up. I had already turned him out, and I put him back in the garage. Mr. Carter came in, and we wrapped them in things I gave him and put them in my car. He didn't say 'Mother's body.' He just said 'her body' and that I had to help him handle it."

"Did he have a box in there?"

"I didn't see one."

"Did you see the limbs lying there in the car?"

"No."

"Did you see a bundle there?"

"No, you see, I didn't go all the way to the automobile."

"Then you brought them into the house?"

"He helped me bring in one, and he brought in one. He told me to bring it in, but I couldn't. So he helped me."

"Did you drop it?"

"Yes."

"Was it wrapped up?"

"Yes. In paper."

"Where did you put it when you brought it in the house?"

"I think we went on back to her room, as I remember."

"Did you stop in the bathroom?"

"I don't remember, but they were wrapped in the house. I thought we went to her room, but we could have gone to the bathroom."

"After they were both in the house, they were washed?"

"No."

"You dropped it on the ground?"

"Just one."

"What did you wrap them in?"

"I gave him some cloths out of the bathroom."

"Was it those striped sacks?"

"I don't remember."

"When he got them wrapped, what did he do?"

"Took them back to my car."

"You had the dog in there, didn't you?"

"I turned the dog out in the backyard."

"Did he make one or two trips?"

"Two."

"Did he put them in your car?"

"Yes, in the back."

"And what did he put them on?"

"*New York Times.*"

"How long was he there?"

"Long enough to do all that."

"What did he tell you then? Anything?"

"Told me to stay there."

"Anything else?"

"Where did he say he was going?"

"Mobile."

"Did he tell you who he was going to see?"

"Miss Adams."

"Where was he going to stay?"

"St. Andrew's Hotel."

"Then where was he going?"

"Evergreen, Alabama."

"Where was he going from there?"

"He said he would be back Wednesday and told me to stay there, and I told him I couldn't."

"Did he tell you to clean up the house?"

"No."

"This kidnapping story?"

"He told me that Wednesday."

"Now, that's the first story you told me. Is that the story he told you to tell?"

"Yes."

"Did you go to bed Sunday after he left?"

"No."

"Stayed in your house all day Sunday?"

"Yes."

"When did you start cleaning up the house?"

"I ran the vacuum over everything Monday, I think it was, or Tuesday."

"When did you destroy your clothes?"

"That night. No, Saturday night."

"Sunday morning?"

"Yes, just as soon as I could take them off."

"How was your mother dressed when she was taken away?"

"Travel tweed crepe."

"Anything else?"

"Her regular things on."

"When did you start cleaning up the fireplace and the floor?"

"Whenever I cleaned up. Monday or Tuesday."

"Did you leave blood on the fireplace until then?"

"It never did come off."

"Did you make any effort before then to get it off?"

"I had, off the mantel."

"What did you use for that?"

"A knife."

"What kind?"

"One that I had in the sink."

"When did you paint the fireplace?"

"I think it was Tuesday. Same day I cleaned house."

"And you painted the fireplace in order to cover up blood?"

"Yes."

"Why didn't you take those legs away that day?"

"I don't know."

"Did he tell you where to take them?"

"Yes."

"Where?"

"Said to put them in the river."

"What river?"

"Just said to put them in the water."

"Did he tell you when?"

"I think it was Monday, but I won't be sure about that."

"Monday morning it rained. Tuesday it snowed. What time did you decide to leave the house?"

"About the time the GM&N came in."

"Around eight o'clock?"

"Yes."

Deavours asked about her route to the woods where she left the bundle. Ouida recalled her journey over the concrete bridge, along the road past Farmer Saul's house, and to the one-lane trail.

"You had been there, I believe you said, after plums, before this?"

"Yes."

"You took the limbs out there?"

"I put them down just as I got them out of the car."

"Right there beside a little pine tree, wasn't it, Ouida?"

"It was where it is a slant in the road, further from where I was stuck."

She recounted her trip home with the help of Kennedy and then told of her phone call to Duckworth. After retrieving her car, she drove home and locked it in the garage.

"Did you go to Mrs. Richeimer's Monday?"

"No."

"Monday night, was the house lighted up?"

"I don't remember, but I guess I must have had on some lights."

"Did you communicate with Mr. Carter Monday, Sunday, or Tuesday?"

"No."

"And Wednesday afternoon, Mr. Carter came back?"

"Yes, somewhere around three o'clock. I was coming up the alley, fixing to go to Mrs. Richeimer's."

"You got in the car?"

"Yes."

"What was your conversation?"

"I told him I couldn't do what he asked me to do."

"What do you mean by that?"

"I mean, putting them over that bridge."

"Did he ask you if you had disposed of them?"

"No, that's the first thing I told him."

"Then what did he say?"

"I went on and asked if he had seen the papers and told him about me getting stuck."

"What did he say to that?"

"He told me that I had been careless."

"What else did he say?"

"I told him that everybody would know it was me."

"And he told you to tell the story you told me?"

"Yes."

"Exactly like he told you to tell it?"

"As near as I could."

"Did you ask him what he did with the rest of the body?"

"Yes, but he wouldn't talk to me about it. He told me he was going to bury her like they do at sea."

"Did he say where?"

"The only thing he mentioned was the Ovett road."

"That's when the body was dismembered?"

"I reckon so."

Then, according to her story, Carter agreed to attend to repairing the frozen water pipe and draining the frozen radiator of her car. He left but returned soon afterward with his hired helper. She said that neither man went into the house.

"Now, you have talked to him in Jackson? I took you over there?"

"Yes."

"Ouida, is there anything else you want to say about this?"

"I think I have told you everything."

"You can't tell us what kind of car he took the body away in? Except that it was a large car?"

"Yes."

"You and you mother hadn't had a fuss?"

"No."

"As I understand it, Ouida, you make this statement voluntarily?"

"Yes."

"Nobody has promised you anything?"

"No."

"It is freely made without any compulsion and represents the whole truth and nothing but the truth?"

"Yes."

"Isn't made with any spite toward Mr. W. M. Carter?"

"No."

"Nothing untruthful?"

"No, except I just guessed at the hours."

Deavours's questions, gentle at first, had moved aggressively to touchy subjects that required candid answers. Only a few times had Ouida, savvy and alert, attempted evasions. They had talked for about an hour. Deavours dismissed Mrs. Martin so that she could go to her office and work on the transcription.

The interim afforded Ouida several hours to muse on the revelations she had admitted. One essential detail should be mentioned, since it would explain her complicity in disposing of Mrs. Keeton's legs. When the lengthy typescript was brought to her bed, she read it, made no corrections, but asked permission to insert an annotation at the end.

"I wish added to the above statement that at the time I assisted in removing my mother's body from our home that Mr. Carter threatened to take my life and pointed at me a pistol."

Her implication was striking. She felt she must dissociate herself from the heinous act. She portrayed herself as a threatened and fearful victim, wary that she, too, might be murdered if she stepped out of line. Upon her further reflection, she supplied one comment more.

"There should also be added to this statement that on Friday morning, January 25th, I found a pistol similar to one stolen from the McRae filling station in the backyard and that is the same pistol Mr. Brown got in the house."

After Mrs. Martin had typed in the addenda, Deavours returned to Ouida's room and presented the revisions to her. This time he watched as she signed her name in the presence of witnesses. Satisfied with his achievement, he was confident that he now had a padlock on the case. For him, this testimony resolved the discrepancies in Ouida's previous accounts of the murder. He and the district attorney would make the document the keystone of their prosecution of both Carter and Ouida. This official confession, the only one with both a signature and a sworn affidavit, would be the subject of one of the most heated and prolonged debates about Carter's guilt or innocence. Had Deavours known that Ouida had even further versions of the murder story to recount, he would not have left the hospital gloating over his success.

Meanwhile, Chief Brown was masterminding the countywide search for pieces of Daisy Keeton's corpse. Fifty convicts and twenty lawmen were dragging the yellowish floodwaters of Jones County. Tallahala Creek, which meandered from northern Jasper County along the eastern side of Laurel and south to Ellisville, and Bogue Homa Creek, which skirted Ovett, seemed likely spots. Ouida's claim that Carter had disposed of body parts near Ovett pinpointed the bottomland below Highway 15.

"If the rest of the body was thrown in the creek, which is not unlikely," Jack Deavours announced, "we will have to wait until the creek goes down to make a thorough search, because the stream is almost two miles wide now."

"I don't believe that the body was taken very far from the house," he supposed, "because the girl says that Carter returned with the legs not so very long after he left the house, and that the other parts of the body had been disposed of then."

Although Chief Brown's crews were responding to most alerts the public offered, all were false alarms and wild goose chases. Behind a rural church a plot of loose dirt aroused suspicion. It proved to be an unused grave. They were called to the GM&N shops to investigate a chunk of meat a dog had dragged out of the creek. It was the remains of a butchered hog. Circling buzzards drew Brown's men to a site where calf carcasses had been left after skinning. From the fire department Wayne Valentine borrowed a rope and two long grappling hooks for use in combing deep, murky waters.

Earl Keeton joined in as the searchers poked through debris beneath bridges and waded into streams. Some swollen creeks had receded slightly after the gushing overflow following the thaw. By that time, putrefaction of the corpse would be a lure both to searchers and to scavengers, but each evening the convicts returned empty-handed to their camp in Ellisville.

In downtown Laurel, the telegraph office, more than the courthouse and the police station, became a mecca for the latest news. In response to the intensity of national news reporting, G. F. Osborne, district superintendent of the Western Union Telegraph Company, was called to Laurel to assist in upgrading wire services. The story was carried in Nevada, New Jersey, Ohio, and every other state reached by the Associated Press. Out-of-towners far and wide followed the mystery as though it were a serialized novelette. Each day correspondents were transmitting fifteen thousand words to regional and national papers and to news syndicates. John Brazeale of the *New Orleans Item-Tribune*; Jack Dale, a staff writer for the Associated Press; and Kenneth Tolar of the *Memphis Commercial Appeal* were filing daily reports, and their papers were giving space for generous coverage, as were the *Leader-Call*, the *Hattiesburg American*, and the morning and evening papers of Jackson. Osborne conjectured that if the case went to trial, Western Union would establish a dispatch office at the courthouse.

When suspicious blood spots and strands of long hair were detected on the upholstery of one of Carter's cars, public joking about his devoted attention to Ouida intensified. By now everyone knew that he gave her car rides and called at the Keeton home after dark. Some Laurelites had no doubts they were fooling around, but Ouida's family objected, claiming his visits to 539 Cross Street as a family friend and adviser occurred only when Mrs. Keeton was present to chaperone.

District Attorney Currie's speculation as to the value of Daisy Keeton's estate drew a retort from Earl. He estimated that it could be no more than $625 from a $500 bond and $125 in a checking account. All of his mother's money and property, he explained, had been signed over to Ouida, and an estate of $10,000 in bonds was out of the question, for probably these had been converted to cash.

"No administrator has been appointed," Earl declared. "Later, if it develops there is an estate to be administered, an administrator will be appointed at that time, if necessary." He brushed aside any further questions about money. He claimed to be concentrating only on two things—the recovery of his mother's remains so that she could be decently buried and helping the police bring his mother's killer to justice.

His sister remained in the Charity Hospital, under guard, but her ten-day respite from the jailhouse was near its end. On Sunday, February 10, her condition was sufficiently improved that she could be returned to jail. When informed of the transfer, the convalescent cried out in exasperation.

"You can take me there or anywhere! I don't care where you take me!"

These were the last spoken words anyone would hear from Ouida until after her trial. Her voice left her. No one, not even her sisters, could compel her to speak. For all they knew, their sensitive sister's ongoing torture had rendered her mute.

The *Leader-Call*'s coverage was headlined "Miss Keeton Goes Back to County Jail." This time when Valentine closed the barred door on her, there was no paroxysm of hysterics. Shivering and withdrawn, Ouida lay solemnly on the prison cot through the long night. On Monday morning the jailer reported that "if she did not sleep, then she was quiet. I did not ask her this morning how she felt."

Had Valentine tried to converse with her, Ouida would not have replied. She either fell into a state of semiconsciousness or withdrew almost completely from reality. Aphasia was her defense. Having wrapped herself in silence, Ouida could not be moved to speak. When her interrogator demanded an answer, she scrawled words on a notepad, if she replied at all. She attempted to contain herself in a safe haven she created. Her gaze remained fixed on spots on the wall, and she was spoon-fed and helped to the toilet. Eloise believed that her sister's tongue was paralyzed, a result of shocking mistreatment. The tantrums and the weeping were over. When the officials prodded her, she remained inert. When David McRae brought her attorneys to meet with her, even they got no answers.

District Attorney Currie, a pragmatic no-nonsense prosecutor, concentrated on assigning a credible motive to the crime. He had studied Ouida's signed statement. When he learned that she had been in control of her mother's assets, he averred before a group of reporters that Ouida had both a motive and an opportunity to kill.

Jack Deavours, however, avoided guessing. He would wait, he said, until facts were more conclusive. Other motives for murder—rage, hate, love, vengeance, and jealousy—could not be discounted. "I am just waiting for some member of the Keeton family to take charge of the estate. As far as I know there has been no inventory made."

Did Mrs. Keeton have life insurance? Deavours was not sure, but he understood that she did not.

He and Dr. Tom Ramsay had gone to New Orleans to turn over crime evidence to the city chemist, John M. Danneker, for examination. On Monday, February 11, Deavours, just returned from the trip, answered questions in a press conference.

"We took all the things that have been found at the Keeton place," he reported. The sanguinary items included a blood-streaked door facing, a piece of floor joist, the butcher knives found on the kitchen counter, foul-smelling silk stockings, vials of bone fragments, a jar of lard-drenched soil, and the brass-handled fire poker.

Reporters pressed him for a comment on the ashes that had been taken from the fireplace.

"I don't know anything about them."

They asked about the search of Carter's automobile, and Deavours hedged. There was a rumor about strands of hair.

"I don't know anything about his car," he said, protecting details of his probable prosecution of Carter, in case of an indictment, "except what you newspaperman have told me and what I have seen in the papers."

J. C. Hamilton and Wayne Valentine, standing beside Deavours, admitted that they had searched the car within a day or two after Carter's arrest, but they declined to make further comment.

The next day, February 12, Ouida was so ill that both the prosecution and the defense called in physicians. Dr. Ramsay declared her health to be "as good as anyone's condition could be when they refuse to eat. Miss Keeton is in a condition that usually accompanies a person who is suffering from mental remorse." He added that the symptoms were nervousness, indigestion, loss of appetite, nervous exhaustion, headache, and subnormal temperature.

"Since her arrest the continuation of these symptoms has produced a condition which is predominated by complete silence."

He said that she was not unconscious and that her pulse beat was regular.

"Every effort is being made to encourage this young lady to eat, and forced feeding will be done if necessary. Miss Keeton is in a satisfactory condition, considering the act with which she is charged." He said that, no, she was not on a hunger strike and that her removal from the Charity Hospital had not been detrimental. "The care she is receiving at the jail is just as good as at a hospital. The essential things are absolute rest, persuasive feeding, and heat. At the present time, electrical appliances have been placed at her disposal in her cell, and every effort is being made to make her comfortable and to give her the proper care." Ouida, he remarked in conclusion, had "not disclosed any idea that would suggest that she wants to die."

The next day Ouida's attorneys, citing a "grave condition" and the minimal jailhouse accommodations as putting her life in jeopardy, threatened to issue a writ of habeas corpus demanding that she be placed in a hospital. Chancellor Amis heard the statements of Drs. J. B. Jarvis, E. A. Bush, J. K. Oates, and Ouida's sister, Maude McRae. The three physicians agreed that "the girl was in a serious condition and should have immediate hospital attention." However, Dr. Ramsay and Dr. Beech were of a different opinion. Both believed that the cell could be made sufficiently comfortable for Ouida's needs. Besides, when Ramsay had attended her on Wednesday morning, she was neither unconscious nor in a coma. She was able to respond to his queries with legibly handwritten notes. The jailer gave Ramsay support by claiming that Ouida had a good night.

When Welch and Cooper threatened to petition, Sheriff Jordan allowed Ouida's transfer without resorting to the courts. As a result Chancellor Amis signed a habeas corpus order allowing Ouida to be hospitalized. Yet confusion resulted when an ambulance drew up to the entrance of the jail but was sent back to the hospital, where Miss Laurendine stood waiting. Both Deavours and Currie deflected blame from themselves, saying they did not know who was responsible for turning the ambulance away.

Later in the day Ouida was transported a few blocks to Laurel General, a short ride down the hill from town. Observers remarked that a trained nurse was attending her as she was helped into the ambulance, the solicitous Miss Laurendine. At first Ouida was confined in a ground-floor room, but because gawkers continued to press their noses against her downstairs window to watch her, she was removed to the second floor. Her guard, Tom Lott, was stationed outside her door to restrict unauthorized visitors and to prevent the possibility of Ouida's escape.

Ouida lay mute in her hospital bed, a notepad and pencil placed nearby. She indicated that she wanted authorities to know she was tormented by remorse for being drawn against her will into the heinous crime. Miss Laurendine pampered and kept a protective eye on the frail patient. Dr. Jarvis, alternating with Dr. Beech, arrived each day to check Ouida's vital signs. Lott followed the letter of the law in permitting only exclusive admissions to the sickroom. From his chair outside, he monitored and screened all comers.

The rooms at Laurel General had swinging half-doors that obstructed a patient's bed from the view of visitors passing along the hallway. If required, a green serge curtain, which could be drawn across the door opening, and a folding screen placed between the doorway and the bed assured a further degree of privacy, but Lott kept himself alert to most of the activity within.

The mute and ashen Ouida remained on retreat within herself and was not able to take solid nourishment. Miss Laurendine bought tomato juice and Coca-Colas, but an intravenous feeding of glucose and sips of liquids sustained her patient. Ouida lay in mental turmoil, her fate outside her control. The whole world had changed. Fearsome adversaries had boxed her into a tight corner. Her health was broken, her life ruined, and no one in power showed any sign of believing her. Since neither obstreperous Earl nor flighty Eloise was capable of taking charge of her affairs, Ouida found support in David McRae when informed that her taxes had not been paid. Her brother-in-law, a man of patience and compunction, ignored the enduring antipathy between his wife and her mother and became Ouida's adviser and guide. With the court's permission, she summoned him and Maude, and they gained entry to the restricted sickroom.

Lott eavesdropped on their murmured responses to Ouida's instructions scribbled on the notepad. One subject they addressed was legal counsel. Another was money. Lott overheard the McRaes' answers to Ouida's queries about her bank account, the paying of taxes on the Keeton property, and a transfer of land. Deducing that Ouida was making a deed of gift to the McRaes' daughter, he heard David reply that they would return with documents for her to sign.

Lott was on duty when David arrived with official paperwork. Accompanying him was a notary public, Maude B. Reed, who would serve as witness to the transaction and apply her legal stamp to the papers. When they approached Ouida's door, they were obstructed, but it was not Mr. Lott who blocked them. Earl, fuming in unsuppressed rage, was standing in the hallway. Somehow he had learned of Ouida's plan, arranged on her sickbed, of giving the McRaes the balance of Mrs. Keeton's bank account. David had brought a check for her signature, but Earl was there to block David and Maude's access to the money.

McRae had not expected him, and there was a scuffle. Earl insisted that he, too, be admitted, but since his name was not on the judge's approved roster, Lott blocked the door and held him at bay as he let McRae and the notary pass. As Earl protested over being excluded from his sister, he lost control.

"If you make her sign those papers, David," he blurted, "I'll kill you!"

Yet Ouida did sign, although she put her name on only one of the two legal instruments. It was a transfer of the Hedgepath house to the McRaes' daughter: "For and in consideration of the sum of $1.00, and other good and valuable considerations, I do hereby convey and specially warrant to my niece, Maude Louise McRae, that certain property together with improvements thereon described as Lot 5 of Block 2 of the Boulevard Addition to the City of Laurel, Jones County, Mississippi. The grantee is to pay taxes for the year 1935. Witness my signature on this the 9th day of February 1935. Ouida Keeton."

Miss Reed signed her name and affixed her seal beneath her oath.

Although the guard's eyes were not privy to the scene, his ears had witnessed the conversation. As McRae and Miss Reed brushed past him and Earl, Miss Laurendine was returning with a Coca-Cola. Earl followed his brother-in-law and Miss Reed to the stairs. As they disappeared, Lott was firm in his opinion. This unquestionably legal procedure of transferring property had been the act of a wholly rational mind.

The search for body parts was at an impasse, and local officers began to express their doubts. They were "frankly skeptical whether the woman's body would be found in a day, a month, or at all." Yet to the north, Jasper County officials were giving the search their full support. They were planning to drain Andrews Mill Pond, west of Sandersville and not far from Corinth Church, because unsubstantiated rumors circulated that Ouida and Carter had been spotted near the site shortly after Mrs. Keeton's murder. South of Laurel, Forrest County officers also lent their aid. A deputy sheriff brought a set of false teeth to Laurel for possible identification.

The revolver found in Ouida's drawer intensified the prosecution's hope that bits of Mrs. Keeton's corpse would be discovered. The three discharged shells in the gun were evidence that she may have been shot rather than bludgeoned. If so, bullets likely would be impacted in body tissue.

At the mortuary the few segmented pieces of the cadaver were stitched back together in an effort to return the dehumanized limbs to a semblance of an actual body. The fleshy tissue had been injected with Sumrall's strongest solution of embalming fluid. L. M. Jones had taken a dozen pictures for the evidence files. Drs. C. H. and Tom Ramsay, father and son, made close analyses for the police. Their report, according to City Hall, declared "that the body was butchered in a crude manner only because the implements used were crude. The manner in which the person or persons dissected the body displayed a certain amount of knowledge of anatomy, possibly the work of a regular butcher or ex-butcher. . . . One of the knees was severed at the exact spot where it would have been most easy to have taken the bone apart and clip the muscles and tendons."

Even though the three-county search had yielded no positive results, the Legs Murder case continued to generate surprise. As Ouida lay under guard in her hospital bed and as Earl tramped the Tallahala swamps searching for the rest of his mother, the irrepressible Eloise claimed her own prominent spot in the family news. In her distress, she repeatedly had turned to Jack Anderson, the handsomest of the police officers, for solace and romance, and on Groundhog Day, thirteen days after Daisy Keeton's murder, they were quietly married in the Keeton home. It was young Eloise's third venture into matrimony. On learning of the nuptials, some waggish Laurelites joked that vows were exchanged before the fatal fireplace. The public merriment over the bad taste and poor judgment shown by the sudden marriage eclipsed the sobering question of whether there was a conflict of interest. Might Anderson's marriage to a Keeton compromise his legitimacy as an police officer investigating Ouida's case?

Daisy Keeton and her daughter Ouida had attended the Presbyterian church, but Eloise's marriage ceremony was solemnized by the Reverend R. A. Thornton, "a friend and neighbor of the Keetons" and an evangelical preacher who ministered mainly in rural churches. Only a few members of the families were present. Earl and Jewel, who had moved into the murder house, were the bride's attendants.

Eloise's most recent sojourn down the aisle was more than a macabre, ill-timed amusement. The marriage documents conveyed serious import, and immediately the press reacted. On the application Eloise had listed Ouida Keeton, not Daisy Keeton, as her next of kin. Until then, despite all Ouida's statements and all the tips and the witnesses who had come forward, the police still had no positive evidence that Daisy Keeton was dead. There were legs, but no proof that they were Daisy Keeton's. The license might serve to establish the family's admission that there was indeed evidence, a corpus delicti proving that a crime had been committed. Was this application a sign that the family was attesting to the truth that Daisy Keeton, so long missing, was dead and that Eloise, in writing Ouida's name in the blank, was acknowledging that the legs refrigerated at the Sumrall mortuary across the street from the courthouse were Mrs. Keeton's? If so, the prosecution might have further basis for proving the corpus delicti.

On the license the alluring Eloise, perpetuating a fib, had entered her age as "twenty-two," and for his, Jack listed "twenty-three." Actually, she was approaching thirty, and from public comments the announcement aroused, her husband likely came to know that Eloise had deceived him and that he was in fact younger than his bride.

Both the *Memphis Commercial Appeal* and the Jackson morning newspaper reported the marriage. The *Jackson Clarion-Ledger*'s page-one headline trumpeted "Cupid Enters Murder Case" and "Sister of Ruby [*sic*] Keeton Weds Cop in Her Third Marriage." In a sly tone the story reported that "last night she married one of the officers, handsome, athletic Jack Anderson, a member of the police force." The marriage, "quite beside the record as far as the investigation of her mother's slaying is concerned," revived interest in the debacle of Eloise's first wedding and the scandalous court case that ensued.

For two weeks Jack and Eloise honeymooned in her room in New Orleans. On February 18 he returned to Laurel while Eloise completed her business course. The marriage would last for just over a year.

On February 17 Ellis B. Cooper, chief defense counsel for Ouida, refuted press reports that a mole on the lower abdomen verified the dismembered corpse to be Daisy Keeton's. No member of the Keeton family, he said, had acknowledged the legs to be those of the mother. This lawyerly ploy was his move to block the prosecution's attempt to establish a corpus delicti on which to build its case.

At Cooper's side, Earl Keeton stepped forward for notice, also declaring the previous report to be untrue. The Keeton children continued to deny that their mother was dead. She merely had disappeared. So far, in this strange ménage there had been no display of grief whatsoever.

"No member of our family," Earl repeated, "has been able to identify the parts."

But would "able" Earl have been aware of moles or distinctive irregularities on his mother's bare privates? Despite disclaimers from Deavours and Currie, the public could assume from his remark that indeed the Keeton children had inspected the pieces of the cadaver, that maybe Earl, Maude, and Eloise together had gone into the Sumrall lab to examine their mother's most intimate flesh. However, they would deny this to be true.

Pressed to comment on Ouida's varied confessions published in the newspaper, her lawyer declared her statements to be mutterings of "an unbalanced person," demanded their removal from the evidence, and hinted that an insanity plea would be central to Ouida's defense.

In Hattiesburg, District Attorney Currie announced that at the convening of the grand jury on February 18 he would seek a joint indictment of Ouida and Carter.

"Ouida will be tried first," Currie declared, "as we will depend entirely on her to prosecute Carter." He told reporters there was evidence, in addition to Ouida's confessions, that would link her to the crime. "If she refuses to take the stand, then she shoulders the crime alone. Her statement that she was afraid to reveal her mother's murder because of Carter's threats offers no defense for her. We know that there were periods of several hours in which she was not under duress and could have reported the crime."

He concluded by announcing that the grand jury would be given a tour of the Keeton home.

Morgan Brassell, a newsman covering Currie's press conference for the *Memphis Commercial Appeal*, focused closely on Jack Deavours. "In assisting Prosecutor Currie, County Attorney Deavours," he wrote, "will not only prosecute a member of his high school graduating class but the sister of a man once indicted for murdering Burns Deavours, a brother of the county attorney." Brassell commented further that "another member of the Keeton family, Mrs. Jack Anderson—formerly Mary Eloise Keeton, a sister of Ouida—is reported residing in New Orleans. Anderson, a former member of the police force in Laurel, who married Eloise three days after Ouida was arrested in the murder case, returned to Laurel Saturday." Anderson had resigned.

When the news corps asked Earl Keeton for a tour of the Keeton home, his surprising reply was yes. He and his wife, Jewel, their six-year-old daughter, and Mrs. A. B. Anderson, Jewel's mother, had moved into Daisy and Ouida's house after Deavours and Chief Brown's investigations were completed and the sheriff had impounded Ouida's car.

Entering the front door from the L-shaped porch, the reporters met a false elegance that overpowered the ordinary dwelling. Guiding the guests as though through a showplace, Earl comported himself as a gracious host. He displayed courtesies that no one in Laurel could have expected in Earl Keeton.

He showed the reporters the fireplace in the "luxuriously furnished" living room, and one or two incorrectly reported it to be the one at which Mrs. Keeton had been struck down. Earl proudly called attention to the coal-burning Heatrola stationed on the hearth. This cast-iron console was coated with a mahogany-colored porcelain that harmonized with the furnishings. Heartily, he explained that it had replaced the old fireplace, although the mantel remained.

He led the guests from the parlor to the dining room and, behind it, the kitchen. Betty Jean, Earl's little daughter, peeked around the swinging door to observe the strangers jotting down notes and inspecting her grandmother's precious knickknacks. Jewel and Mrs. Anderson had secluded themselves from view.

Earl made no display of shock over the horrific events that had occurred on the premises. He ushered the guests through a short hallway and into the chamber of horrors and showed them the repainted hearth and fireplace.

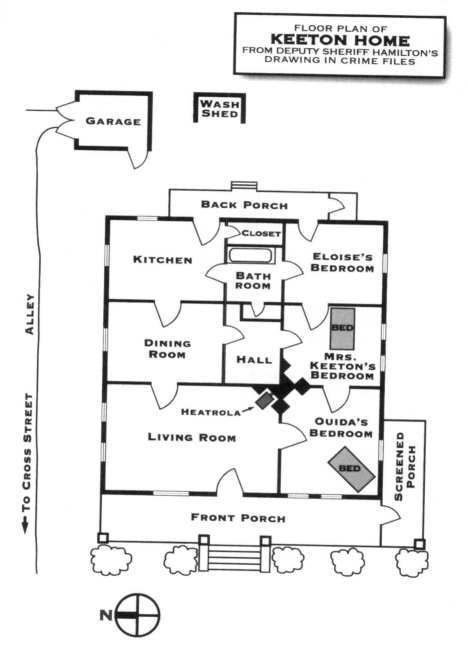

FLOOR PLAN OF
KEETON HOME
FROM DEPUTY SHERIFF HAMILTON'S
DRAWING IN CRIME FILES

GARAGE

WASH
SHED

BACK PORCH

CLOSET

KITCHEN

BATH
ROOM

ELOISE'S
BEDROOM

ALLEY

BED

DINING
ROOM

HALL

MRS.
KEETON'S
BEDROOM

TO CROSS STREET

HEATROLA

OUIDA'S
BEDROOM

LIVING ROOM

SCREENED PORCH

BED

FRONT PORCH

N

Floor plan of the Keeton home, adapted from a drawing in the crime files, Jones
County courthouse. (Illustration by Bill Pitts)

"Whether there were bloodstains on it before it was painted I don't know," Earl ingenuously remarked. "But Ouida says there were."

The newsmen and women did not enter the bathroom. Had they been allowed there, surely someone's report would have described the ghastly bathtub and its probable function in the dismemberment. A repulsive thought was inescapable. The residents at 539 Cross Street must be taking their baths in the tub where a human corpse had been slaughtered.

Although not allowed to inspect all the rooms, the reporters sensed that Ouida's bedroom was adjacent to the living room. Its significance would come to light at Carter's trial in another titillating disclosure, for Ouida had not yet finished giving confessions that took surprising new turns.

The floor plan was typical of houses on Cross Street. Daisy Keeton, as the press noted, preferred a somewhat overrich decor. The *Commercial Appeal* described the home itself as modest and noted that the four temporarily in residence were keeping Mrs. Keeton's costly possessions safe and sound.

Had Earl reformed? The handsome but volatile son seemed out of character as he poured servings of his mother's homemade cordial for his visitors, and tossed back a sampling or two himself.

"I can hardly believe that Mother is dead," he commented, as though to make a favorable impression. "I keep waiting for her to come back just like she used to when she was away on a visit. Maybe someday, after all," he continued fatuously, "she will come back."

On Monday, February 18, after taking their own tour of the murder house, a grand jury convened to weigh the charges against Ouida and Carter. Two hours later they returned with two indictments. In the jail in Jackson, when Carter heard, he declared the accusations were "a pack of lies."

For the first time since the arrest, Will Watkins allowed his client to face reporters and answer questions. Restricted to responding only to preapproved topics, Carter was emphatic in his denial of any connection with Mrs. Keeton's murder: "With my right hand raised to heaven and in the presence of God above, I do here, now, and forever deny any knowledge of the crime or any connection with it. Even if I die on the gallows, that is the truth, so help me God."

Standing beside Watkins in the receiving room, he was reported to be in good spirits.

"I have heard reports of mobs," he continued, gratifying his interviewers with information, "and have told my family that if I was mobbed to get hold of my lawyers and defend my name as though I was alive."

Watkins interceded and warned him to respond only to the questions they had agreed to answer.

Two reporters told Carter of having visited in the Keeton home and being served a fruit wine by Ouida's brother, but neither could identify the fruit flavor.

"That was scuppernong wine," Carter quickly replied. "That old woman made good wine."

"Hush, Mr. Carter," his attorney admonished.

He declined to allow his client to answer queries about the trip to Mobile.

"We have nothing to say about that yet. Ouida has said that her mother was murdered on Sunday night, and later when she found out that Carter was in Mobile that night, she changed her story and said that the murder was done on Saturday night."

The interview was concluded as Carter identified himself as basically a plain and simple man.

"I am a member of the Masonic lodge, Woodmen of the World, the Lumbermen's Association, and the Presbyterian church." He denied any mistreatment by jailers and reported that he was "eating plenty of good food."

By February 2 Carter had been relocated to the fifth floor. For four days he had remained locked on death row across from "the giant Negro ghoul."

Currie, quizzed in Jones County for a comment about the motive for Mrs. Keeton's murder, replied that he and Deavours were reassessing Ouida's statement. In accusing Carter, she had given a strange reason for her mother's murder—that Mrs. Keeton's death would give Ouida more personal liberty. The prosecuting counsel again emphasized a more likely motive—greed for Mrs. Keeton's money.

"In my opinion," Currie said, "both this motive and the motive that Miss Keeton assigned in her original confession are possible." From research of the family history he recounted the story of Mrs. Keeton's transferring several thousand dollars in bonds and real estate to Ouida, hoping to safeguard them from being attached in the Robinson lawsuit. Since the statute of limitations on the suit had passed, Currie said, "there was no longer any reason why the property she deeded to her daughter could not have been returned to her."

Ouida herself was apparently too ill or too unnerved to participate in laying plans for her own defense, but David McRae remained the Keetons' ever-reliable in-law. In a family gathering that he moderated, Cooper and Welch outlined their plan. The strangeness of the circumstances warranted a plea of insanity, of "an unstable mind." Apparently, their proposal so incensed Eloise and Earl that negotiations with the attorneys broke down.

Cooper and Welch backed away from the case.

"We withdrew because we are not in sympathy with the views of some members of the family in regard to the conduct of the defense that was proposed to be made," Welch remarked to newsmen. He did not elaborate and turned away further questions.

Hoping to put the best possible face on the disturbing decision to discharge seasoned attorneys who had served the Keetons well in previous legal business, Earl explained it as a family matter, rather than as his and Eloise's objection to the insanity plea. However, ill will between the former clients and the attorneys would fester. Through the trials and in the months afterward Welch and Cooper remained unpaid. After the trial, the firm would petition to garnish Daisy's estate for compensation.

Who would replace them?

In all probability, McRae announced to the press, F. Burkitt Collins of Laurel and Frank Clark of Waynesboro would take over. Collins would serve as chief defense counsel, assisted by Clark.

Collins, who had defended McRae in the garnishment suit ten years previously, seemed a good choice, considering the possible jury pool. Although no longer in office, he once had served as an elected county judge. In Mississippi, once a judge, always addressed as judge. The title was like a halo to which the public gave reverence. "Judge Collins" was a Laurelite of proven legal stature and a figure known for his civic profile and his churchgoing. He was a family man, a veteran, a Baptist, and a scion of one of Jones County's oldest, largest, and most popular pioneer families. It was happenstance that the Collins residence at 610 Ellisville Boulevard was next door to the house Ouida owned and transferred to her niece. Judge Collins was forty-eight and the father of a son of fourteen.

Clark, a resident in Waynesboro, was in general law practice. The *Leader-Call* praised him as "a comparatively young attorney with a good reputation for criminal work." In appearance he looked younger than Judge Collins. "Young," was the adjective the Laurel newspaper repeatedly used to identify him, although he was forty and the father of a twenty-year-old son.

Carter's team of attorneys, headed by Watkins, was a more mighty force of four, chosen both for legal clout and for power of influence. William H. Watkins of Jackson, sixty-four and the senior partner in the firm of Watkins

& Eager, was touted for having scored the highest grade average in the history of the University of Mississippi School of Law. His magnificent home in the mansion district of North State Street presided from a crest between the Jewish cemetery and Millsaps College. Its Grecian columns and Palladian appointments simulated antebellum grandeur. Will Watkins's executive offices were conveniently near the Hinds County courthouse. From high up in the Plaza Building he could gaze down on Congress Street and into the east lawn of the Governor's Mansion. He kept his client abreast of the latest developments in Laurel by sending the morning newspaper and day- old copies of the *Leader-Call* to Carter's cell a few blocks away.

Associate counsel was Marion W. Reily of Meridian, once a candidate for governor and known as one of the state's leading criminal lawyers. Since Daisy had hired Reily to defend Earl in the rape trial, the Keetons were sure to remember him. To offset the presence of F. Burkitt Collins as Ouida's senior attorney, the Carter team countered by including Jeff Collins, Burkitt's brother, a former member of the state legislature and an ordained preacher whose presence likely would sway the stereotypical evangelicals on the jury. Quitman Ross, the fourth member, was a rising young Laurel attorney with a reputation for skill with criminal cases. Ross and Collins were monitoring proceedings at the Laurel courthouse and posting news to Watkins in Jackson.

During the short term of his incarceration, the frazzled Carter had lost his good looks and commanding demeanor. The strain of jail time was giving him a prison pallor. He had little command of the events taking control of him like some fatal sickness. Shuddering over the reality of prison, he turned to denial, anger, and the expectation that authorities would see their grave mistake and set it to rights with apologies for the public humiliation. At this most inconvenient of times phantasmagorical forces had leaped out of the dark to wreck Carter's life. He was Ouida's scapegoat. She had loaded all blame on him and then set him adrift for Jack Deavours to slaughter. No one seemed to understand his attempts to explain himself. Of course they cared, but none of his listeners was penetrating the meaning of his feelings. Legalistic ploys did not connect with his own perceptions of what had occurred. The press, the public, his persecutors, his family—all were wrenching his explanations out of context. Things couldn't get any worse. It was so confusing that he felt like crying out, "That is not the way it was! That is not the way it was at all!"

With the permission of Watkins, he agreed to allow a reporter from Associated Press an interview at his cell.

"His thinning hair is white-grey," the newsman wrote for the *Clarion-Ledger*, "and he appears nervous when questioned about the girl's accusations. The man, a grandfather who four days ago looked younger than his reputed sixty-seven years of age, now looks older."

Peering through the bars at the newsman, the frail Carter seemed fallen and broken. Yet he had not remained entirely in isolation from outside contacts. Visitors had been allowed to see him, including his minister, the Reverend Grayson L. Tucker, and other prominent friends from Laurel. Will Watkins already had spent three hours with him in planning the defense.

But swallowed up in the monotonous minutes and hours of waiting, Carter mainly was keeping to himself as he meditated on the charges against him and on how best to build his case. Fuming, he had declared to his attorneys that he was an innocent man being railroaded for a love affair with a pretty woman rather than for murder. He wondered about the emotional cost of this shameful episode for his children. The worrisome expense of four lawyers' fees would distress his dwindling assets, but he had spouted off in false merriment that he was eating well. By special arrangements of his family, a Jackson restaurant was delivering his meals. His daughters had provided him with little luxuries like a change of underwear and socks. But how did a modest man of his status and dignity react to a forced association with convicts? Of using the toilet publicly? Of stripping for a communal cleansing in a mildewed shower bath? Of enduring the inescapable filth and stench and noise? In his businesses Carter was a fellow who had mixed with all types and classes and who knew how to consort with them. He had excelled in the art of managing resentful hired hands and of taking difficult clients to court. In the jail he was high-bred and exceptional yet handled no differently from other accused felons awaiting their day in court. Against the cacophony of jail mates playing dominoes in the adjoining bullpen, the Associated Press newsman had to strain to hear Carter's softly spoken answers.

On his cell wall were clippings from newspapers and magazines, tacked up by previous occupants. These were photos of sports celebrities and movie stars. Without much of anything else to do, Carter had been studying the faces. Idle and alone, he sat quietly in this incongruous setting. Who ever would have thought W. M. Carter would be sitting in a sordid jailhouse looking at images of movie stars?

"They remind me of friends back home," he reflected to the reporter, glad to change the subject from the murder charge. "You know," he mused, peering through the dirty bars, "there are familiar characteristics in pictures."

Despite his history of philandering, Carter had foreseen no signs pointing to this trouble or to his awakened conscience and its hurtful companion, remorse. In his solitude he suffered a more punishing reflection. A man, whether he is a murderer or a saint, has absolutely no power to dominate the forces that change the direction of life in an instant. He knew, win or lose, no matter the outcome of this misery, that the sun and the moon would shine forever after on a shamed and ostracized man.

However, one hope sustained him: that the court would allow him to post bond and suffer at home.

At the opening of the February court term, the grand jury indicted both Ouida Keeton and W. M. Carter for the murder of Daisy Keeton. The two defendants would be arraigned and tried separately. Ouida's arraignment would take place on February 20, and Carter's a day later. It was agreed that Ouida Keeton would be the first to face the jury.

Judge William Joseph Pack, a Baptist layman of steadfast principles, would preside over both trials. Better known as "W. Joe Pack," he was, at sixty, in the second term as circuit judge of the second district. Previously he had gained respect in Laurel as an attorney for leading lumber companies; as a director of Commercial National Bank & Trust Company, Laurel Oil and Fertilizer Company, and the Merchants Company; as president of the Home Building and Loan Association; and as a trustee of Woman's College in Hattiesburg. In 1928 he was appointed to be a justice of the Mississippi Supreme Court but had failed to retain the office in the election that year. He ran for and won the circuit judgeship in the elections of 1930 and 1934.

On Wednesday, exactly one month after the murder, Ouida was roused from her hospital bed and delivered to the courthouse for her arraignment. Dodging oglers stationed near the main door on the western side, Deputy Sheriff Hamilton brought her through the northern entrance. In a *Clarion-Ledger* photograph documenting their arrival, Hamilton carries Ouida in his arms. Tom Lott, her special day guard, awaits with a wheelchair, and Nurse Laurendine trails at Hamilton's elbow. Behind them are the intersection of Fifth Avenue and Fifth Street and the image of the old high school Ouida attended fifteen years previously. Once inside, Hamilton, still wearing his hat, carried the limp defendant up three marble steps to a landing, made a turn to the left, and then tramped up twenty-two more steps. In his best suit and with his felt hat tipped over his eyebrow, Lott came up backward, bumping the wheelchair to the top. Miss Laurendine removed her navy-blue cape, plumped a soft cushion into position, and then spread Ouida's open mink jacket over the chair back. After Hamilton had placed the invalid on top of the cozy nest, Miss Laurendine swept the fur lapels upward to warm Ouida's neck and shoulders.

JACKSON, MISS., MONDAY MORNING, FEBRUARY 25, 1935

OUIDA KEETON IS CARRIED INTO COURT

Ouida Keeton, 32 year old Laurel woman, is shown being carried into the Jones county courthouse to hear the indictment against her of the murder of her mother. When she did not reply to Judge Joe Pack's question in answering the indictment, a plea of not guilty was entered by the court. The young woman is in the arms of Deputy Sheriff J. C. Hamilton. She is attended by her nurse Miss Lettie Laurendine. Shortly after placing her in the roller chair to descend the steps in returning to the jail, Miss Keeton slipped from the chair and fell. Ouida is facing joint indictment with W. M. Carter, prominent Laurel business man, whom she charged with the actual fire-poker slaying and butchering of Mrs. Daisy Keeton, 62, wealthy widow, mother of the girl. Miss Keeton will go on trial on Wednesday, January 27.

Ouida Keeton in the arms of Deputy Sheriff J. C. Hamilton, arriving at the Jones County courthouse for her arraignment. (Permission of the *Clarion-Ledger*)

News of the arraignment had spread at a velocity only flocks of gossips can generate. Every courtroom seat was taken, and bailiffs were instructed to keep the aisles clear. When the double back doors were pulled open, it was like the parting of a theater curtain. The watchful onlookers jamming the packed room turned in unison to observe the pageantry of Ouida's entrance along the left aisle. In Laurel, not even Greta Garbo, Tallulah Bankhead, or Myrna Loy could have aroused a more appreciatory response. If the day had been radiant rather than gray, sunbeams shooting through the stained-glass skylight would have heightened the drama.

Every eye absorbed the almost majestic procession, impressed both by Ouida's bruised beauty and by her truehearted handmaiden, the soul of professionalism in her crisp white uniform. Miss Laurendine would remain

Ouida's personal attendant on and off for the next two years. Lott walked alongside. He took charge of pushing when a bailiff began giving hand signals about placement. In Laurel, no courtroom spectacle in memory surpassed this exhibition. As the guard wheeled the marked woman up the rise and to a stop before the judge's bench, all saw that her mouth was fixed as though she would refuse to speak. Her posture was rigid, and her thin hands were tightly knotted together. After Lott had parked her before the bench, most of the audience could see only the top of her head and the back of her chair. Spectators in side seating craned to view the beautiful face, but it was almost entirely concealed by the soft lapels of her mink. Yet some of the women achieved a close look, and afterward they gladly told that for Ouida's first day in court her attire was a black dress of silk crepe with a white satin collar. She was not wearing any makeup. Her dark hair, somewhat tousled, sprang up from her high forehead.

Ouida's lawyers rose to receive her, and Miss Laurendine comforted Ouida, listless and limp, by positioning Ouida's head against the back of the chair and then taking hold of the patient's fists and placing them against her chin as supports.

A low iron-rail fence topped with golden-oak coping separated the general seating from the judge's bench, the jury box, the witness stand, and the two tables for defense and prosecution attorneys. As Judge Pack faced the courtroom, the jury and any testifying witness were to his right.

Against the railing, Maude and David McRae and Earl Keeton squeezed into the cramped space behind Ouida and the front row of seats. Stirring close against their necks were the morning breaths of the curious crowd.

The legal procedure was short and quick, taking only thirty minutes. Ouida's attorney Burkitt Collins stood to make strenuous protest that the arraignment was scheduled for this inconvenient time. The defendant's family had contended, as a result of her nervous prostration, that the defendant was not able to talk or hear. New to the case, Collins and his co-counsel claimed severe disadvantage. Having been retained for less than twenty-four hours, they had not yet held a productive meeting with their hospitalized client, and Ouida's physician had barred them from seeing her before the arraignment. Collins moved for a delay.

"Is it not true that you saw your client yesterday?" Judge Pack responded.

"I did go to see her, your honor," Collins replied, "but I did not get a word out of her, only some writing that was not coherent enough to make sense."

Judge Pack overruled the motion, informing Collins that four court-appointed doctors had determined that the defendant was well enough for the arraignment. He then proceeded.

He asked Ouida to state her plea.

There was silence.

She did not look at the judge but directed her gaze to the space above his head. Her chin rested on her hand, and her face was pallid. Her eyes were ringed by brownish shadows. Spectators closest to her noted a tear rolling down her cheek. Miss Laurendine leaned forward and blotted it with a handkerchief.

There was whispering.

The judge pounded his gavel and again asked Ouida if she wished to enter a plea.

She made no reply.

"The prisoner failing to enter," Judge Pack intoned, "it now becomes my duty to enter a formal plea of 'not guilty' for this young woman."

At once Ouida relaxed. Then she was dismissed.

Lott rolled her slowly through the throng to the back door. Hamilton and the sheriff appeared from the cloud of spectators and took charge, lifting Ouida, still reclining in the chair, down the two flights to the first floor. She was rolled past spittoons and dust bins as silent clerks peeped out of office doors. When she and her three attendants had moved through the north exit, the chair was borne ceremoniously down the steps the way pallbearers carry a heavy coffin from a stuffy church and into open air.

Along the sidewalk a small crowd of sightseers had assembled to ogle the exciting presence. To them she seemed to be both troubled and, in her costly fur, privileged. In every mind was a common thought: how could she have done what she did to her own mother? As they watched her being rolled toward the sheriff's car in the "reserved" parking lot, a shout rang out, and a man with a camera came running toward Ouida. It was L. M. Jones, who had snapped the pictures of the Keeton house, the severed limbs at the mortuary, and Dan Evans kneeling at the crime site with his dogs. He motioned for Lott to wheel Ouida against the brick wall next to the jail. None of the authorities turned him away, and the five figures settled into a pose. Miss Laurendine pushed back Ouida's mink coat to expose her pretty dress. Ouida appeared gaunt and exploited, almost lifeless. Her loss of weight was remarkable. Her black slippers were now too wide for her feet, and her legs, crossed at the ankles, had shrunk to the size of a child's. She raised her chin and winced

Ouida Keeton and her handlers, the signature image of the Legs Murder case, published worldwide. This detail shows the defendant with her nurse, Lettie Laurendine; her jailer, Lonnie Valentine; and her day guard, Tom Lott. (Courtesy of the *Laurel Leader-Call*)

but did not turn away when Jones lifted his camera and snapped the shutter. Spotlighting Ouida, with Miss Laurendine, Jailer Valentine, Lott, and Hamilton crowding together behind her, this shocking photo of official power and helpless vulnerability gives the appearance of an execution. Published worldwide, it would become the signature image of the Legs Murder case.

Ouida's sister and brother-in-law rushed forward to help place the fragile patient on the backseat of the car, minding that her head did not strike against the metal door frame. This was as far as they could go. They still were not allowed, except by the court's permission, to visit the hospital room. Miss Laurendine pulled Ouida upright, plumped pillows around the delicate body, and then crowded in against her. The day guard got up front beside Hamilton, and away they went.

The weary McRaes and a cluster of sightseers continued watching until the car had passed the schools, dipped down the hill at the Magnolia Street intersection, and vanished from sight.

Judge Pack's court order, issued two days later, specified Ouida's responsibilities and restrictions: "Ouida Keeton is hereby placed in the Laurel General Hospital, under guard both day and night; said defendant to bear all expenses of her incarceration in said hospital, together with the expenses of maintaining two guards, one each day and one each night." The judge further ordered that she be allowed no visitors except her two attorneys and her physicians and other doctors they specifically invited to accompany them.

On Thursday, February 21, the day after Ouida's arraignment, W. M. Carter came to the courtroom to hear his criminal charge and to enter a plea. His schedule had been kept secret from any potential mob. Deputy Sheriffs Hamilton and Valentine had driven to Jackson on the previous night and brought him to the Laurel jail at 2:00 a.m.

Accompanied by the two deputy sheriffs, the defendant, dignified and well dressed, moved across the room to his attorneys' table. Some thought he had aged considerably since his arrest, for his brow and cheeks were furrowed and his hair more silvered. Though he appeared frail and tired, he walked with a firm step. When he saw familiar faces in the audience, his eyes flashed in recognition. He read sympathy in their glances.

Because the proceedings, announced for 9:30, began thirty minutes early, the courtroom was only half filled, and Carter's family had not yet arrived. Upon a motion by Watkins, the judge decreed a severance of the two trials. They would begin the first week of the term. Carter rose to hear the district attorney read his indictment, and when Currie asked for his plea, Carter responded with "Not guilty." He spoke in a firm voice, but spectators could barely hear him.

Deputy Sheriff Hamilton guided Carter from the courtroom. In the cell where he had passed the night, the prisoner was permitted a brief reunion with his children. By ten o'clock he was on his way back to Jackson. He had succeeded in dodging an ugly scene.

The following morning, however, drama returned to the courtroom in the wake of Ouida's second appearance. Scheduled for Judge Pack's announcement of the trial date, the Friday court session involved a full day of legal wrangling. For both morning and afternoon sessions, Ouida was hauled up and down the stairs. Wearing the same frock she had worn on Wednesday, she clutched a white handkerchief in her left hand. As before, she remained as inert as an ice-cold statue, her eyes wide and staring into space while the boisterous proceedings whirled around her. According to one meticulous observer, "At odd moments her eyes showed interest." The audience could only imagine the world into which she had retreated.

Giving her familial support, her brother and brother-in-law were sitting at the defense table. Her lawyers first argued for a continuance on account of the precarious state of Ouida's health, and then later curiously retracted the request. They asked that the jury venire include 300 to 350 people instead of the customary 100 and that they be chosen from the entire county, rather than from only the district in which the crime occurred. They requested more time to prepare their case. The prosecution asked for a change in Ouida's medical supervision.

At day's end, Judge Pack confirmed that Ouida's trial would begin with jury selection the following Wednesday, February 27. The venire would come from the entire county, and the number was raised to 150. He overruled the other pleadings. Before adjournment, the judge ordered all in the courtroom to remain seated while the defendant was removed. Bailiffs stood ready to quell any disorder.

The obedient spectators watched the semirecumbent figure being rolled along the aisle. After Ouida's party had passed out of view and into the outside corridor, the courtroom was rocked by a shocking cry of alarm. But it was not Ouida's. Itching with curiosity but restricted by Judge Pack's order, all stayed in their seats. When they read the evening papers, most would learn about the sudden mishap. As Ouida's chair rolled toward the edge of the marble steps, it had struck a banister post. Male voices gasped as she tipped out and fell forward. She thrust her hands before her to break her fall,

Staircase, Jones County courthouse. (Photo by Hunter Cole)

and tumbled in dead weight to the staircase. Before she could topple all the way down, Hamilton and his assistant Red Robinson caught her up in their arms. Together they carried her to the first floor.

Outside, they broke through a small flock of spectators and carried the swooning defendant to the sheriff's car. Ouida collapsed in complete exhaustion. The inquisitive crowd ganged against the windows and blocked the driver's pathway. Angry Sheriff Jordan, monitoring the departure from the side entrance, rushed down the steps, yelling, "Clear the way, you curiosity seekers!"

They grumbled as they stepped aside so that the car could pass, yet they managed to claim an intimate peek inside. Miss Laurendine was holding Ouida's head upright. Ouida had produced another day of theatrics, and her trial had not even started.

■ ■ ■

In the year Daisy Keeton was murdered W. M. Carter had no legal restrictions to keep him from courting and marrying Ouida, Harriet Adams, or any other woman. Nettie Newton Carter had died two years earlier at the age of sixty-three. She was ill for about ten days before her death at the Crawford Infirmary in Hattiesburg on May 25, 1933. Dr. W. W. Crawford had operated on her for intestinal adhesions, and she died two days later of cardiac failure. She was buried the next day close by her daughter Mary Lou in Hickory Grove Cemetery. The plainness of her gravestone and the lavishness of the late daughter's may indicate how quickly Carter's fortune was eroding during the Great Depression.

When hard times struck Laurel, the roaring days of the lumber trade were over, and by the 1930s the building of the downtown had been virtually completed. Small businesses collapsed, and a midsize operation such as Carter's felt an economic blow that was almost devastating. His base of customers vanished, unpaid accounts were uncollectible, and W. M. Carter Lumber Company was near bankruptcy. Although neither of Laurel's banks failed, large-scale milling was past, and housing construction in Laurel was sharply curtailed. Scrabbling to remain solvent, Carter reorganized his business as the Carter Building and Supply Company, focusing mainly upon retailing lumber and hardware.

Hard up for cash, he offered to sell Ouida a piece of rental property, the house on Ellisville Boulevard occupied by the Hedgepaths. Actually the real estate belonged to Nettie Carter. The deed bore only her name. The Hedgepaths and the Smallwoods, Mrs. Hedgepath's brother and sister-in-law, treated the home as a duplex, and each family paid $20 a month in rent. As a favor—or as a way to gain money quickly—Carter sacrificed this property to Ouida for $1,500 under its value. In Ouida's behalf he continued collecting the monthly rent checks. Delivering them to Ouida at home was an excuse for visits.

During the Depression, few in Laurel, except the very rich, were spared economic suffering. In the downturn Carter retained only a few employees— the McLeod brothers and a small crew of laborers. He and his son managed the operation, but Carter was so pinched that he had to reduce Ouida's salary to $50 a month. In 1932 she left his employ.

At home Carter economized as well. His son Newton's family (a wife and two children) moved into the Carter residence on Sixth Avenue, and after Nettie Carter died, the front bedroom and bath were rented out to a roomer. Newton's wife, Carolyn, took over Ouida's former duties at the office. Carter's automobiles were fairly old and out of style, but he kept them—a Buick, a Lincoln, and a Whippet. The rich sedans fell into use occasionally for small deliveries. In 1934 he acquired the Pontiac coupe, a two-seater he bought in Memphis secondhand. He used it himself for business trips because it was more economical and newer. For several months many noticed it driven about town with its original Arkansas tag, an infraction perhaps tolerated only in a local dignitary. Sometimes seated beside Carter was beautiful Ouida Keeton.

During the years of his prosperity, a surprising number of Carter's travels took him to Mobile, about 125 miles away. The business part of these trips, however, was merely pro forma. When Carter became free for courtship, he still made it a point to keep his trips confidential. In wooing Harriet Adams, he no longer could be classified as an adulterer, yet he preferred that their affair be cloaked in secrecy. For their periodic trysts he made arrangements by mail. Over the years their flurry of correspondence was seen only by their eyes. For these exchanges he devised a cunning plan, the secret mailbox Ouida had exposed to Deavours. Business mail was delivered to the office, personal mail to his home, and backstairs mail to Box 74 at the Laurel post office. When an employee, one J. R. (Joe) Sampey, had moved away, Carter had taken over his personal mailbox and paid the yearly rental. So far as Sampey knew, it was no longer his, but Carter did not change the assigned name, and Harriet's intimate correspondence to him was addressed thereafter to "Mr. J. R. Sampey."

When Ouida moved to Washington, D.C., in 1932, Carter, then sixty-five, peppered her with fond letters. Intending to remain in her path, he collected and mailed her the Hedgepaths' rent payments. His giddy scheme of correspondence was designed so that a letter with Sampey's return address would be in her mailbox each Sunday morning. After her arrest, she tried to distance herself from suspicions of any romantic entanglement, claiming that she never replied to these mailings and that his correspondence served only to transfer the checks from her renters.

For a long time before she left Carter's employ, she was wise to his amours with Harriet. They came as no accidental disclosure. He intentionally took her into his confidence. Perhaps by taunting her with a rival, he goaded her to take occasional trips with him. He may have had a scheme for a ménage à trois. Ouida knew therefore that he had at least one other woman, but she told herself that she was the one he favored, the one he saw every day and visited in the evenings.

He wound her further into this out-of-town alliance by introducing her to Harriet. Once Carter lured both women to the Jung Hotel in New Orleans, and at another time he gave Ouida a train ticket to that destination, planning to join her there. There is no evidence that Ouida protested or that she herself engineered the acquaintance with the rival. Although Harriet was some ten years older than Ouida, Carter thought they should be friends. Ouida seems not to have been averse to the suggestion. Though she seldom was separated from her mother, she accepted a week's invitation to visit Harriet in Mobile, as she had confessed to Deavours. She also got to know Harriet's sister Mesalena and enjoyed the short vacation in the Adams home. Later, when Harriet made the furtive visits to Laurel and stayed with the Keetons, Daisy was kept unaware of ulterior motives.

Until the prosecuting attorney's aggressive interrogations broke her silence, Ouida had told no one about her employer's secret life. As his personal secretary she kept both business and private matters in confidence. On the pretended business trips to Mobile, it was Carter's custom to check into the St. Andrew's Hotel for a night or two, but his stay was mainly amatory. Over the years of their love affair, Harriet had remained unmarried, living with her family on Ann Street. She had left the nursing profession and in the 1930s was a truancy officer for the Mobile schools. During two decades of his comings and goings, Harriet's family got to know Carter well as an out-of-towner in Mobile on business. He was in their home many times.

In the Jackson jail Carter had little to do except reflect and suffer. He continually worried that his good name was forever ruined. As a contaminated figure, he imagined that his business cronies would no longer accept him. If he should tender his resignation from the board at the bank and from the deaconry of his church, he wondered if there would be sighs of relief.

Some days seemed longer than others. Incarceration gave Carter over a month of solitude to assess the folly of his frisky extramarital meetings and to suffer dread of his unknown future. In the stink and dirt of prison, he could realize that the bloom was gone. He was no longer the man he was. His virile power had vanished with the onset of an ailment that was euphemistically termed bladder trouble. Ouida, once pink with youth and comeliness, had been astonishingly disloyal, even treacherous, and Harriet, on the far side of menopause, was no longer a Lorelei.

There is a commonly perceived idea that a respectable man abides on a plateau more morally elevated than the ordinary. Carter was of the first quality, a dignified citizen of the better class. However, in these seamy romances he became common. The straitlaced public viewed such misbehavior in a notable person not only as astonishing but also as unacceptably vulgar. When his love affair with Harriet became an open fact, gossip was rife. For him to take up with not just one hussy, but with two, seemed an outrage.

However, he considered the story of his double life, like his moon-sick notes left on Daisy Keeton's sofa, as nobody else's business. The two affairs should be regarded as his own dirty secret. They had remained so, until Jack Deavours began his probe of the fragile, angry Ouida.

■ ■ ■

Deavours proceeded to gather useful evidence for prosecuting his case against his former schoolmate. Focusing on her activity after she left Carter, he learned that in Washington, D.C., she had enjoyed a way of life free from her mother's intrusions and from Carter's impromptu visits. Her classes met at the Lewis Hotel, but she did not reside there. She had a room instead at the Blackstone and lived among women who introduced themselves as war widows. Far from home, Ouida kept closely in touch with her mother and shared reports about how her courses were progressing. Daisy liked to be kept posted.

Later in his investigation Deavours would learn that Ouida had written home about a fascinating Mr. Grace who was showing her around Washington. Ouida liked him, and she informed her mother that she was receptive to his suggestion of investing in Capitol Bank stock. She of course asked Daisy's permission. Daisy agreed, and in January 1933, after Ouida's Christmas visit in Laurel, they risked $6,500 in this speculation.

In deepening his investigation, Deavours obtained a syllabus of Ouida's course of study. One class would constitute a loathsome revelation for the case, certain to produce public shock, but Deavours was saving its announcement for later. His use of this new information was substantiated by evidence that Ouida had completed all her studies with honorable grades.

He would learn too that upon her return to Laurel in the summer she made an unanticipated announcement. Mr. Grace had asked her to marry him. Ouida informed Mr. Carter that she had accepted the proposal. Deavours concluded that the engagement should have terminated Carter's furtive attentions and that the marriage also would separate mother and daughter after more than three decades of intimate connection. Deavours saw how Carter's behavior reflected his unhappy reaction. The prospective marriage brought a turnabout that he did not welcome. Hoping to renew her interest in him, he began again to dog Ouida with compliments and visits. What did prospective matrimony mean for Daisy and her intention to purchase a hotel? The plans were at a standstill, and she was highly displeased.

What Deavours did not learn was that after Ouida left her job at the Carter Lumber Company, and then after returning from Washington, her physical and mental health disclosed a remarkable change. She began to put on weight, and her pleasing plumpness turned to fat. She wasn't pregnant, however. Rather, idle in the gloom of home, she took on a habit of snacking and lying about the house. When she reached approximately 160 pounds, she was horrified by the assault on her vanity. Her chic wardrobe had become obsolete. Her mirror did not lie. Nor did her nosey aunts. Always vain, Ouida began dieting so that she could regain her allure. She purchased a reducing machine and for a time used it faithfully in an exercise regimen. She stored it out of sight in the bathroom closet. It remained there after she shed the extra pounds and became trim again.

Her weight, however, continued to drop, and she was stricken by frequent spells of upset stomach and vomiting. Vomiting caused her pretty teeth to decay. Now she faced a new challenge, retaining her weight. Possibly Ouida was anorexic. Beside her hefty mother, she was a wraith. The period of this swing in her increase and reduction of weight can be pinpointed as the time that she began having serious episodes with psychosis. The malady can be traced to her adolescence, although it was dismissed then as teenage moodiness. After she turned thirty, her demeanor grew peculiar, marked by long periods of staring blankly into space. Her mother and her aunts commented among themselves on the strange behavior. At times Ouida had been demanding and difficult, but now she had begun to engage in nonsensical prattle. The tantrums of childhood were now charged with high rage that alternated with pouting and self-isolation. Although she did not tell anyone, Ouida frequently would hear her name being called, but when she turned to answer, no one was there. For the moments of turmoil, Daisy found a remedy. A glass of buttermilk would calm Ouida. Mrs. Lott, a Cross Street resident who kept a cow in her backyard, sold milk to neighbors. Ouida would drink a glassful and become quiet.

The Ouida who had returned to Laurel seemed truly a different person. In addition to fluctuating weight and strange behavior, Ouida lost all interest in the hotel venture. Daisy harped that the course and expenses had been considerable, but for the first time, she surmised, Ouida was in a real courtship. Her daughter's strange moods could be attributed to love and separation. She began receiving beautiful bouquets of roses and fancy boxes of chocolate bonbons. From time to time these were presented at the front door for "Miss Ouida Keeton," but in accepting them from the delivery man, Daisy could not sniff out a gift card. Curious, she and her sisters tried to tease out the name of the admirer. By nosy wangling they solved the mystery. They had to laugh. It was not Mr. Grace who had been sending the gifts, but Ouida herself.

Who was this "Mr. Grace"? Unless Eloise met him during the getaway visit in Washington, no one in Laurel knew him or had ever seen him. Since Ouida left no other clues in the public records, almost all that is known about him is his surname. The Washington, D.C., census of 1930 enumerates a list of nineteen Graces. The male names include an Irish immigrant, a few blacks, some who are old or married, and a student or two. One salient Grace pops out of the listing as a possibility. He is W. Eugene Grace of 3920 Seventeenth Street, born in 1898 and therefore thirty-two, a fitting age for a match with Ouida. However, in 1930 he was married to a wife born in Tennessee. Two or three years later, when Ouida met him, he could have been divorced and free for courtship. Or, like Mr. Carter, he could have been a philanderer. In the roster he is the only Grace whose occupation connects in some way with investments. He is mentioned as an underwriter at a casualty company.

Were they actually engaged? Were there real plans for a wedding? If so, why did Mr. Grace not figure more prominently in Ouida's case? He seems not to have been just a figment in an unsound mind, for while she was hospitalized at Laurel General, the press learned that the mysterious fiancé made a quick visit to Laurel. When Ouida's financial records were examined, the Capitol Bank stock was not listed among her assets. Mr. Grace and the invested money had vanished.

As Ouida's trial date approached, Burkitt Collins refused to declare what tactics he and Clark were planning for her defense. Their client still seemed to be in shock, not able to face what had happened. Madness had its own rules, and she had acted irrationally in covering up the crime. Word was circulating that Collins and Clark had called in psychiatrists. Soon after Dr. O. E. Schmid of the Wallace Sanitarium of Memphis, Dr. C. D. McCool of Meridian, and Dr. C. D. Mitchell of Jackson and the Gulf Coast had arrived in Laurel to examine Ouida, a headline in the *Memphis Commercial Appeal* announced that "Ouida's Defense May Be Insanity" and, capitalizing on the Laurel litigation, the page featured an adjacent story headlined "England Has New Legs Murder Case, Parts of Man's Body Found on Train."

Collins would affirm publicly only that Ouida had undergone a medical examination. "Aside from telling you that Miss Keeton was yesterday and today examined by three eminent physicians who are specialists in the treatment of diseases of the brain, I have no other statement to make at this time."

Anticipating the eventuality of an insanity plea, the Jackson newspaper speculated about a turn in the prosecution should she be declared insane. "Then the state cannot bring her to trial. She would be confined in an institution where in all probability she would remain for the rest of her life. If so, Carter likely would be released."

In response to Collins's use of psychiatrists, Currie and Deavours summoned their chosen alienists to counteract any defense on grounds of insanity.

In preparation for what promised to be a big draw and huge crowds, Judge Pack prepared the courtroom for the onslaught. He ordered that his bench be shoved four feet toward the north wall to make way for the journalists' station. He wanted members of the press to be seated to his right, advantageously near the witness stand, the jury box, and the defendant's side of her counsel's table. Jack Dale of the Associated Press, John B. Hudson of the *New Orleans Times-Picayune*, L. C. McGlohn of the *Jackson Daily News*, Irwin Bradford of the *Mobile Press*, Kenneth Tolar of the *Memphis Commercial Appeal*, John Brazeale of the *New Orleans Item*, William Barksdale of the *Hattiesburg American*, and E. E. Hoffman and Harriet Gibbons of the *Laurel Leader-Call* came in to draw numbers for assigned seating. Odell McRae, a freelance reporter, represented the *Jackson Clarion-Ledger*. He was a brother of David McRae. The judge advised them that they would be crowded and cautioned that picture taking in the courtroom was prohibited.

On February 26 almost everyone in Laurel seemed to be lining up outside and clamoring for admittance, but with seating for only five hundred, many would be disappointed. The venire of 150 prospective jurors reported to the courthouse. Each had answered a summons to be present by nine o'clock. At that hour the defendant was wheeled in for the lengthy process. A bailiff motioned for twelve of the talismen to take seats in the jury box, and from these the unacceptable would be culled one by one. As a man was dismissed, another would take his seat. After being sworn in as a group, each was processed singly during a seemingly interminable two days in which every man was interrogated by the state and by the defense. Among the procedural questions: Your place of residence? Do you favor the death penalty? Would you convict a woman as quickly as you would a man? Do you object to the execution of a woman? Are you prejudiced by the news reports of the case?

Have you formed an opinion? Do you know the defendant or her former employer? Most of the veniremen were farmers. None resided in the city itself.

Although their trials were separate, Ouida and her former employer were permanently conjoined in both the public and the legal minds. The defense admonished the veniremen that the prosecution must prove first of all that Daisy Keeton was dead, that she was slain, and that the legs discovered in the woods were in fact hers. The prosecution countered by maintaining the legs were sufficient to prove the corpus delicti.

Throughout two days the opposing attorneys battled over the jury selection, and during the ordeal Ouida lay in her chair in a state of apparent collapse. Much of the time her eyes were closed. It was noted that she was breathing hard and that when she did open her eyes, she continued to stare almost lifelessly at the ceiling.

By two o'clock on the afternoon of February 27 the prosecution and the defense had selected the twelve men who would decide Ouida's fate. As their names were announced, she gave no sign that she was awake. As they shuffled to seats in the jury box, everyone in the room surveyed them, surmising their social conditions, assessing their attire, and guessing how each might vote in deciding the verdict.

Suddenly Ouida's body tilted forward, and Miss Laurendine gave a frantic signal that the defendant was in acute distress. She had fallen into a faint. The spotlight moved from the jurors back to the limp figure in the wheelchair. With a grave gesture Judge Pack motioned that she be taken to an anteroom. Although wan and pitiful, Ouida, like an exciting star exiting a theater stage, commanded the focus of every eye.

For an hour and a half the restless courtroom waited. When the side door opened, Lott wheeled Ouida to her former place near the defense table. Judge Pack gave the long interruption little notice, although all attention again was beamed on Ouida.

"All right, gentlemen," he stated without exasperation, "let's proceed with the case."

From the skylight, fragments of color sparkled over Ouida's tousled hair.

On Monday, March 1, as the first day of testimonies was about to begin, police investigators scotched Ouida's defense by making two startling announcements to the press. The first: Ouida Keeton once had taken instruction in butchering. The brochure Deavours had obtained from Washington told that her curriculum at the Lewis Hotel Training School from September through March 1932–1933 ranged over some fifty subjects. Her grades had been high, from 84 to 100, and the descriptive brochure of the courses stated that Lessons 15–32 included tips on butchering. No grades had been given for this particular instruction, but Ouida scored a mark of A on the overall final test.

The electrifying revelation heightened curiosity by recalling newspaper depictions of the death as a slaying by a human butcher and of body parts severed with the precision of an expert. The public questioned again how so beautiful and loving a daughter whom they had greeted day by day in the normal course of events could commit such an outrage.

Unclaimed and unhonored through a second month, the mutilated thighs and pelvis remained in refrigeration at the Sumrall Funeral Home. Daisy Keeton's children made no move to claim them or to display grief or mourning. Since the finality of a mother's death should not be meaningless, Laurel residents believed that the murdered woman was deserving of respectful pomp and commemoration. Instead, they saw how her children clustered around Ouida, supported her claim of innocence, but did nothing to honor their parent. It was rumored that Earl Keeton had offered to give the legs as fine a burial as he would give his own mother but that on the counsel of his sister's attorneys he refused to sign any affidavit identifying the limbs as Mrs. Keeton's. Collins and Clark advised the family to remain silent and commit no act that would disrupt a basic strategy of the defense—of pleading that there was no actual evidence that the missing Mrs. Keeton was dead. There was officially no corpus delicti.

The second announcement in the newspaper, however, showed that one Keeton had edged on a violation of legal counsel. Maude McRae had become administrator of Daisy Keeton's estate. The public record in the chancery court, signed by Maude, stated that she did believe her mother was dead. Also complicating the defense's claim of no corpus delicti was the marriage license on which Eloise had named Ouida, not her mother, as next of kin.

As latecomers to the case, Burkitt Collins and Frank Clark had no more than a week to make their plans for Ouida's defense. The flamboyant Collins, who would take the lead, was rich in experience not only from his former term as a county judge but also as an entertaining courtroom tactician with a folksy style. Without doubt, such down-home assets could be effective in swinging this Jones County jury.

When an occasion called for ferocity to heighten rhetoric, Collins could be quick and snide. In addition to standard trial tactics of pestering the opposition with denunciations of unsound testimonies as incompetent, irrelevant, or immaterial, Collins and his associate would rely on a master plan of four parts. First, they would hold the prosecution to proving the corpus delicti. Without it, their client was an innocent woman. In gadfly fashion they planned to voice harassing objections to any testimonies based on the assumption that the unidentifiable legs were those of Daisy Keeton. In fact, the prosecution had only a piece of body with no head or breast, no hands or feet, no fingerprints or telltale scars. Second, they would force the prosecution to prove the currency of any concrete crime evidence taken from the family home and presented to the court. Third, they would attempt to block the introduction of Ouida's purported confessions, but if these should be declared admissible, Collins and Clark would assail them as being the products of coercion and her fear of mob violence. Fourth, throughout the trial they would showcase their client's fragile physical health. A last resort, a corollary, would be to plead that she was insane. In doing so, they would demand that the prosecution place the one signed and notarized confession into evidence so that it could serve the defense in proving Ouida's mental instability. For the insanity plea they also would lay the precedent for bringing their medical experts to the stand. Three notable alienists, having examined Ouida, would give testimonies that she was insane.

The courthouse resounded with the frenzied buzz of voices debating the rumors. Just minutes before court was to be convened at 1:30, Judge Pack was summoned from his chambers to address a critical problem. He hastened through a side entrance adjacent to his bench and at once saw the trouble. The courtroom was alarmingly overfilled. Since early morning, avid spectators had been jamming into every space and were spilling out into the corridor. Still more were entering the courthouse minute by minute. He nodded in agreement with the bailiff who had come for him. Indeed, the balcony was so dangerously thronged with spectators that it could collapse at any moment. The teeming crowd from both town and country had shoved and jostled into the limited seating. In its design the balcony, high up near the stained-glass skylight, jutted into the middle of the courtroom above two-thirds of the downstairs, where benches resembling church pews were placed east to west with two aisles dividing them. Although the balcony was braced by a stout oak post at each end, the middle was sagging almost twelve inches under the load of human bodies.

Like a prelude to rousing entertainment, the din of voices cast a dizzying roar that reverberated against the walls and the ceiling and seemed to transform Judge Pack's tidy sphere of jurisprudence into a gymnasium, a circus tent, or a movie house. At any second another sound, a riving of wood and screams of panic, could pierce this festive scene.

Spectators continued to monger rumors and greet one another. Most were nestling themselves and staking claim to the uncushioned benches for the long duration. Preparing for it, some women took out their embroidery hoops or crochet needles. The defendant, like a star attraction, had not yet been brought into their midst. She and her retinue awaited in a side chamber as though for a grand entrance. Having filed in from across the street under close escort, the jury also was on hold.

Annoyed that the spectators were not heeding the peril of the tilting balcony, Jack Deavours began issuing orders for the aisles to be cleared. Waving his arms, he signaled directions to stationary figures wedged into corners and crevices. Some deflected his warnings by giving nonchalant nods that they were aware of risks. It was time for decisive action. Judge Pack stepped to the bench and pounded his gavel for attention. Noise subsided as everyone looked in his direction and saw him motioning for the bailiffs to clear the balcony.

"We must protect the lives of the people," he called out.

Very few made a move, for every person in the audience was mad to see Ouida Keeton.

"The court will not proceed until that is accomplished," Judge Pack warned above the din of protests.

With bailiffs shooing the reluctant from their roosts, the room reverberated anew, this time with tramping feet and griping. As the crowd vacated the cramped confines, the weight lifted, and the balcony, resuming its somewhat horizontal alignment, gave out a low groan.

After thinning the upstairs crowd, Judge Pack surveyed the empty space and gauged its limits. Following a whispered discussion with his bailiffs, he ruled that a limited number of spectators would be allowed there, and at once a lucky few clambered to reclaim seats. As others drifted into the aisles near the downstairs windows and onto the upstairs porch that fronted Fifth Avenue, the courtroom remained jammed and uncomfortable. There was no longer even standing-room-only space. The number of spectators sitting downstairs and in the balcony, herding at the top of the stairs, and pressing against the interior walls and windows was estimated to be one thousand. Some had arrived before seven o'clock that morning to claim seats for the afternoon proceedings, scheduled as the first session of testimonies. Many had brought their lunches, intending to spend the entire day. Hundreds from the county had appeared, the men in overalls and the women and children in their Sunday attire. Some mothers were carrying babies. Most of the lucky spectators held a lock on their prized seats and through the long session to come would refuse to take breaks for restroom visits. They munched peanuts and sipped colas and waited for the entertainment to begin. Families without seating gathered near the Confederate monument outdoors, standing around till the clock over at the bank tolled the noon hour. Then they would spread their lunches and litter on the winter lawn. Denied access to see Ouida, they would rely on secondhand reports or witness her exit from the building toward evening.

When all were settled after the readjustment of the seating plan, Judge Pack pounded the gavel again and called the court to order. His intimidating gaze slowly swept right and left as he took a survey of the crowd. Marion Reily and Quitman Ross, attorneys for Ouida's accused partner in crime, were seated together. They were present to take notes for planning W. M. Carter's defense in the subsequent trial.

The judge motioned for the jury to be brought in, and eleven stern-faced farmers and a bricklayer, uncomfortably attired in their Sunday best, trooped in a line to the jury box.

Hattie Belle Stevens, the court reporter, took her seat near the witness stand. She was, however, not the only skilled stenographer in the courtroom. The *Leader-Call* had hired its own to take shorthand notation of every testimony. The newspaper would publish transcripts for the readers who had been crowded from the courtroom.

Before the state's witnesses were called in to take the oath together, the defendant's immediate kin adjusted their chairs to accommodate Ouida as she was rolled in from the anteroom. The craning spectators noted the presence of family support. Her sister Maude McRae, her brother-in-law David McRae, and her uncle M. A Sherrill already were cramped close to the defense attorneys' table. Earl was waiting downstairs with other witnesses. Eloise was in the Crescent City.

The defendant's pitiable state stimulated wonder. A day or so previously a nurse at Laurel General Hospital had been quizzed about Ouida's health and, unable to restrain herself while in the spotlight, divulged insider information to a reporter from the Memphis newspaper:

"She is unable to talk," she declared, "because her tongue is apparently paralyzed. The only words that she has spoken since she entered the hospital were in her sleep during her first night here. She incoherently muttered something about her covers. She writes notes when she wants anything, and I believe that she is aware of everything that goes on. I don't think that she cares about what happens to her—whether she gets well or is freed or convicted. . . . She was a brilliant and beautiful girl until a short while ago."

District Attorney Currie took charge of the proceedings by summoning the state's sixty-one witnesses from their quarters below the courtroom. Trudging in with the mass were Earl; his wife, Jewel; and two of Daisy Keeton's sisters, Paula Richeimer and Stella Sherrill. After the group oath-taking, Currie called for any defense witnesses in the courtroom to approach the bench to be sworn in. Afterward, all except Miss Laurendine and Mr. Lott were removed to await being called one by one to give testimonies. With the agreement of the prosecution Judge Pack also allowed physicians summoned as the defense's expert witnesses to remain.

Spellbound eyes continued to be riveted on Ouida, although she could be viewed only from the back and sides. Those seated at the press table and in the jury box, however, had a full and open view of her. One note-taking reporter described her as the "once lovely Ouida Keeton, now a nervous wreck and her beauty ravaged." Some spectators thought she appeared less wan than on previous days. "A faint color showed in her face and lips," one journalist remarked. "She indicated that she was too warm and assisted the nurse in taking off a light-weight navy blue coat which covered a blouse of blue-and-white gingham. Then she settled back into her wheelchair, facing the jury. She lifted her hand and wiped her own forehead. She raised her elbow, helping the nurse to arrange her wraps." Thereafter, Ouida seemed to doze into oblivion. Some surmised her sleep was due to a sedative administered during the lunch hour or to the stuffy air in the courtroom. Lying on her back, she excited compassion.

The crowd watched as the opposing attorneys bristled in postures of professionalism while getting ready for the long afternoon of interrogations. Defense attorneys Collins and Clark were keeping both the public and the prosecution in suspense. They had not yet divulged two matters of the greatest importance to this case: First, would their client be capable of testifying in her own defense? If so, would they put her on the witness stand? The consensus of those gazing on the dozing defendant was that she was too ill. Second, how would they support the not guilty plea they had entered for her? It was certain that if they could prevail in establishing the absence of a corpus delicti, Collins and Clark would deny that any crime had been committed.

If Ouida's attorneys should fail in this defense, the public was betting on an insanity plea. By common logic, any daughter who murdered and chopped up her own mother had to be insane. The presence of three psychiatrists in the roster of defense witnesses gave credence to this speculation.

"We will prove the corpus delicti," District Attorney Currie had boomed to a Memphis reporter. Moreover, the prosecution would emphasize greed for money as the likely motive for Daisy Keeton's murder. Since both had been indicted for separate trials, it little mattered whether Carter and Ouida were partners in crime or whether Ouida acted alone, for in each defendant there was probable cause. Rayburn Robinson's statue of limitations had expired, yet Ouida continued to hold on to her mother's assets; Carter, Mrs. Keeton's financial adviser, had suffered a business failure and a shortfall and was in need of cash, which he could grasp from Ouida; and Ouida evidently had grown accustomed to presiding over the large bank account that she did not intend to relinquish.

Shocking sensitive observers was the possibility that a convicted murderess would face execution. If Ouida should be judged guilty, the prosecution already had signaled the likelihood, in interviewing the venire, that the state would press for the death penalty. Each potential juror had been asked his views on capital punishment and whether he could inflict it on a woman as readily as on a man. The twelve had agreed on execution, either way.

Aroused not only by the horror of madness, matricide, and mutilation but also by the taunting image of this beautiful "Keeton girl" being led to the gallows or to the electric chair, the public mind throbbed in excitation.

■　■　■

The prosecution's first witness was W. E. Kennedy. Currie and Deavours were starting off with a bang by placing the accused at a scene of the crime. Kennedy began his testimony by saying he had never seen the defendant before the morning of January 21. He had picked her up on Highway 11 around 8:45 a.m., some four-tenths of a mile from where her car was mired on a muddy lane.

"She began to flag me, and I saw it was a lady and slowed up. I stopped and asked her what she was doing walking along a highway in the rain and sleet."

After describing her appearance—her green-striped dress, her fur coat, her bare head and legs—he recounted her story of the stalled car and of her purported reason for being on the lonely trail. He told of letting her out on Cross Street at a location he since had learned to be directly across from her family's house. He recalled her remark as they drove toward Laurel: "I'm just completely given out, just a nervous wreck."

Spectators could not resist staring at Ouida. The babble of the attorneys and the witness was giving no evident stir to her torpor. Some thought she was pretending to be invisible to every eye, her mind a million miles away. Some imagined her like a deaf woman unaware of being the subject of discussion. Then, suddenly, the few who were seated closest to her gave a start. Indeed, Ouida was awake. As Kennedy was telling of her plight on the rainy highway, they saw Ouida's response. A tear glistening on her cheek showed that she was listening to every word. She wiped it away herself.

After Kennedy was dismissed, the bailiff called out the name of the second witness, Dan Evans Jr., the black hunter who had discovered the legs.

He came through the back door, holding his cap in both hands. L. M. Jones's photo of Evans had drawn much comment among both whites and blacks. He took the seat between Judge Pack and the jury and watched the district attorney moving toward him.

"Your name is Dan Evans?"

"Yes, sir, Dan Evans, Jr.," he replied politely.

Judge Pack interrupted.

"Dan, it is mighty hard to hear in the courtroom. You don't mind speaking loud, do you?"

"No, sir, I don't mind speaking loud."

The witness stated that he was thirty-seven and that he lived a little more than a quarter mile from where he found the bundle.

"On which side of the road were these limbs and the body found as you travel toward Heidelberg?"

"Well, it's on the right going north and the left coming south. I was walking along looking along the road. I figured I might see some rabbits sitting in their bed. So my dogs run on ahead of me. They was already ahead of me, and about twenty steps ahead of me my big black dog began growling, and I taken notice of the growling, and there was some packages laying there. And the dogs was growling so that I stopped them from growling. And I saw it was flesh in the bundles, and I got a stick about twelve inches long off a plum bush there. I rolled one of the bundles over, and when it rolled over I began to see it wasn't hog flesh and it wasn't beef. I stood there for four or five minutes studying what it was, and while I was studying, it run across my mind I seed a fellow killed one time at a saw mill, and it put me in the mind of his flesh. And when I discovered it was human flesh, I left there. I rolled it back up and left."

Evans gave a clownish grimace of pretended fright and widened his eyes.

Titters rippled from the crowd.

Judge Pack, a stickler for courtroom decorum, rapped for order, motioning for bailiffs to quell the outburst.

"There's no reason why you should not be here," he said with firmness. "I wish we had room enough for all who want to come. But order must be preserved at all times, and no demonstration whatever will be tolerated."

Bailiffs were empowered to remove anyone disrupting the dignity of the court. He turned to Currie and nodded for him to proceed.

"Describe how many packages or bundles you saw there on the ground."

"Just them two bundles. It was white. It was in a white cloth that looked to me like sugar sacks. It was just laid in there and rolled right on up. That one I unrolled, that was the one I was taking notice of. Doubled up at the end. And when I rolled it over there was a little of it showing, about that much, and I rolled it back after I unrolled it. And I left there."

He said he had hurried home and told his wife.

"I went on down and told four colored fellows. They was killing hogs. I told them about it."

Then he got word to a white man who notified authorities.

Currie turned to select an item from the crime exhibits on the table. He lifted a piece of striped cloth, asked Evans to identify it, and then paraded it past the jurors. Several wrinkled their noses as though the wrapping must carry a bad smell.

"Well, that is one of the cloths all right."

For the cross-examination, Ouida's attorney Frank Clark took charge. He intended to set a precedent in motion by implying that a traveling stranger may have dumped the legs while passing the dark road. He tried to confuse Evans by pressing him to identify the many blind roads and trails connecting with the main highway and to admit that they were heavily traveled by anonymous tourists. His legal rhetoric was too complex for Evans.

"Don't you know, Dan, there isn't a thing in the world there and that the place where you saw the fragments of the body is in plain view of Highway 11, and that a person that walked down the little blind road where you say you found the limbs couldn't have helped but see them?"

"Well, if I had looked up, I could have seen them when I got in twenty steps of them, but I wasn't looking for them, and I wasn't noticing until the dog growled. I wasn't paying no attention."

Moving past his opposition, the district attorney stepped forward for redirect examination.

"What time of day would you estimate or figure you found them?"

"It was more twelve than it was eleven. I don't know what time it was, but it was between eleven and twelve o'clock, more twelve than it was eleven."

The witness was excused, and Dan Evans hastened to the exit door at the back of the courtroom.

Next, Will Saul, the farmer who claimed he saw Ouida in her car, was called.

He recounted having seen a woman that early morning as she drove past his farmhouse on the rain-slick road. She arrived from the south. He had come out on the porch to take a look at the peculiar winter weather. Instead, he watched this mysterious stranger. He had stood on tiptoe to peer into the passing car. Since the way the woman drove was, to him, a little strange, he had tried to note if anyone was with her, attempting to hide. Something, but not a person, was on the front seat or on the floorboard.

Ouida's Willis Knight had been impounded, and officers already had escorted Saul to take a look at it. He testified that it was the same car he had seen passing his house around eight o'clock on January 21 and that the defendant, now lying in the wheelchair, had been the driver.

As the slow stream of witnesses flowed to the stand, the courtroom remained overfilled. No one wanted to leave. Reporters at the news table checked their watches and nodded to one another. Since each testimony was averaging thirty minutes, at least five days would be consumed if the state questioned every person on the roster.

Griffin Cook, constable of Beat Five of Jasper County, was called next. After telling of serving on the coroner's jury and of delivering the legs to the Laurel undertaker, he testified that one set of tire tracks led to the spot where they had been discovered. In attempting to turn around, an automobile had backed into a pine sapling. Publicity had stirred such curiosity that the site, a dirt trail that led to a field and barn, had become like a highway. Judge Pack asked Constable Cook to bring the small tree to the courtroom at the next session and submit it as evidence.

After the five witnesses had given their testimonies, Judge Park ordered a recess. It was 4:45. The trial had continued for two and three-quarters hours with no break.

"There is a limit to human endurance," he sympathized, peering down on the recumbent Ouida. She was ill from exposure. After three days of being hauled to the courthouse, she had the look of utter exhaustion.

Concerned for the jurors' comfort, Judge Pack instructed bailiffs to give them special care and attention for the duration of the trial. When not in court, the twelve men were isolated across the street in the Pinehurst Hotel. Some had complained of chilly rooms the previous night, and the judge now ordered an additional supply of blankets.

"And get some exercise," he advised, reminding them that they were permitted to take walks. "If they want to ride," he told their handlers, "provide them with a conveyance. They can visit any place in the county, being careful that all previous instructions under the law are followed."

The trial would be in recess over the weekend. Saturday was a day for recuperation, except for Ouida. She was treated like a scientist's specimen as a series of examining physicians passed in and out the swinging door of her room. Tom Lott monitored every comer and wrote down the names.

Sunday fell on March 3, and just as Judge Pack had advised, the jury was packed up for a suitable excursion. Since all were churchgoers, they were collected from the hotel, piled into a county vehicle, and driven around the block for services at First Baptist Church. Shielded from contact with the public and ushered in by two bailiffs, they filed in after the rest of the congregation was settled. Their reserved seating was a row only a few feet behind Judge Pack's pew. He was a member of First Baptist.

From the pulpit the Reverend L. G. Gates announced it to be a phenomenal Sunday, the first time in his long ministry that he had preached to an entire jury. His topic was "the unrecognized Christ," and completing his sermon required both the morning and evening services. Ouida's jurors attended both.

■ ■ ■

Laurel cemeteries give surprise in their lack of elaborate statuary. Though in a town with pockets of great wealth, the well-tended graveyards proliferate with unadorned marble slabs and plain gray markers. In most of the shoeless South a cemetery was a small community's sole repository of art, but in early Laurel the only public statuary was the fantastical Confederate monument erected on the northwest corner of the courthouse lawn. This graying marble emblem of downtown beautification had enhanced this plot since before the Keetons moved to Laurel.

It seems odd and out of place, since Jones County could claim only few Confederate connections. Indeed, in a prevailing legend the county had seceded from the Confederacy, since there were virtually no slaves and thus little call to fight. The gist of this tale is one reason some called the occasionally defiant county the Free State of Jones.

In elaborate conception there are few finer Confederate monuments in the entire state of Mississippi. Erected by the local United Daughters of the Confederacy, it is designed as a Roman temple of one open room. Four columns at each corner of the edifice support the heavy load above. On the roof, as upright as a spire, the statue of a lean foot soldier holding a rifle stands guard and gazes toward a western threat. Sheltered inside is a dolorous beauty with lowered eyelids and carved tresses that flow over her back and shoulders. She is imperfect, for long ago someone chipped off the tip of her nose. The sculptor has captured her seated on a marble block in a pose of languid submission to an endless wait. She is womankind protected by watchful manliness lording from on high.

Each morning Ouida Keeton's guards wheeled her past the eastern side of the statuary. Because the front courthouse entrance, on the west, admitted most of the spectator traffic, Ouida's entourage, dodging crowds, continued to enter by the north door. If Ouida was seeking comforting answers from symbols as she was rolled behind the monument, the marble lady offered none, unless it was to suggest that Ouida was not alone in her depression, isolation, and subjugation to men. The statue was slumped forward as

Marble statuary, the grieving lady in the Confederate
monument, Jones County courthouse, 1960s. (Photo by
Hunter Cole)

though turning her back on the accused murderess. If Ouida saw the lady's
melancholy face each day, it told her the cause was forlorn.

On various mornings Ouida's arriving delegation thinned or grew. At
times it was composed of Maude, her aunts, Miss Laurendine, the guard, and
occasionally Earl. The strength of two men was required to lift the wheelchair and Ouida up the concrete steps and then to lug it up the staircase to
the courtroom.

In the Jackson prison cell, Carter was following trial reports in the newspaper. He held to his hope of being granted bail, but the court had announced
no decision. He read that on the second day of testimonies the courtroom
was treated to a phenomenal display edging on outright entertainment.
Constable Cook paraded down the aisle bearing the aforementioned pine
sapling. His crew had winched it, roots and all, from the mushy ground at

the crime site. Although bent and broken, it rose to ten feet. Cook estimated its trunk was two and a half inches thick. The bark at about the height of a car's bumper had been knocked off.

"It has not been shown," Collins protested, staunchly maintaining the absence of the corpus delicti, "that it is any part of the body of the person named in the indictment or that the person named in the indictment has even been killed."

However, Judge Pack allowed the pine to be placed in evidence. As it was lifted high and conveyed toward the front table, all gazes for a moment roved from the amusement and fell on Ouida. What could she be thinking of this ridiculous scene? No one could discern whether she was even aware that a tree had been brought past the back of her chair. Her dark eyes sunken in brown hollows were directed upward. It was the look of a martyred saint in some old portrait.

Next on the stand was E. S. Conliff, who had served on the coroner's jury during that cold afternoon after the discovery. By 2:15 he had arrived at the scene, which was best known, he said, as a lovers' lane. Could a car have turned around on that one-lane trail? Only by backing up, he said, could it turn and go down to the highway.

Mrs. C. H. Nicholson came next. Mrs. Nicholson, a former neighbor of the Keetons, had conversed with Ouida on Saturday afternoon, January 19, when buying gasoline at McRae's Service Station. When asked about her mother, Ouida had replied that Daisy was visiting in New Orleans. Actually, Mrs. Keeton was thought to be alive at that hour and, as everyone in the audience was surmising, at home awaiting her awful fate. Mrs. Nicholson, who now lived a few blocks from the Keetons, had known them for some twenty years. When Ouida's attorneys, playing up Ouida's frailty as a sign of mental illness, asked her to comment on Ouida's physical condition, Mrs. Nicholson agreed that she had lost a considerable amount of weight.

Neville G. Allen, an undertaker at the Sumrall Funeral Home, was called to testify. On January 21, he stated, he had received the legs from Constable Cook between four and five in the afternoon. He reported the details of embalming the bloodless tissue with the strongest solution available in his lab.

Following Allen, L. M. Jones testified that he took photographs of the body parts at the mortuary. Over the objection of Collins, who continued to protest that there had been no proof of a corpus delicti, he was allowed to identify the pictures. They depicted the pieces of the corpse in various positions, shot from different angles. After the district attorney introduced these as crime exhibits, he turned toward the jury box. No spectator seemed squeamish. Craning with hopes of gaining a peek, the closest watched him place the stack of pictures in the outreaching grasp of the nearest juror. As the photographs of the mutilated limbs were passed from hand to hand, the reporters noticed the jurors' reactions. The *Leader-Call* described "tense frowns and straining attitudes" and "faces swept with horror."

Ouida never showed the least evidence of interest. An observant reporter noted on his pad that "sometimes wide-eyed, sometimes she closes her eyes but lies practically motionless in her chair." Another described the defendant in this memorable moment: "Ouida lies asleep while they look at those photographs, but not many of the jurors look her way to see if she is sleeping or waking. She droops against the padded back of the wheelchair, utterly relaxed, breathing the regular, deep breaths of undisturbed repose, the embodiment of utter mystery to the hundreds who crowd the courtroom and listen to the testimony in one of the most baffling murder stories ever heard before the court of justice."

Currie called Cammie Cook to take the witness chair. She had come from the bedside of her little grandson, sick at home with pneumonia, and was eager to return to him. Clearly a woman of dignity and reserve, she did not like swearing to divulge facts about the intimate lives of the people next door. As she came forward, her face paled when she looked down on Ouida, her children's former playmate. The witness was still coping with the psychological shock of her neighbor's violent death. Both she and Mrs. Keeton were widows and mothers of girls. The two Cook daughters, Clayton and Bertie Belle, still lived at home. The elder was the mother of the sick boy. After Mr. Cook's death, Walton Therrell, Clayton's husband, had become the man of the house.

Mrs. Cook testified about the alley serving as shared driveway separating her house from the Keetons'. She last had seen Mrs. Keeton on Saturday morning, the nineteenth. Late that afternoon Mrs. Keeton had given Mrs. Cook's grandson some cookies. During the day Mrs. Cook had noticed her working in the garden with a hired man. She provided the court with a description of the rooms in Mrs. Keeton's house and explained the configuration of the fireplaces, all sharing the same stack, and mentioned that the Heatrola provided warmth for the living room.

"Were you there at your home on Sunday?"

She told of having gone to church and then to the cemetery. Again on Sunday evening she went to church. When she returned she had not seen any of the Keetons.

"State whether or not you saw any lights in the Keeton home on Sunday night."

"Yes, sir, the house was light Sunday night. The living room had lights in it, but I don't remember any lights in the kitchen or anywhere else, but as I passed the living room, there was a light in there."

"When did you next see Miss Ouida Keeton that you recall definitely?"

"I saw her Wednesday morning."

"Where and what was the occasion for your seeing her Wednesday?"

"I saw her coming from her aunt's, where she spent the night. I saw her coming from over there Wednesday morning."

Collins then stepped forward for the cross-examination and ascertained how long she had lived on Cross Street.

"In May it will be twenty-five years."

He directed her gaze toward Ouida.

"Mrs. Cook, the defendant there—in all of your acquaintance with her, and noticing her, the defendant here has appeared very much devoted to her mother, hasn't she?"

"Yes, sir."

"Even more than any of the other children, didn't she?"

"Well, her mother seemed to think she was."

"In other words, Mrs. Keeton was more devoted to her, wasn't she, than any other child, seemingly, she had?"

"Well, I couldn't say, Mr. Collins."

"Well, from hearing her talk, she was more devoted to her, wasn't she? And from general appearances? You saw all the children?"

"Yes, sir.

"Well, Mrs. Cook, you have seen them sit out on that back porch for hours at the time, just those two alone, and laugh and talk for hours at the time, as though they were having the best time in the world?"

He was putting words into her mouth.

"Yes, sir."

"For hours at the time and laugh and talk as though they were having the best kind of time?"

"Yes, sir."

"And you know from all appearances, both parties were very much devoted to each other?"

"It seemed that they were."

"Now, Mrs. Cook, the defendant here used to be a pretty stout girl, didn't she?"

"Yes, sir."

"Weighed around 160 pounds, didn't she?"

"Well, I'm not much judge of weight, Mr. Collins."

"But she was considerably stouter than she is now?"

"Yes, she was stouter than she is now."

Some took note that Mrs. Cook seemed reluctant to speak of personal subjects. She cast a beseeching glance toward Ouida, but obliged to respond to Collins's questions, she agreed that Ouida formerly had been stouter.

"Mrs. Cook, during the last two years she has been sick a lot, hasn't she? That is, sick at home?"

"Well, she was there at home, Mr. Collins. I don't know whether she was sick or not."

"You didn't visit over there?"

"Well, not so much. I heard her mother say she was reducing, taking exercise and things to reduce. She was too large, but as far as she being sick—"

"Well, you knew she went to Hot Springs two or three times in the last two years for treatment?"

"Yes, sir."

"And you know she has fallen off considerably in the last two years?"

Collins was laying the precedent for possible questions about Ouida's mental decline.

"Yes, I know she is not nearly as large as she was."

"That is all."

Currie came forward for redirect examination.

"On that Saturday and before that she had been working down at the filling station, hadn't she?"

"Yes, sir, I think so."

"Of course, you don't know what kind of work she did down there or how many hours she put in?"

"No, her mother just told me she was working down there."

Mrs. Cook's son-in-law, Walton C. Therrell, was introduced next. He testified to having seen Ouida around five o'clock on Saturday afternoon and then again about eight on Monday morning as he and his wife were leaving for work. Collins tried to bear down on the subject of Ouida's loss of weight, but Therrell wouldn't oblige him with confirmation.

Mrs. E. W. Lott, another neighbor, came to the stand. She also had seen Mrs. Keeton on Saturday when selling her a bottle of buttermilk. She told that Mrs. Keeton reserved milk for the following Monday but failed to come for it.

She stepped down, and Earl Keeton was called. He answered the district attorney's questions about the floor plan of the Keeton house and about Chief Brown's searching the premises while Ouida was being interrogated downtown.

"Did she turn the home over to you?"

"Well, it wasn't turned over to me at the time because it was under charge of the law. They had guards there."

"Were you with Mr. Brown and other persons when they went to the home to investigate this matter?"

"I was."

"I will ask you if Miss Ouida didn't tell Mr. Brown to go ahead and make the investigations."

"If I was with him."

In the cross-examination Collins planted thoughts that news of Ouida's being in police custody had stirred up a frightening mob that could have agitated her into making self-incriminating statements. His objective was to steer Earl to comment that a sizable crowd was gathering outside the bank when he arrived between 3:30 and 4:00 o'clock Wednesday afternoon.

"Well, there wasn't any crowd," Earl corrected. "There was a good many people around."

"Good many people, there," Collins repeated, not giving up, "coming in and out all the time? And they kept Miss Ouida there in that office for twenty hours, didn't they? Four o'clock the next morning?"

"Yes, sir, but it was about four o'clock that afternoon she gave permission to go to the house."

"And one person right after another grilled her, didn't they?"

He was attempting to show coercion.

"Well, she was asked questions."

"By first one and then another?"

"Yes, sir."

"All night long, that's true, isn't it?"

"Yes, sir."

"And nobody in that room warned her that anything she might say would be used against her, and that she didn't have to talk if she didn't want to?"

"Not that I know of."

"Yet, on the other hand, they questioned her, one of them right after another, trying to elicit something out of her? Mr. Keeton, that night from about dark up until late at night, there was a big crowd down on the streets, wasn't there?"

Again, he was hoping to underscore the image of a threatening mob.

"Yes, sir."

"And you couldn't hardly get up and down the staircase there?"

"Well, I had trouble getting up and down."

Collins hoped next to maneuver Earl into describing how the inseparable mother and daughter were utterly devoted to each other, but Earl reminded the court that on occasions Eloise also lived with them, but Ouida was there with Daisy all the time.

"Ouida was practically always the one that lived with Mother, the only one that stayed with her."

"Fact is, Earl, she was, seemed to be, more devoted to your mother than any of the other children, didn't she?"

"She was."

"That's right. Now, Earl, in the last two and a half years, Ouida has been rapidly failing in health, hasn't she?"

"She has. She has been sick off and on."

"While you lived there in the house with them, night after night your wife has gone in, when Miss Ouida would be complaining with her head and back, and bathe her shoulders and her back, hasn't she?"

"She went in at times and worked two and a half or three hours putting hot towels on her back."

"And sometimes your wife would take water in there to bathe her back? That would be so hot your wife would have to wear rubber gloves? Couldn't stand her hands in the water?"

"She has."

"Notwithstanding that, Ouida let her put it on her naked back?"

"She did."

"Earl, she has been to Hot Springs three or four times in the last two years for treatment, hasn't she?"

"Been a good many. I don't know just exactly, but she had been over there several times."

"And she has been to the doctors here in town for treatment, hasn't she?"

"She has."

"Earl, for the last two years, there has been a definite change in Ouida, physically and from all appearances, hasn't there?"

"Well, she hasn't been the same girl she has always been, because she had been sick a lot."

"And you have noticed a kind of blank, absent-minded look out of her eyes in the last two years, haven't you, Earl?"

He kept playing up Ouida's mental state.

"Well, I haven't paid so much attention to it. I knew she hadn't been the same girl, but I just thought it was on account of her feeling so bad."

"She had, in other words, a kind of melancholy expression?"

"Well, she just wasn't the same person she always had been."

"State whether or not she had some kind of reducing machine back there."

"She has."

Earl was dismissed, and Bill Hinton, a carpenter, was called to the witness chair.

He told Currie of going to the Keeton house with Earl and Dr. Tom Ramsay to collect crime evidence. He had noted a trail of blood specks from the victim's bed to the bathroom and kitchen. He had followed orders to remove a segment of woodwork that bore traces of blood and a section of cross joist from beneath the house.

"I cut a piece of door facing and a piece of jamb and the stop off of the bathroom door and a base joist from under the middle bedroom, right next to the fireplace."

Currie signaled for bailiffs to bring these pieces of wood into the courtroom.

Hinton identified them and explained their functions.

The prosecution next called Deputy Sheriff Hamilton. After corroborating Hinton's testimony, he told of having gone with Chief Brown to investigate the legs found in the woods. Currie passed photographs of the legs to him and asked for verification of the images.

Again, Collins rose to object, continuing to protest that the legs had not been proved to be Mrs. Keeton's. Judge Pack overruled him.

Hamilton reported on the confrontation with Ouida at the Keeton home. Then he told of returning to look for crime evidence. After identifying the piece of floor joist Hinton had cut, he commented on its greasy spotting and its odor of tallow. He described the concrete hearth in Mrs. Keeton's bedroom, recently given a new coat of green paint. It extended toward a rug and bore a crack through which grease had dripped onto the joist and cobwebs and then to the ground below. From the soil he had collected a sample that he placed in a jar and sent to Deavours's office. He testified that when he, Deavours, and Chief Brown arrived on Wednesday, Ouida had been housecleaning.

"She was scrubbing—between the rug and the fireplace. It was a highly varnished floor, but she had scrubbed the paint all up, and there were two or three little spots that had showed up. At that time the floor was wet with water, but the spots looked like grease."

He said that on his return Friday evening he found small specks of blood on the floor and on the wall at the right head of Mrs. Keeton's bed. At the center of Mrs. Keeton's mattress was a blot of blood measuring about fifteen inches in diameter. He followed the trail of droplets to the back bedroom and into the bathroom, where he detected a blood smear on the door molding.

Next, Wayne Valentine, one of the investigating police officers, took the stand to corroborate both Hinton's and Hamilton's testimonies. He identified a pair of dark gray silk hose as stockings Chief Brown had found in Ouida's fireplace Friday evening. When Currie asked about a foul odor on them, the defense objected on the grounds that no corpus delicti had been proved. This was overruled.

"The right stocking," Valentine continued, "had a very strong odor." It was the same that had been detected on the body parts. Over objections by the defense, the stockings were placed in evidence.

He also identified Ouida's brown suede shoes that emitted the same odor. The chief had taken these from her bedroom as well.

Valentine reported on other evidence the search had brought to light. The hearth and front of Mrs. Keeton's fireplace, as Hamilton had testified, had been freshly repainted and the floor before the hearth scrubbed very recently. Dried blood had trickled down the fire grate and splashed on the inside left wall of the fireplace. A sifting of ashes had disclosed pieces of bone. In the fireplace were burned articles of clothing, including a piece of hat and a steel brace from a corset. An iron poker with a brass handle bore traces of blood.

To these appalling particulars Ouida made no response, but Miss Laurendine signaled to the judge that her patient needed a recess. At 10:30 she was wheeled to an anteroom. Her attorneys, making a play for the jury to recognize Ouida's fragile health and possible insanity, insisted that the court stenographer's record show that the defendant had been removed to be given nourishment. Judge Pack, however, ordered that the record show only that there had been a ten-minute recess.

As Miss Laurendine wheeled the chair back into the courtroom, everyone could view Ouida's face directly. There were hollows and brown circles around her eyes. She was looking at no one, only at some faraway spot on high. Throughout the rest of the day she would pay absolutely no attention to the courtroom rituals.

"She lies in her wheelchair, facing the jury," noted a *Leader-Call* reporter staring at her directly from the press table. "She wears the same smart black crepe dress she wore at her arraignment. Her toilet is more careful than on that appearance, however. Her dark hair, softly wound, is becomingly arranged around her face. Her face is faintly powdered. Neither movement of hand or facial expression disturbs her appearance. Occasionally she shifts her head slightly." Each day spectators remarked that Ouida was becoming more gaunt. She seemed to be declining before their eyes.

John M. Danneker, chemist for the city of New Orleans, was the next witness. He answered Currie's questions about the kinds of tests he performed on the block of wood and the soil sample from under the house, on the blood-marked molding from the bathroom door, on the brass-handled fire poker, on the serum-spotted cloths that had wrapped the severed legs, on the stockings taken from Ouida's fireplace, and on the brown suede shoes from Ouida's room. His chemical analysis revealed grease or tallow on the wood block and human blood on the molding and on the handle of the fire poker. The soil sample was impregnated with grease or tallow whose odor was distinctive. One of the stockings was stained from the knee to the ankle with "undigested vegetable matter." A similar stain appeared on one of the shoes.

"Mr. Danneker," Currie asked, "would a human body heated to a high temperature give off oily tissues or a greasy matter such as you have indicated and testified you found in the soil and in the wood?"

"The heating of the human body would necessitate some fatty material being given off when the tissues were burned," he replied.

The revolting image of a mother's gore roasting in the family fireplace made several spectators recoil. Ouida continued to train her eyes upward and gave no visible reaction.

Claiming absence of proof of the corpus delicti, the defense counsel objected to Danneker's testifying but was overruled. In the cross-examination Collins attempted to cast doubt on the timeliness of the evidence.

"The substance you say you found on that piece of wood—you don't know how it came to be there, do you? And you don't know how long it had been there? You don't know how long that blood had been on that piece of material?"

"I do not."

"Mr. Danneker, did you ever have your mother treat you for croup when you were little, with tallow? Get down before a fire and melt tallow before the fire and wet a cloth with the tallow and other mixtures and heat it and treat you with it?"

"I may have, but I don't remember it."

"You weren't reared in the country, were you then, Mr. Danneker?"

"No, sir, I wasn't."

By connecting the tallow to an old-timey chest-cold treatment, Collins was alienating Danneker as a slick outsider with little connection to local customs and was upholding the defense's stance of making the prosecution verify that crime evidence was current.

"So far as you know, Mr. Danneker, this might have been tallow from melting tallow in front of the fireplace, or it might have been grease that was poured up under the house, and so far as you know, it might have been there for a year or two years?"

The chemist replied that he made certain physical and chemical tests with a limited amount of material. He had his figures in his notes if Collins cared to examine them.

"But, Mr. Danneker, the question I asked you is, so far as you know, you don't know how long that grease had been there in that soil."

"I don't."

Nor could he identify the kind of grease. Pleased that he had scored a point or two, Collins released the chemist.

"Your name is Bruce Jordan?" the district attorney asked the next witness. He then lifted an object from the exhibits table and held it up. It was the gun Chief Brown had taken from Ouida's chifforobe. Jordan identified the revolver and testified to having sold it to Ouida's brother-in-law three years previously.

"By what means do you identify it?"

"By its being a thirty-two-twenty, made in Spain, black-handled, and by a mark on the under part of the left handle and by a mark on the barrel."

Currie took the gun from the witness and said he wanted it to be labeled as an exhibit.

For cross-examination Frank Clark came forward.

He removed the shells, handed them to Jordan, and then asked him to comment on any other distinctive marking on the gun.

"Notch here on the left handle."

"Can you tell the jury who put that notch there?"

"Well, it's a long story, but I can tell it. I notched the pistol because one time I killed a cat and a dog with that pistol, and at the time I notched the gun I was at outs with a Negro that wanted to kill me. He had threatened me and sent me word, and I told Dr. Matthews if this Negro came back again there would be another notch on the gun."

"Are you willing to tell the jury that this is the pistol you had?"

"That is the gun."

He told of having bought it from Officer Wayne Valentine.

"Wayne Valentine was the one that come to me and told me to go to see Chief Brown and ask to look at it."

"Now, if the court please, Mr. Jordan has three loaded cartridges that came out of the gun and three empties have been taken out of the chamber, and I am calling attention to that physical fact, and I want the three empties and the three loaded cartridges placed here as exhibits."

Though the defense objected to the testimony, Currie had achieved his objective before the jury. The history of the Spanish gun could be traced. Valentine, a police officer, had sold the revolver to Jordan. Jordan had sold it to David McRae, and the gun had been discovered in Ouida's bedroom. However, Ouida had stated that her mother had been bludgeoned, and so far in the trial, gunfire had not been connected with Mrs. Keeton's means of death.

On the Sunday following the night assigned for Mrs. Keeton's murder, the families in the vicinity of Cross Street were assailed by a pungent stench that wafted over their houses and through their doors. Beginning about the time it snowed, the nauseating reek was noted during a few days and nights. Whatever could it be? Across the tracks was the distribution station for Texaco oil and gasoline, but the odor wasn't smoky petroleum. Nor was the Lorimor gas station on the corner the offender. Trains passed by during all hours, but residents were accustomed to the billows from coal-burning locomotives. Beyond the intersection of Cross and Daughdrill the building of the new viaduct was under way, but it occasioned no malodorous offenses. The smoldering stink was ubiquitous. Neighbors began to complain and inquire. The emission seemed to come from the Keetons' house. Then it went away. Then it returned. Some also recalled hearing gunfire in the wee hours of Sunday.

Despite objections from Collins and Clark, Cross Street residents took the stand to testify about their experiences during the period of Mrs. Keeton's death.

Willie Trigg, a Southern Bell Telephone lineman who lived diagonally some one hundred yards from the Keeton house, told of hearing gunfire as he was getting into bed next to his wife after coming home from a coon hunt.

"It said 'pow-pow-pow,' just that way. Just a few minutes after two. A muffled sound, I would say, like somebody was holding a gun next to cloth or the ground or something another. It didn't sound clear, like it was shot out into the open or up in the air or like that. I am positive it was around two o'clock, or a little after, on Sunday morning." His testimony left suspicion that perhaps Mrs. Keeton had died by gunshot rather than by blows with a poker.

Collins, for the defense, questioned Trigg about Ouida's state of health.

"You used to know Miss Keeton when she was much heavier and stronger-appearing than she is now, didn't you?" Collins was inching toward showing that Ouida was a mentally sick woman.

"Well, she looked stouter than she does now, yes, sir."

"And at that time she was the picture of health, wasn't she, Mr. Trigg?"

"I would say she was, yes, sir."

Trigg's wife was called to the stand. She too had heard three pistol shots around two o'clock. She replied "yes" to Currie's asking if she recalled hearing about the discovery of body parts north of Laurel. She said moreover that the pistol shots were fired late on the Saturday night prior to the discovery of the legs.

For cross-examination Clark asked for how long she had been seeing Ouida.

"I don't know her personally. I do know her when I see her, but I never met her."

As to Ouida's declining health and loss of weight, Mrs. Trigg replied, "I couldn't say. I never did pay close enough attention to know just what size she was. She was usually in the car when I would see her."

He asked if she could be mistaken about a pistol shot.

"It was a pistol shot." She said firmly that the gunfire came from the direction of the Keeton house.

The state brought nine more neighbors to testify to the shots and to the foul odor.

Mrs. O. H. Gibson refused to consider that the offensive smell had been rubber tires burning at the filling station, since it was nighttime and it was a Sunday. Her first notice of it was just before the snow. It was like burning wool or old tires.

J. W. Smith first smelled it on Sunday, January 20, around ten in the evening. He described it to be like wool, hair, or horn burning. It was blowing from the south of his residence. When Clark cross-examined him, Smith held to his testimony.

"I don't know what it was, mister, but it was a different odor just to hair alone."

Mrs. Harrison Goff, who lived north of the Keeton home, also reported her experience with the odor. She noticed it first on Sunday afternoon around four or five o'clock. She was on her back porch but soon went inside and paid little attention to it thereafter.

Plummer Rowell testified that he noticed it first on January 21 about two blocks north of the Keetons'. Never before had he smelled anything like it, and the farther he traveled from their house, the less he noted its pungency.

Zeb Norris, walking north past the Keeton house Sunday night about ten o'clock, told that he was assailed by the stink.

"It smelled like wool, leather, and rubber—a kind of mixture."

A half an hour later when he returned, going south, the odor had not diminished.

The prosecution's most damning witness came next. Virgil Sumrall, new to Cross Street, told that he had never seen Ouida or Mrs. Keeton but had passed their house many times. At about eight o'clock on the Monday of snow and sleet he sensed the odor.

"Well, it smelled like wool and grease, or something like that, is the nearest I could tell you."

"State whether or not you had ever smelled anything that had the exact odor that you smelled on that night," Currie asked.

"Well, yes, sir, I have."

Ears were piqued by this new answer. Most in the audience leaned forward. Knitting needles and crochet hooks became still.

"Where was it that you experienced such a smell?" the district attorney asked.

Currie was primed for the damaging answer.

"It was in the Canal Zone, at the crematory, where they burn bodies."

Currie took a seat and gave Deavours a confiding smile.

Collins rose for cross-examination. He planned to give this young authority a work over.

"Mr. Sumrall, you say that was Monday night when you smelled that?"

"Yes, sir."

"How long did you smell it?"

"Well, I never noticed about the time that I smelled it how long it lasted."

"Never noticed about the time?"

"I know about what time it was, but I didn't keep up with how long it lasted."

"Well, give us your best judgment about how long it lasted."

"Well, I guess it was something like about thirty minutes before I went to bed."

"Lasted about thirty minutes? And you say now that you have smelled human bodies burn? How many times did you ever smell human bodies burn there?"

"Well now, that would be hard to say because I was there for seven months, and they burned most of the bodies that die there."

"Burned most of the bodies that die there?"

"Well, yes, sir."

"Now who burns them?"

"I was working for the Canal Zone Government, and it was at the Canal Zone Hospital, and I suppose it was the government had charge of it."

"Mr. Sumrall, do you mean to tell the jury they don't bury the bodies? They just burn them?"

"They burn some of them. When you go to work there, they ask you if you die how you want to be buried—like that or some other way."

Collins's tone turned vicious. He would demolish this know-it-all.

"Mr. Sumrall, don't you know that in all those crematories where they burn any portion of a human body even, they are sealed and you don't get any odor from them at all? Now don't you know that is the truth?"

"No, sir, you smell them."

"They weren't sealed, were they?"

Front page of local newspaper after testimonies about offensive odors of burning, Tuesday, March 5, 1935. (Courtesy of the *Laurel Leader-Call*)

"They go in there, but you are going to smell the odor."

"Why you don't know anything about it. Then if you don't know anything about the crematory, you don't know what is burned there, do you?"

"Yes, sir."

"How do you know?"

Collins was going to split hairs.

"Because I was there, and the officers said it was bodies."

"Well, I didn't ask you what they said. I'm asking what you know of your own personal knowledge, and that is what you are telling, isn't it? Isn't that what you are telling, what you know of your own personal knowledge?"

"Well, sir, they burned the bodies there."

"I'm not asking you that, Mr. Sumrall. Did you see them put the bodies in there?"

"I saw them take the ashes out."

"I didn't ask you that, did I? Was that what I asked you?"

His tone was snide. It let everybody know he was addressing a young whippersnapper who had come to grandstand with bogus, flamboyant information.

Collins looked toward the bench and feigned a face of exasperation. Judge Pack prodded Sumrall to answer the question, and Collins asked it again.

"All right, Mr. Sumrall, did you see them put the bodies in there?"

"No, sir, I didn't see them put the bodies in there."

"All right, then, you don't know what it was that was burned, do you?"

"Well, they built that to burn human bodies in."

Some witnesses are easily browbeaten by aggressive attorneys, but Sumrall held his own.

"I didn't ask you that, did I, Mr. Sumrall?" Collins snapped. "Did I ask you that?"

"No, sir."

"Why did you want to volunteer that?"

"I answered."

"You want to be fair in this case, don't you?"

"Sure."

The courtroom was tense, for the drama of the confrontation was highly entertaining.

"And you want to tell the truth about it?"

"I will tell the truth."

"All right, let's see, Mr. Sumrall, you didn't see them put the bodies in there, did you?"

"I said no, sir."

"And you don't know what it was they were burning, do you?"

"I have their word is all."

"I didn't ask you that. You don't know what it was they were burning, do you?"

"Mr. Collins, I—"

"Why do you hesitate, Mr. Sumrall? You don't know, do you?"

"I have only their word for it."

"And that is what you tell the jury? That is the only way you know to answer it? And so you don't know what it was you were smelling, do you?"

"I know they burned the bodies there, and they said they were burning the bodies when we were smelling the odor."

"I didn't ask you what they said, Mr. Sumrall. Why do you want to be dodging around? Don't you want to tell the truth about it?"

"Sure."

"Then can't you tell the jury whether you know whether or not they put human bodies in the crematory?"

"I didn't see them put them in there."

"Well, then, you don't know whether they put them in there or not."

"Well, I didn't see them."

"Well, then, you don't know whether they were in there or not."

"Well, they put them somewhere and burned them, because they disappeared."

"Well, you can stand aside."

Eight neighbors had testified about the offensive odor, but Sumrall's grisly testimony had been explosive. How could any juror not be influenced? Next, Currie and Deavours would focus on Ouida's reported confessions. The chief of police was called to the stand.

The chief was expecting a merciless grilling by the defense, yet confident in himself and in the punctilious attention he had given to every detail of this messy case, he was prepared. Now and then he had found time to compile a timetable of the confusing events. In spare moments he had put a pencil to paper to jot down their sequence and the progress of the investigation. It was all in his head now almost as clearly as the words on his tablet.

On Saturday, January 19, Carter had conferred with Miss Ouida when he stopped by the McRaes to gas up his car. In the afternoon Mrs. Nicholson came by and bought some gas and, during a chat with Ouida, learned that Daisy Keeton was in New Orleans. All the while Daisy was still at home and alive, but sometime about midnight or later she was murdered and chopped up. After midnight a near neighbor back home from a coon hunt said he heard gunfire.

On early Sunday, the twentieth, Carter departed for his business matter in Alabama. Yet some had reported seeing a black car like his coupe parked at the curb near the Keetons' after midnight on Saturday. Later on Sunday and thereafter, several Keeton neighbors began noticing the terrible smell. In the late afternoon the same Mrs. Nicholson claimed she saw Ouida and a man in a tan car with red wheels.

On Monday, the twenty-first, it rained and then turned cold. That was the morning Ouida left the legs in the woods, hailed a ride back home, and then got Duckworth to help her retrieve her automobile. Then, sometime before noon, Dan Evans's dogs found the bundles.

On Tuesday, the twenty-second, it snowed and nearly the whole town shut down. Ouida spent the day cleaning up the house, even putting a coat of green paint on the hearth and around the fireplace.

On Wednesday, the twenty-third, men warming themselves in front of the Lorimar gas station watched Carter stop his automobile at the Keetons'. Ouida got in and sat beside him, and they talked for about an hour. Then he left but soon afterward came back with his store handyman to make a few repairs at the back of the house.

He had learned that on Thursday, the twenty-fourth, Ouida had driven downtown to get her hair fixed and to do a little shopping at Fine Bros.-Matison Company. By this time Kennedy had given his report by mail about picking Ouida up on the highway, Will Saul had come in with his claim of seeing her driving the Willis Knight car past his farmhouse on the twenty-first, and Duckworth had come forth telling about how he'd pulled her car out of the rut. With their information, Brown saw the case break open.

On Friday, January 25, he, Deavours, and Hamilton had placed Ouida under arrest. While Deavours was interrogating her, he and his men had gone back to the Keeton house with Earl and completed the investigation. They found an abundance of crime evidence. Late on Friday, Ouida could take no more. On that date she confessed to assisting Carter. Then Carter was brought in.

On Saturday, the twenty-sixth, Ouida was in the Jones County jail having a crying jag.

The next day, Sunday, District Attorney Currie interrogated her in her cell. She gave still another confession and fell over on the cot in hysterics.

On Monday, the twenty-eighth, Deavours charged Carter and put him under arrest. All this time the woods were being searched and creeks were being dragged for the rest of Daisy Keeton's body. Carter was taken to Jackson for incarceration, and Ouida was brought into the room to confront him. Crying and accusing, she created as trying a scene as Chief Brown had ever witnessed.

Having organized the chronology of the case, he was ready to testify. The chief was a bold and dominant figure in Laurel. As many feared him for authority as respected him for law and order. He came from the back of the room, stepped up on the low platform, and took a seat in the witness's chair. It would be a tight fit because of the holster and pistol.

Currie came forward with questions.

Brown told of being notified at police headquarters that a pair of severed legs had been found north of Laurel. He had arrived at the crime scene after three o'clock in the afternoon. The vicinity he described as a narrow "one-horse wagon road" on the east side of Highway 11. The cloths were rather clean, but the stubs of the legs were caked with black mud.

"The skin portion then of the limbs was clean?" Currie asked.

"Yes, sir, blue-looking."

On a later day, Brown testified, he went to Farmer Saul's house and examined the tire tracks. Rain and snow had not obliterated them. The tracks appeared similar at both sites.

The district attorney inched closer to the matter of Ouida's confessions.

"State whether or not if sometime thereafter you went to the house of Mrs. Daisy Keeton."

"I went there on Friday morning."

He mentioned that the hour was between nine and ten and that only Ouida and Jean Richeimer were present. Ouida had answered the knock at the door.

To ward off any closer approach to whether Mrs. Keeton actually was dead, Collins rose to voice an objection.

In order to examine this objection, Judge Pack dismissed the jury, and Currie was allowed to press on. He asked the chief to tell of his encounter with Ouida, and Brown complied.

When the jury had been reseated, he resumed by describing Ouida's automobile.

"Well, it is a sedan car, Willis Knight, and maroon-colored with black fenders. Well, the right-hand fender, right up on the top of the fender, looking down over it like that, you couldn't see anything, but you could get back and look at it, and it looked as though something had been drug across it, some sticky object. I just asked her, I says, 'I wonder what that is on the fender,' and she taken her hand like that, and begin trying to rub it off."

He told that after examining the car, he "come on back around, and she went in the house and dressed, and we told her we were going to take her up town to Mr. Deavours's office."

"For the purpose of investigating the cause of Mrs. Keeton's death?"

Collins broke in to object on the basis that the corpus delicti was not proved.

"I taken a pair of gray stockings, or hose, out of the fireplace of Miss Ouida's room," he continued, "and laid them upon a little bench that was setting to the right of the fireplace."

Currie selected an item from the exhibits table.

"I will ask you to look at this pair of hose and state whether or not that is the pair of hose that you took from defendant's room."

"It was a pair just exactly like it."

"Same color?"

"Well, they had a very offensive odor."

"What was the character of the odor, as best you can describe it?"

"Well, it just had a kind of sour, stinking smell to it, is all I know."

"You said you saw the portion of the body that was found?"

"Yes, sir."

"And examined it? State whether or not there were some of the intestines attached to the portion of the body that you found."

"Yes, sir."

"How did the odor of the stocking compare in quality and character to the body?"

Collins objected, but the court overruled him.

"I never got any odor from the body," Brown replied.

"You didn't?"

"No, sir, I couldn't smell any odor to the body or the part that I seen."

"You didn't see it down at the undertaking parlor?"

"No, sir, I never seen it after I left up there where it was in Jasper County."

Currie then displayed the stained suede shoes found in Ouida's bedroom.

"State what the condition of the shoes were with reference to the odor of them."

"Well, sir, them shoes had the same kind of odor on them that was on the pair of stockings."

Currie asked him to recount what he found in Mrs. Keeton's bedroom.

The chief described the scoured flouring, the freshly painted hearth and fireplace, a sprinkling of blood drops, the hearth rug, and residue of cleansing powder.

"Where else, if any place, did you see blood in the house?"

"Right back next to the door leading out of this room into the third bedroom. The bed, this side, come up pretty close to the door, the head of the bed, and there was a few drops of blood on the floor right near the door facing to the right, and just a few little specks on the wall."

"As you passed out of this room, what, if anything, did you find?"

"Well, we went out of that room into the bathroom, and the bathroom door leads out into the kitchen, and there was some blood on the door facing leading from the bathroom to the kitchen and about, I judge, eight inches from the floor maybe, there was a little more."

He told also that on the morning he called on Ouida the water in the bathtub was running full force.

"Full force, and the cork was out, and it was going down. The water was running out of the faucet and going out as fast as it come in. There is one end of the bathtub that comes up right near the door, right near the kitchen door, and the blood was on the bathroom door facing leading in the kitchen to the right."

He left the impression that Mrs. Keeton's corpse could have been dismembered in the bathroom.

The prosecutor took the Spanish firearm from the exhibits table and handed it to the chief.

"Mr. Brown, the gun was unloaded yesterday. I will ask you to insert the loads and empties in the chambers as they were when you found it. What was the condition of the gun when you first saw it, with reference to how it was loaded?"

"It had three empties and three bullets, three loaded shells."

"I will ask you if you have had a large experience in the handling of guns."

"Yes, sir, I have handled them."

"Are you familiar with the results of firing guns under different conditions?"

"Yes, sir. I don't claim to be an expert, but I know something."

"Mr. Brown, I will ask you to examine the cylinder of that pistol and state to the court and jury what if any difference you see or is observable on the side of the cylinder containing the three fired shells and the side of the cylinder containing the three unfired shells with reference to powder burns or any other evidence."

"Well, there was a smoky powder around the cylinder where the three shells had been fired and also smoky powder on the barrel when I got the gun."

"Mr. Brown, I will show you one of the shots or discharged shells. What, if any, observation do you make as to the condition of the cap of that shell?"

"Well, the cap in that shell projects out. The shell that hasn't been shot. The cap in the shell isn't even, flush, with the top of the shell, and this cap projects out more than flush with the end of the empty shell."

"Do you know of your own knowledge, Mr. Brown, what will make a cap do that?"

"If you foul a pistol barrel, or the end of the pistol, why the combustion will push the cap back. I mean if you take the pistol and hold it right up close to my leg and fire it—"

"Firing a gun at close range then?"

"That is, if it is close enough. You confine part of the power. If you shoot it out in the open, all of the force will go out in front, but if you confine it, why part of it will come back the other way."

Currie had planted the thought that Mrs. Keeton had been killed by gunshot rather than with the fire poker. He moved on to the next phase of his strategy.

"Mr. Brown, you said that you saw the limbs as they lay on the ground up there where they were first found?"

"Yes, sir."

"And that the nubs or ends of them were filled with dirt?"

Perceiving his ploy to establish the limbs as Mrs. Keeton's, Collins objected.

"We object to that as repetition."

"Sustained," Judge Pack pronounced.

Currie would attempt to achieve the same result, though with a different approach.

"I want to lead into another question," he said to the chief. "Have you been in the Keeton backyard?"

"Yes, sir."

"State whether or not you have made observation as to the character of the soil and dirt in that place."

"Yes, sir, it is kind of blue-looking soil, black-looking."

"How did the color of the dirt or soil that you saw on the ends of the limbs compare to the soil that was in the backyard of the Keeton home?"

"They was about the same color. Same kind of dirt."

"Sir?"

"About the same kind of dirt, same color."

"Same color."

"We want to ask one more question. Mr. Brown, state whether or not there is a toilet or commode in the Keeton bathroom."

"Yes, sir, there is."

With this answer, the crafty district attorney insinuated a gruesome thought: bits of Mrs. Keeton's corpse had been flushed through the plumbing.

"I think it would be proper to retire the jury," he advised.

He intended next to lay the precedent for bringing Ouida's confessions into the proceedings. He would introduce testimonies of Chief Brown, three newspapermen, Earl Keeton, and Deputy Sheriff Hamilton. All had been present at Deavours's office during the marathon interrogation, and all knew what had transpired.

When the jury box had been vacated and the door had been closed, Currie resumed.

"Mr. Brown, I will ask you if on Sunday, January 27th of this year, if you visited or saw the defendant, Miss Ouida Keeton, here in the Jones County jail."

Perceiving the prosecution's intent, Collins jumped to his feet.

"If the court please," he cried out, "we want the record to show now if they propose to introduce any statement or confession of this defendant, that we object to the evidence for the reason, first, that the corpus delicti has not been established, and, second, because the confession is not free and voluntary and it is therefore inadmissible and incompetent."

The response from the bench changed the direction of the defense.

"The court holds," Judge Pack announced, "that there has been sufficient evidence introduced into the record to make it competent, so far as the corpus delicti is concerned. Any testimony the state has to offer touching a confession the court will hear further testimony with reference to the competency of a confession."

With evidence of the corpus delicti established, Judge Pack nodded for the district attorney to proceed. Defeated, Collins would now to rely on alternate options: a coerced confession and the insanity plea.

Chief Brown told of being present when Ouida made her confession in her jail cell and assured the court that she wanted to make her statement even though advised that it could be used in subsequent prosecution.

In the cross-examination Collins reviewed the schedule of Ouida's arrest, intending that it show she had been subjected to inhumane grilling. He implied that she, a frail and fragile woman, was alone, threatened, and fearful in the presence of Deavours, Brown, Hamilton, Sheriff Jordan, and their aides. With his questioning of previous witnesses he had shown her to be emaciated and ill. Collins gave Ouida a pitying look, then attached a staged and compassionate gaze on the eyes of a juryman, and carried it to the helpless shape in the wheelchair, a suffering woman whom he would show had been terrified of being harmed.

Turning the direction of his questions, Collins again attempted to prove there had been a frightful mob outside Deavours's office and around the jail.

"The only ones I remember seeing around there," the chief replied, "was Mr. Jordan and Mr. Deavours and Miss Keeton on the outside of the office, and Mrs. Daly was on the outside in her office, and Mr. Montgomery, the newspaper reporter, was sitting out there on a bench in an outside office. I seen a few around the jail. Most of them was on the lawn, hanging over the fence."

"Then on Sunday it was virtually the same? The street down there and all on the lawn and the courthouse around there, people were standing all around? There was a considerable crowd of people milling around?"

"As well as I remember, there was quite a few people scattered around out there in different places."

"And of course her being in jail, she could see them out there, couldn't she? Out the windows?"

"She never looked out while I was up in the jail."

"And it is your understanding and information that she was kept in Mr. Jack Deavours's office until four o'clock in the morning?"

One or two jurymen were shaking their heads as though to comment on the punishing agenda for a woman to endure. Collapsed in her wheelchair, the emaciated defendant continued to give the illusion of being far removed from the courtroom.

"I don't know how long she was kept there. I don't know as I had that information. I asked next morning when I come down where she was, and I was told she was in the county jail, but I did not know what time they left Mr. Deavours's office."

The next witnesses were three newsmen who had sat in Deavours's office during Ouida's lengthy interrogation. Waiting for news to break, they had lingered in the reception room from 6:30 until nearly midnight. Collins pressed them for comments on the size of the crowd in the street but got little support to his claim that it could be defined as a threatening mob.

After Collins had completed this line of questioning, Currie asked permission to offer testimony about events in Deavours's office, events that would sanction the admissibility of the confessions.

He called Earl Keeton back to the stand.

"I was in and out all night, but I was in Deavours's office something like four or five times," Earl recalled. Ouida had been provided food, and he himself went out for Coca-Colas. He was present when Ouida was allowed to phone Eloise in New Orleans.

Collins came forward for cross-examination.

"Mr. Keeton, while you were in there, did anybody warn Miss Keeton that any statement she made might be used against her?"

"No, sir."

"Popped questions to her all the time you were there?"

"Well, one would ask questions and he would get through, and another one would ask her a question. There was practically somebody asking her questions all the time."

"You didn't see her eat or drink a mouthful while you were there?"

"Well, she taken one swallow of coffee and drank one Coca-Cola, to my knowledge."

"And then they put you out along the latter part of the night?"

"Well, at times they would let me go to the door, and Jack Anderson come out and told me to meet the train and bring Miss Eloise back. He wanted to see her."

Intending to vindicate the prosecution from Collins's implication of brutality, Currie brought Deputy Sheriff Hamilton back to the stand and asked him to testify that Ouida had been fed and afforded occasions to use the toilet.

"And all of that time, Mr. Hamilton," Collins asked in the cross-examination, "they had been grilling and questioning this defendant?"

"They had been talking to her," he replied, downplaying the interrogation. "The only ones I saw talking to her was Mr. Deavours and Chief Brown and Wayne Valentine, and I asked her one question myself."

"And she didn't sleep any from the time she was carried to Mr. Deavours's office Friday morning at ten o'clock until the time you left there at midnight?"

"No, sir, she didn't sleep any that day."

After Hamilton was excused, Currie asked the court to rule on introducing the statements Ouida made in her cell.

Collins immediately objected.

"We object because under the evidence it is not shown that it was free and voluntary. On the other hand, the evidence in this record discloses that it was made by coercion."

"Overruled."

It was another setback for the defense. Collins could not block the confessions. The time had come for the insanity plea. He asked if the court would allow him to recall Chief Brown to the stand. Collins intended to show that Ouida's strange behavior was caused by an unsound mind. With the jury retired, he established that Chief Brown had known and observed Ouida for more than twenty years and that on the morning he went to the Keeton home to question her he had noted a definite change in her weight, appearance, and behavior.

"Well, she had an unusual expression on her face," the chief admitted.

"Well, what was that unusual expression, Mr. Brown? A blank, starey look, wasn't it? And you have seen insane people, haven't you, Mr. Brown?"

"Yes, I have seen them."

"Good many of them. And you have had a great deal of experience in running down crime and tracking people and dealing with more or less people in connection with crime, haven't you, Mr. Brown?"

"Yes, sir."

"Now, Mr. Brown, from what you have observed about the girl and what you saw there that day, isn't it your opinion that at that time this girl was insane?"

"No, sir, I won't say that."

"You wouldn't say that?"

"No, sir."

"Mr. Brown, you did notice a very definite change in her at that time, didn't you?"

"Yes, sir, but under the circumstances that might have brought that change on."

"Mr. Brown, regardless of what brought it on, isn't it your opinion that at that time she was insane?"

"No, sir."

"It isn't? Now, Mr. Brown, you have talked to me about this, haven't you?"

"Yes, I have talked to you about it. I expressed my opinion that it looked to me like the whole job was an insane act. That is the way I expressed it."

"That in your honest opinion she was insane?"

"I don't remember telling you that."

"Then do you state, Mr. Brown, that it was or was not your opinion at the time she was insane?"

"Not at that time."

Judge Pack ordered the bailiff to summon the jury, and Collins resumed. The chief reported on Ouida's strange behavior while she was giving him and District Attorney Currie a new statement in her jail cell. With the jury-men listening, Collins achieved his ploy of imprinting them with thoughts of her probable insanity. However, in this same testimony Ouida's references to Mrs. Keeton's dismembered legs were a bitter pill for the defense. Indeed, proof of the corpus delicti had been established.

Jack Deavours intended to win this case by leaving an indelible imprint in the courtroom. Before the state rested, he had yet one more exhibit to introduce, planned as an end-of-day event and as the climax of dramatic prosecution. It could clinch the jury's decision to convict Ouida. Already on the table lay the sugar sacking, the gory photographs, the fire poker, the butcher knives, the vials of tallow and bone fragments, the stained shoes and stockings, the segment of blood-streaked woodwork, the piece of tallow-saturated floor joist, and the Spanish revolver. The withered pine sapling was there too, in a far corner of the room. The ultimate exhibit, an unforgettable spectacle, would surpass all of these.

Many in the courtroom edged forward in their seats and craned their necks as the district attorney made the announcement. Daisy Keeton's legs would be displayed before the jury. On signal, the bailiffs and Neville Allen, the mortician, marched in with a case that resembled a small coffin and set it on the floor in front of the jury box. It had a clear glass lid. Specta-tors stretched and gaped, but only the judge, jurors, and a few members of the press corps could see the intimate contents. Ouida was unfazed, though what were alleged to be her mother's thighs were within ten feet of the wheelchair.

Dr. C. H. Ramsay, the final witness, gave a description of the limbs and specified their weight and measurements. He reported that Mrs. Keeton had been somewhat large, had weighed around 180 pounds, and was between five feet seven and five feet nine inches tall. The legs, 40 percent of Mrs. Keeton's weight, weighed thirty-two to thirty-seven pounds. In response to questioning from the defense, he told that the weight of the blood in the body amounted to 12 percent of the total.

"The state rests," Jack Deavours announced to the stunned courtroom.

In a procedural formality Frank Clark rose with a motion to exclude all testimony and asked the judge to direct the jury to give a verdict of not guilty. He was, of course, overruled.

■　■　■

Public confusion about the meaning of corpus delicti sparked arguments throughout the county. Few, other than specialists, knew the true definition. Burkitt Collins and Frank Clark kept spouting the legal jargon, and the citizenry assumed that the term simply meant Mrs. Keeton's corpse and that, so far as the defense attorneys were concerned, until the rest of her body parts were located or identified, the prosecution had no sound case. This literal interpretation was flawed.

An editorial writer for the *Leader-Call* attempted to clear away the confusion: "You have been seeing the term *corpus delicti* very frequently in these news columns of late." So that there would be no further misinterpretations, the paper reprinted a definition from Judge W. W. Magruder of the Sixteenth Judicial District. "Few people except lawyers," he stated, "know the true meaning of the term. It is currently supposed to refer to the corpse or body of a human being, which is correct only in a limited sense. It is in fact applicable to any and all criminal cases, homicide, arson, burglary, larceny, etc. It merely means that the body or substance of a crime must be established."

The *Leader-Call* pointed out one other point of confusion in the Legs Murder case. Although the first half of Ouida's trial had been concluded, no one had determined by what means Mrs. Keeton had been killed. "Whether the victim had been shot dead in her own bed [or beside] the fireplace, or whether the death blow had been struck with a poker, the body carried elsewhere for disarticulation and disposal, only the legs being returned, was the unsolved mystery."

On the afternoon of Wednesday, March 6, the second half of Ouida's trial began as the defense launched its attack on the prosecution. Thirty-four witnesses were scheduled to take the stand. Since Currie and Deavours had established the outrageous belief that much of Daisy Keeton's corpse had been cremated in her own fireplace and that its incineration had emitted a stench that pervaded the homes of Cross Street, the initial shot in Collins and Clark's strategy would aim to demolish all testimonies about the worrisome odor. They would offer a mundane explanation.

Mrs. A. V. Shull came to the stand as the key witness. She lived on Front and Seventh streets, across the railroad tracks and two or three blocks from the Keeton house. An open space between the two homes would allow smoke to drift up Cross Street. In January she too had sensed the unsettling smell and had wondered about its source. On the day it snowed, she discovered that a fire was burning within her own premises. When it was extinguished, the stink went away. She told that the combustion, undetected for two days, had smoldered in a box containing sheets, pillow cases, old quilts, woolen blankets made from men's suits, rubber swimming caps, and a container of olive oil. Just as a blanket was beginning to flame, she dragged the box from the house into the snow.

The blanket was submitted as evidence.

Collins's smiles conveyed his satisfaction as his witness gave this plausible explanation. In the cold weather the woolen and rubber items had never burst into flames but had continued to waft the obnoxious smell through the neighborhood.

Four others also came to the stand to tell of the burning box. But with their testimonies had the defense achieved its purpose? If the box had been confined in Mrs. Shull's room until Tuesday, could the odor have circulated over to Cross Street on Saturday, Sunday, and Monday? Was it truly the source?

Next, having laid the precedent for an insanity plea with cross-examination of Chief Brown's testimony for the prosecution, Collins and Clark were poised to argue that their client was insane and therefore not responsible for any criminal act that could be attributed to her. Their interrogations would dwell on the signs and the symptoms, namely, her loss of weight and her unusual behavior. The questioning would be sharply focused on Ouida's past two years, a time after she had returned from Washington, D.C.

Clark took over and called one of Daisy Keeton's sisters. Stella Sherrill came to the stand as the first of four family members brought in to give evidence of Ouida's physical and mental frailty. How closely had she observed Ouida? Mrs. Sherrill testified that she had seen Ouida at least once a week over the past ten or fifteen years. Had she noted any physical changes in her niece? She replied that Ouida had lost a considerable amount of weight and had been sick off and on during the past two years.

"Ouida was unusually bright mentally," she continued, "and a good conversationalist. In the last two years she would come in and seem to try to avoid us, have little to say, appeared restless and nervous. She would turn pages in magazines, running through them rapidly without reading a line. Then she would suddenly say, 'Well, I've read them all, Mama. Let's go.' Her eyes had a wild, staring look."

She praised Ouida as "the most devoted child to her mother I had ever seen. Ouida seemed to prefer to stay with her mother to going out to play with other children."

In the cross-examination Mrs. Sherrill told that "for years back Ouida would take little pouting spells. We didn't know what about." She said Ouida liked to look at herself in the mirror and she had a strange laugh.

Deavours asked how many of the McKinstry brothers and sisters were still living.

"Two boys and three—no four—girls, if my sister is alive. You haven't proved to me that she is dead yet," she added, seeming to remember Collins's advice to the family about refusing to admit there was a corpus delicti. She stated that the McKinstrys were reared in Jasper County, north of Sandersville and near Corinth Church. She was not certain about Daisy Keeton's age.

"Fifty-seven or fifty-eight. I'm not sure. You know," she chuckled, "women don't keep up much with their ages, and they stop having birthdays." She hesitated before replying to a question about Ouida's age. She estimated it to be thirty-four, although "the newspapers say she was thirty-three."

For the court she reviewed her recollection of Ouida's schooling and her going "to Washington to take a special course." She said that Ouida's employment with W. M. Carter had been devoted to collecting bills, acting as Carter's secretary, and performing usual office work.

Stella Sherrill's husband, M. A. Sherrill, was the next witness. Clark asked him to state how often he observed Ouida and to comment on her physical condition. Sherrill replied that he saw Ouida about once a week, sometimes less often. Yes, he had noted some changes in the past two years, especially in her weight. She now weighed only 115 or 118 but formerly had weighed 155 or 160.

Her demeanor?

"She couldn't carry on a conversation like she used to. Her eyes looked dull. They had no luster." She had been frequently ill within the past two years, and her mental and physical condition had been a subject of family discussion.

The district attorney came forward for the cross-examination. He asked if Mr. Sherrill himself had conducted any investigation into Mrs. Keeton's disappearance.

"No, I thought the officers were doing all that could be done."

"How long has Mr. Carter been a widower?" Currie asked.

"About two years."

As her family spoke for her, Ouida remained unresponsive, disclosing neither embarrassment nor resentment that her personal life was being aired so publicly.

Earl Keeton's wife, Jewel, was called. She told that for about three years after 1930 she and Earl had lived in the Keeton house with Daisy and Ouida and were there, she said, to observe Ouida's breaking health.

"I massaged her back and shoulder and put hot cloths on her for hours at a time nearly every night." Her sister-in-law's behavior? "Ouida paid no attention to what was said to her and had a faraway look in her eyes." She and Mrs. Keeton had traveled to Hot Springs twice and stayed for three weeks. Both had received treatments, Daisy for her rheumatism. Jewel told that Ouida had "an electrical reducing machine."

And Mr. Carter?

"Mr. Carter was there lots of times. He had been a widower for two years."

When Jewel stepped down, Dr. J. D. Smith was called. Smith, age sixty-two, had practiced medicine around the town of Sandersville for thirty-one years after graduating from medical school in Alabama. He had known the Keetons and McKinstrys all his life.

"We were old families in that section." He said also that he was acquainted with Ouida and had done business with her at Carter Lumber Company.

"She struck me as a very thorough business woman, and transacted business with me in a very nice way." She was "strictly business."

Collins thrashed over the question of Ouida's falling weight.

Dr. Smith had observed that she had "lost quite a lot of weight" and had "a sort of half-anxious, half-blank stare." She had been his patient only once, but he had chanced to see her, off and on, a number of times. One unusual encounter with her had occurred about six months back. As he was driving in downtown Laurel, she suddenly had crossed the street directly in front of his car. He blew the horn, applied his brakes, and came to an abrupt stop to avoid hitting her.

"She never noticed."

He said that he had seen her only once since she was taken to the hospital.

Collins asked whether he was of the opinion that Ouida was sane or insane.

Deavours immediately objected, questioning the competency of such testimony from Dr. Smith.

Judge Pack excused the jury so that Deavours and Collins could debate.

"If Dr. Smith is in a position to give an opinion as to the sanity or insanity of the defendant from personal observation made by him on facts known by him, he may give it, otherwise not," Judge Pack ruled.

When the jury returned, Collins rephrased the question.

"She's insane, in my opinion," Dr. Smith replied.

The district attorney took over for cross-examination. First, he inquired about the Keeton and McKinstry home places and the family members. In responding, Dr. Smith told that John Keeton, Ouida's father, had been killed by a passenger train. Next, Currie asked if Dr. Smith knew W. M. Carter. He replied that he had known Carter well, since 1901, when Carter operated a sawmill north of Sandersville.

Before the break for the day there was time for Collins and Clark to bring only two witnesses to the stand. Both, like the family members, were focused on showing Ouida to be insane.

Dr. J. B. Jarvis, a Laurel physician for forty-two years and W. M. Carter's former neighbor, was serving the court as Ouida's physician. He had been seeing her as a patient at least twice a day since first examining her in the Jones County jail on January 27 and 28. He had treated her both in her cell and at the hospital. Though not an expert on insanity, he claimed general knowledge of mental cases.

"After she had been assigned as my patient, the second day after she was put on trial," he replied to Collins, "I considered her insane."

But on cross-examination the district attorney found this testimony in conflict with Dr. Jarvis's earlier statement attributing Ouida's collapse to mental worry and nervous shock. Jarvis had remarked that any woman accused of killing her mother could be expected to fall into melancholy. Currie asked for clarification.

"I considered her insane the first time I saw her."

"What about now?"

"I consider her quite insane."

"What kind of insanity do you say she has?"

"Dementia praecox."

To most ears in the courtroom this was a strange technical term, but to the physicians in the room it specified a type of psychological disorder begun in adolescence and characterized by cognitive disintegration, loss of attention, and the breakdown of other mental functions. In later years it would be classified as a form of schizophrenia.

Currie queried the doctor about Ouida's medication. Jarvis replied that on the recommendation of Dr. C. E. Holbrook, a nerve specialist at Tulane University Hospital summoned by the state, he had given Ouida a grain and a half of sodium luminol. The dosage should have been only one-half grain, for it proved to overmedicate her. He reminded that as her jurors were being processed, Ouida had fallen into a sound sleep despite the courtroom babble. However, Jarvis held that the seeming stupor his patient continued to display in the courtroom was not caused by medicine but by her mental condition. He testified that his examinations at the hospital revealed neither fever nor irregular pulse beat. To detect possible syphilitic infection, a cause for some cases of dementia, he had administered a Wassermann test, which proved negative. A drawing of spinal fluid "showed a low pressure and lack of vitality."

The district attorney rebuked him "for puncturing the spine of this poor, defenseless girl."

Dr. Jarvis refused to admit that Ouida's health was improving, although she was now taking nourishment. When asked what she had eaten on that morning, he replied, "Toast, bacon, egg, but I can't remember the whole menu."

The hour was five o'clock, and Judge Pack prepared for adjournment. He signaled that spectators remain seated while Ouida was wheeled toward the exit. As he was lifting the gavel to pound for adjournment, the opposing lawyers fell into heated debate. They were face to face, almost in physical combat. Now that the defense had turned toward the insanity plea, Collins was demanding that the state produce Ouida's signed confession, and Currie and Deavours were refusing. Judge Pack broke up the wrangle, calmed the room, and called for adjournment.

Collins continued to bluster. The turn in the defense required that he thrash it out with the prosecution and gain access to the official confession. Ouida's statements in Deavours's office, in her jail cell, and on her hospital bed, as well as those reported in newspapers, were riddled with sensational contradictions. Only Jack Deavours's interview at the hospital included Ouida's witnessed signature. Relying now on proving Ouida's mental instability, the defense intended to bring this authorized confession to the attention of the jury and to mine it for elements of insanity.

When court was reconvened, he and Clark came to the courtroom armed with a subpoena duces tecum that called for the judge to admit the confession into the evidence. Caught by this surprise move, Currie and Deavours demurred with vigorous and angry resistance. They were reluctant to explain their reasons, but releasing it too soon, during Ouida's trial, could endanger their subsequent prosecution of Carter. Judge Pack calmed their clash and took the matter under advisement, saying he would rule on the admissibility of the confession on the following day.

Musings in the courtroom supposed that the state attorneys had not introduced the confession themselves because if it contained wild conjectures and was of rambling character it could give support to the defense strategy. Collins and Clark held to their claim that the signed document, as yet unexamined by them, would clinch their case for Ouida's insanity and would bolster the testimonies of the four psychiatrists scheduled to testify later in the week.

When court was reconvened on March 7, Judge Pack was prepared to address the admissibility of the confession. Both the prosecution and the defense had passed a long night in legal research and in plotting strategies. Collins and Clark came to the courtroom flourishing the writ of subpoena. Jack Deavours came prepared with a demurrer and an eloquent defense of the prosecution's position of withholding the confession. Placed on the table before him was a waist-high stack of casebooks and precedents they had consulted. Deavours charged that Collins and Clark were merely on a fishing expedition.

"There is no law on earth that would compel us to turn over to the defense any evidence we might have that could be used in prosecution of another case." He cited case after case in support of his position.

Most of the morning session was consumed by the battle over the confession.

Judge Pack gave his ruling. Deavours demurrer was sustained, and after Collins's petition was denied, the defense resorted to a new tactic. Collins called Currie to the stand.

"State whether this defendant has made written confessions," Collins confronted him.

"I have not seen a written confession with her name signed to it," Currie replied.

"Has the defendant made any statement that was taken in writing?"

"I understand that one was taken by a stenographer."

"Did that statement differ from the one introduced here as evidence?"

Deavours rose to object, and Judge Pack sustained the objection but sent the jury from the room.

When the judge gave his ruling, it was a victory for the prosecution. Currie and Deavours could withhold the confession. Collins and Clark would have to rely on other ways to prove Ouida was insane.

They resumed the interrogation of her immediate family and called on her aunt to portray Ouida as mentally troubled.

Paula Richeimer described Ouida as a strange girl who had always preferred to live her life alone. Ouida, she said, had been unusually attached to her mother after suffering an accidental fall during childhood. She told that, while in high school, Ouida had no dates. Mrs. Richeimer recalled how Ouida sometimes shut herself in her bedroom, refusing to come out and requiring that her meals be served to her there. Such a retreat became customary during her annual two weeks of summer vacation while she was employed by Carter, although in recent years this habit had been broken by her bouts with illness.

Mrs. Richeimer spoke of the plan her sister and niece had made of buying and operating a hotel or boardinghouse in New Orleans. Mother and daughter had traveled there together to see about renting an eighteen- or twenty-room hotel. However, Daisy's hopes were dashed when Ouida's interest in the project waned. For no given reason, she balked at conferring further with their real-estate agent about it. The family thought this behavior strange in one who formerly had taken such interest in the project. In fact, for some months Ouida's mental state had been a subject of discussion among her aunts. Mrs. Richeimer was especially alarmed by Ouida's fixations.

"On a Saturday night in January she sat and picked at her face until blood ran out. W. M. Carter was present."

She denied that her niece had undue affection for Carter, although he visited the Keetons often. Ouida, she said, was never alone with him in the house, nor did she ever go out alone with him. In her view, her niece had regarded him only as a good friend. In the recent past Ouida's behavior, she asserted, had become remarkably mysterious.

"I have seen her sit on the porch for half a day at a time, just looking into space."

The aunt also recalled "gorgeous American Beauty roses and expensive boxes of candy" that were showered on Ouida at Christmas time. No one knew the name of the admirer, but the family eventually found out. Ouida had sent them to herself.

"The family enjoyed the candy, but Ouida never took a single piece."

"Is it unusual for a pretty girl to receive flowers?"

"I never did."

In addition, there was other odd behavior. Ouida had been purchasing baby clothing and storing it in her chifforobe. No one knew why.

In the cross-examination, when District Attorney Currie asked if the baby clothes could have belonged to her sister when Eloise was married to James Daniel, or to Jewel Keeton. Mrs. Richeimer did not agree. The baby things were "a part of Ouida's dreams."

As he was pressing her for family information, she told him that Eloise had gone to Washington to visit Ouida and then returned to take a business course in New Orleans. Ouida had remained in the capital.

"When did you last see your sister?"

"She was at my home on the afternoon of January 19. I telephoned her Sunday night [January 20], but no one answered. I telephoned Monday afternoon and talked to Ouida. Using the word 'we,' Ouida spoke about their bringing in the potted ferns from the porch to keep them from freezing. She telephoned me the next day and said that her mother had gone to New Orleans on a business trip and that she was going to stay with me while her mother was gone. Ouida went back to her home Friday [January 24] to see if she had received a letter from her mother."

Mrs. Richeimer said she believed her sister was still alive.

When Currie questioned her about Ouida's reducing machine, she replied that Ouida probably had not used it for two years. In fact, a day or two after Mrs. Keeton was reported as missing, Mrs. Richeimer saw the machine still stored in the bathroom closet with scales placed against the door.

"She had ten or twelve bad spells of illness during the past two years, and instead of trying to reduce, she has been trying to gain weight. She would eat seven or eight meals a day in an effort to gain."

When Currie inquired about Ouida's employment at the Carter Lumber Company, Mrs. Richeimer commented on Carter's finances.

"Ouida stayed with him until he failed two or three years ago." However, since then she believed he had made a financial recovery. In fact, she said,

Carter had told her that "he is richer now than he ever was in his lifetime because [his assets] were 'all on paper before.'" After Carter's business failure and after Ouida was no longer his employee, she reminded Currie that Ouida had gone to Washington to enroll in the classes in hotel management.

Up to this point Collins and Clark seemed satisfied with their course in shaping the defense. Though having lost their attempt to disprove the corpus delicti, they felt a sense of success with the insanity plea. Among the twelve men gazing down upon their pitiable client, a spirit of sympathy may be supplanting vicious feelings for retribution and harsh justice. In her wheelchair, the pathetic Ouida herself gave the plea graphic support merely by lying in semiconsciousness for the jury to observe and pity. She looked like a wounded and persecuted innocent. On the stand two local physicians who were fairly well acquainted with the defendant had declared her to be insane, and her own kin, who had observed her intimately during the past two years, had given the jury a sad picture of a troubled young woman of shifting moods and inexplicable behavior.

Thursday was the doctors' day in court. It was, as well, yet another in which a horde of curious and jostling spectators rushed the doors early in hopes of achieving the prime seating. Collins and Clark had masterminded a plan that they thought could not fail to influence the jury and outflank the prosecution. Their assembly of experts, the best in the region and the best in the community, was present to give dire pronouncements about Ouida's mental health. In order to monitor the defendant and to take notes as they observed her for a few days, some who would be called to the stand had sat incognito in the crowded courtroom amid the Jones County citizens embroidering, munching peanuts, and slurping soda pop.

Included too were four homegrown practitioners who from time to time had administered to deranged patients, mainly in referring them to the state asylum. Two of them had examined Ouida. Always mindful of the country character of the jury deciding this delicate case, the defense evidently inter-mingled these local authorities to counteract any negative feelings some jurors could harbor for uppity outsiders, as well as to bring any high-flown medical jargon back to earth. Dr. A. J. Carter was superintendent of the South Mississippi State Hospital (Charity Hospital) in Laurel, where Ouida temporarily had been interned recently. Dr. R. H. Cranford and Dr. Robert McLaurin, Laurel physicians in general practice, had treated patients with mental disorders. Dr. Joe Green was a colorful country doctor known in the community as an expert in any disease from mental illness to foot itch.

Laurel's Dr. Jarvis and the two Drs. Ramsay, father and son, already had testified and were not included in this day's medical roundup. The son had examined and treated Ouida at the jail, but by having declared that her ailments could be addressed as readily in her cell as in Laurel General Hospital, young Dr. Ramsay had proved himself unsympathetic to the case Collins and Clark were trying to build.

The local physicians were called to the stand first. Collins and Clark were saving the high-powered guns for last.

Dr. Carter told of Ouida's admission to the Charity Hospital on January 30, a Wednesday, and of her release on February 10, a Wednesday. He had given her a routine examination on the first day and assigned her to a private ward on the third floor of the west end of the building.

"I concluded she was mentally off."

"Was she insane when she was brought to the hospital?"

The district attorney objected but was overruled.

"I'd say she was insane."

"In your opinion was Miss Keeton sane or insane on January 19?"

Deavours objected.

Judge Pack asked Dr. Carter if he was qualified to answer.

"I have an opinion based on the history of the case."

The objection was overruled, but Deavours, continuing to fume, discredited the doctor's statement.

Currie took over for the cross-examination.

"I don't claim to be an expert," the doctor advised.

"You stopped giving her medicine?" Currie asked.

"At her own request."

"This defendant had been employed in a responsible position the very day of the crime," Currie reminded the jury. He emphasized that Ouida was known around town as a capable businesswoman serving as cashier at the McRae gas station.

"We just decide if a person is sane or insane," the doctor replied. "There are varying degrees of insanity, and some of the brightest people go crazy."

The district attorney moved to strike all of Dr. Carter's testimony, since he himself had claimed not be an expert.

Judge Pack, however, disagreed, and overruled the motion.

Young Dr. Robert McLaurin, a graduate of the University of Mississippi and of the medical school in Richmond, Virginia, took the stand next. He had been in practice for seven years, since 1928, but disclaimed to be a qualified mental expert. He had examined Ouida ten days previously. Her blood pressure at that time was exceptionally low, and there was almost a complete absence of reflexes. Under the circumstances he believed he had gained the best possible history of the patient.

"In your opinion, is she sane or insane?" Collins asked.

"She is insane."

When Dr. Joe E. Green was called to the stand, he gazed piteously on the defendant lying so complacently in the wheelchair, not ten feet from where he sat. He was a graduate of the medical school at Tulane University, with a practice that extended over nearly fifty years, mostly in Laurel. He was the physician of the local Masonite Corporation, and he specialized in diseases of women and children. He first had seen Ouida in W. M. Carter's office some years back. His impression: "She is different."

"In my opinion," he replied to Collins, "from the history and physical conditions, from the red-blood count and all that goes with it, this girl was suffering and had been suffering for some time from dementia praecox. In my opinion she was insane on January 19."

Ouida lay almost motionless. Her head was propped up somewhat higher than on previous days and her face more visible to the jury.

"Ouida was a beautiful girl," Dr. Green volunteered in a compassionate tone, "but when you met her, she gave you the impression of being very different. I first examined her ten days ago and found that she has been suffering with catatonic dementia praecox since she was a child of six years. At the time I examined her, she insisted that she was not crazy, but there is no doubt about her condition."

He pointed toward Ouida, so obviously a sick woman, and in a firm voice made his declaration.

"She is undoubtedly insane."

Dr. Green then made a dire announcement.

"She will probably be dead in six months."

If the defendant heard his prediction, she did not stir. In the audience heads rocked gently, resigned to the pitiful plight of Ouida Keeton.

"On January 19," Collins asked, "was the defendant able to distinguish right from wrong?"

"No more than space," Dr. Green answered. "It's a blank space in her life."

There was no noticeable response from the jury, but suddenly the defendant stirred in her chair and seemed awakened from her stupor. Had Dr. Green's prognosis riled her? She squirmed as though uncomfortable and placed her hands on her head. Was she signaling her protest of the doctor's candid remark? Then she grew calm. Perhaps she had merely been nestling to smooth out a hard wrinkle against her aching back.

When the district attorney came forward to question the witness, he asked about the doctor's qualifications for testifying about Ouida's alleged insanity.

"I knew you were going after me, a country doctor, for qualifying as a mental expert."

Deavours asked him to explain dementia praecox.

Dr. Green launched a picturesque analogy to convey a simplistic definition.

"You look up at a sky, and it is cloudless and blue. Then a few clouds scuttle across, and the sun is dimmer for a while and then comes out again. After that, the clouds pile up suddenly into a funnel-shaped thing, and a cyclone descends on the earth and brings death and disaster. After it is all over, the sky is blue again. The mind afflicted with this disease is like that sky."

The awaiting alienists from New Orleans, Jackson, and Memphis rolled their eyes, but the faces of the jurymen seemed to brighten with understanding.

When Currie asked if Dr. Green was acquainted with W. M. Carter, the doctor replied that he frequently bought building supplies from him but denied that Carter was in his thoughts at present. Giving a subtle implication to the jury that perhaps Dr. Green could be biased, Currie reminded him that Carter, jointly indicted with Ouida, was the father-in-law of Paul Decker, now an executive at Masonite Corporation, that Carter sold Masonite products in his company, and that Dr. Green was a physician for the corporation.

He continued by asking what history he had obtained from Ouida when examining her.

"She wanted me to understand that she wasn't crazy, that when she was six years old she had a fall and since then had suffered, that in the last two and one-half years she had suffered much pain in the back of her neck and down to the middle of her spine."

"Do you believe she is in pain?"

"You could stick a pin in her and she couldn't feel it, but rub your hand up and down her spine and she'll come out of that chair."

When Dr. Cranford, the next to testify, took his seat on the witness stand, he too was of the opinion that Ouida was insane. He had practiced medicine for thirty years and had known Ouida for about thirteen. He had met her at W. M. Carter's office in 1924.

"I tried at that time to hire her as my secretary and bookkeeper."

More than a year ago he had chanced to see her at a reception held for the opening of Laurel's new starch plant. She had told him of wanting to make an appointment. She expressed her concern about having lost thirty-five to fifty pounds. He observed then that Ouida's appearance was drastically altered.

"She wasn't the same girl."

Then he reported that three weeks ago Dr. Jarvis had called him to come for a consultation about the Keeton case, a "hideous crime" Dr. Cranford classified as the "act of a crazy person or lunatic." As he studied the family history and Ouida's medical report, he decided that "she hadn't developed her glandular structure since she was two years old." He continued: "The whole thing began to unfold, and I decided she was a victim of dementia praecox." In the many faces of insanity, he said, "some want to love everybody, and some want to fight." He added that Ouida's "reflexes were all wrong," and he offered to perform "infallible tests" on her there in the courtroom to show that she was abnormal and to "prove she is insane now."

Deavours rose to suggest that the jury retire, and his colleague went on record to claim for the state the same right of running experiments on the prisoner. Judge Pack inquired what Dr. Cranford planned to do.

"Shove something down her throat."

He proposed, also, if the court would allow, to place Ouida in grotesque postures "in which she would remain until she collapsed from weakness or until someone moved her."

From the audience came gasps of protest. Judge Pack rapped for order. Currie objected, claiming that the defendant had overhead his plan and would perform accordingly. Judge Pack interceded.

"The court will disallow any demonstration that might be taxing on the strength of the defendant."

Dr. Cranford acquiesced, saying he would rely then on one of his experiments in the sickroom.

"I stuck a pin in her and she didn't flinch. I can run my finger down her throat, but she won't gag. A week ago we made tests, repeatedly asking her who killed her mother. She wrote that she did not know and said that God and her mother visited her every day and that her mother was happy and beautiful. Not an expression crossed her face as she wrote this."

The doctor had even more to report in his awesome portrayal of Ouida's serious distress.

"There has been no glandular development in her body since she was two years old."

Dr. Cranford announced this discovery in a tone of grave authority. But he was not finished, for he made a more startling revelation.

"She has no thyroid gland."

On hearing this medical opinion, sophisticated physicians cast darting looks at each other. How could such a bold assertion be medically true? Astonished eyes rolled to and fro, and some in the audience began to press fingers upon their own throats.

Collins turned the witness over to District Attorney Currie.

In the cross-examination Dr. Cranford ascribed Mrs. Keeton's death to Ouida's insanity, and as he hastily pressed forward to offer his magisterial views, he blurted out his opinion that as an insane person she was subject to whim and suggestibility and could lay the blame for the crime on anybody and everybody, no matter who.

"It might have been you or me instead of Carter implicated for the murder, had our names been suggested to Ouida Keeton at the right moment. Why W. M. Carter is as innocent as a man can be," he exclaimed, "no more guilty than I am!"

Dr. Cranford's gratuitous outburst was like a punch, and the whole room rocked in a unified knee jerk. Interlocked bodies were jostled from their confines and had to be rewedged and settled. At the far edges of the side aisles chair legs scraped and bumped during the scramble. Ouida, alone in her stupor, did not flutter. The district attorney was appalled. He moved that Dr. Cranford's testimony be stricken from the record. Collins leaped up to object, his feet loud on the floor. Currie's face was red with passion, and Jack Deavours was running his palms over his hair in exasperation. Judge Pack honored their request that the jury be retired.

"The state contends," Currie protested, "the doctor's statement on Carter's guilt shows interest in the case." "If the defense of insanity is proved for Ouida," he continued, "it will go far in obliterating the alleged guilt of Carter. Therefore, this man's interest in the case makes his testimony incompetent."

Collins interjected his view.

"The question of whether or not Carter is guilty is not material to the issue of this defendant's guilt or innocence."

Deavours rose to support Currie.

"Dr. Cranford's opinion on Carter's guilt or innocence shows his interest in Carter and would reflect on the testimony in this case."

Judge Pack overruled, and the jury was returned.

Collins asked Dr. Cranford to rephrase his answer, and he did so in a modified tone.

"Ouida in her present state," he said, "is so susceptible to suggestion that she might have named anyone as the murderer of her mother. I said that if she were so susceptible to suggestions as I indicated by her condition, that, had it been suggested to her, you or me might have been indicted and not Carter."

"You also said Carter was no more guilty than you are?"

"I did under those circumstances."

"You tried to hire her for your office?"

"I offered her $150 a month to come to the hospital and run the office."

"What did she say?"

"To come back tomorrow and she'd give me her answer."

"Did you go, and what was the answer?"

"She said that Mr. Carter had told her if she was worth $150 a month to me she was worth $175 a month to him."

The district attorney came forward for cross-examination.

"Did you know Carter was so familiar at the Keeton house that he walked in unannounced?"

Dr. Cranford replied that he was not privileged to know details of Ouida's social life. Her aunt Paula Richeimer had commented on it, however. "She told me that Ouida never received company unchaperoned."

"You asked her who killed her mother?" Currie asked.

"A number of times."

"What did she tell you?"

"She said she did not know. She said her mother comes to visit her every day. And she says she looks beautiful."

"Isn't that a normal way to remember a mother?"

"It is."

■　■　■

Heavy rain would fall throughout Friday, March 8. Many county roads were blocked by flooding, yet spectators filled the courtroom by early morning. Ouida arrived under a shield of umbrellas.

The first witness Collins and Clark called was Leila Mae Martin, vital to the case as an insider who had taken down Ouida's statements of confession. Mrs. Martin, a woman of about thirty, was serving the county as deputy circuit clerk. The defense attorneys intended to squeeze her testimony for details in the signed confession. Since Deavours and Currie had balked at privileging the jury with contents of this document, perhaps the defense could tease out useful facts during Mrs. Martin's interrogation.

Mrs. Martin replied that she was not present when Ouida made her confession to the district attorney and Chief Brown at the jail. However, she had taken down Ouida's statements in Deavours's office and at the Charity Hospital. The latter amounted to five or six pages, and the total of all the confessions was about eighty pages of typescript. As Collins demanded to see the one that bore Ouida's signature, Currie sprang to his feet, insisting that the court ruling prevented the defense from gaining the details of the document.

Deavours rose to voice support of his colleague.

"We have no objection to turning the statements over to you," he advised Judge Pack, "but we don't want to turn them over to the defense so they can fish around to see what they can find. The sole purpose of this is to expose the state's evidence in the case of the co-defendant."

Collins bellowed in protest. Deavours responded in stentorian shouts. Their reverberating word battle rocked the room. Both grew red in the face and clinched their fists. Despite their bustling on each side of her, Ouida remained an enigma, her eyes fixed on the spot of ceiling immediately above Judge Pack's head. He was pounding his gavel, declaiming that the court must come to order. Mrs. Martin sat in solemn amusement, awaiting the next question. Judge Pack dismissed the jury until the room became calm again.

Collins, subdued but angry, explained that he could not know whether the statements would be introduced as testimony since he was not privileged to know their contents. He was seeking to show how concealing this and other statements made by Ouida was preventing him from responding to Chief Brown's testimony about the confession Ouida made in her cell. To contradict the chief, he had to rely upon the statements, for the defendant was not able physically and mentally to speak for herself.

Mrs. Martin was asked for clarifications.

She said again that she did not take any statement on Sunday, the day Chief Brown and the district attorney had questioned Ouida. The only statements she had taken down in shorthand were those made in Deavours's office and in Ouida's hospital room.

As Collins attempted again to probe for details, Currie objected a second time.

"The state cannot be compelled to disclose its evidence," he protested, "and the state is not bound to accept as true every statement this girl made. If that were true, we'd have to accept her story that her mother was in New Orleans."

Judge Pack sustained the objection, and yet again the defense was stymied in attempting to bring the written confession to light.

Collins next turned to his panel of experts, the three psychiatrists.

Dr. P. C. McCool of the state hospital took the witness chair. He had examined Ouida on a Sunday two weeks previously.

"I found the defendant in much the same condition as now." She had no reflexes, he said, and she had not been able to gag. "She showed no emotion. I also stuck a straight pin in her eyelids, lips, and other parts of her body, and she showed no pain. It is my opinion that the defendant is insane, with the qualifications in the use of the word. My opinion is that this disease started approximately two months before, and I conclude that she was insane at that time. I do not believe she was able to distinguish right from wrong at that time. The 'intent' filled her mind to the exclusion of other things."

In the cross-examination Currie recalled for the court that Dr. Cranford had spoken of insanity within the hearing of the defendant.

"In your opinion, can she hear? She has heard all that has been going on in the courtroom?"

"Yes."

"Can she talk?"

"She is unable to talk, but her tongue is not paralyzed."

Currie reminded the court that Ouida had talked at the time she was arrested and at the time she was hospitalized. He asked if it was possible that her aphasia had developed when she realized there were plans for her prosecution.

"I don't think that had anything to do with it."

"You heard the doctor predict she would be dead in three months. Do you agree with that?"

"I neither agree nor disagree. I couldn't make that statement."

He stated, however, that insane persons generally have a long life. He also declared that each of the various physical tests made by local physicians was useless.

"It just eliminates something and doesn't prove anything."

And as for the statements made about her alleged failure of glandular development, he remarked that "she would be unable to reach womanhood without development of certain glands." Yet he could not contradict Dr. Cranford's claim that none of her glands had developed since she was two. Dr. Cranford had been present both times he saw and examined Ouida.

"Is there any infallible test for dementia praecox?"

"The only thing in medicine that is infallible, so far as I know, is death."

Dr. O. A. Schmid took the chair when Dr. McCool stepped down. He had examined Ouida on Monday, a week previously, spending about two and a half hours with her in taking her history and in making his diagnosis.

Collins asked him to explain the meaning of dementia praecox.

He replied that the term meant insanity in youth, before adolescence. The illness might go undetected for a period of years until some act or change in social contacts revealed it. He said that some who suffer from dementia praecox are intelligent, one whom he had treated having graduated from the state college with honors.

Collins asked if those with the illness were "responsible"?

"The acts are committed under a clouded or semiclouded condition. They may obey an impulse over which they have no control."

"Do they have lucid moments?"

"They have moments when they can talk to you intelligently, but they are not normal."

"What is the mental condition of the defendant, in your opinion?"

"I believe her to be insane."

He added that Ouida was not able to be melancholy, for "her emotions are dead." He believed her to be "particularly susceptible to suggestions."

Dr. C. D. Mitchell, the last of the alienists for the defense and the final witness Collins and Clark had scheduled, took the chair and to defense attorney Clark's immediate question stated: "She is insane now and was insane at the time the act was committed."

Three of the region's most noteworthy psychiatrists had pronounced that Ouida Keeton was insane. Dr. Mitchell's pronouncement rang in the air but drew no reaction from the inert woman in the wheelchair. The eyes probing her face for a visible tear or frown saw only the pallid cheeks, the wrinkled brow, and the blank expression. Her glance seemed glazed or focused on some minuscule, faraway item no one else could see.

Clark asked the alienist to state his qualifications to give this opinion.

Dr. Mitchell answered that he had treated many cases of mental illness, "probably fifteen thousand." Many of these had been persons, like Ouida Keeton, who could "plan and scheme" and "may be unable to control their temper. They are very susceptible to suggestion and are powerless to refrain from doing whatever the impulse is to do. There are times when they can appear outwardly natural and normal, [but] they are controlled and predominated by hallucinations."

"Can the defendant talk?" Clark asked.

"I think she could talk, but she just won't. For what reason I don't know."

"If she were malingering, Doctor, would she write?"

"I don't think so."

He clarified by stating that "a malingerer stops talking to avoid the possibility of being trapped."

"Do you think this defendant can walk?"

"If she is not too weak, she can walk."

Moreover, he said that her refusal to take nourishment would be a cause for her weakness and her wan appearance.

Currie took over for the cross-examination.

"If this defendant has a normal eye," he asked, "then it would indicate sanity?"

"It would remove one symptom. The normal eye reflects, ordinarily, a normal mind. The dilated pupil is not always an indicator of insanity. It might be dope."

Defense attorney Clark stepped forward to follow up. He wanted to drop a psychological term he had heard whispered by the prosecution.

"Do you recognize 'prison psychosis' when you see it? Is this a prison psychosis?"

"I don't think so."

"A prison psychosis doesn't have those earlier history symptoms, does it?"

"No, sir."

He believed that on January 19 she could not tell right from wrong and that at present, while she was not unconscious, she was emotionless and indifferent.

The trial was now in its final battle. Had the defense won the combat to free Ouida from the harshest of sentences, and if so, had it condemned her forever by proving that she was insane? Even if this pitiable beauty should escape execution, would she be doomed permanently to an asylum?

Judge Pack called for rebuttals. Nearly everyone was weary—judge, jury, Collins, Clark, Currie, Deavours, and the defendant perhaps most of all—nearly everyone except the avid throng of spectators. Before them the prosecution and the defense were taking their positions for the last skirmishes. Currie and Deavours stood prepared to counteract the defense plea of insanity. In the room downstairs, their twenty-three witnesses were waiting to be called. Each would claim that Ouida behaved rationally both before and after she was arrested. Each was called, and whereas alienists for the defense had been authoritative and succinct, those for the prosecution were authoritative and verbose.

First was Dr. C. S. Holbrook, the New Orleans psychiatrist who had advised Dr. Jarvis on Ouida's medication. Practicing at the medical school of Tulane University, he also was chief of the department of nervous diseases at Touro Infirmary in New Orleans. His stated qualifications included service to some twenty-six thousand cases of people with mental problems during the past eleven years. He had examined Ouida first on February 28 at the Laurel General Hospital and had spent more than an hour with her then and had seen her five more times, as well as having observed her attentively during sessions of court. In addition, he had questioned a few members of the Keeton family and others who knew Ouida.

Of all the specialists drawn to Laurel to give testimonies, Dr. Holbrook turned out to be the most voluble and time-consuming. Although he claimed to have been obstructed by Ouida's attorneys, he believed he had gained sufficient information about her by speaking with her physicians and a few neighbors. Most of her family had refused his request for interviews.

Dr. Holbrook's drawn-out reply about his physical examination of the defendant revealed nothing abnormal except Ouida's considerable loss of weight. "She was lying quietly in bed and seemed conscious of everything that was going on. She was rather thin and pale."

He had found Ouida to be sound organically. He verified his tests with four physical examinations. During the gag test he said she seemed on the verge of vomiting. In the direct examination he was never able to ascertain evidence of hallucinations or delusions.

"The patient would not talk," he continued. "This was not due to paralysis of any of the mechanism of speech. Her voice box was quite normal. Her tongue was normal. There was no physical reason why she couldn't talk if she wanted to."

During a second examination that followed her trying day in court, Ouida had been sluggish, uncooperative, and close to exhaustion.

"Now, Doctor," Currie asked, "from the history of this case as you have it and from the physical examination and observation and tests that you have given to this defendant, from what you have heard and observed here in the courtroom, in your professional opinion, is the defendant a catatonic dementia praecox or not?"

"I see nothing that leads me to believe she is in any way different from the average individual, certainly not different to a marked degree at least. Prior to January 20 there was no evidence that I could obtain that she was suffering from mental disorder in January or in December. I can't see any evidence of a serious mental disorder."

"What was her condition as compared to anyone suffering with catatonic dementia praecox?"

"The catatonic dementia praecox simulates this condition somewhat. I think upon these observations one would certainly be impressed with the resemblance of this patient to a catatonic, except there are a number of things. One is the fact that no serious mental disability, especially her inability to speak, developed prior to a considerable time after her arrest. There is no evidence she is suffering from delusions or hallucinations."

"Then, Doctor, what is your opinion of her condition now?"

Every ear in the courtroom was keenly attuned for the answer. Judge Pack gazed down on the inert woman in the wheelchair. The reporters at the press table awaited the decisive remark. The court reporter and the stenographer for the *Leader-Call* had their pencils ready to write the words in shorthand.

"I think," Dr. Holbrook said after his dramatic pause, "that she is suffering from a minor mental disability which is very closely related to hysteria and is a result of the situation in which she finds herself."

"What is it commonly called?"

His answer was exactly what Clark and Collins had heard whispered.

"That is known as *prison psychosis.*"

Currie let the sound of the terminology ring through the courtroom before pressing on.

Collins would be taxed in refuting Dr. Holbrook's expositions. His recourse was that of pushing the witness to apply Ouida's behavior to symptoms of dementia praecox. In the witness's answers he would watch for an opening for a pestering attack. Collins took over as Currie sat down.

He began by asking if patients suffering from hysteria sometimes reached a stage when they were not responsible for their actions.

Dr. Holbrook replied that usually they are held responsible. He did not believe that Ouida was confused. Some dementia praecox patients would answer questions intelligently, but usually they did not.

"Upon superficial examination," Holbrook continued, honing his response to best advantage, "I would say she has many of the symptoms of dementia praecox. I mean this, however, that I don't for a minute consider she is a dementia praecox."

"Could you be mistaken about that?" Collins snapped.

"I don't think I am. I could be mistaken. I am not infallible."

Collins paused and let the last sentence sink into the jurors' ears.

"Tell the jury what symptoms she has of dementia praecox."

"She doesn't talk, and this condition is found in hysteria. It is found in dementia praecox and is found in several other types of diseases. In dementia praecox one would expect to see that she wouldn't write and if she did write that there would be some unusual indications in her writing, some showing a disturbed mental condition."

When court was reconvened, Dr. Frederick L. Fenno, also from New Orleans, was introduced as an expert on mental diseases. Among his qualifications to serve as an expert witness he listed his teaching at Tulane, his practice at Touro Infirmary and Charity Hospital, and his consulting work for the Illinois Central Railroad and at the federal jail in New Orleans. His testimony was similar to Dr. Holbrook's. He, too, had examined Ouida at the hospital and had observed her behavior in the courtroom.

"My opinion," Dr. Fenno stated, "is that this young lady is afflicted by situational psychosis because it developed in characteristic form after the occasion arose for it to develop."

Currie asked if she knew right from wrong.

"It is my opinion that she knows right from wrong, and it is my opinion that she was perfectly all right on or prior to January 19. Her condition is due to the consequences of an act. It is self-produced, but she is not a malingerer."

Currie inquired if he had an opinion about the question Dr. Cranford had raised about Ouida's glands.

"If none of the ductless glands had developed since she was two years old," he replied diplomatically, "I don't know if she would be alive today."

Clark took over for cross-examination.

"I came here to be absolutely fair and impartial," Dr. Fenno told him, "regardless if she is found guilty or not guilty, sane or insane."

He said he considered her to be sane.

"You're willing to take the responsibility of telling the jury that this girl is not insane, even if by your testimony it costs her her life?"

"Yes."

"You'll admit you could be mistaken?"

"I could be mistaken, but I believe she is sane."

He conceded that her reported peculiarities could be interpreted in some as symptoms of insanity.

"Could the baby clothing found in her drawer," Clark queried, "also be a symptom?"

"I don't know. It might."

Clark asked him to give his opinion on whether Ouida suffered from dementia praecox.

"She may be a praecox of the catatonic type, but it would be far-fetched. Casually, every hysteria may be a praecox, and every praecox may be only hysteria. After investigation, the line of demarcation is usually farther apart."

After Dr. Fenno left the stand, the next witnesses were altogether less academic. The prosecution would show Ouida's behavior, only three days after the murder, had been evidently normal.

Evelyn Adams, a beautician at Mrs. Buntyn's Marcelle Beauty Shop on Central Avenue, told that on Thursday, January 24, three days after Mrs. Keeton's legs had been discovered, Ouida had come downtown to have her hair washed. The beautician had given Ouida "a shampoo and a finger wave." She quoted Ouida's request that the beautician "fix my hair the way I'll look the best." She had noted nothing unusual in Ouida's appearance during the hour and a half she worked on the hairdo. There was, she said, no "starey look in her eyes."

Dr. C. H. Ramsay was recalled. The defense objected to any testimony he might give, claiming it would violate confidentiality between patient and physician, but the objection again was overruled.

"I've known Ouida practically all her life," Dr. Ramsay responded. He was first in the Keeton home fifteen or twenty years back. He recently had treated her, on the Monday after she was jailed.

"Her mind was perfectly clear. She was very much concerned about her health. She had a little fever and complained of pains in her left chest."

He recalled that she had talked freely with him before being taken to the state hospital, and in his opinion she was sane then, as well as on January 19, and was able to tell right from wrong.

"She is sane now and is able to talk."

Cammie Cook, returned to the witness chair for the rebuttal, declared that Ouida was sane. In the cross-examination she refused to comment that Ouida had been frequently ill in the past two years.

"I always considered her a nice, sweet girl."

She never saw her out with beaus or alone with any man.

"I never saw anybody but Mr. Carter come there to see her."

Mrs. Cook's daughter, Mrs. Walton Therrell, came next to the witness chair. She had been a neighbor and a close observer ever since she and Ouida had played together as children.

"She is sane, so far as I know."

In the cross-examination she remarked that she had seen Ouida out with a man only one time.

Bill Hinton, the carpenter who removed blood-streaked wood from the Keeton home, testified that he had had business dealings with W. M. Carter many times. He saw Ouida there in the office and had no reason to doubt her sanity, although he had not seen her in the past two years.

Currie next proposed to introduce a public record into evidence. It was the deed transfer that documented Ouida's giving property to her niece on February 9. Currie held that the transaction, witnessed by a notary public, was evidence that Ouida was rational and competent. He called Charles T. Walters of the chancery office to take the witness chair. Walters identified *Land Book Z* and showed that on page 636 the transfer was recorded in the amount of "one dollar and other good and valuable considerations."

The prosecution continued to amass testimonies that Ouida was sane.

McWhorter Beers, cashier at the First National Bank, stated, "I always considered her sane." Currie's interrogation of him implied that Ouida's banking transactions had been decisive acts of a rational person. Beers detailed her management of large accounts.

Maude Reed, the notary public, testified to having witnessed Ouida's signing of the deed transfer. Currie held that this was a rational act. Reed told that David McRae and Earl Keeton had been present when Ouida willingly signed her own name. She added that Earl Keeton had objected to the transaction "for personal reasons."

Dr. J. K. Oates, a Laurel physician who had attended Ouida, came to the stand to testify that he considered her sane.

"The only thing the matter with the defendant is hysteria."

Albert Hammett, a building contractor and a longtime customer of W. M. Carter's, came next. From his experience in buying building supplies, he knew Ouida well as a capable businesswoman.

"I believe she is sane."

D. W. McLendon, another contractor, was of the same opinion. She had given him excellent service at Carter's company.

Virginia Buchanan was called to the stand. An employee at R. C. Gaddis Department Store, she had been acquainted with Ouida for many years. On Thursday before the arrest, she and Ouida had conversed. Ouida had discussed her hopes of getting a job.

"She seemed perfectly all right to me that day."

Mrs. E. W. Lott, the next witness and the neighbor from whom the Keetons bought milk, remarked, "Ouida was sane when I knew her."

Currie and Deavours were closing Ouida within a wide circle ranging from family to business associates and to courthouse staff. The accumulation of testimonies was becoming monotonous, every witness being of the same opinion. Yet two more, O. R. Robinson and Archie Valentine, were called. Robinson, a courthouse janitor, had assisted in helping transport Ouida to and from the hospital.

Currie asked if she acted any differently outside the courtroom.

"My observation is that she is quite different outside." He said she raised and lowered her arms and held her Coca-Cola herself. "On Thursday as we rolled her wheelchair to her auto to go back to the hospital, the wind blew her dress up. She calmly leaned over and pushed her dress back in place with her hands." Some jurors nodded that this was a natural act of a modest, normal woman.

Valentine, a door guard, witnessed Ouida's behavior each day after the trial.

"She seemed relaxed," he said. "She stretched and yawned and seemed completely relaxed. She did this several times."

When Judge Pack called for a lunch break, he gave Nurse Laurendine strict advice.

"See that the defendant is not bothered by anyone whatsoever during the recess."

Ouida was wheeled toward the anteroom. A cold Coca-Cola and a light snack were on Ouida's menu. Judge Pack motioned for the jurymen to leave, and then he himself swiftly vanished. The attorneys rushed out ahead of the crowd. In their wake the courtroom did not clear. Many a spectator broke open a paper sack and took out a warm soda pop, peanuts, and a Baby Ruth. Virtually no one was yielding a seat.

Outside, the burgeoning springtime was cloaked in a gray cloud, threatening more rain. Because the wet lawn around the Confederate statuary deterred picnickers, the courthouse corridors and porches were jammed. One fortunate woman blessed with good seating sent her husband to fetch her hat. She said that without it her head was chilled. Earlier, her sister had decided they should not wear hats indoors and gave a boy a nickel to go and put them in the car. The two spread themselves and their lunches over the three seats so that no interloper could horn in while the spouse was on his errand. A small stir ruffled the wife and sister when he returned, for he brought word that both hats were missing. Aghast, they shook their heads and surmised that some shiftless tramp had probably stolen them from the backseat. They told everyone around them that one was black and one was brown and both were felt, with colored feathers in their grosgrain bands. For the moment, while they explored the misfortune of the hapless hats, the plight of Ouida Keeton faded for later.

Page ten in the afternoon newspaper featured a group photograph of eight men who had served Jones County as sheriff and tax collector. On the far right in the lineup was Luther Jordan, the current officeholder. Beside the photo appeared a brief notice posted by a man named D. S. Boliver of Route 1. It announced that by mistake someone had placed two women's hats in his parked automobile near the courthouse while he was attending the Keeton trial. The owner could claim them at the offices of the *Leader-Call.*

Golda E. Kennon was the first witness called to the stand when Judge Pack reconvened court for the afternoon session. She identified herself as the office manager at Laurel General Hospital. She had been on duty when Ouida was admitted at 5:25 p.m. on February 13. Mrs. Kennon's testimony served to show Ouida in full possession of her senses at that time, even though not able to speak. She had completed the admissions questionnaire herself, something that very few patients undertook.

Josie Mills, a clerk at Fine Bros.-Matison Company, testified next, telling that Ouida had come in on Thursday, the day before she was arrested. Her two aunts, Laura McKinstry and Paula Richeimer, were with her. Laura was supervisor in the credit office at the store. They had strolled through the ladies' department admiring spring dresses.

Did Ouida's making choices among the racks of spring frocks imply, as the prosecution hoped, that she was of a sound mental state? Would jurors conclude that any woman able to admire new frills and furbelows had a rational mind? But could Mrs. Mills's testimony serve the defense equally well? Perhaps only the mind of a crazy person could oscillate from murderous mutilation to the latest fashions.

"How did the defendant look?" the defense counsel asked.

"She looked very beautiful to me."

The remark sent a few hundred gazes toward the dozing woman in the wheelchair, known about town as one who favored pretty clothes. She did not look beautiful now.

Dr. Barentine, an eyes-ears-nose-and-throat specialist in Laurel, was called.

"I found nothing wrong with her," he said matter-of-factly. Accompanying Dr. Holbrook, he had examined Ouida's throat and vocal chords a week after her admission to the hospital. He declared that nothing prevented Ouida from speaking if she wanted to do so.

"How about her eyes?"

"I found no defects. They appeared perfectly normal."

Tom A. Lott, Ouida's hospital guard and courtroom attendant, came to the stand, emerging from the back of the room when he heard his name called. Easing around Ouida, he proceeded to the witness's chair. Facing her, he told that he had met Dr. Tom Ramsay on Monday or Tuesday and had inquired about the condition of the patient he was guarding. He repeated what he said the doctor had told him.

"They don't have anybody in the state asylum any crazier than she is."

Yet when the defense took over the witness for cross-examination, Lott implied that Ouida was sane enough to interpret and sign a legal document, the land transfer.

"Earl," he said, "told Mr. McRae if she signed any more papers he would kill him."

"Did the defendant sign the documents?"

"She signed one."

"You don't know where they came from?"

"Mr. McRae brought them."

"Did the defendant act any differently outside the courtroom?"

"She would relax, and she seemed pert. And she feeds herself."

The district attorney asked about Ouida's writing of notes.

"She wrote a lot of them," he replied, looking down at the reclining Ouida. This man, whose wages, by court order, she was paying, who had lifted her day after day and wheeled her to and from the car, was divulging intimate facts that in more normal times a patient could regard as an act of betrayal. But Ouida's face was a blank. She seemed unaware that her guard was speaking. Her eyes were focused on a space far above Judge Pack's head.

"Did the county attorney ask you to collect any notes the defendant wrote?"

Lott replied that he had tried to claim one scrap on which Ouida had written, but she had seized it and torn it to pieces. He denied also that he had made any effort to take a note away from her.

Dr. Thomas R. Beech was called next. In his position as the county health officer, he had observed Ouida while she was in jail and had examined her at Laurel General Hospital on February 13. He said he had seen her every day since. He revealed that she walked to the bath alone, took nourishment, and fed herself. In his opinion she was not insane.

The final witness for the rebuttals was Thelma Valentine, deputy tax collector for the county. After she had been seated, a bailiff brought forward two tomes from her office. With these the district attorney would show that Ouida, while hospitalized, was sensible and focused. Entries in the books showed that on February 1 she had paid her land taxes. Miss Valentine told that in payment Ouida had written two checks. One was drawn on the First

National Bank of Laurel, the other on the Citizens State Bank of Hattiesburg. She handed Currie the two receipts of the transaction, and he placed them in evidence.

When Miss Valentine had stepped down, Judge Pack asked if the prosecution had completed its rebuttal.

"We have, your honor. She was the last witness."

All that remained was the defense's sur-rebuttal, followed by the opposing attorneys' closing statements. Judge Pack asked them to convene amicably after the recess and then to meet with him over the weekend to decide the final agenda.

After court was recessed, Lott rolled Ouida toward the anteroom to wait until the courthouse was clear of spectators. For an instant she was aroused from her seeming stupor. She was beyond the view of the last of the crowd trickling out the back door near the center aisle. As Lott leaned to turn the doorknob, he bumped the wheelchair. Ouida's hand flew up and gave his face a staggering smack. A few stragglers turned to see what had happened. They told reporters it was Ouida's revenge on her guard for giving testimony against her.

It was to be a long night for the opposing lawyers. In late-hour preparation, each side drew up its special list of jurors' instructions for Judge Pack to consider for the closing arguments. After studying them, he summoned prosecution and defense attorneys to his chambers to debate which he should accept or reject. The composite list would be passed on to the jury to guide them in deciding the verdict.

Of the twenty-seven instructions the attorneys disputed through the weekend of March 9–11, only four were marked "refused." Judge Pack accepted their proposals and turned them over to the stenographer. Both the prosecution and the defense approved the nineteenth and the twenty-fourth instructions—"that if you believe from all of the evidence in the case beyond a reasonable doubt that there was a conspiracy, scheme, understanding, or plan entered into by and between the defendant and W. M. Carter to murder Mrs. Daisy Keeton, a human being, and that the defendant and W. M. Carter, or either of them, murdered the said Mrs. Daisy Keeton in the presence of the other, while acting in the furtherance of such conspiracy, scheme, understanding, or plan, if any, and in the execution of its object, the defendant would be guilty under the law, no matter whether both or only one of them did the actual killing, and no matter which one did the actual killing." And that if the jury should vote to convict Ouida, the form of the verdict should be *We, the jury, find the defendant guilty as charged*; or *We, the jury, find the defendant guilty as charged and fix her punishment at life imprisonment in the State Penitentiary*; or the last, which gave Judge Pack leeway to pronounce the death sentence, *We, the jury, find the defendant guilty as charged but are unable to agree as to her punishment.*

On Sunday Judge Pack allowed the jurors a time-out from their stuffy hotel rooms. They were not treated to church services as on the previous weekend but to a ride in the country. A county truck that customarily hauled sawdust drew up at the Pinehurst entrance. The twelve men climbed into the back and stood for about hour during the afternoon outing.

The judge declined to relax other standards for the last day of the trial. Although many citizens continued to demand access, Judge Pack could not be swayed to make the proceedings available to a more wide-scale audience. The local radio station offered to broadcast the closing arguments. Fed up with the carnival air, Judge Pack refused.

"I do not intend to make a show of the trial."

He was assailed on all sides. W. M. Carter remained in the Hinds County jail, and his attorneys were hectoring Judge Pack to give their client an immediate trial and not to delay it until the fall session of the circuit court.

■ ■ ■

On Monday, March 11, the courtroom filled before 7:00 a.m., two hours before court was scheduled to convene for the closing arguments. It was jammed beyond capacity, with an estimated count of a thousand persons. Chairs and stools placed along the walls clogged the side aisles. No fewer than a thousand additional hopefuls milled in the hallways, ready to spring toward any seat that might be vacated. Outside the building, the cloudy day did not deter a congregation from assembling on the sidewalks and the lawn. Many perched on the railing of the iron fence fronting Fifth Avenue and waited for a report from inside.

At nine o'clock Ouida was rolled in and parked within two feet of the closest spectators. At 9:18 Judge Pack took his seat at the bench. At his signal a bailiff led the jurors in. The judge had ruled that each side would be allowed a maximum of three hours for closing arguments. Deavours would be first, followed by Clark. Collins was next, and Currie would speak last. The day promised a morning and afternoon of legal bombast.

It was 9:30. Deavours was ready. He knew that this case, the biggest in his career, could be his springboard. Though the public was divided on the question of Ouida's real mental state, no one could blame him for going all out for a conviction. Doing so was his duty. In the glare of sensation his name was appearing each day in the *Leader-Call*'s roster of candidates seeking public office. What happened in the courtroom today could clinch his goal to be Currie's successor in the August election. The throng riveting their eyes on him, a composite of the district, would be assessing his prosecutorial skills. Every reporter seated at the news table was watching, pencils raised and ready to record his crafty words. So far, he and Currie had given the public an accomplished performance of legal professionalism. Long past midnight they had continued to hone their arguments for a vivid final day. Deavours would ask for the death penalty.

He stepped to the front and center, turning to face the jurymen. In his hand were sheets of paper that outlined his oration.

The courtroom was in a solemn mood. Many strained to watch Ouida, but she registered no reaction to her former schoolmate's ringing condemnations.

Her face was without any expression. Her gaze remained fixed on the invisible, faraway spot on the ceiling. Miss Laurendine sat close at her elbow. As Deavours took his seat and surveyed his colleague's face for a signal of approbation, Clark inched around Ouida's obstructing chair to take over the central spot in the room.

It was past midmorning. He planned to consume only an hour of his allotted time of ninety minutes. The extra half an hour would be allocated for Collins's extended oratory.

For two and a half hours the vast crowd listened to steady legal argument. There were few interruptions and only a brief interval between speeches. Judge Pack pounded the gavel and recessed the court until 1:15. As Ouida was wheeled to the anteroom in the company of her family, nurse, and guard, and as rival attorneys and Judge Pack hied to private regions for an hour of rest, virtually every spectator in the room remained intact and unwilling to move. Since the afternoon forecast even more intense oration from Collins and Currie, the crowd held fast to seating claimed from very early hours in the morning. It was common understanding that whoever rose and slipped away even for a moment would return to find the seat appropriated. As the hawkers floated into the room with their baskets of eats and colas, the crowd got ready to feed.

At 1:15, it was F. Burkitt Collins's turn at persuading the jury to an acquittal. Immediately, holding to his defense that no corpus delicti had been established, he proclaimed that the state had failed to prove that Daisy Keeton was dead or that the defendant Ouida Keeton had committed any crime. He spoke for one hour and twenty minutes, using his full allotment and a portion of his colleague's. At 2:35 he rested his plea and thanked the jury.

Ouida seemed to be dozing as he slipped past her. If she was conscious, many spectators wondered what it must be like to hear herself described as an object to be pitied, to hear others classify her as a lunatic not capable of discerning appropriate actions. Some thought her chic crepe frock was somewhat tired after her days of lying in the wheelchair. In this attire, which once added dash to her allure, she now appeared even more shockingly gaunt. Her expression was neither grave nor bitter, but rather world-weary.

The district attorney waited until his adversary was seated and then stepped toward the jurors, ready to have the final say in the closing arguments. Whatever points Collins had achieved in his laboring eloquence were vulnerable now to the most memorable words the jurors would hear, the final argument of the trial.

The jury was retired at 4:10 p.m., the footsteps of the departing twelve men resounding in the silent courtroom. Judge Pack rapped for a recess, and the notables quickly disappeared. Tom Lott and Miss Laurendine wheeled Ouida back to the anteroom to wait for the verdict. Miss Laurendine then slipped away to bring Ouida a bite of supper. Once the prisoner was settled, Lott stationed himself outside the door. No report had come of any further slap to his cheek. On the chance that the decision should be announced later in the evening, Judge Pack went to his chambers to remove his robe, left instructions that he be notified instantly if the jury returned prematurely, and then drove home for a quick meal with his wife and daughter.

The spectators who had crowded the courtroom throughout the day remained motionless. They seemed not to realize that the first trial in this legal drama, a battle for life or death in the most repellant murder case Laurel had ever known, was almost over.

Again, peanut, pop, and candy vendors broke the spell and began to do a rushing business. Scores of those who waited had been in court since early morning, with only scant breakfast and little if any lunch. Some arranged for bystanders to hold their seats while they looked for a toilet, even paying for this service. An hour passed, and not one peep had sounded from the secluded room. Resigned that the day, for them, had ended, a few spectators drifted from the courthouse and to responsibilities at home.

When Judge Pack returned from supper, the jury was still undecided. The courtroom remained jammed and charged. Everyone kept consulting watches as the minutes ticked by. The floor was deep in the debris of peanut hulls, empty cola bottles, candy wrappers, and cigarette stubs. There was buzz that a copy of the *Leader-Call* had found its way to the anteroom. The issue included a photo of Ouida, Miss Laurendine, and Lott. It was rumored that, on seeing her picture, Ouida had stirred.

Others whispered that a bailiff had delivered chewing tobacco and cigarettes to the jurors' door. Some of the crowd that had scattered for supper returned to claim a place in the courtroom as soon as possible. It was fortunate that this was not a Wednesday evening, or the faithful would be missing midweek prayer meeting, but since this was Monday, the churches both in town and country were dark.

At nearly nine o'clock Judge Pack emerged from his chambers.

Everyone came to attention.

The jurymen, he announced, were not yet prepared to declare their verdict. On that disappointing note, the tingling suspense would extend into another day. He instructed the sheriff to lock up the jurors until morning and then recessed court until nine. Sheriff Jordan ordered the courtroom cleared, and the crowd rose slowly and then slouched toward the bottle-necked exits.

Crossing the dark street and trailing their assiduous guard, the jurymen seemed like a line of obedient ants. As quiet fell upon the empty courthouse and the lights began to dim, Lott wheeled Ouida to the stairs. A bailiff met them and assisted in lifting her to the first floor. The party headed back to the hospital to pass uneasy hours of waiting.

On Tuesday morning the jurors returned to their room at the courthouse. For sixteen hours and fifty minutes they had remained secluded. When the foreman Alonzo Blackwell popped his head around the door to announce that they were ready, Judge Pack notified the sheriff to bring Ouida from the hospital.

In the afternoon when the jury had returned to the jury box, Judge Pack asked if they had reached a verdict. The twelve nodded, and the courtroom watched Foreman Blackwell hand the folded paper to Talmage Sumrall, the circuit clerk. After only two ballots, the vote, the foreman later would report, was unanimous. The first had been eleven to one. The holdout had "wished to sleep over the matter."

Sumrall cleared his throat, the only fanfare to the decisive announcement every eager ear had anticipated since Ouida was arrested. Was she guilty? Was she not? Each spectator was guessing. Sumrall quietly read the verdict, then turned to face Judge Pack. At one table the attorneys were jubilant. At the other the opposition was glum.

■ ■ ■

"We the jury find the defendant guilty as charged and sentence her to life imprisonment."

The *Leader-Call* described the scene. The audience "remained motionless. They seemed unable to realize for the moment that Ouida Keeton's legal drama, a battle for life or death in the most gruesome murder case this section has ever known, was at an end."

"Guilty as charged and life imprisonment the punishment." Ouida did not face execution.

The verdict stunned the hushed courtroom, but Ouida lay quiet and unperturbed. Her head was turned slightly. Her fair skin was accented by the brown circles around her languid eyes. A *Leader-Call* reporter who earlier had seen "a ghost of a smile on her lips, as if pleasant dreams had carried her mind far away from the tragic courtroom drama," now saw only the blank face.

As she heard the verdict, Miss Laurendine rested her hand on Ouida's forearm in a comforting stroke. Maude McRae and Paula Richeimer, gripping the arms of her chair, looked at each other with disbelief. David McRae whispered something to his wife. Some, reading his lips, thought his words were, "We will appeal." In the family members rather than in Ouida the spectators read signs of tension. The dependable David McRae was unquestionably haggard. He must shoulder yet again the enduring Keeton burden.

Ouida's conviction was daunting news for trial regulars Reily and Ross, joined by Will Watkins, who had come from Jackson to observe the day's proceedings and to hear the verdict. Defending Carter promised to be a Herculean challenge, for in the Keeton trial, both the prosecution and the defense had fouled the atmosphere with damaging images of W. M. Carter. The closing arguments on both sides left prejudice in the air. In the public mind Carter was damaged goods. If Ouida was guilty, so, too, was he.

Judge Pack then polled each juror. Each nodded that he had voted guilty.

"There is only one duty left for the judge," Judge Pack announced, "and that is to fix the sentence ordered by the jury at life imprisonment. It is so ordered."

Front page of the Laurel newspaper, Tuesday, March 12, 1935. (Courtesy of the *Laurel Leader-Call*)

The audience watched as he documented the verdict and sentence in the court record.

"It is therefore the judgment of this court," he resumed, "that Ouida Keeton be sentenced to the state penitentiary for the rest of her natural life."

Judge Pack rapped his gavel and dismissed the jury. They were free to go. The twelve men vacated the jury box and tramped from the courtroom.

Frank Clark sprang from his seat to make a motion that Ouida be admitted bail.

"I understand that you want bail for Miss Keeton on account of her health only," the judge responded. "She is certainly not in the strongest physical condition. The court was advised that she might not be able to stand this trial, but she has stood it and it is now over. But due to her health the court is going to allow bail pending the appeal to the supreme court and is going to set the amount at $15,000."

Carter's attorneys rose to address the court. Will Watkins demanded that the court grant his client an immediate trial. Joining him were Carter's other counsel, Quitman Ross and Jeff Collins. At this moment the two Collins brothers were in the courtroom as adversaries.

"Now, gentlemen," Judge Pack acknowledged, "we have another case before us at this time, the State vs. W. M. Carter. But here is a very serious impediment. The court ends here by law at the end of the week, that is, Saturday of this week. The court at New Augusta opens under law Monday morning, and there has not been a court there in more than a year. The court feels duty-bound to go there and hold court. I do not know if the state is ready in this case or not. If Mr. Currie wants to make an announcement at this time."

"I understand that Mr. Carter has been sent for and is on his way here at this time," Currie said.

"I understand that the defendant must be here for the setting of the trial," the judge advised, "but not in a continuation. Are there objections?"

"No, your honor," Watkins replied. "This is just an informal discussion."

"The state has been wholly occupied for two full weeks," Currie clarified. "That is, tomorrow it will have been two weeks, but the state can be prepared for trial in twenty-four to forty-eight hours. But the same court that your honor must attend in Perry County is also in my district. I can safely say that forty-eight hours is needed to prepare for the case against Mr. Carter."

"Mr. Carter is in jail," Jeff Collins reminded, "and has been now more than a month. The defendant is ready for trial. Under the constitution the defendant has a right to it. And we demand it."

Judge Pack's response was to ask if attorneys for both sides were ready to discuss the amount of bail in the case of Carter.

"Then are we to understand that the court is refusing a trial?" Ross questioned.

"No, sir, the court will not be put in that attitude. There have been full and sufficient reasons given for the continuance of the case. There are times when the state must continue cases. The case of W. M. Carter will be continued until the May term, and I am fixing the bond at $15,000 and upon the approval of the clerk Mr. Carter will be released."

"We are sorry that we can have no trial," Jeff Collins replied, "but the bond is excessive. If you could reduce the figure to one we can make—"

Watkins interrupted, adding, "Make it $10,000. I feel sure we can make that."

"If you can make a $10,000 bond, you can make a $15,000 bond," the judge retorted.

"Your honor," Collins pleaded, "things are different now from what they were several years ago. So many people have lost their property. It is our contention that where a person could make a $5,000 or $6,000 bond several years ago, it is hard for them to make $500 today."

"Well, give it a try, using due diligence."

"We are of the same attitude with reference to our client," Clark added. "If the court could reduce her bond—"

Jack Deavours broke in.

"Why, the woman has more than enough money in the bank to make a bond of that size, according to the testimony."

"Use due diligence, gentlemen. Make an honest effort and then we will see about it."

As though he had not just completed one of the most monumental cases in the jurisprudence of the county, Judge Pack moved routinely to the next case on the docket, that of *Annie Sumrall v. Thomas Bus Lines*, and, after a recess, issued a call for forming the next jury.

It was past twilight when he signaled for Lott to take Ouida back to the hospital. In awe and silence the crowd watched. The hour was seven o'clock, and storm clouds hovered. Ouida had awakened from her afternoon doze and was attentive as her chair bearers took her head-first down the staircase. She blinked as an Associated Press photographer's flash captured the moment.

Hawkers of edibles sprang back to life. The courtroom was suddenly animated. After sitting in cramped confinement hour after hour for nearly two weeks as prosecution and defense attorneys postured, orated, and battled to punish or rescue the limp creature in the wheelchair, no one seemed quite ready to leave, although guards had carried Ouida outside for the short ride to the hospital.

The clustered family shielded her from intruders as Lott rolled her to the car. If Ouida happened to glance toward the rain-drenched Confederate lady in the little temple, she saw another lost cause and a mocking rejoinder of defeat and humiliation. Both the felon and the mournful sculpture were beneath a master's feet. Gusts of late-winter air were nipping the green of false springtime, and under the their umbrellas the Keeton women shivered in the marble chill. Miss Laurendine bent low to draw the mink lapels over Ouida's frail bosom. Newsmen watching their sad departure were restricted from drawing close.

Carter's local attorneys learned that harried David McRae stayed behind to go through the formality of demanding a retrial. As expected, the writ would be denied. Collins and Clark processed the formality of an appeal and began arrangements for meeting the demands of Ouida's bond. Until posting it, she would remain under guard in Laurel General.

After living out thirty-eight winter days and nights in sunless and stinking cells, Carter was elated that the court would release him if he could post the $15,000. Since his attorneys' fees promised to be hefty, this was a punishing sum for his pocketbook. Family members and friends came forward with contributions, and Carter was scheduled for release. He said farewell to the movie-star clippings, eagerly packed his few belongings, and sat impatiently on his bunk to wait. He would be delivered to Jones County authorities in company with two convicts picked up at the state prison at Parchman. However, as time lagged, Carter's hopes were foiled by rainy weather and high water. Lightning flashes and a steady downpour continued. The Pearl River was cresting, and its tributaries were rising east of the capital city and along central Mississippi's gravel highways. Laurel was southeast of Jackson, and the roads were closed. Only three blocks from the jail a section of South State Street was under water, and the Pearl River Bridge was posted with warning signs that barricaded the route to Laurel. Frustrated, Carter endured the interminable delay. He knew that his family was waiting in anticipation.

Then things took a positive turn. Although highway traffic was impeded, trains continued to run. Carter would be escorted to the town of Forest by rail. Officers from Laurel had arranged to meet him there. After the unhappy delay, the jailer unlocked his cell.

It was seven in the evening when Carter reached home. His son and daughters welcomed him, and that night, for the first time in more than a month, he took his bath in privacy and slept in the strange comfort of his own bed.

Although he and Ouida were temporarily settled, Daisy Keeton still lay in limbo. Her legs remained unclaimed at Sumrall's. On March 13 Jack Deavours announced that the county would cover the expense of their burial. The Keetons had been given permission to claim them, but Daisy's children had not come forward. Some in Laurel continued to speculate that the pieces of cadaver would be held as evidence for the Carter trial.

Carter sequestered himself from public view, but Ross kept him informed about late developments in Ouida's case. Her bond had not yet been raised, and she continued to be under guard at the hospital. Meanwhile her attorneys were filing a motion for retrial, as well as to appeal her conviction to the state's supreme court. Hattie Belle Stevens was preparing the colossal paperwork from her shorthand notes. Collins and Clark's motion for a new trial claimed six causes: "The court erred in overruling the defendant's motion for a directed verdict. The verdict and judgment were contrary to the evidence. The verdict and judgment were contrary to the law. The verdict and judgment were contrary to the law and the evidence. The verdict and judgment were against the overwhelming evidence. The verdict and judgment were against the weight and preponderance of evidence as shown in the record. And for other cause to be assigned on the hearing here."

Carter learned that his old friend Judge Pack was ill. After the marathon of Ouida's trial and the additional load of cases, the judge was exhausted. Under doctor's orders he was put to bed at home. On Thursday afternoon, March 14, he had signed the minutes at the courthouse, thereby officially adjourning the March term. Including Ouida's trial, he had processed thirty cases in what the Laurel newspaper called "the most widely publicized term of circuit court in the history of the Free State of Jones." With regret, he notified Governor Connor that he was not physically able to travel to New Augusta to preside at the next session in the circuit, and the governor appointed a proxy.

By Friday, March 15, the $15,000 for Ouida's surety bond had been raised and approved. The heftiest part, $10,000, was posted by the United States Fidelity and Guaranty Company. The remaining $5,000, arranged by David McRae, included contributions by McRae and Maude, Ouida's uncle M. A. Sherrill, Earl, and Eloise. The children had dipped into their mother's funds for their portion of the bond. Carter knew that Ouida's family was euphoric over her reprieve from a death sentence and over the prospect that during her appeal she would be at home and not at Parchman prison. Yet her release was tempered by the ominous terms of the bond: "If the judgment of the conviction be affirmed," it stated, "said Ouida Keeton shall surrender to the sheriff of Jones County, Mississippi, within one week after the judgment of affirmation shall be certified to said circuit court to answer the charge of the state." It would take perhaps nine months or a full year for the appeals court to announce its decision. Until then Ouida was free.

Since Earl's family and his mother-in-law had taken up residence at 539 Cross Street, Ouida was temporarily lodged at the McRaes' home on Short Seventh Avenue. Out of the spotlight, Ouida would try to regain her strength and her equilibrium. Her aphasia soon disappeared, and she began to take nourishment, but after her nearly two months of torment, she was shy and reclusive. How, her family figured, could anyone expect her to behave normally after the horrific circumstances she had endured? They tried to screen her from the public, but her mere presence in their bungalow became a formidable test. As the fourth in the small household she loomed as a notorious and disruptive figure. By April there were rumors of outbursts and strife, and Dr. Jarvis was summoned. McRae's brother Odell, a freelance reporter with a keen nose for news, resided in his mother's house, almost next door. Carter guessed he was the unnamed newsman who cornered Earl Keeton to ask if it was true that the family was considering committing Ouida to the asylum.

"Ouida is doing nicely," he retorted in a statement published in the *Leader-Call*, "and there is no thought of her being sent away." With an air suggesting that his convicted sister was merely a victim of misunderstanding, he resisted further questions.

Carter read further information about Ouida's case. Ten days after her release, the unclaimed limbs were back in the news. It was mid-March, and since January 21 they had lain in cold storage. According to Jack Deavours's edict, they seemed destined for a pauper's grave. David McRae had put out feelers on how to avoid this fate. He learned from the state registrar of deaths that in order to proceed with the required formalities the heirs must sign an affidavit declaring that the legs were Daisy Keeton's. The announcement brought yet another family dispute. Certain of the Keetons refused to acknowledge that the pieces of cadaver were their mother's. They agreed to put their names on such a statement only if allowed to affix qualifiers. As a result, there was no official death certificate, but the registrar agreed for them to go ahead with a burial.

Word got around that whether Daisy Keeton was dead or alive, the McRaes had arranged for the saintly minister of First Presbyterian Church to hold a memorial prayer service for her at their home. The Reverend Grayson L. Tucker was their pastor and Daisy's. In the early evening of March 23, he and his wife, Harriet, arrived at 449 Short Seventh Avenue. They exchanged their soft condolences and then got down to the difficult business. Carter guessed that the circumstances of murder and conviction presented a challenging test like none this man of God would ever face again. Carter, another sinner of Tucker's congregation, was in need of spiritual consolation himself, but on the scale of griefs, his seemed a degree less unusual than the horror that throbbed in this home. Only inspiration from a greater power could guide the minister to appropriate thoughts and expressions for such an occasion. After a reading of scripture and offering a delicate prayer for the mutilated woman, he spoke his homily to the fragmented family. At the minister's invitation the McRaes and their teenager; Earl, Jewel, and their little girl; Eloise and Jack; and Ouida bowed their heads to express memorial grief and reverence, though some in the room were still in psychological denial that the mother was dead and that the beautiful sister was terribly ill.

Even with her conviction, were they still accepting her conflicting accounts of the murder? Were any of them able to suppose that she alone, and not Carter, might be guilty? Surely the siblings wondered how their own sister, on whom their mother had doted, actually might be such a she-devil. In profound quandary, the shaken family sat listening to the minister's prayers and consolations. This home service is the only time on record that Daisy Keeton's children openly displayed their grief.

Three days later, on Tuesday, March 26, an undertaker in Pearl River County had the family plot opened and buried the meager remains. Carter thought it ironic that Daisy Keeton's burial occurred on Ouida's birthday and that not one of Daisy's children was present for the interment.

■　■　■

Would the jury also convict him? Aware that his reputation was damaged and his case already pretty much decided in public opinion, Carter faced this besetting question. Supporters voiced their encouragement that his alibi was perfect and that no jury could discount such positive testimonies as to his whereabouts at the time Daisy Keeton was murdered. Despite their uplifting words, their faces conveyed a look of suspicion that not even old friendship could conceal. Carter wondered what had happened to trust. When he looked hopefully into an old friend's eyes, he perceived not only doubt but also the lewd reflection of himself, a presumed murderer with libidinous stirrings relieved by love affairs with young women.

Deavours and Currie were fierce prosecutors, but Carter was certain of one thing. He believed that he could have hired no better team of attorneys for his defense. Watkins was renowned for his brilliant legal mind, flawless research, and steel-trap responses. He told Carter he would not rest until he had forced the prosecution attorneys, despite their defiance, to turn over a copy of Ouida's signed confession. To Carter the lumber dealer, Watkins's painstaking preparation for his defense was similar to building a house. First came the planning, then the foundation, then the frame to be meticulously filled.

He hoped the trial would be quick and businesslike, not a carnival, like Ouida's. Yet even with bolstering from family, friends, and legal counsel, he remained discouraged. The town and county were against him, and Jack Deavours, making a name for himself with spontaneous announcements and posturing, remained no less a menacing threat than Earl Keeton.

Piteous Ouida, convicted and on bail, remained an alluring curiosity, especially for reporters. Although she was out of sight and guarded by her family, Carter sensed her venom and was sure she intended to wreak vengeance. In her possession were his deepest secrets. A segment of the county was siding with her as a vulnerable and submissive girl who had been afraid not to follow her taskmaster's will. Carter's lawyers had informed him that she was cooperating with Deavours and was scheduled to be the prosecution's star witness. "She went over the case with me yesterday," Deavours told the *Leader-Call* on May 22. "I have talked with her on several occasions previously." To handicap Carter's defense, she had betrayed him and turned over the letters he posted to her in Washington, D.C. He worried that she might also have saved the delicate notes he had made a habit of dropping on Mrs. Keeton's sofa.

Carter's unease could not be reasoned away. During Ouida's trial, even with Deavours and Currie shielding Carter's forthcoming prosecution from possible contamination, Ouida's attorneys had portrayed him as a monster. Burkitt Collins's explosive closing argument had polluted Carter's case with unforgettable images. Depicting Ouida as an orphan girl driven insane by seeing her beloved mother battered with a fire poker and then by finding herself coerced to dispose of the mutilated corpse, Collins had pictured her boss as a dominating ogre. Thereafter, Carter reasoned, who in the county, when hearing the name Carter, would not link it to the terms "adulterer," "failed and desperate businessman," "duplicitous schemer after the Keeton money," and "heinous murderer"? What possible juror could efface such damaging impressions and consider Carter's ensuing case fairly? Carter told Watkins the jury pool most certainly would be influenced.

"She stayed there for twelve years, answering every command," Collins had bawled before the court in vivid denunciation of Carter. "She considered him as a father."

The denigrated boss was dumbfounded when he had news of this rhetorical onslaught. He saw himself neither as Ouida's parent nor as the predator Collins was depicting. Carter the lover had loved Ouida Keeton as a man.

"All the way through this thing," Collins had continued in belabored bombast, "she relied on her beloved mother for protection. And then, as that poor girl worked in that office and sacrificed and worried about the responsibilities of life, taking care of the one she loved, the ravages of disease overtook her. She became diseased and weakened in body and mind. And on that fateful night when that weakened mind saw that man take that poker and destroy the one she loved, how would it have affected you? She saw this dominating mind take this poker and destroy the life of the best friend she ever had. Why wouldn't it destroy her mind?"

Then, as Collins was urging the jury not to send Ouida to the gallows, the bombast took a crazy turn and really got out of control.

"God knows, I think the guilty culprit ought to be brought to justice. I have seen this prostrate girl brought into court and tried where she is not physically able, yet that man she says killed her mother—the date of his trial has not even been set. Any statement that she made could be used against this man. We want the guilty party brought to justice. And if you will commit her to an insane asylum to have her health restored, then when she is well, she can return and you can bring this guilty culprit to justice and put her on the witness stand."

From the start, Carter's four attorneys had agreed unanimously that he must testify in his own defense. His testimony could clinch the jury's decision to acquit or convict. It was an ordeal Carter confronted with dread, and since he was a soft-spoken man, he was not sure he would be effective. In the lengthy line-up for the defense he would be the final witness. Watkins, Reily, Collins, and Ross coached him on how to be candid and direct. It was important that he show himself as honest and trustworthy and not give the appearance of cloaking possible guilt. If there were questions about his amours with Ouida Keeton and Harriet Adams, he should speak frankly, since there was nothing criminal about such love affairs.

The defense required, in addition, that almost his entire family testify. To support his alibi, their testimonies, even those of his spinster sister Rosa and his young granddaughter Carolyn, were essential. Carter realized that delicate matters would be exposed to the public eye, that genteel Rosa, after taking the oath, would have to answer a barrage of embarrassing questions. She was more suited to conversing quietly with a circle of Presbyterian women and to sitting alone at her piano. Crass confrontations in a criminal trial could sully spotless reputations and precious innocence. For just over a decade, women had been exercising their right to vote. Carter still disliked seeing ladies in dirty, public places where careless rustics and nonchalant farmers almost always missed their aim at the tarnished spittoons set here and there along the courthouse corridors. Before mounting the marble staircase, the Carter daughters, sister, and granddaughter would have to traipse through spittle as their coattails brushed against squirts of tobacco juice streaking the downstairs walls.

Forget scruples. Forget decorum. A murder trial would trounce privacies by making them public property. To prepare for the unknowns in such a crucible, Watkins convened a family meeting. Carter recalled his attorney's explanations of legalistic interrogation, an artful process. Watkins reminded the Carters that it was in the nature of prosecutors to paint the accused in black. Moreover, since none of this family ever had been witnesses in a criminal court, they needed instruction in protocol. The team of defense lawyers, they learned, would rotate with the questioning, but Watkins, as lead attorney, would be in command and would take charge of interrogating Ouida Keeton.

It was all-important, he advised, for the witnesses to answer questions directly and briefly and to say no more than necessary. They must allow the attorneys to lay precedents for testimonies so that responses might predicate them with useful details the defense attorneys would summon. It was unwise to blurt gratuitous information or to reveal facts too soon. Nor should a witness report what someone else had said. The opposition would surely pounce and voice an objection. Such information would be regarded as hearsay and not as evidence. Although legal interrogation seemed a perilous trail laid with traps and pitfalls, the Carters were reminded that, except for a few subpoenaed specialists, almost every witness taking the stand was an amateur.

On Thursday, May 23, the trial began in what Carter considered tainted air.

Two hundred men answered the summons to report to the courthouse as prospective jurors. In a tedious process, the mass was reduced, one by one, to twelve, who were seated. Then, to the astonishment of the court, every juror turned out to be from the same beat in the county. Throwing up his hands, Judge Pack declared that the screening must start over. Already, Carter was weary.

In the midst of this pretrial turmoil, Jack Deavours played a cruel trick. On the same day Judge Pack was redressing a bungled jury, the *Leader-Call* scooped all other newspapers with an astonishing story that promised to stun Carter's defense.

Four scraps of paper bearing notations Ouida scrawled while she lay mute and hospitalized had come into Deavours's possession. Without explaining how he obtained them, he had released a transcript to the newspaper. Presumably these notations were Ouida's responses to questions from her attendants and family. At this critical moment Deavours's intent was obvious. Carter and his attorneys exploded in anger.

Published in a format without the questions, they seemed disconnected and incoherent. In typing the transcription, Deavours's secretary had numbered each of the four sheets:

No. 1: "Mother was beautiful in gray."

No. 2: "I try not to cry but those in inside family knew how much I loved Mother. Seems like I go on without her. I try for all to do what I know is right. But I have always felt that she was all I had."

To whom was Ouida writing these notes? Was she answering questions posed by Eloise, Maude, or Miss Laurendine from her sickbed?

No. 3: "*Fight, strength, nothing will give me Mother. That is all I want, or ever want. Tired unto death pleading with others. Words do not express my thoughts or feelings. Go on each day eating and trying—but nothing develops to clear up conditions. All is wrong. God didn't do this—the devil did it.*"

No. 4: "*How did they find out. / Death to me would have been more prefera-ble than all this. It is killing me to think a wholly good woman had to go under such conditions. / You know, the public knows, that somebody helped him. / He didn't and won't say who. / I am so tired waiting and waiting for all to clear up. I am getting blamed for it all. He has witnesses to prove that he wasn't there—you know you can prove anything—truth or lies. / I've decided all else so smart, until it was intended that I be placed as I am. / He is prominent—such good lawyers / I know they are working to put everything on me. Everything I did is known. Nobody knows he did anything. He is smart and shrewd. / When you love people you break down. I suppose, everyone else would do the same. / He had nothing to lose—gains ruining my life. Further shame my family fixed my future life with* [name deleted, possibly Mr. Grace's] *away. / Enough to make me insane, but I am not. / Only wish I were at times. / Eloise understands—she needs me to live and I am going to do the things to make possible—God knows. / Do you think God forgives everything but self murder? / No time to pray. / I pray for God to forgive Mother, take her and not let her suffer. / My father had no time to pray—she always prayed for him to be forgiven.*"

Forgiven? Ouida's reflections were focused on the troublesome enigma of her father's early death. Carter wondered if she herself were considering suicide. To the contrary, the note expressed a deep-seated instinct for self-preservation.

Incensed by the outrage of publishing these scribblings, Watkins charged that Deavours had released this "vicious and inflammatory" evidence only to influence Carter's prospective jurors.

"The article was delivered to the public press," Watkins stormed, "when two hundred special veniremen were around the courthouse, thereby obstructing public justice."

Many in the venire, of course, likely would read the newspaper circulated by eager newsboys. Holding that this beautiful woman for whom his client once held romantic daydreams was perverse and deceitful, Watkins accused the prosecution of trying the case in the press. Judge Pack downplayed the uproar. He explained that the prospective jurors had been confined in courthouse rooms at the time the article appeared. "Until it is shown that the special veniremen have read the article, the motion is overruled."

In addition to the two hundred packed in for screening, a furious rush for seats cast an unabating holiday aura over the courtroom. As Carter watched attendees greeting one another, the bluster and jostling did not dissipate. With sad amusement he listened as noisy collegiality marred the serious purpose of his being there. Lawmen habituated to the rules of a criminal trial did not tone down the banter. It reverberated like the din in a country church, where exuberant cacophony precedes the opening of a revival service. Rubes were munching snacks in an irritating display of casualness. Carter noticed that, just as at his indictment, courthouse regulars in overalls and straw hats always managed to claim preferred seating. Gossips and reporters kept sharing late-breaking rumors, and posturing swellheads were present to impart authoritative know-how to tyros. The phenomenon of parti-colored dresses, like a sea of bright flowers, violated the gravity the case mandated. In a small town these folksy rituals of spectatorship appeared to be as codified as the statutes in law books. Until Judge Pack pounded for order, clamor was unchecked. Even after he had achieved a seeming order, a crying baby and paroxysms of coughing punctuated the sober proceedings.

Toward Friday evening, when he was back home again and reading the afternoon paper, Carter spotted a new item about Ouida that could stir up trouble. It announced that she had left her retreat at the McRaes' and was living at home. This change of address seemed predictable, for Carter knew how Ouida and Maude got on each other's nerves. She was there on Cross Street, crowded in with Earl, Jewel, Jewel's mother, and little Betty Jean. Ouida would have Earl's ear, and he could be riled into violent acts. The drunken bully might come after Carter.

Near the Keeton house work crews had dug a wide tunnel beneath the railroad trestles. Through it the new roadway would curve north over the hillside Daisy Keeton had sold to the government with Carter's help. He read that the underpass was scheduled for completion in 150 working days. The recent spell of good weather was a blessing, but in driving to town, the Keetons, their neighbors, and travelers coming into Laurel would be inconvenienced by a detour as workers reshaped the intersection of Daughdrill and Cross streets.

Another item in the paper detailed a newsman's recent encounter with Ouida. His report, the first public glimpse since her conviction, could stir up sympathy for the fragile felon and therefore more gloom for Carter. In snooping out an intimate story, Jack Dale had knocked on her door while the screening of Carter's potential jurors was under way at the courthouse. Just before noon, he peeked through the glass and watched Ouida approaching him from the shadowy parlor, "much like a casual housewife prepared to send a salesman on his way."

She peeked back at him and spoke a polite greeting.

"Miss Keeton," he said by way of introduction, "I am a representative of the Associated Press, and I would like an opportunity to talk to you."

He thought Ouida seemed pleased over the attention, but she refused to admit him into the house.

"I am sorry, but I cannot make any statement."

She was wearing a "simple white dress, over which she wore a spotlessly white apron. She was thin and pale, but her dark brown eyes sparkled, with only a trace of the stare that marked her fixed gaze throughout her trial."

Dale asked if she would tell him about her life, her health, and her plans for the future.

"I'm sorry that I am unable to make a statement."

"Is it true, Miss Keeton, that you wrote certain notes that were published yesterday, notes written while you were in the hospital?"

"I cannot answer that. I cannot make a statement."

She made a polite curtsy and closed the door.

However, Dale had achieved his scoop. His story, read by Carter and all of Laurel, was published in the afternoon paper under the headline "Ouida Keeton Courteous / In Refusing to Talk to / Associated Press Today."

For three days the selecting of jurors continued at a tiresome pace. In the stuffy courtroom Carter sat nervously as opposing attorneys queried, challenged, and bickered. During the Saturday-night session the seating was never more than half filled. Spectators not able to endure the tedium of jury screening slipped in and out. By nine o'clock the venire had been filtered to twelve, and their names were announced. With businesslike figuring, Carter calculated the composition of the panel that would try him. Most were farmers, or farming preachers. Two were laborers. All but one were in their twenties or thirties. A majority were from Beats Four and Five. When all was done, Carter watched as Judge Pack conducted a brief conference with all attorneys, admonished the jurors, and dismissed them to the care of bailiffs until court was reconvened at 1:30 on Monday afternoon.

Afterward at home, Carter agonized over the local newspaper report describing him as "broken by the few brief months he has been under indictment." He flushed in reading that he had "lost flesh," that his hair had thinned and grayed, and that he was possessed by "a noticeable nervousness." No man appreciates having his distress paraded before the public. How could he not be nervous? He was now the central attraction, a prominent business figure in disgrace, a family man and a deacon belittled and ridiculed.

The long weekend passed, and on Monday an overheated crowd scrambled into the courthouse several hours before the session was scheduled to open. The human swarm was clogging the hallways when Carter arrived for the first day of testimonies. Pressing against the locked doors of the courtroom, the early birds were taking no chance at missing out on seating.

Newton Carter had driven his father to the courthouse, and at one o'clock Carter was permitted to enter and take his place before the bar. Bristling over preliminaries, his four attorneys clustered around him. Shortly afterward, when the back door was unlocked, a stampede of spectators broke through the opening to claim every seat. Carter estimated that more than half of the number pouring into the room were women. He had the unpleasant sensation of being minutely observed. Women whispered close behind him, and ten scribbling reporters, like artists sketching his portrait, sat at the press table stationed between the judge's bench and the jury box.

To mask any traces of jailbird persona, Carter had chosen to wear his gray suit speckled with black. He hoped to evince an air of dignity and respectability, but even in his best clothes he knew he looked diminished and plunged in gloom. Watkins leaned over and whispered for him to take note of Dr. McCool, the psychiatrist from the asylum, and recall that he had declared Ouida to be insane. Carter carefully turned to look. Watkins would be defending him on the premise that Ouida was not insane but sly and conniving. Dr. McCool was present both as a courtroom observer and as a witness for the prosecution.

Judge Pack called court to order at 1:30. With the exception of that one witness every spectator was most eager to see, all who would testify for the prosecution were summoned in for group swearing. The absent witness was Ouida Keeton.

The afternoon proceeded without turmoil. Six men who had testified at Ouida's trial took the stand. For almost all except Carter, who was present to hear their testimonies for the first time, these were familiar figures. Coming in turn were Dan Evans Jr., who had discovered the legs; Jasper County Constable E. S. Conliff, who had transported the legs to Laurel; Griffin Cook,

"The Legs," L. M. Jones's photographs circulated to jurors at the two trials. From the crime files, Jones County courthouse. (Photo by Hunter Cole)

who had notified the Laurel and the Sandersville police; Neville Allen, the mortician who received the legs; L. M. Jones, who photographed them; and W. P. Duckworth, who gave Ouida a ride.

To the defendant a criminal trial appeared to career between good and evil. In the urgency to win, both sides attempted to convert twelve jurors by shading truth and fact to fit their particular arguments. In discrediting the opposition, each side painted the other in dark and evil hues. Carter knew, however, that outside the courtroom these adversaries could be the jolliest of professional comrades. As a businessman he had at least a nodding acquaintance with almost every witness brought to the stand. By testifying for the prosecution, some of these gave indication that they disliked him.

Spectators were forgetful or ignorant of the fact that like all murder trials, this one should be a sober proceeding. Instead, it was to them like a diverting entertainment. The testimony about Mrs. Keeton's corpse provoked much whispering. Neville Allen, the undertaker, confirmed that the cloth-wrapped parts had been delivered to Sumrall's on the day before it snowed. The flesh, which he said weighed around thirty-seven pounds, had been soft and drained of all blood, with no evidence of putrefaction. He told of stitching the sections back together and then specified the clinical procedures of embalming the cadaverous tissue. Most of the audience seemed pleasantly captivated by Allen's grisly vignette, as though the particulars of the murdered woman's horrible fate were news to take home and share around the supper table.

Next, L. M. Jones testified that he had come to the mortuary's "preparation room" to snap pictures of Neville's completed restoration. Since Mrs. Keeton's legs had been interred in the week following Ouida's trial, Carter's jurors would be denied any display. Jones's provocative black-and-white glossies were the only documentation. When these were circulated up and down the rows of grimacing jurors, spectators on their side of the courtroom craned hopefully for a peek.

The prosecution called a flock of neighbors who had been offended by the nauseating odors emanating from the Keeton property. A few of these had testified at the Keeton trial. Then, W. T. Trigg and his wife again told of having heard muffled gunfire after he returned very early on Sunday from a coon hunt. L. S. Brown testified that he saw a black car parked at the Keetons' house at six o'clock on Saturday evening. Jesse Woods claimed he saw it at eleven. W. H. Morrison saw it at 1:30 p.m. on Wednesday.

R. C. Buckalew, a pretrial witness before the grand jury that indicted Carter, took the stand to testify that he too had seen the much-mentioned Pontiac. He recounted a convincing story of noticing the car between 2:00 and 3:00 a.m. on Sunday, approximately an hour after Mrs. Keeton reportedly was murdered. His recollection was vivid, since on that wintry morning he happened to be completing his furlough from the prison farm. He was serving time for whiskey possession, but because his whole family was down with flu, he received a temporary release to doctor them. He claimed that while walking along Front Street to catch the early-morning train back to the Ellisville prison camp, he had said hello to Carter outside his place of business. Although it was dark, Carter, he claimed, was standing at the curb beside the black coupe while talking to two black men.

Deavours intended that this circumstantial evidence from the wee hours of Sunday would show Carter as he was plotting to dispose of Mrs. Keeton's corpse. Ouida had stated that he took the corpse away in a sedan, but Buckalew claimed Carter had been standing next to the two-passenger coupe. If so, where was the body? Was Buckalew's testimony genuine, or was he merely a trifler hoping to be noticed?

When Monday court was recessed, Carter and his family waited in an anteroom for the crowd to leave. Then, wanting to be free from notice, they walked quickly to their cars and drove home for supper.

Carter passed another night of insomnia. Turning and tossing, he antici-pated the most damaging testimony of all. The *Leader-Call* had announced that Ouida Keeton would break her long silence and take the stand. From her own once-mute lips the courtroom would hear her name W. M. Carter as her mother's murderer. After conferring with her, Deavours told reporters that she seemed "to be in fairly good health and spirits." Because her "highly contradictory" testimonies about the murder remained disputed, Carter's attorneys continued their demand to see all her statements held by the pros-ecution. If Deavours and Currie continued to refuse, Watkins planned to pry them loose with a court order.

By the time Carter arrived on Tuesday morning, spectators already had packed the courtroom. When Judge Pack pounded the gavel for order, every seat had been claimed, and latecomers were lining the walls. At 9:30, when Ouida's name was called, heads turned in the direction of the staircase. A bailiff had summoned her from a waiting room downstairs. The image of the wretched, mute creature in her wheelchair flickered in every mind. Hoping for high drama, the full house quivered in anticipation. Carter also turned, looking toward the back door and waiting for her to appear.

It opened, and everyone held breathlessly still.

■ ■ ■

The click of Ouida's high heels echoed on the marble staircase as she approached. Then in quietness the star witness, this beautiful woman sentenced to life imprisonment, appeared in the doorway, paused for an instant as a protective bailiff released her arm, and then proceeded along the aisle toward the witness chair. Carter heard whispers. Her white silk suit and white beret were being much admired. They invested her with an elegance no other woman in the room achieved. Squirming to get a good look, spectators saw that the mute broken doll had been restored to genteel grace and beauty, as though for her finest hour. She had been transformed, a stunning picture. But would this delicate woman survive the battering the morning promised? The sweet scent of her perfume touched Carter's nostrils as she eased past, careful not to brush against him. Then for the first time since their confrontation in Jackson, he beheld her fully. She was standing before him, no more than five feet from his chair. The brim of the chic beret was like a dusky veil masking defects by casting a shadow over her thin cheeks. There she stood, dazzling his eyes. Despite all this legal turmoil, his obsession had not entirely waned.

He knew her so well that he could predict the substance of her testimony in this sorry case. It would arise out of her rancor and her powerful will to save herself. She would be crafty and articulate. Upon her conviction she had forfeited her rights to privacy, and already she had portrayed herself convincingly as the pitiful victim and him as the disgusting predator. The positions of their chairs meant that the two of them would continue facing each other while she was testifying. The jury box was immediately to her right, the bench to her left, and Carter's table in front of her. He lowered his eyes. She was wearing new white pumps.

In the light of the day's purpose she was disgracefully alluring, as though she were en route to a wedding or a social. Groomed to perfection in her pretty suit, she looked sweet and virginal. Standing there before everyone, she made the other women in the courtroom seem unspeakably dowdy. Carter could feel the sting of ambivalence, for Ouida—so close to where he was sitting that he quickened to the whiff of her perfume—was both a lovely vision and a horrid adversary. The scent was no less redolent than honeysuckle wet with rain, yet the tang of copperhead venom lurked within.

A bailiff holding a Bible asked her to take the oath. She raised a white-gloved hand and listened to him.

Every ear was tense in anticipation of hearing the formerly paralyzed voice.

"I do," she said, and then seated herself.

Carter saw that she was nervous. He watched her bosom rise and fall each time she took a breath.

The district attorney approached her. When she raised her head, she was looking in the direction of Carter's face but would not allow their eyes to meet. He knew she was shy and frightened. Was she going to make a fool of him today? Would she recount the now shameful episodes? Was she going to embarrass his family by airing the contents of those private letters?

Her nervous hands, clasping and unclasping, could not keep still. She constantly bit her lip. Her agitation mesmerized the courtroom.

The questioning started. Carter and those seated nearest her watched the pulsing of her carotid artery. When she turned to look at Currie, the shadow of her brim lifted. Her dark brown eyes had an alarming, glassy stare.

"Miss Keeton, you are co-defendant with W. M. Carter, charged with the murder of Mrs. Daisy Keeton?"

"Yes."

"Under the law you are not required to give any testimony that would incriminate yourself," Currie intoned in a way that was meant to ease Ouida's anxiety, "and under the guidance of the court I am advising you of your constitutional rights, to claim that if you wish. Are you willing and do you desire to testify in this case?"

"I do."

Everyone heard a soft, somewhat girlish contralto, pleasant to the ear. Her accent was to a degree refined. Because she was speaking so low, her words were not clear. Politely, Judge Pack asked her to speak up.

"When, if at all, did you begin your work for this defendant?" Currie resumed.

"Around fifteen years ago."

"You are now thirty-three or thirty-four years of age?"

"Thirty-three."

Carter knew that this answer was not quite true, yet no one questioned it. Ouida continued to flex her nervous hands.

"So you began working with him when you were a girl of approximately seventeen years of age?"

"Yes, sir."

Carter whispered to Watkins that she was at least twenty then.

"Prior or shortly prior to January 19 of this year, where have you been working?"

"McRae's Filling Station."

"How long have you been working there? Approximately."

"About six weeks."

"Did the defendant W. M. Carter trade or come to that filling station while you were there?"

"Yes."

"State whether or not you frequently saw him at the station while you were employed there."

"I did."

"When was the last time you saw Mr. Carter at the station?"

"Saturday afternoon, January 19."

"Now, do you know his handwriting?"

"Yes."

Carter watched him hand her a small pad of sales receipts. He understood the prosecution's strategy. They were preparing to establish the incriminating fact that he had been whispering to Ouida several hours before her mother was murdered. The district attorney was contriving to use this circumstantial evidence to suggest their planning the crime.

"I will ask you to look at this memorandum," Currie said to Ouida again, "and state whether or not that is W. M. Carter's handwriting and signature."

"It is."

Carter had filled the tanks of his automobiles, and the memorandums were receipts for gasoline he purchased. They connected him with Ouida on the day of the murder.

"Did you have any conversation with him there at the station?"

"Yes."

"Miss Ouida, tell the court and jury whether or not in the period of your early employment with him there was established an intimate relationship between the defendant Carter and yourself."

"There was."

Currie was keeping the terminology clean, but here the snake began to peep from beneath the flower. A shaking of heads was evident in the courtroom.

"How soon after you began or were in his employ that this relationship was established?"

"A little over a year."

"What was your mother's attitude toward that relationship?"

"She did not approve of his coming to the house as often as he did, but she did not know of the relationship."

"Did the defendant Carter know of your mother's disapproval? State whether or not the defendant Carter knew of your mother's objections."

"Yes."

"State to the court and jury what, if anything, was ever said between you and the defendant or by the defendant with reference to her objections and what threat, if any, was made. Just tell the jury the facts about it."

Ouida told that after Eloise moved to New Orleans, Carter began insisting that she take trips with him. If she refused, she testified, he had announced that he would kill her mother.

"State whether or not you agreed to go with him and make these trips as he suggested."

"I told him I could not leave Mother. I wasn't willing to leave her there in the house alone."

"When did this conversation take place with reference to the death of your mother?"

"The latter part of September, 1934."

"Miss Ouida, what conversation, if any, did you have with the defendant on the date of January 19 of this year?"

"I told him I wouldn't be working at the filling station after that Saturday for two weeks, and this trip to Mobile was discussed, and he asked me to go with him, and this same conversation regarding the threats of my mother at that time. I told him I couldn't go with him."

"You said the same conversation took place, similar. State whether or not you did or did not consent to go to Mobile with him."

"Not and leave my mother alone."

"State the place and when it was."

"The place was at the filling station on Saturday afternoon."

"What time did you leave the filling station on that Saturday afternoon?"

She replied that she had gone home at five o'clock and had taken her mother for a thirty-minute drive. When they returned, they prepared supper. At about six, Carter stopped by with a pint of vanilla ice cream and handed it to her mother at the front door but did not come inside. She told that he returned at eight o'clock and remained for about an hour. She and her mother were alone.

Ouida seemed sure of her facts and was making a show of stating them positively and clearly.

"Where was he entertained?"

"Mother's bedroom."

"State whether or not your mother remained present during the time he was there."

"She was present during the entire time."

"After he had gone away that time, state whether or not he again returned on that Saturday night."

Ouida told that he returned after midnight, since the northbound train had passed.

"Miss Ouida, by what means did he enter your house on this late visit?"

"I let him in the side window."

A flurry of soft whispers swept through the room. The side window? An illicit rendezvous at midnight? Here was fresh fuel for the scandal. Carter's face flushed bright red. He knew everyone must be wondering if he was a tempter of the night, a seducer who sneaked through Ouida's window for lovemaking. Nudges and murmurs caused Judge Pack to rap his gavel a few times for order and give the audience a stern look of authority. However, it was not Judge Pack who was in control, but the seductive woman in white.

"Tell the jury what transpired when he came back on this last visit and you let him in by the side window," the district attorney continued.

"He had only been in my room a very short time when we heard a slight noise in Mother's room, and he ran in there, and I heard shots fired, and I went into the room, and Mother—I sat down on the side of Mother's bed and tried to get her to speak to me, and she wouldn't. While I was sitting there holding her, the man I thought was always my friend started abusing me and said, 'Get up or I will do to you just what I did to your mother.' I went all to pieces and I don't remember anything else."

She was giving an electrifying performance. Her new story made no mention of the fire poker as the instrument of death. Carter began to shake his head. With beseeching eyes he looked into Watkins's face to express denial. All gazes suddenly had fallen upon him. He hoped that judge and jurors were aware that this testimony recounted yet another of Ouida's versions of the murder. Death by a gun or by a fire poker? Which story was to be believed?

"Miss Ouida, where was your mother when you entered the room and first saw her?"

"She was in bed."

"Where was she shot?"

"Right side of her head."

"Who shot and killed your mother, Mrs. Daisy Keeton, if you know?"

"Mr. Carter."

"What date was it?"

"After midnight, making it January 20."

"After you saw him on this Saturday night, the nineteenth, or the morning of January 20, when did you next see Mr. Carter?"

"No more until Wednesday afternoon."

This answer caused a stirring in the audience and at the defense attorneys' table. Was Ouida forgetting her previous accounts, in which she reported that Carter took the body away, returning later with only the legs, which she claimed he ordered her to dispose of? Here was a chink in her accounts of the murder.

"Where did you see him on Wednesday afternoon."

"In front of our house."

"Miss Ouida, while the defendant was there, state whether or not he asked you to give him a check for any money?"

Ouida replied that as they sat in his Pontiac he asked her to make out a check for $10,000. It would be used in her defense, should she be arrested. She denied having given him a check.

"What other conversation did you have with him there at that time? Tell the jury about it."

"This kidnap story principally, as I recall."

"Tell the court and jury what his object or purpose of slaying your mother was."

"So that we could have more privileges."

The district attorney kept still for a long moment so that her answer would register in the jurors' minds. It gave them the motive. Then he asked her about the lawsuit Rayburn Robinson filed in 1925. The district attorney was dragging up that old case. Carter knew this would include a discussion of Mrs. Keeton's money and an implication that the motive for killing her had been his greed to gain control of it.

"I will ask you to state if in the progress of that lawsuit whether or not, whether money belonging to Mrs. Daisy Keeton was turned over to you and deposited by you to your credit in the bank."

"It was."

"State whether or not at the time of this lawsuit in which the defendant Carter was jointly sued had he frequently consulted with and counseled with Daisy Keeton about this."

"Yes."

"Then describe just what his relationship has been toward the family in a business way. How you have looked upon him."

"We have gone to him for everything, looked upon his advice as being absolutely perfect."

"During the course of your acquaintanceship with the defendant Carter, I will ask you to state to the court and jury whether or not you carried on a correspondence between the two of you and how it was done."

Carter felt perspiration on his brow. She was making ready to divulge the words of his foolish love letters.

"There was some correspondence, some letters written while I was in his employ but not very many. Most of the letters were written after I was at home."

"How did you receive those letters?"

"I was usually the one to go to the front door. If I wasn't, I would always see him to the door, and he would bring the letters to the house and hand them to me."

"Miss Ouida, state to the court and jury whether or not prior to the date of the death of his wife you received any of these letters from him."

"I did."

Carter's fate had been blessed. He relaxed as the interrogation moved to another subject. The love letters were not submitted as evidence to be read before the court.

"Miss Ouida, do you know Dr. McCool of Jackson, Mississippi, doctor and alienist who testified in your case of the state against you?"

"I met the young doctor."

She added that she neither authorized his or Dr. Mitchell's services nor paid them to testify.

Ouida had answered questions for much of the morning. Before the cross-examination began, she was dismissed so that Watkins could renew his demand to see all transcripts of her interrogations. Armed with this new writ, Watkins entered a motion that the prosecution turn over this vital evidence. Judge Pack, sensing a furor in the offing, asked the jury to retire.

Watkins handed Judge Pack three sheets.

"If your honor please," he intoned, "we state to the court that the prosecuting witness upon the stand has given, according to all information, her *twelfth* different account of this killing, and the stenographic notes of the examinations had by the prosecuting officers will reveal this and enable us to lay proper grounds for impeachment. Which we are not able to do with entire accuracy without them."

Judge Pack reminded the court that at Ouida's trial he had withheld these statements from the defense until it was ascertained whether she would take the stand and testify.

Having prepared for this confrontation, the district attorney pleaded that the defense would be accorded full and sufficient access to Ouida during cross-examination. He protested that turning over any such statements to Carter's attorneys would be "an unwarranted invasion of the state's prerogatives."

Judge Pack took a minute or two to digest the district attorney's rhetoric, then announced that he did not agree. "The court now holds and directs the prosecuting attorneys, if they have in their possession any of the alleged documents set out in the motion, to produce the same instanter for the investigation of the defendant and defense counsel."

Currie relented, but he offered only one document.

"Let the record show, if your honor please, that the county and the district attorneys deliver into the keeping of the court the *only* signed copy of the *only* statement we now possess of Ouida Keeton."

He submitted a typescript to the judge, who in turn made a dramatic gesture of handing it to Watkins. Watkins and Reily whispered for a moment to organize their plan of action.

"If your honor please," Reily said, turning to face Judge Pack, "we desire to take a little proof, in view of the statement just delivered to us, and we call Mrs. Leila Mae Martin as a witness."

While Watkins, Reily, and Collins began poring over the papers they were seeing for the first time, Mrs. Martin emerged from the back of the room and stepped up on the witness stand. Quitman Ross came forward to question her.

She told the court exactly what she had testified at Ouida's trial, of having taken down three statements, for a total of some eighty pages of transcript.

"Where," Ross asked, "are the original shorthand notes or the notebooks that you took the original notes in?"

"I don't know. I turned them over to Mr. Deavours."

"Did he require you to turn them over to him?"

"Yes."

Ross asked about any variation in the three statements.

She replied that two were entirely different and that the other included some variation. She recalled no mention of a pistol as the murder weapon. The document the district attorney had turned over to the defense was the statement Ouida had given at the hospital.

Ross took the typescript from his colleagues and, riffling the pages, made a hasty inspection of information he had never before seen.

Jack Deavours came forward for the cross-examination. He ascertained that Mrs. Martin recalled other versions of Ouida's statements and that they identified only Carter as her mother's killer.

Not satisfied with the single item the prosecution had relinquished, Watkins reminded that his motion called for the release of all statements, and Judge Pack asked Currie and Deavours to deliver any others in their possession. When Deavours denied having them, Reily exclaimed in protest, "If it is true that this lady made a number of statements contradicting what she said on the witness stand, it would be a crime before God and man for this man to be tried for his life and that the jury not know what is in the statements. We have got a right to know where they are or what became of them."

Quentin Ross leaped into the fray, and the court recognized him.

"Yes, sir, I now call Mr. Jack Deavours as a witness."

Deavours, taken by surprise, exchanged quizzical glances with Currie. Then he walked toward the stand, shaking his head and giving Ross a stern look.

Ross asked what became of the statements not delivered to the defense.

"They were destroyed right after the Keeton case."

"Why were they destroyed?" he asked, flabbergasted.

"Because I had that last one acknowledged by the Circuit Clerk, and that one being the only sworn statement we had. That was the only one I considered of any value."

"What became of the original notebooks or shorthand notes?"

"These were destroyed at the time they were turned over to me."

"How were they destroyed?"

"Torn up and thrown in the wastebasket."

"I will ask you, Mr. Deavours, to state whether or not she stated in one statement made to you that the homicide occurred on Sunday night, January 20, instead of Saturday night."

"The only time she ever told me her mother was killed was on Saturday night. She didn't say anything about Sunday night, and the morning we went to Jackson was the first time she ever admitted to me she knew her mother was dead."

After the lawyerly fray died down, the jury was returned. Since the relinquished transcript was entirely new information for the defense, Watkins faced a difficult task of grilling Ouida without having read her written testimony. His touted skills were about to be mightily tested.

Ouida was called for cross-examination. Watkins intended to crack her testimony. It was a little past eleven o'clock as she took the witness chair. Carter watched her smooth telltale wrinkles from her silk skirt. He hoped her soft allure would not deceive the jury as Watkins's gruff interrogation attempted to wring truth from her lips.

"Miss Ouida," he began in a voice of seeming friendliness, "I will get over a little closer where you can hear me and I can hear you too. Your name is Ouida Keeton?"

"Yes."

"And your age, Miss Keeton?"

"Thirty-three."

"When were you thirty-three?"

"October 26."

Watkins moved on, questioning her amicably about her schooling, family, life in Laurel, and employment. Procedural questions were a way of establishing a warmth that could put a witness off guard.

"Miss Keeton, I wish to ask you if from the year 1922 or 1920, when you entered Mr. Carter's service, up until the nineteenth of January 1935 if the most cordial relationships did not exist between your mother and Mr. Carter."

"On the surface."

"M'am?"

"On the surface, yes. They seemed to be the best of friends, because she was always courteous to him."

"I will ask you if, during the intervening time between 1920 and the date of her death, Mr. Carter didn't extend many acts of neighborliness and kindness to your mother and other members of your family."

"Up until this we considered Mr. Carter a good friend."

"He had done many acts of friendship and kindness for your family, hadn't he?"

"Yes."

"I am going to take you over a few of them."

He reviewed the Robinson suit and Carter's aid to the family in that crisis.

"And as a result of that friendship, the first thing you knew he was mixed up in a great big lawsuit. Made defendant in a great big lawsuit, wasn't he? As a result of this neighborly friendliness, he was made defendant in that lawsuit, wasn't he?"

"Yes."

Watkins next asked her about Carter's kindness to her brother when Earl was indicted for rape.

"Miss Keeton, don't you remember that in order to protect your brother from a mob, they had to take him from here, and Mr. Carter protected him by—"

"We object, if the court please," the district attorney spoke up in protest.

"I want to show the lack of motive and show the circumstances," Watkins responded. "Whenever her people got in trouble, he was the good friend and neighbor Carter."

Judge Pack overruled.

"That's true, isn't it? You knew they had to take your brother away from here to save his life?"

"All of those kindly acts, Mr. Watkins, is why this relationship existed between Mr. Carter and myself."

"And out of this friendship he protected your brother's life upon this occasion."

"With words, yes."

"You were grateful to him, weren't you?"

"Why certainly, yes."

"Your mother was grateful to him?"

"Yes."

"Has your brother any gratitude?"

"Yes."

"Now from that time on down, your mother advised with Mr. Carter as a good businessman, didn't she? And he freely gave her good business advice?"

"He did."

"I mean to say he didn't want any personal profit. He had no selfish interest or interest in her personal property?"

"He didn't express any to me."

"I will ask you if in the year 1934 the question of the acquisition of her property for the city or county for a highway didn't come up. And I will ask you if both public authorities and your mother didn't submit to Mr. Carter the question of fixing the value upon that property."

"Not Mother, myself."

"But you did it as your mother's agent? And he did it, serving your mother as well as the community, didn't he?"

"Yes."

"And satisfactorily to your mother? And she was grateful to him, was she not?"

"She was."

"I will ask you then if on account of these things the most cordial relationship didn't exist between your mother and Mr. Carter."

"On the surface, yes."

"Miss Keeton, your mother is dead, isn't she?"

"She is."

"There have been people who have gone about over this town and said unkind things about your mother and Mr. Carter, and they are here in this courtroom today. And I want you now, in justice to your mother's memory, and in the presence of this court and jury, to say as to whether any improper relations existed between your mother and Mr. Carter."

"Positively no."

"Miss Ouida, when Mr. Carter would come there at night, he would talk to the three of you, freely, yourself and your mother and Eloise? He would sit down in that room and talk to you?"

"It was very seldom that Eloise would come in."

"Isn't it true that your mother was hospitality itself?"

"That is correct."

"And when Mr. Carter would go there even on the most casual occasion, your mother would sit down with you and the three of you would talk together? There was never a cross word between them, was there?"

"Not between Mother and Mr. Carter, no."

"You never heard your mother say a cross word to Mr. Carter, did you, up to that night?"

"Oh, they would disagree on things, but nothing—"

"What I mean is, there was nothing cross about it, no disagreement."

"No, I wouldn't say that."

"Of course, Mr. Carter would argue with anybody, wouldn't he? He was a great arguer, wasn't he, m'am?"

"Yes."

"You have told the jury about your relationships, your intimacy with Mr. Carter. Who did give you a thousand-dollar diamond pin?"

"Mr. Carter."

"Mr. Carter? And Mr. Pierce never gave you that?"

"I don't know 'Mr. Pierce.'"

"Did Mr. Pierce ever meet you at Hot Springs?"

"I don't know Mr. Pierce."

"You never knew any such man at Hot Springs?"

"No."

Carter knew his attorney had botched the surname in attempting to insinuate the identity of other suitors. The correct name was "Price."

"Well, you knew a man by the name of Grace, didn't you? In Washington?"

"I did."

Watkins quizzed her about her stay in the capital in 1932.

"And you became quite intimate with Mr. Grace, didn't you?"

"We were good friends."

"Well, you became more than friends, did you not?"

"We did not!"

"Well, you let him have $6,500, didn't you?"

She replied that she and her mother had given Grace the money to invest in real estate through the Capitol Bank. In January 1933 she had given him a cashier's check. After coming home, she informed Carter of this investment. She told the court that she became engaged in November 1932.

"Now when did you go down to work for your brother-in-law Dave McRae at the filling station?"

She said she took the job in late November 1934 and explained why McRae hired her. "My sister noticed the nervous strain I was under, and she felt like if maybe I was busy part of the day, that would help me overcome it."

Watkins next explored her knowledge of the Carter land in Evergreen and learned that she was aware of the oil boom there.

"I knew of his affairs, just as he did mine."

As Watkins proceeded to trace her activities on Saturday when Carter stopped by the station, Ouida told that he came by during midafternoon. She had processed his charge ticket for gasoline. She claimed that later he stopped by her house with ice cream and at about eight or nine o'clock he returned and then left. She and her mother retired around 10:30 or 11:00.

"Did you shut the door between your room and your mother's?"

"Yes."

"Pretty good sleeper?"

"Sound sleeper."

"What time did you say Mr. Carter came back there?"

"Little after midnight. It was after the midnight train had gone up, and it doesn't go until one."

Watkins next questioned her for details not covered sufficiently in her previous testimony.

"And he came in your room, did he? You let him in. Is that true?"

"That's true."

"Then after he came in your room, what happened?"

"He had been in my room just a short time. We heard a noise in Mother's room."

"What kind of noise?"

"As though she was turning over in bed."

"There had been no loud talking between you and Mr. Carter? If you talked at all you talked in whispers?"

"That's right."

"The door was closed?"

"The door was closed. The transom was up is all."

"He did what now?"

"He went from my room into her room."

"And did what?"

"Shot Mother."

Here the court heard again the latest version of the homicide, that Mrs. Keeton died by gunshot while in bed. Was Ouida forgetting that already she had established the fire poker was the instrument of death?

"Where were you at the time he shot her?"

"In bed."

"Whose pistol did he shoot her with?"

"I'm not positive about whose pistol he shot her with. I just know it was a pistol and was left there at the house, the one I gave the officers."

"How many times did he shoot?"

"I heard shots. I wouldn't say how many. I immediately went in her room."

"All right, when you got in there, what did you do?"

"I sat on the side of Mother's bed."

"Where was Mr. Carter?"

"Standing there by the bed."

"Where was your mother shot? What portion of her body?"

"In her head."

"What part of her head?"

"She was lying on her left side."

"Then what became of Mr. Carter?"

"As I said, after the little incident that I described a while ago, that happened at the bed, I don't know anything about it. I don't know where he went."

"What did you do then?"

"I don't know."

"Well, did you telephone anybody that your mother was shot?"

"I didn't know anything. I was completely torn up."

"Did you call your brother, Earl Keeton?"

"I was completely torn up, Mr. Watkins. I didn't know what I did."

Her voice had become a touch whiney, yet she kept her composure.

"Well, what became of your mother's body?"

"I can't give you the details of it."

"When did you come to yourself again?"

"Well, I have a faint remembrance of trying to go to Corinth Church, and I don't remember now what day that was."

"Going where?"

"Trying to go to Corinth Church. As I said, I went completely to pieces. I was torn up from seeing Mother there in that shape."

Ouida gave him a fierce look.

"Well, when did you come to yourself?"

"I have a faint recollection of going—trying to go to Corinth Church. I don't remember the day."

"Where is the Corinth Church?"

"That is the McKinstry burial place."

"Well, when did you try to go out there?"

"I don't recall the date. I can only tell you what I have been told about that. I have been told that it was day, but I don't remember."

"Who told you you went to the McKinstry church?"

"What I have read in the paper."

"I see. Now then, when you went out of that room, your mother was lying on the bed shot, wasn't she?"

"I don't recall even leaving the room."

"What became of the body?"

She claimed not to know. Her emotional stress, she said, had obliterated horrible events from her memory, and the facts she had given about the murder came from her conversation with Carter as they sat in his car after he returned from Mobile. She claimed he had coached her to tell the far-fetched stories about the old woman hitchhiker and about the kidnapping.

Carter whispered to his attorneys beside him that this was a lie.

Ouida claimed only a dim memory of seeing Mrs. Nicholson at the filling station and denied having informed her that Mrs. Keeton was in New Orleans.

"No, I told Mrs. Nicholson since Eloise was in New Orleans and that my aunt's husband was going down that we were anxious that Mother join him and go down."

"Did you tell her your mother was in New Orleans or was going in the next day or so?"

"Told her we wanted her to go down for Mardi Gras."

"Miss Keeton, you said you were engaged to Mr. Grace. Well, notwithstanding the fact that you were engaged to be married to Mr. Grace, you say you let a man into your room at one o'clock in the night, on Saturday, January 19, 1935?"

"That's right."

Watkins let this news of the immoral streak in the witness settle in the jurors' ears.

Judge Pack stopped the interrogation and announced a break for lunch. Court would resume at 1:30. The interruption occurred just as Watkins was mounting steam. Ouida would have over an hour to rest and regain any loss of composure, but Watkins would use the recess to mine her written statement for questionable passages. Carter nudged him and whispered that he had got the Birmingham boyfriend's name wrong. The correct name was *Price*. They agreed that Ouida had been alert and cagey in the way she denied knowing any Mr. Pierce. Her performance had been exceptionally effective.

"You say this killing occurred Saturday night a little after one o'clock?" Watkins questioned as the cross-examination resumed after the noon recess. "Where did you spend the night that night?"

"I presume I was at home. I don't know," Ouida replied in a controlled voice.

"Did you sleep in your bed?"

"After seeing the condition that Mr. Carter had placed my mother in, I was so shocked and nervous and torn up until I couldn't relate just what I did."

Carter heard her repeat that she could not remember anything else that happened Saturday night. She was holding to the claim of amnesia caused by shock. He saw how Watkins kept trying to make her slip with an inconsistency.

"Do you remember Monday morning, January 21, 1935?"

This was the time the legs were left on the trail.

"I have a faint remembrance of that," Ouida replied wearily. "I can remember trying to go to Corinth Church."

"Where did you go on Monday?" Watkins's tone was becoming less friendly.

"I have a recollection of making a trip up in the country."

"Well, you recollect taking a portion of your mother's body and going up the road above Sandersville and throwing it out in the woods for the dogs to fight over?"

The district attorney leaped up to object.

"I will ask you whether or not on Monday morning, about half past seven o'clock, you took all the remains of your mother's body that has ever been found and went up north of Sandersville and turned into a small private road and threw it off into the woods."

Ouida again avoided giving a direct reply. "I can remember trying to go to the McKinstry burial place."

"I don't like to ask you an unkind question, but I will ask you if you didn't carve your mother's body up, either during the day Sunday or Sunday night, burn part of it, throw a portion of it through the commode or bathtub, and take the balance up there and throw it off on the side of that little road."

"No, Mr. Watkins," Ouida bristled, an angry edge in her voice. "I would like to tell you confidentially what Mr. Carter told me on Wednesday afternoon that was done with my mother."

"You have already been asked by the District Attorney on direct examination about that," Watkins snapped.

"You asked me for statements I was to tell, not anything that was said confidentially."

"All right, what did he tell you he had done with the body?"

"He told me that was the part that I carried off, that he gave me there, that it was wrapped right there at home, and he told me I had been most careless in leaving it and disposing of it in the manner that I did."

"I understood you to say you didn't remember it."

Carter thought Ouida's answer was calculated and clever. She kept claiming a memory lapse. She could report, she said, only what she had learned from him and others.

"I remember what Mr. Carter told me on Wednesday afternoon."

"Then you had come back to yourself on Wednesday afternoon?"

"I didn't come back to myself entirely. I was still very nervous and torn up. Then I asked him—I said, 'Where is the rest of my mother's body?' And he said, 'It is just as though buried at sea.'"

Hearing this, Carter began shaking his head.

"Coming back to the question I asked you: I will ask you if Monday morning about half past seven you didn't take all that has ever been found of your mother's body, take it in your car up above Sandersville, and throw it out."

"He says I carried it there."

"I'm asking you, Miss Keeton."

"And I will say I did. There is every evidence in the world that I did."

"Have you any recollection now of taking the portion of your mother's body up the road Monday morning and throwing it out on the road?"

"If it hadn't been that I was so shocked and torn up, my mother's body wouldn't have been taken there."

"You left it there?"

"It has been proven that I left it there."

"I'm asking you now if you remember it?"

"No, if I did, it wouldn't have been there. I can only tell you what he told on Wednesday."

"Then you have no knowledge of throwing it out?"

"The recollection I have is of trying to go to the McKinstry burial place."

"Now I will ask you as you came out from there after you had thrown your mother's body out of the car, if your car didn't get caught on a little pine tree and you couldn't come on out."

"All of that has been established."

Watkins asked her to admit she had hitchhiked with Kennedy and had phoned Duckworth to pull her car from the rut.

"Anything any of those witnesses said I am not denying. Mr. Watkins, if you were to go to the bedside and pick up your mother's head and see the blood stream out of her nose and see the man that you thought had always been your friend—"

All four of Carter's attorneys rose up to object.

"You have no recollection of what you did Monday?"

"Only vague ideas of the things I did."

"What did you do on Tuesday?"

"I sat there in that house, went in Mother's room and stayed there in Mother's room a good, long time Tuesday morning. I don't know anything I did Tuesday afternoon."

"Well, when was the next time you saw Mr. Carter?"

"Wednesday afternoon."

"Now your mind comes back. You remember that, do you? Remember that Mr. Carter came up there Wednesday afternoon?"

"I remember some things that happened Wednesday morning."

"What happened Wednesday morning?"

"I was over at my aunt's house."

"Did you tell her Mr. Carter shot your mother?"

"No."

"Did you say anything to your brother about it?"

"I hadn't seen my brother."

"Well, you learned that it happened, did you?"

"I knew my mother was gone."

"Did you know Mr. Carter had shot her, Wednesday morning?"

"Yes, I knew it."

"Why didn't you go and tell your brother?"

"Because if I had gone and told my brother what had happened, the state of Mississippi would have been saved the trial of Ouida Keeton and W. M. Carter."

Her facial expression reflected her inner turmoil, yet she showed little evidence of losing command.

"There was your mother, you say, shot down Saturday night. You were back conscious Wednesday morning, and you didn't tell the chief of police, the sheriff, anything about it. Is that true?"

"Mother was gone. There was nothing I could do to bring her back and be just where I am today."

Watkins asked her about sitting with Carter in his car on Wednesday.

"Didn't you go out there and say to him, 'Mother's gone to New Orleans'?"

"I made that statement."

But Ouida claimed a reasonable explanation for telling Carter her mother was away.

"And in the presence of hearing of Mrs. Cook you said to Mr. Carter, 'Mother's gone to New Orleans'?"

"Before making that statement to Mr. Carter, I had seen the boys across the street out in front, the filling-station attendants."

"Yes, but you didn't have to say 'Mother's gone to New Orleans,' did you?"

"If you had had your life threatened as I had, and Mother was gone—"

"You went out there in the broad open daylight, about two o'clock in the afternoon, walked out in front with Mr. Carter and got in his car and sat there and talked, didn't you? Sat there and talked to Mr. Carter over an hour right out in the broad open daylight?"

"I talked to him. I don't know exactly how long."

"You knew he had a friend named Miss Adams in Mobile?"

"She has been a guest in my home."

"She sent you a message by him, didn't she?"

"It wasn't delivered."

Carter listened as his attorney asked Ouida about the frozen pipes and about the man brought to repair them.

"And isn't it a fact that you were standing there in the yard, and as Mr. Carter went around the house, he threw a snowball at you?"

"I don't recall."

"His usual playful attitude, right there in the broad open daylight?"

"It was in the afternoon."

"And when the pipe was fixed, Mr. McLeod and Mr. Carter got in the car and drove off?"

"That is correct."

"And Mr. Carter didn't come back to see you that night, did he?"

"I was at my aunts.'"

"And you never saw Mr. Carter again until you met him in jail in Jackson, Mississippi, to accuse him of the killing of your mother?"

"That was understood."

"Was it Wednesday or Thursday you went to the beauty parlor to get your hair curled?"

"I understand it was Thursday."

"Well, you remember that, don't you?"

"I don't remember the day. I had a shampoo."

"Had yourself shampooed? You had yourself fixed up? That is true, isn't it?"

"I had a shampoo."

"Did you tell anybody there about the death of your mother?"

"It wasn't mentioned."

"And up to that time you had never told a living soul, had you?"

"No. Nobody knew it but Mr. Carter and myself."

"Now where did you spend Thursday night?"

"I spent the balance of that time at my aunts' house."

"Did you tell any of your aunts or anybody about Mr. Carter killing your mother?"

"I mentioned it to no one."

"Your recollection was clear then, wasn't it? All perfectly clear, wasn't it?"

"Not perfectly clear on many things."

Watkins turned to events on Friday, when Police Chief Brown was questioning her. Watkins emphasized that by then she was in his care and safe from any reprisals she had claimed Carter could make if she reported the crime.

He next asked her about knives that Chief Brown had discovered in Ouida's kitchen.

"I will ask you if he didn't pick up one of these long, bright knives and call your attention to something which looked like human hair down next to the handle."

"I don't recall."

"And don't you know you told him it wasn't human hair. You had been cutting some kind of vegetable matter?"

"No, I was trimming ferns when they came."

"Why, Miss Keeton," Watkins corrected her, "when he came there, you were down there washing up bloodstains in front of the fireplace!"

"Not as I recall. I already had cleaned up the house on Friday morning, and we had had a freeze, and there was a great deal dead in the ferns, and I was cutting it out."

Ouida was looking very fatigued, but although Watkins kept bearing down, she did not waver.

"Now I want to go back to this. Isn't it a fact that the Chief of Police found a container of water there by your fireplace? That it had been used in washing the blood from off of that hearth and around the fireplace?"

"I don't know that to be a fact," she said wearily.

"Hadn't you repainted around the hearth? Repainted in the last day or two in order to cover up bloodstains?"

"The hearth had been painted green."

"When did you have it repainted?"

"Well, I don't know that I recall the exact date. I don't remember who did the painting. I think I told them I did, but I have no recollection of it. W. M. Carter said I painted it."

"But that paint had been put on there to cover the blood of your mother, which had been shed around the fireplace, hadn't it?"

"My mother was killed in bed," Ouida insisted.

"Your mother was killed in bed. Then what were you painting to cover up? What were blood spots doing around the fireplace then?"

Ouida replied that they must have come from her mother's pillows, bed linens, and a small rug beside the bed. She had burned them on Wednesday afternoon.

"You deny that when you burned the bed linens you also burned your sleeping garment because it was covered with the blood of your mother?"

"I won't deny it."

"You won't deny it? Why, Miss Keeton, on Wednesday the blood would have been dry and wouldn't have gotten on the fireplace, wouldn't it?"

Ouida quickly turned his question and gave a useful answer.

"That was just the trouble. It wouldn't come up. It was dry."

"How was that?"

"It wouldn't come up."

"Why, if you took the bed linens off your mother's bed Wednesday and took them there to that fireplace Wednesday, that blood was already dry, wasn't it? Ain't that true, m'am?"

"Possibly so."

"All right then. That wasn't the blood you were painting to cover up, was it? I'm asking you about the bloodstains around the fireplace, around the hearth. I will ask you to state if you hadn't taken a knife or something and scraped the paint off the floor around that fireplace in order to get rid of the bloodstains."

"I have no memory of that."

"I will ask you if it isn't a fact that in front of that fireplace there was a rug and that Mr. Brown lifted that rug up and under it was the soap or material—some kind of material—that you had been using in washing up around the hearth? Isn't that true."

"I wasn't with him at the time he was in Mother's room."

"You weren't with him? Well, they went out there with the ashes, didn't they, in your yard, and they found pieces of human bone, didn't they?"

"Not in my presence. I understand that was done after I was arrested, but I didn't hear anything about that then."

"Found a piece of human skull, didn't they?"

"I don't know."

"Found pieces of human fingers, didn't they?"

"I don't know."

"Found pieces of human hair, didn't they?"

"I don't know."

"You will not deny it?"

"I have never seen any of those things."

"I will ask you if it isn't true that every time thereafter you made a fire in the fireplace, grease would steam up in the floor up around the fireplace."

"I hadn't stayed there. I had stayed up at my aunts'."

"Isn't it true it could be seen there where grease and tallow had dripped through the hearth and through the floor of the house underneath the house?"

"I have understood that."

"When that grease had run down through the floor to the ground under the house, that was done after Saturday night, wasn't it?"

"I don't know."

"Miss Ouida, I will ask you to state if there weren't bloodstains leading into the bathroom."

"I never saw them."

"Miss Keeton, when Mr. Brown went up there that Friday morning, your hands and wrists were scratched, weren't they? How did you get those scratches and cuts?"

"I had done a great deal of heavy housework. We did all of our housework practically."

"Isn't it a fact that Chief Brown asked you how you got those scars, and you told him you did it bringing wood in?"

"I brought wood in."

"And isn't it true that your left leg was blue from your knee down to your ankle?"

"There were bruises on both of them."

"Where did you get those bruises?"

"From the man—I was sitting on the side of the bed, with those sleeping garments of mine on that they say were burned because they had blood on them. That was Mother's blood all right, because I was holding her head."

"All right, I asked you about the bruises."

"And while I was sitting there holding her head, he kicked me and said, 'If you don't stop and get up, I will do to you what I have done to your mother.'"

"Was that when the shots were fired?"

"It was after the shots were fired."

"I thought you said you didn't remember anything after the shots were fired."

"I beg your pardon," she replied deftly. "I said this morning that the man I had always thought was my friend abused me while I was sitting there."

"But you didn't say he kicked you."

"I said he abused me. You asked me about the bruises. I wouldn't have told it if you hadn't."

"Well, Miss Keeton, you didn't state this morning that your leg became bruised by reason of his kicking you, did you?"

"I said he abused me."

"Is that what you meant? That he kicked you?"

"That is exactly what I meant."

"Bad bruises, wasn't it? Perfectly blue, wasn't it? On both of your limbs from your knee down?"

"I don't remember the extent of the bruises now."

"Miss Keeton, did you and your mother have any difficulty that night?"

"No."

"Miss Keeton, did you take her body in there to that bathtub and put it into the bathtub and cut her body up?"

"That would have been impossible."

"And you didn't do it? You didn't do it?"

"I have no—with the shock, I have no knowledge of anything after I was sitting there on her bed, but to take my mother in there, with the weight that she was, that would have been impossible, Mr. Watkins."

"And you didn't do it? If you did, you have no recollection of it, have you?"

"I say it would have been impossible."

"And you say your mind went blank just because Mr. Carter said that to you and he abused you?"

"The shock of seeing Mother there in that condition is really what brought it on."

Watkins moved on, questioning her next about the Robinson lawsuit, about the amount of money her mother feared she might lose to him, and about her entrusting her estate to Ouida. He was implying a motive for a fatal dispute between Ouida and Mrs. Keeton.

"And if you mother wanted any money, she had to get it from you, didn't she?"

"We established a checking account for her so I wouldn't have to be bothered with writing checks."

"Miss Keeton, at the time your mother died, this judgment this man had gotten against your mother had gone out of date?"

"Something over a year ago."

"I will ask you then if your mother didn't want that money put back in her name."

"If she had wished the money transferred to her name, it would have been transferred."

"Hadn't she requested it to be transferred?"

"There had been no mention of that."

"There had been no disagreement about that?"

"No."

"Didn't she tell you she wanted it, and didn't you tell Mr. Carter she wanted it transferred, and he told you to go talk to a lawyer? To go talk to Lawyer Welch about it?"

"It was never mentioned."

"And you had an account, kept in the name of 'Miss Ouida Keeton,' No. 7374, and you had a balance on January 17, 1932, of $20,000, didn't you?"

"I don't remember exactly."

"Approximately that? And that account had run down to where at the time of your mother's death it was approximately $2,000?"

"Correct."

"In other words, you had spent the money from approximately $21,000 to about $2,000?"

Carter heard whispering. Spectators behind him were wondering about the vanishing of $19,000.

As Ouida reminded the court that "$6,500 had been invested with Mr. Grace," Carter detected a hint of self-defensiveness in her quick reply. It astonished him that Mrs. Keeton's holdings had dwindled so drastically. But he perceived in Watkins's planted questions about the bank account the trick of puzzling the jurymen with sinister possibilities about the true motive for the murder. They would wonder whether Ouida genuinely had lost all interest in the hotel venture, whether her shift occurred only because she knew her mother's money had vanished and there were no investment dollars left, and whether, on learning that a lion's share of her assets had disappeared while in Ouida's trust, Mrs. Keeton's explosive confrontation with Ouida had caused her daughter to retaliate in violence.

When he asked if Ouida's share of the Keeton money remained in the bank, she replied, "I did not accept any of Mother's money. Mother's estate has all been settled."

Of course, Ouida's legal expenses had been enormous. Later, with a clarification, he pointed out that $5,000 from the bank account had been applied to Ouida's bail bond, with contributions from Mrs. Keeton's children. Each had received $2,368.55 in the estate settlement.

Relentlessly pressing Ouida into a corner, Watkins questioned her fabrication that the missing Mrs. Keeton had gone to New Orleans. Chief Brown's inquiries and Deavours's investigation of train ticket sales had disproved it.

He also examined the conflicting nature of her statements about how her mother disappeared.

"I will ask you if you didn't make then this statement: That on Monday morning, which was the twenty-first, you were expecting Mr. Grace, your beau from Washington, to visit you. That you and your mother went out in the car to get some help to clean up the house, and that up about the Gilchrist Fordney Mill you saw an old, tall, skinny, lean-looking white woman who asked you to take her to Sandersville. And that you and your mother felt sorry for her and agreed to do so, and that you took her up the road, up the same road where you had deposited the body on Monday, and let the old lady out, and that the old lady walked off in the field, and that when you started home, you found two men crouching in the back of the car. That these men demanded $5,000, either in money or in bonds. That you gave them the

$5,000 in bonds and asked them to turn your mother aloose, and they said no, they would take your mother on to New Orleans to get the money and would then turn her aloose, and then that you got out of the car and caught a ride to Laurel and that your mother and the two men got in your car?"

"That was part of the kidnapping story I was to trying to get over. I did make a statement. I will say yes."

"It wasn't true, was it?"

"No."

"All right, I will ask you if you didn't tell them that two men had come to your home on Sunday, kidnapped you, and locked you up in the closet, and that whenever the telephone would ring, they would come get you out of the closet to answer the telephone, and the next morning those were the two men that got in the back of your mother's car and went up the road with you and kidnapped your mother on that occasion."

"I made quite a few conflicting statements. The kidnapping was discussed Wednesday afternoon."

With eyes flaring, she kept blaming Carter for suggesting these creations.

"I was very confused, and as I said, I tried to tell it in exactly the words that Mr. Carter said."

Ouida was visibly flustered. Her gloved hands were clinched tightly. She refused to alter her accusation that Carter had instructed her on what to say if interrogated about her mother's death. Watkins challenged her to repeat it.

"Oh, he gave me a good many pointers," she replied with a shrug.

"Just tell me what pointers he gave you. About going out on the highway and picking up a party and turning off on the side road and two men coming up and demanding this cash payment, or this bond payment."

"If I would be allowed to, I could give one answer that covered all these statements."

"That ain't what I asked you. I asked you, did you make that statement to Mr. Deavours and Mr. Brown?"

Judge Pack interceded.

"One minute, Miss Keeton. Answer yes or no. Then you have a perfect right to explain. The question is: Did you make that statement? Answer that question. Then if you want to explain, you may do so."

"I made so many statements I just don't remember the details of all the statements I made."

"Well, did you make the statement?" Watkins demanded. "I ask you to either admit or deny whether you made that statement. I will ask you this: When you were in Mr. Deavours's office that evening, you were put under oath, were you not?"

"I suppose I was. I don't remember."

"I will ask you now if you didn't, in giving an account of the death of your mother, state that the night she was killed, the Saturday night she was killed, that she fell against the mantelpiece, injuring herself, and fell to the floor. That Mr. Carter was present, took your mother and said he would take her to the hospital to be treated. That he went out the front way, took her in his car, and later you called up the hospital and found that neither Mr. Carter nor your mother were there. Did you make that statement?"

"I don't remember that particular statement."

Seeing Ouida's agitation by being cornered, Watkins hammered on and on, next asking her to account for the pistol Chief Brown found in her room.

"Isn't it a fact that he left you and went up there, came back with your purse and with the pistol which I now hold in my hand?"

"That looks like the same one."

"I will ask you if you didn't tell him that you found that pistol on top of a hen's nest at the chicken house."

Ouida shrugged.

"Just another conflicting statement."

"As a matter of fact, you had left the pistol in your wardrobe, tied up in a handkerchief, wasn't it?"

"That is not the fact about it. The pistol was left there in Mother's room."

"How did it get in your wardrobe?"

"I put it in my wardrobe."

"Some time during that week?"

"As I recall, it was that Friday morning when I was cleaning up."

"You will say yes, that you had put the pistol in the wardrobe and wrapped it up in a handkerchief that Friday morning?"

"Well, it was just in the wardrobe. I don't think it was wrapped up."

"You hadn't found it in any chicken nest in the chicken house, had you?"

"No."

"You found it in your mother's room?"

"Yes."

"And it stayed there until Friday?"

"Friday I think is the day it was put in the wardrobe."

"The pistol is one which belonged to Dave McRae, isn't it?"

"I don't know. I understand it has been identified as that."

"Well, don't you know it is his pistol?"

"Personally I don't know it."

"And if your mother was shot with a pistol, she was shot with the pistol of Mr. McRae, your brother-in-law, wasn't she?"

"I don't know if that is David McRae's pistol or not. That looks like the pistol that was there."

"How did the pistol get to your mother's house?"

"I don't know."

Watkins next asked her if the plans to kill Mrs. Keeton had not been set in motion back in September.

"The first threat was made the latter part of September."

"And didn't you tell Chief Brown that Saturday, the nineteenth, Mr. Carter came to the filling station on the Boulevard, the McRae filling station, twice, and it was planned to be done that night?"

"Threats were renewed that afternoon."

"Did you and him enter into a plan that evening at the filling station that your mother would be killed that night?"

"Didn't enter into any plan."

"Well, did you make that statement to Mr. Brown?"

"I don't recall making that statement."

"Didn't you tell Mr. Brown that he said to you 'I have got my alibi made. All you have got to do is do like I tell you to'? Did you make that statement to Mr. Brown as coming from Mr. Carter? That he said, 'I have got my alibi made, and all you have to do is to do like I tell you to'?"

"That is correct."

"And didn't you tell him Mr. Carter went to the house where your mother lived that Saturday afternoon about six o'clock and brought some ice cream to the front door and left there and was gone until about eight or eight-thirty and came back?"

"I did."

"And then didn't you tell him that at that time, that is to say, eight-thirty, he came into the house and the three of you were sitting in your mother's room in front of the fireplace, your mother on the right, you in the center, and Mr. Carter to the left? That there was a question or argument come up on how some people raised their children, and Mrs. Keeton took exception to it, and you said it didn't amount to much? And that at that time your mother walked out of the room and went into the kitchen and came back with a bottle of wine or brandy and was pouring wine into a glass, standing at the corner of the mantel? And that Mr. Carter struck her down with a poker, striking her again as she lay on the floor?"

"Yes, I made that to avoid baring our personal relationship."

"Then you did make the statement?"

"I did."

"Then didn't you state to Mr. Brown that Mr. Carter struck your mother on the right-hand side of the head, just above her ear, with the big end of the poker, and she fell, and that you got down over her, got her by the hand, felt of her pulse, and that your mother was dead? Did you make that statement?"

"Yes, all statements were made for the same purpose."

"For the same purpose."

"So then you stated that Mr. Carter had you pack her clothes and that you got a brown zipper bag and packed your mother's clothes in it and that they were taken out and loaded up in a big automobile on the north side of the house?"

"Yes, all those statements I made were to avoid baring our personal relationship, each and every one of them."

"And you stated that he drove away and came back with two limbs from the knees up to the hips and brought them in and said, 'Here's your part to dispose of. I have disposed of mine'?"

"Quoting his conversation Wednesday, yes."

"I said did you make that statement to Mr. Brown in the jail Sunday afternoon?"

"Yes."

"You will understand that I am not asking about what occurred Wednesday afternoon. I'm asking what you told Chief Brown took place Saturday night. Understand? With that explanation, I will ask you if, that afternoon in the jail, you told Chief Brown that Mr. Carter drove away, took your mother's body, was gone a short time, and came back with two limbs of the knees up to the hips, and brought them in there and said, 'Here's your part to dispose of. I have disposed of mine.'"

"Yes."

"Did you make that statement?"

"Yes."

"And didn't you tell him that you said, 'What in the world did you do with the rest of my mother's body?' And that he said 'I left it down on the

Ovett road, and now I'm going to Mobile in my Pontiac'? Did you make that statement?"

"Yes."

"And in that statement you state that your mother was struck between eight and nine o'clock on Saturday night, January 19, 1935? Is that statement true?"

"It was not."

Carter watched in wonder as Ouida squirmed. She was exhausted.

"And you now state it was after one o'clock at night on Saturday, the nineteenth of January 1935?"

"Yes."

"I will ask you to state if about ten days later, or after you went to the hospital, and three days before you were sent back to jail, while you were in the Charity Hospital, if you were not interviewed by Mr. Jack Deavours and Mr. Brown, and if they didn't again ask you what time Mr. Carter killed your mother. And you said it was between eight and ten o'clock that night, not later than ten? Did you make that statement?"

"As I recall, yes."

"You did? And isn't it a fact that at that time Mr. Brown said to you that you could be of a great deal of assistance to them in helping to locate the body?"

Ouida did not answer.

"And up to that time you had stated to them that Mr. Carter had killed your mother with the poker, took her body and went off with it, and came back with part of the body and told you to dispose of it? And when Mr. Brown called your attention to the fact that from the blood and grease there, it looked like that body was disposed of in the house? And didn't you tell him that Mr. Carter came back with something wrapped up in a bundle about 2½ or 3 feet in length? Put it on the fire and told you to keep the fire burning?"

"I don't recall that statement."

"Will you deny you made that statement?"

"I made too many statements to do that."

"In other words, you made so many contradictory and conflicting and inconsistent statements that you couldn't admit or deny them all? Is that true?"

Carter was hoping the jurors were concluding that Ouida could not be believed.

"With the explanation I gave you a while ago," she answered, somehow managing to hold up.

"Isn't it a fact that Chief Brown called on you to help locate your mother's body? And you had told him Mr. Carter knocked your mother down with the poker, took her body off and brought back a portion of it and asked you to dispose of it? And you had stated that you had taken that part of the body up the road and disposed of it yourself? And didn't he call attention to the fact that anybody could look and see that part of the body had been burned in the house? And didn't you tell him Mr. Carter had come back in there with a package and laid it on the fire and told you to keep the fire burning?"

"I don't recall that statement."

"And you neither admit nor deny it?"

"That's right."

"Isn't it a fact that in that same conversation you were asked 'How much did your mother weigh?' And you said 'Between 175 and '80 pounds.' And I will ask you to state if Mr. Brown didn't call your attention to the fact that Mr. Carter couldn't have taken your mother's body and gone out with it and put it in that car. And I will ask you to state if you didn't tell him he put it in a wheelbarrow and rolled it out. Didn't you?"

"As I recall, I remember something like that."

"When they called your attention to the fact that your mother weighed around 175 pounds and that obviously your statement was untrue, that Mr. Carter had taken the body himself and taken it and put it out in the car, you stated that the body was put in a wheelbarrow and rolled out?"

"I don't remember Chief Brown making that statement to me."

Watkins shifted the interrogation back to Ouida's engagement.

"Mr. Grace came from Washington to see you, Miss Keeton, didn't he, since this case came up? Came down there with Mr. Deavours to see you, didn't he? At the jail or in the hospital?"

"Out at the hospital."

"And you repeated this story to Mr. Grace about Mr. Carter striking your mother down and taking her body off?"

"No, as I recall the conversation, he said—the family had told him, or he had read the statement, or some way he knew—"

"Didn't he tell you if you would stand by your statement, you would come out all right, and Mr. Deavours ordered him to leave the room?"

"No, I'm quite sure Mr. Deavours didn't order him to leave the room."

"But he did tell you to stand by your statement?"

"I don't remember about the statement."

"But I'm asking you, at the time during the day Friday or Saturday, did you tell them Mr. Carter had shot your mother?"

"I didn't admit the shooting at all."

Carter saw how she was holding to her claim that until she was questioned on the witness stand she had neither told that her mother died of gunshot nor divulged the correct hour or day of her death. She had told only that he was the murderer.

"I knew well enough to try to keep the facts away from them," she admitted. "I gave them a great deal of the facts but not all of the facts."

"When you came to the time or how he killed her, you told a falsehood?"

"I placed it at an earlier hour."

During a minute of silence Carter watched as Watkins examined a page of the signed confession. The lawyer ran his finger down the typescript and seized on a passage.

"Now in this statement which you have sworn to under date of the second day of February 1935, I will ask you if you didn't under oath state that about eight or nine o'clock at night Mr. Carter and your mother got into an argument about the proper way to raise children."

"I admit the statement as I explained."

"You stated under oath that the killing occurred about nine o'clock at night, didn't you?"

"I don't recall exactly what hour I named in that statement."

"I will ask you if in that statement you didn't say that Mr. Carter came back in his Pontiac car before daylight and brought you part of the body to dispose of."

"Many of the facts in that statement were facts he gave me, and if I have misquoted those facts ten days or a week later, then they were not things I know of my own personal knowledge. They were just what I can remember of what I was told by him."

"You mean Wednesday?"

"Wednesday."

She was referring to Wednesday, when she and Carter were sitting in his car.

"Mr. Carter didn't tell you to say he struck your mother down, took her body off, and brought part of it back, did he?"

"He said, 'You can't ever blame anything on me,' and I said, 'No, I can't, because it was done in my house and not yours.'"

"All right, now you say, and you tell the jury on your oath that you have not the slightest recollection of a thing you did on Sunday?"

"I tell this jury on oath that I don't know what I did on Sunday, and I tell the jury on oath that in that statement I was still trying to shield Mr. Carter and myself."

Watkins did not desist in trying to trap her, but she artfully dodged each attempt by stating that she didn't recall, that she had been coached by Carter, or that she had given evasive statements to Deavours only to protect herself. In exasperation with both this star witness and with the defense attorney, Jack Deavours broke into the interrogation.

"This is going to be a tedious matter, going into this statement as he is doing, a statement consisting of thirty-eight pages, as shown by the record, and we are willing for him to read every line of it, but to read every line, one at a time, and ask this witness whether or not she remembers that she made each statement will be a very tedious matter, and we are objecting to it."

Tedium, Judge Pack reminded him, was not a concern of the court. "The court hasn't any right to control the manner in which he conducts his examination."

Watkins resumed, mining the written statement line by line for any possible slip in the witness's testimony that might benefit his client. He reminded Ouida that although she denied any memory of events after the murder, one of her signed statements mentioned that she had stayed inside the house all day on Sunday.

"I don't deny making that statement under the conditions explained."

"But you deny now, say you haven't any recollection of what you did on that day? Isn't that true?"

"My statement today is true."

"You were asked if you stayed in your house all day Sunday, and you said that no one came there or telephoned."

"I don't remember."

"All right now, you say you don't know what took place Monday, do you?"

"Not all of it."

"Haven't you told the jury you didn't know anything about what you did?"

"I said I have a faint recollection of trying to go to the McKinstry burial ground."

"That is all you do remember on Monday?"

"Yes."

She claimed to have no memory of having told the officers of running the vacuum cleaner and burning bloody bed linens and night clothes on Monday.

"Don't remember" had become a tiresome response to Watkins's badgering.

Judge Pack perceived the witness's extreme weariness.

"If you get too tired, Miss Keeton," he advised, "let the court know."

"Thank you."

It was now midafternoon, but Watkins did not ease up, and in questioning each admission in her signed statement, he failed to break her. Ouida responded by claiming she had no memory of any part of the murder until the events of Wednesday, "not the faintest recollection" of driving the car to the lonely trail, of leaving the bundle, of hailing a ride home.

"To my own knowledge I don't know that I was even there."

Watkins held his finger on a passage in the transcript. Looking down at it, he resumed. He asked her about the pine sapling that had obstructed her car, then about her wheels on her stalled car, about newspapers on which the severed legs had been placed in the car, and about having hailed a ride with W. P. Duckworth.

"I have no personal knowledge of it" was Ouida's reply to each. The facts she had expressed in her statements, she repeated, had come from overhearing discussions, from reading accounts in the newspaper, and from her conversation with Carter.

"Why did you state here that you did then? Why didn't you tell them you had no recollection of riding back home in Mr. Kennedy's car?"

"Still trying to cover up."

"Well, you are still trying to cover up, aren't you?"

"No.

"You now state that you did not help remove your mother's body from your house?"

"I now state that I don't know what happened to my mother after she was shot."

"All right, when you made and signed this statement on the second day of February 1935, the following language is contained in the statement just above your signature: 'I wish added to the above statement that at the time I assisted in removing my mother's body from our home that Mr. Carter threatened to take my life and pointed at me a pistol.'

"In this examination, taken down by Mrs. Martin, which you signed and swore to under date of February 2, 1935, didn't you state that after your mother and Mr. Carter got into a fuss that Mr. Carter killed your mother with the poker, hit her after she was down, and that you and Mr. Carter took the body out and put in his car?"

"I remember making a statement something like that."

"But that is as far as you will go with me? You will not expressly admit or deny that you made the statement in the substance that I have asked?"

"I'm afraid I can't answer that. I just really don't know. I remember the argument part—part of the statement—but I don't remember it all."

Watkins expressed his utter exasperation.

"If your honor please, I don't think we can possibly get through with this cross-examination tonight."

"Gentlemen, you have had all day," Judge Pack responded. "I want to get through with this trial. Let's work an hour longer."

The district attorney, seeing how wan Ouida looked, beseeched the court to ease up on the witness.

"Judge, I am going to say this—in solicitation—speaking of my own responsibility. I think I am a strong man, entirely well, but it is made apparent that this witness has been subjected to the most grueling cross-examination."

All three of Carter's attorneys voiced objection. It was sustained.

"And we move that the jury be instructed not to consider it," Collins added.

"Let the motion be sustained," Judge Pack responded. "Gentlemen of the jury, of course you won't consider what counsel said with reference to the nature of the cross-examination. That will not be considered by you."

Watkins resumed examining her signed statement a line at a time. He asked her to identify the fire poker and her previous claim that it had been the fatal weapon and to recall her remark that pieces of cloth from the Keeton house had bound up the pieces of corpse and that the bundle had been placed on sheets of the *New York Times*. Ouida kept answering the she had no recollection.

"Are you suffering another of your lapses of memory today, Miss Keeton? You have had frequent lapses of memory since this killing, haven't you. Since the killing and the death of your mother, haven't you?"

Ouida did not reply, but Judge Pack pressed her to answer.

"Since the death of my mother I have suffered greatly, and I really can't answer that question."

"Well, do you know when you have had a lapse of memory and when you haven't had one?"

"Anyone that has suffered as much as I have, it is very difficult to answer all those questions. Impossible."

"And very difficult to tell when you have had a lapse of memory and when you haven't? That is true, isn't it?"

"I described the lapse of my memory yesterday to the best of my ability."

"And the first time your memory came back to you was on Wednesday afternoon, or Wednesday when Mr. Carter came back from Mobile to incriminate him?"

"No one knows better than he how I have suffered."

Carter knew her chronic backache was killing her. Every eye in the room was trained on her face, watching for the subtlest revelation of guilt that her voice was refusing to express.

"Now you never saw Mr. Carter any more from that Wednesday afternoon until you saw him the following Monday in Jackson, isn't that true?"

"If I did, I do not recall it."

"And so Mr. Carter remained in jail in Jackson, Mississippi, until after your trial here in Laurel, Mississippi?"

"So I have been informed."

"Your trial occurred when?"

"I don't recall the date."

Watkins emphasized her selective loss of memory. "Do you remember that you had a trial? Do you not remember? Have you not been convicted for the killing of your mother?"

Ouida's response supplied an answer to a question that curious Jones Countians had been dying to ask: had she been faking her semiconsciousness as she lay in the wheelchair?

"I remember every detail of my trial. Every detail."

She said this in a bitter tone, as though she wished to obliterate him.

"Then you have been tried, indicted, tried—"

"And convicted and sentenced to life," she said, finishing the statement for him.

"For the murder of your mother?"

"Yes."

Judge Pack, shaking his head, intruded.

"Miss Keeton, one minute, please. Let the court admonish you to control yourself and let your answers be responsive to the questions."

Ouida nodded, and Watkins resumed.

"Then you do remember your trial?"

"In detail."

"You remember every detail of it? Is that true?"

"That is true."

"You sat here in this courtroom and heard the witnesses testify against you?"

"I did."

"And looked at the ceiling and never said a word, didn't you?"

"True."

"While you were making out like you didn't understand it? Weren't you, Miss Keeton?"

"Yes."

"And you did understand it?"

"I did."

"Well, Miss Keeton, Mr. Carter was in jail, wasn't he, in Jackson?"

"So I have been informed."

"Well, you knew he was in jail because you went up there and saw him with the officers, didn't you?"

"I left him in Jackson."

"Miss Keeton, if the testimony you gave yesterday on the stand is true, you were not guilty of the killing of your mother."

"Correct."

"Didn't you make out during the entire trial you were unable to talk and had to write?"

"Prior to my trial, during my trial, and for a great while after my trial I was unable to speak."

"And in communicating with your attorneys you communicated by writing?"

"Everything I had to say then was in writing."

"When did your power of speech come back to you?"

"I don't recall the day."

"It was after your trial, wasn't it?"

"A great deal of time had elapsed after my trial."

"I will ask you if you didn't sit here in this courtroom and hear Mr. Lott testify, and when you got out of this courtroom there wasn't anything the matter with you, your talking or anything else."

"I heard Mr. Lott testify."

"And when he got outside in the room here, didn't you slap him?"

"I did not. I didn't hit Mr. Lott."

"You heard them ask the jury to inflict capital punishment upon you for the death of your mother, didn't you?"

"I heard everything about my trial, Mr. Watkins."

She gave him a withering stare.

It was growing dark, and Judge Pack decided to bring the session to a close. Everyone in the room, even the crowd packed into the seats before him, was ready to call it a day. He adjourned the court until nine on Wednesday.

■ ■ ■

Watkins intended to cast doubt on Ouida's claim that Mrs. Keeton refused to be left at home alone. When court was reconvened, he brought up Ouida's trips to Mobile, New Orleans, and Washington, D.C., without her mother.

"Oh, my brother and his people were living in the house at that time. They were living in the home with Mother."

"And didn't you go to New Orleans with your aunt for the purpose of buying a hotel and setting yourself up in business?"

"I did, and for medical treatment too."

"You had a bank account of your own of over $2,000 and over $20,000 of your mother's in your exclusive possession, didn't you?"

"I had a great deal in my name."

"Now what did you say Mr. Carter said to you Wednesday afternoon about the $10,000?"

"For my defense."

"I don't understand what you mean by that. He didn't offer to lend you $10,000 for your defense, did he?"

"No, he said they wouldn't be able to prove anything on him, but I had better get the money out of the bank and give it to him so he could protect me."

"You remember that?"

"Emphatically."

"Your memory is all right on that? I will ask you if in this examination on February 2, 1935, you didn't testify that he never asked you for any money at that time."

"That was our confidential conversation, and I wasn't relating it to the officers."

"Asked you for $10,000 to be used in your defense?"

"For mine, yes."

"And at that time you never had been arrested, had you?"

"I had not."

"You just sat there and talked casually? Just casually, in a normal manner?"

"No."

"Well, what was the matter? Why, he played with you and threw a snowball at you, didn't he?"

"I have no recollection of any snowball being thrown."

Watkins cagily stirred his notes on the defense table as though to let the jury note still another of Ouida's memory lapses. After this had time to sink in, he wheeled around to confront her with another subject.

"You took a course in hotel training, did you not, m'am?"

"That's right."

"What different courses did you take?"

"It was divided into three sections."

"What were they?"

"Front of the house, hearth, and back of the house."

"Didn't you take a course in butchering?"

"I did not."

She denied that butchering was taught.

Watkins pushed the school brochure toward her.

"Isn't this that I hand you a catalog of the Lewis Hotel Training School?"

Her gloved hand accepted the brochure he was extending toward her.

"It is."

"I call your attention to the fact that this is a 1935 catalog. I haven't got a catalog for 1932, but at the time you were there, didn't they teach butchering?"

"No."

"And didn't they issue that identical catalog?"

"Do you wish me to tell you what this book is for?"

"Yes."

"They train you there at the Lewis Training School to go into the markets and be a purchasing agent. If you will read in there, you will find where they teach you to be a good purchasing agent, to buy furnishing for a hotel, such as bed linens, furnishings, everything that goes into a hotel."

"Including butchering?"

"Just a minute, please."

"Just answer the question."

"And you are also advised how to go out and buy proper cuts of meat. In other words, become a good purchasing agent, but you do not have a course in butchering."

"Don't they take you out to a packing plant and give you actual demon-strations of cutting up beeves?"

"They take you in a packing plant and have their agent show you the good cuts of meat, the different kinds, and what are good cuts."

"And they show you how to cut it up, don't they?"

"No, it isn't how to cut it up."

"Is that the kind of catalog they issue?"

"This is just part of it. They have others for different things."

"I mean to say, is that what they call the butchery department?"

"They don't have a butchery department. Why not call the Lewis Hotel Training School and ask them if Ouida Keeton took a course in butchery?"

"I know, but I'm asking you."

"But you won't take my statement."

"Is that a catalog for what they call the butchery department?"

"No. They had no such course."

"I ask you to look at that picture on that page."

An illustration he held up showed a butchered side of beef.

"As I explained, that is just to go out and be a purchasing agent, buy the proper cuts of meat."

"They did use these pamphlets with these photographs?"

"I don't recall just this pamphlet."

"Or one just like it?"

"Not this particular one. As I said, I had a lesson in how to buy proper cuts of meat."

"And in this book at page five they had set out there these particular cuts, and how to cut the hind quarter and those photographs are in there to illus-trate it?"

"They carried us in these markets and told us how to buy this kind or that kind."

"But I mean in this cut they give you these particular cuts of beef. Look on page five there and see it."

He held a page of photos before her.

"I don't recall these particular cuts."

"And when you would go to the packing plant, an expert butcher stood there with a knife and demonstrated how to carve up a beef?"

"They had their agent show us the different cuts of meat."

"In other words, they took you to these expert carving exhibitions?"

"It wasn't termed as that."

"Then what did they call it?"

"They are purchasing lessons."

"How many times did you go to that demonstration?"

"I only had one purchasing lesson in meats."

Watkins moved on, asking her about Mrs. Keeton's estate.

"Earl took possession of the house, the residence, didn't he?"

"Mother's estate has been satisfactorily settled."

"All right, I will ask you if the day following your mother's death, or in less than a week, if Earl didn't take possession of your mother's residence."

"At my request that Earl go over and take charge and take care of it and stay over there."

"And Dave McRae, as soon as you got in jail, brought a deed and asked you to sign a deed to his daughter for property that you owned, didn't he?"

"I sold a piece of property to Maude Louise McRae."

"And isn't it true that your brother Earl told you not to sign it?"

"I know nothing of it."

"Where were you when the wedding took place? Did you know of your sister's marriage in the week following your mother's death?"

"I did."

"Were you present at the wedding?"

"I was not."

"You were then in jail, were you not?"

"No, I was in the hospital."

"Do you know who was present at the wedding?"

"I have been informed."

"Coming just a minute to a division of the money which was left in the bank from your mother's estate: $10,000 was put up for your appearance, wasn't it? Your bond?"

"As I recall."

"The balance was divided into four parts of $2,368.55, Mrs. McRae getting one, your sister Eloise one, Earl Keeton one, and your part is in the bank. Is that true?"

"Untrue. Parts of it."

"In what respect is it untrue?"

"I did not accept any of Mother's money."

"You haven't taken any of it? Then the balance, $2,368.55, is in the bank?"

"I have no knowledge. Mother's estate has been settled."

She turned her face away to let him know she had said all she intended to state about the money.

"Now you say you left Mr. Carter following the Depression?"

"Yes."

"You afterwards went back to him and wanted to buy an interest in his business, didn't you?"

"I did not."

"Didn't you try to get him to sell you an interest in his place of business? After he reorganized his business, didn't you then want to buy an undivided interest in it?"

"No."

"All right, then. Didn't you then want him to take you back in his employ?"

"No."

"Didn't you offer to work for as little as $25 a month if he would take you back in his employ?"

"No."

"You did not desire to go back into his employment?"

"No."

"I will ask you if, in the statement taken down in Mr. Deavours's office on Saturday afternoon by Mrs. Martin, if you didn't state that your mother was killed on Sunday night."

"I don't recall that statement made on Saturday afternoon."

"I will ask you to state if in each of the other examinations taken down by Mrs. Martin, other than that of February 2, 1935, that the death of your mother occurred Sunday night instead of Saturday night."

"I have no knowledge of saying it occurred any other time than Saturday night. It was after midnight, and that was Sunday."

Carter watched Currie rising from his table, ready to take over. He launched his attempt to put a different perspective on the testimony his witness had given to Watkins. He first asked her to clarify exactly when her mother was killed.

"My mother was killed after midnight January 20, in the morning."

That settled, Currie moved on.

"He has asked you about a Mr. Grace and your going to Washington and taking a course there. Now he has examined you with reference to the course you took there."

He held up a photostatic copy of a brochure.

"Miss Ouida, state whether or not that it correctly represents the course that you took at this institution, your course there?"

"It is."

"Miss Ouida, state to the court and jury whether or not you ever sustained intimate or illicit relations with any man other than this defendant."

"I have not."

He asked her next to clarify the matter of transferring her property on Ellisville Boulevard.

"State whether or not the deeding of this piece of property to this niece in any way was involved with the murder of your mother."

"Has nothing to do with it."

Currie asked her to affirm that some of the statements Watkins had read to her from the signed confession were from information that she had gained from Carter.

Ouida recalled that parts were from Carter and parts she had fabricated as she attempted to keep Deavours from knowing about her sexual relationship with Carter.

"Miss Ouida, did you see the defendant W. M. Carter in the Jackson jail after the death of your mother?"

"I did."

"State to the court and jury whether or not you then begged Mr. Carter to tell you where the other remains of your mother's body was."

"I did."

He asked her to confirm that she had overheard all that was said in the courtroom during her trial.

"I heard what you and Mr. Deavours had to say about me, and I heard what Mr. Collins and Mr. Clark had to say about Mr. Carter."

When the high-pitched drama ended and Judge Pack excused her, Ouida's time on the stand Tuesday and Wednesday had totaled more than five and a half hours. Carter glanced at her white slippers as she stepped down and threaded her way around him. Their eyes did not meet. Sensing acrimony as she passed, he did not turn to watch her proceeding to the back door. In the weighty moment, he noted the stirring of the spectators as they absorbed the quiet spectacle of the departure. Like a star who suddenly exits the stage after a thrilling act, Ouida left an awesome void.

■ ■ ■

During her lengthy interrogation Ouida had shown defiance, anger, and pronounced weariness but had not wilted. Her generally graceful demeanor perhaps fooled the jurors. Though she may have been forgetful, her composure while under great stress appeared to contradict any claim that she was insane. In her notes, the *Leader-Call* reporter concluded that Ouida had weathered the storm: "She had been on the stand approximately six hours and had not been shaken in her testimony."

The prosecution resumed by bringing three Keeton neighbors in turn to the stand. As each testified about the offensive odors wafting from the direction of the Keeton home, none could hold a light to Ouida's unforgettable performance.

After them, three men who claimed to have seen Carter's Pontiac parked at Ouida's were called. L. S. Brown stated he saw the car at six o'clock on Saturday evening. Jesse Woods remembered seeing it that same night at eleven o'clock. W. H. Morrison saw the black coupe at 1:30 p.m. on Wednesday, the afternoon Carter returned from Alabama. Ouida and Carter were seated inside talking.

Cammie Cook returned to the courtroom, and spectators recalled her lengthy testimony at Ouida's trial. She appeared nervous to be testifying about Carter.

Again Mrs. Cook told the court that mother and daughter always had been compatible.

"Well, they looked like they were just as happy as could be together. They looked like they just thought the world of each other, and you wouldn't think there was anything between them that was in any way wrong."

As for Carter, "Well, I would see him there maybe once or twice a week and sometimes longer. I just don't remember, but I just noticed his coming at times."

She repeated her earlier testimony about having noticed Daisy Keeton in her backyard on Saturday morning, January 19, at about eleven o'clock. Then on Wednesday, she witnessed Carter in front of the Keeton home. She iterated much that she had stated at Ouida's trial. As though to compliment the accused man sitting so closely to her, Mrs. Cook told that Mr. Carter was a family friend who occasionally had visited in her home.

"He and Ouida were sitting in the car talking out in the front and I went in. I don't know how long they stayed there." Repeating most of what she had stated at Ouida's trial, she told that on the night of the murder she and her family were on the north side of their house, the side away from the Keetons', and had heard no disturbance whatsoever. Her guard dog did not bark, nor did the Keetons'.

"When it barks, the other one barks."

Mrs. Cook was pressed to recall Ouida's trips to Hot Springs, New Orleans, and Washington, D.C. Except for the trip to Washington, Mrs. Cook said she thought that Mrs. Keeton always accompanied Ouida. On the Wednesday morning following the murder, she observed Ouida returning home from her aunt's house, and on Wednesday afternoon Carter stopped by to see Ouida.

"She stepped across the walk that leads to the steps," she continued, "and he threw a snowball at her, and she dodged her head, and they stood there a few minutes and then she went out and got in the car and they sat there and talked. That's when I first knew that Mrs. Keeton had gone to New Orleans."

In the cross-examination she replied with an answer that the defense hoped would be indelibly impressed on the jury. She repeated what she had overheard Ouida say to Carter—that Mrs. Keeton had gone to New Orleans. While sweeping snow from her porch, Mrs. Cook had been present for only an instant, but she had overheard this important disclosure. The remark satisfied Carter's defense. If he were guilty, why should Ouida be imparting such obvious news?

After she was dismissed, the prosecution called C. A. Rowell. His residence on Highway 84, a block or two north of the Keeton house, was close enough for him to hear three gunshots the night of the murder. The rest of his family had been asleep. Rowell, a fan of hillbilly music, was in the habit of listening to late-night broadcasts. After the Nashville signoff at midnight, he customarily turned the radio dial to a Wheeling, West Virginia, station. He recalled hearing the sound of gunfire just as the announcer was saying it was 2:30 a.m. there. He clarified by explaining that in Mississippi the time would have been an hour earlier.

"How fast were the shots?"

"About as fast as a man can work his finger. That's about how fast it was. Towards town."

He pointed out the difference in the sound in a backfiring car and a pistol shot. His testimony left the impression that Mrs. Keeton had *not* been killed by bludgeoning.

Currie called Dr. D. C. McCool, a psychiatrist at the state mental hospital. A recognized witness who had testified for the defense at Ouida's trial, he told the court that Carter's chief counsel had conferred with him at his office.

In rebuttal, Collins hoped to impeach Ouida's testimony by showing her to be sane and cunning.

"Ouida Keeton is the only witness that tends to incriminate this defendant, W. M. Carter. She claimed a lapse of memory from the time of her mother's death until the following Wednesday. Now she says she knew everything that was going on and was playing a game."

He objected to the doctor's divulging any reported conversation with her as being immaterial and irrelevant. Judge Pack sustained.

Currie inquired how Dr. McCool had been retained by Ouida's lawyers. The doctor replied that this was done in an interview and an exchange of correspondence. He then reminded the court that for three days of Ouida's trial he had been present to monitor her behavior. As a witness for the prosecution, the psychiatrist was present again to testify that Ouida was insane.

"We propose to show that at the time she was tried for her life she was playing a game, according to her statement, just like she is playing it here," Collins remarked during the cross-examination. He asked that the record show Ouida's impeachable bias and prejudice in the case.

But Collins's line of defense did not hold up. It fell apart as the psychiatrist told that Ouida's past was clouded by mental turmoil. He had examined her while she was in Laurel General Hospital, and at the request of Deavours and Currie, he had been in the courtroom to observe her. He classified her disorder at that time as "catatonic dementia praecox."

Collins, holding to his position that Ouida was not insane and only pretending to have memory lapses, protested that by divulging privileged testimony Dr. McCool would violate the confidentiality existing between a patient and her physician.

Dr. McCool corrected him. Neither Ouida nor her family had retained him. He said, furthermore, that she had been unable to speak at the time of her trial, and, at present, he could not give a pronouncement on her current state of mental health.

He was dismissed, and at four o'clock the prosecution rested its case.

As the defense took over, Jeff Collins called C. H. Nicholson. Carter, as his former landlord, knew this man fairly well. Nicholson and his wife lived on Meridian Avenue, but a year previously Carter had been renting them a house he owned at 316 Walters Avenue, near the GM&N depot. Before that, for two years, the Nicholsons had lived immediately south of the Keetons. That residence was the one razed to make way for the new viaduct. They were the couple who claimed to have seen Ouida riding around with a man on Sunday several hours after Mrs. Keeton's murder. Mrs. Nicholson also had spoken to Ouida at the filling station on Saturday.

Nicholson told that he and his wife were returning from Union, sixty-one miles north. On Highway 15, about eight miles above Laurel, a tan car with red wheel hubs had overtaken them. The speed of Nicholson's car he estimated at thirty miles per hour. The driver of the tan car, a man Nicholson could not identify, sounded the horn and sped around them. Nicholson said that his wife recognized the passenger in the tan car.

"She said, 'There goes Ouida.'"

Mrs. Nicholson was called next. She was present to repeat testimony she had given at Ouida's trial. The defense hoped Mrs. Nicholson's remarks would show that Ouida, in having gone on this outing, was of a rational mind on the day of the murder. Again, the witness told of greeting Ouida at the McRae station. "I asked her how her mother was getting along, and she said, all right, she reckoned. She was visiting in New Orleans."

District Attorney Currie took charge of the cross-examination.

"Have you ever seen Mr. Carter's handwriting, Mrs. Nicholson?"

"Yes, I have."

He wanted her to examine his signature on the gas station's sales pad. She had seen it on house-rent receipts.

"But Mr. Carter didn't sign all the receipts," she reminded. "Sometimes Mr. Newton—and sometimes Mrs. Newton Carter—was in there and would sign the receipts."

"Did you know that he personally supervised the repair and reconstruction of the home in which his co-defendant lived?"

"I have heard it."

Collins next called Mrs. W. C. Therrell, reared next door to the Keeton girls. She too had testified at Ouida's trial. She gave the court an idea of the situation on Cross Street the night of the murder. When she and her husband returned from a movie between 9:30 and 10:00, no cars were parked at the Keeton house. The next evening, Sunday, she recalled "yellowish lamplight" in the Keetons' living room. On Monday while leaving for work, she encountered Ouida coming from the Keetons' back porch.

"It was raining and the wind was high. I was standing in the garage waiting for my husband to back the car out. She was just across the fence in her backyard. She was going to the back porch, walking. She had on a green dress without any sleeves. She mentioned something about the weather being bad and about her work, and I didn't understand what she said, so I asked her if she had said her mother was sick in bed. She faced me and said, 'No, Mother isn't sick.'"

Mrs. Therrell did not see Ouida after this.

Currie conducted the cross-examination.

"Tell the jury your observation of the association between Ouida and her mother throughout these years."

"Well, she seemed very fond of her mother. They were inseparable and usually there on the porch together."

Mrs. Therrell agreed with Currie's leading descriptions—"companionable," "devoted to each other," "apparent love for each other," "really beautiful devotion."

He asked about the routine of Carter's visits to the Keeton home.

"I couldn't say exactly. I have noticed him there two or three times a week and sometimes not so often. I have noticed Mr. Carter and his wife there."

She seemed to add this last remark as a forgiving afterthought, for she saw that Carter was studying her closely.

"You and Ouida were reared up as girls together?"

Mrs. Therrell said yes, adding that sometimes she rode to work at noon with Ouida and Mr. Carter.

"Carter's custom was to carry her back and forth, wasn't it?"

"Yes, sir," she replied softly, giving a meek look at Carter.

Currie pressed her to agree that she had seen Carter as the only male visitor at the Keeton home. He nudged her too to recall that his Pontiac carried an Arkansas license plate.

Collins rose for redirect examination of the witness.

"You never did see them when Ouida was mad at her mother, did you?"

"No, sir."

He asked if it was true that Maude Keeton McRae and her husband had not been inside the Keeton home in the past three or four years.

Mrs. Therrell was hesitant to say.

Hadn't Earl Keeton and his wife been living there?

"Since about two weeks after Mrs. Keeton's death."

Pressuring her, Collins asked her to state how much time had passed between the mother's death and Eloise Keeton's marriage at the Keeton house.

"About ten days, I guess. I don't know if she married there or not."

Next, C. L. Griffin, a night watchman, was called. His testimony was not heard at the Keeton trial. It cast a new light on the relationship by negating the cordial picture of mother and daughter Mrs. Therrell had described. Griffin testified that his duties began at eight in the evening and throughout the night he strolled the downtown streets checking for signs of mischief or crime. After making a complete round to his employers' businesses each hour, he terminated his shift between 5:30 and 6:30 and then returned home. He lived at 643 Cross Street, one block beyond the Keeton residence. In walking to work just after dark, he made a habit of crossing the street in front of their house and then proceeding to town. His recollection of Saturday, September 19, gave the court a glimpse of possible family turmoil.

"That night," Watkins asked him, "did you notice anything in front of the Keeton home?"

"Well, I noticed the house was lit up."

"Did you hear any conversation?"

"Yes, sir, I did."

"What conversation did you hear and between whom was it?"

"Well, I couldn't say who it was between."

"Women or men?"

"Women."

"Tell the jury so they can hear you what conversation did you hear there in the Keeton home."

"I heard the loud talking before I got to the house, and just as I got in front of the house I heard a remark made. Somebody says, 'I didn't do it,' and the other one says, 'You did do it. You done all you could have done.' And the other one said, 'Don't accuse me of that anymore. If you do, I'm going to knock hell out of you.' I moved on across the street and stopped at the filling station and stood there and heard the other one say, 'Don't accuse me of that again. I didn't have anything to do with it.'"

"Where did you go then?"

"I come on to town."

"And there was a car parked there that night?"

"Yes, sir, just north of the driveway."

"What kind of car was it?"

"A one-seated car. I didn't pay any attention to it. It was more in front of the other home than the Keeton home."

"What kind of car? You said it was a one-seated car."

"I never paid any attention to what make it was."

"In the conversation did you hear any man's voice?"

"No, sir, I didn't hear any man's voice."

Then his testimony took a surprising turn. On the next night, Sunday, while walking to town, he heard voices again.

"What did you hear at the Keeton home that night?"

"Well, there was some kind of argument going on there that night."

"Between men and women?"

"It was women."

"Women?"

"Yes, sir, but it wasn't loud enough that night for me to understand what they said, and I didn't stop because I wanted to get on to my work."

Carter, who had been in Mobile on Sunday night, was mystified over the two reported female voices. Whose was this second voice overheard that night after the murder?

"Did you see any car parked there that night anywhere?" Watkins continued.

"Yes, sir, there was a car parked about the same place, just north of the driveway."

"On either one of those nights did you hear any shots fired?"

His answer astonished the courtroom.

"Yes, sir, I did. Saturday night."

"Where were you on Saturday night?"

"I was right there by this county barn."

"How many shots did you hear fired?"

"Three."

"And about what time of night was that?"

"It was between twelve and one o'clock."

Jack Deavours took over for the cross-examination.

He reminded the court that Griffin had testified before the grand jury before it brought an indictment of Ouida Keeton and Carter.

"Isn't it a fact that you testified that those three shots came from the direction of the Keeton home? That the three shots you heard were over that way?"

"Yes, sir."

"And you also testified that there in front of that driveway leading to the Negro drug store on Front Street you saw a black coupe there?" the district attorney asked, trying to place Carter on the scene.

"No, sir, I didn't do that, Mr. Deavours. I said it was across the street in front of Freeman's."

Freeman's was a hardware store southwest of the Carter business.

"Between two and three o'clock in the morning?"

"Yes, sir."

"After the shots were fired?"

"Yes, sir. It was afterwards."

Carter appreciated being called a handsome man, a respected citizen. Although graying, he was confident in being a trim 165 pounds and in Miss Adams's good graces, the proof that he was not yet too old to cut the mustard. His heart was young, and his thoughts this Saturday evening were amorous. Now that he was a widower, his occasional trysts with his Mobile lady friend were no longer adulterous, yet he was quiet about his private life, since he was certain that his children, so devoted to their late mother, would not cotton to his courtship with this particular woman. He knew that gossips surmised he would remarry. A decent two years had passed.

He claimed to his attorneys that the remainder of January 19 was routine. The alibi revealed nothing unusual. With night falling fast, he had driven to his barber's for a shave and a haircut. He wanted to look nice for Miss Adams. He turned the Pontiac right onto Oak Street. In the middle of the block Cross's newsstand was still open. The overhead light in the front room cast a yellowish glow over the stacks of newspapers, comic books, magazines, and candy bars. Mrs. Cross, encamped on her chair beside the cash register, was waiting to lock the door. Her husband, as was his custom, was straightening up and getting ready for the next morning, when customers heading to Sunday school would drop by for the Jackson or the New Orleans newspaper.

Approaching the intersection of Magnolia Street, Carter turned right. Beech's Barber Shop was just ahead on the left. As businesses shut their doors and clerks hurried home, the thoroughfare was a picture of weariness that typified the end of a week in winter. The Commercial National Bank, on the corner, was dark on Saturday, of course.

In no time at all Carter took his seat in W. T. Chisholm's chair. He told Chisholm some of his plans. A customer often loosened up with his barber. Already he had gassed up his Pontiac at McRae's filling station. Except for advising his children of the business part of his plans and packing his suitcase, he was ready to go. His Sunday would be spent on the road and in Alabama.

Just as Chisholm was finishing with him, Ethel Hicks, the next customer, arrived to take his turn. He and Carter fell into conversation. Hicks needed gun cartridges, but he remarked that all the stores had closed. Carter said he could oblige. After paying Chishom, Carter returned to his store for the shells and delivered them to Hicks just as Chisholm was whisking hair off his customer's shoulders. Hicks settled up both with the barber and with Carter. It happened to be an easy, methodical transaction, one that Hicks would remember. He had shown no reluctance when asked to testify. Chisholm likewise had come to the stand to substantiate Carter's whereabouts on Saturday in the six o'clock hour.

Carter would assure his attorneys that the rest of the day, from seven till midnight, had progressed routinely. At the trial family eyewitnesses recalled every stage of Carter's trek home, and each stop served as a link in an unbroken chain. As the family patriarch and provider, he was a figure for his family to make note of.

Passing the post office, the hotel, the Methodist and Presbyterian churches, and the courthouse, he drove a few blocks north and popped in at his daughter Pauline's house. Her husband had gone hunting. After telling her of his plans to go to Alabama to check on their oil interests, Carter gave her a goodbye kiss. In her testimony she had accounted for this time spent with her. Back in the car and still heading north, Carter drove two blocks and stopped by his sisters Rosa and Ida's house, on Seventh Avenue. They were entertaining their brother Eugene and his wife, visiting from Louisiana. Supper was over, and the guests and Charles, a second brother who lived nearby, were in the process of leaving just as Carter arrived. Carter, the eldest, recalled telling them his plans of traveling to Evergreen (but, of course, with no mention of Mobile), and after they left, he too went on his way. Newton and Carolyn were driving away just as he approached home. They were going to the Saturday-night spaghetti supper at the Catholic church. In a cozy setup, father and children resided together in the fine house Carter had built in 1922.

The family of his only other daughter, Helen, lived directly across the street. Carter recalled that it was about eight o'clock when he pulled his car to the curb in front of their house and went in to tell Helen his travel plans. At the front door Walter, Helen's young husband, greeted him. She was upstairs putting their two boys to bed. While reading, Walter was listening to Wayne King's orchestra on the radio. Carter went to tell the grandsons goodnight and gave the younger one fifty cents to be applied toward a birthday gift.

When he and Helen came downstairs, Carolyn, Newton's little daughter, was seated beside her uncle Walter. At about 8:30 she had arrived from a wiener roast up Sixth Avenue at a young friend's house. She and her grandfather then drove across the street into the driveway and locked the Pontiac in the garage. Carolyn's older brother Matt, already in bed, was recovering from an upset stomach his mother had doctored before leaving. The grandfather was the babysitter until the parents came home.

Carter would recall the testimonies of his family. His sister Rosa, his brother Charles, both daughters, his son and daughter-in-law, both sons-in-law, and even young Carolyn had given support to his alibi.

On the stand the fifth grader had recalled the mundane details of the fateful Saturday evening. Watkins considered her testimony essential in establishing the alibi. Who would not believe a lovely ten-year-old child? Her vivid account was impressive. She told the court that she had plopped onto her bed in her pajamas and played games until it was time to turn out the lights. Her grandfather, she remembered, came out of the bath wet-headed and wearing his nightshirt. She watched him drying his hair over a gas heater. On the bed across from hers, her sick brother was sleeping. Their bedroom was situated between their parents' room and their grandfather's. Creeping about in his nightshirt, he was packing his suitcase and putting himself in order for the Sunday trip. She remembered too that the telephone rang once. It was a family friend wanting to speak with her father, and when he and her mother returned, the little girl advised them of the call. Her report of this evening was remarkably mature in specific revelations.

From her testimony, the intimacy of the Carters' sleeping arrangement became general knowledge, the kind of revelation that could be embarrassing, but the urgency of the case demanded that such private matters be aired. The family bathroom was adjacent to the parents' room and two rooms beyond Carter's. A candid part of the daughter-in-law Carolyn's testimony revealed that bedroom doors remained open during the night so that there was a line of vision from room to room. She told the court that from her bed she could hear the two sleeping children as well as her husband's father. If Carter rose to go to the toilet, he had to pass through the grandchildren's and their parents' bedrooms. To show evidence of the interconnection of rooms, Carter's son-in-law from across the street, at the request of defense counsel, had sketched a detailed layout of the floor plan and the yard, and during Newton's testimony this had been presented as one of the crime exhibits.

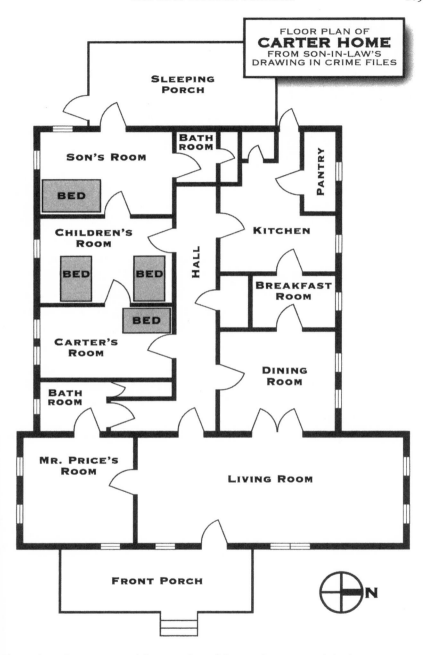

Floor plan of W. M. Carter's home, adapted from a drawing made by his son-in-law and filed with crime documents in the Jones County courthouse. (Illustration by Bill Pitts)

However, the bedroom on the front of the house, separated from Carter's by a second bathroom, was occupied by a roomer named J. B. Price. Although classed among the well-to-do, the Carters were bedded close together and rented out the front room to the town's deliveryman of the *Jackson Clarion-Ledger*. His quarters did not communicate with the rest of the house, and his doors always remained locked. Carolyn told that Price arose at 3:30 a.m. to go on his paper route. Two hours afterward, her father-in-law was in the habit of getting up. She testified that he seldom was able to sleep for more than six hours, and for insomnia he took his medication.

On the stand Carolyn admitted that she and Ouida had been students at the high school together but that they were hardly friends. Carolyn held her distance, implying a dislike for Ouida and a distinct separateness from her. Her haughty tone, not a bit concealed, was snobbish and cutting, as though down at the office Ouida were merely hired help who had risen imperti-nently above her station.

Carter sat stoically as Carolyn discussed her duty of attending to the laun-dry. He wore a fresh white shirt each day, but she waited until there was a sufficient collection of soiled shirts before phoning the laundryman. She revealed that Carter changed his underwear three times a week and that, in gathering the wash, she had not detected any blood on his garments. The court heard also about his bladder and kidney problem, which necessitated several ups and downs between bedtime and daylight. For the modest Carter this was humiliating exposure.

The whole family suffered from this intimate peek behind their closed doors. Pressed to continue, Carolyn told that while the family slumbered, some in the household might be awakened by sounds from what she called "the chamber," the metal slop jar Carter kept under his bed. At the spaghetti supper on January 19 Carolyn had drunk too much coffee. High-strung on caffeine, she had passed a fitful night, never falling into a sound sleep. For the sake of his alibi, she told that two times after midnight her father-in-law got up to urinate. She had heard the noise of the metal pot sliding from beneath his bed.

In his testimony Carter's son stated that his father had been in bed when he and Carolyn returned from the spaghetti supper at midnight.

Carter had arisen at five o'clock, had dressed quickly, and then had gone on tiptoe through the children's room with his suitcase. Carolyn, still awake, got up too and asked if she should prepare breakfast for him. He shook his head and said he'd eat downtown. Exhausted from lack of sleep, Carolyn had

Intersection of Oak and Magnolia streets, Laurel, post–World War II. Jack Deavours's office, where Ouida was interrogated, was upstairs in the building on the left. Note the town clock hanging on the southwest corner. Across the street is Lucas Café, where Carter ate breakfast the morning after the murder. (Photo from the collection of Hunter Cole)

returned to bed, she told the court, and slept until 8:30. The night before, she had laid out the children's clothes for Sunday school. From her testimony the curious might conclude that the well-to-do in their fine homes actually were not much different from the hoi polloi.

Carter recalled opening the garage door, putting his suitcase on the floorboard, and then backing his coupe down the sloping driveway. Their roomer and his car were gone, already making the rounds of his paper route.

This was the dawn after Daisy Keeton's murder. His memory of the day was firmly fixed. The weather that morning was blustery, seeming to promise rain and cold. As he drove south in the direction of town, the two yellow cones of the headlights shone on the brick paving of Sixth Avenue. He proceeded to Fifth Street, took a left, and pressed on past the Confederate statuary on the north side of the courthouse to Magnolia Street and took a right turn. He pulled up to Lucas Café, just a few doors past his barber's, and stopped behind Charlie Thompson's ambulance parked at the curb. Across the street the lit faces on the bank's iron clock said the time was closer to 5:30 than to 6:00.

More a diner than a café, it was just one narrow room with a long counter and stools screwed into the floor. He took a seat next to Thompson and gave his order (coffee and toast) to Ernest Edwards, the all-night waiter rounding up his ten-to-six shift. Thompson had just finished an ambulance call. He told Carter of being summoned to Pine Street to pick up some woman who had been knocked in the head. He had delivered her to Laurel General Hospital and then stopped at the café for coffee. Carter told him he was bound for Evergreen to check on oil drilling near family property. They discussed the best routes.

At the trial Thompson's testimony about the encounter, along with that of Edwards, was given to help establish the alibi. But Thompson, an undertaker, a popular fellow of thirty-nine, and a prospective candidate for sheriff of Jones County, also would be called to serve the other side of the case. Wanting to refute experts testifying for the defense, the prosecution solicited his professional views on the time it took for a body to decompose. If accurately determined, the time could establish that Mrs. Keeton had been slain on a Sunday, when there was no question about Carter's whereabouts. Thompson and the undertaker for the defense did not agree.

Carter thought his own account for his activities on the night of the murder had been satisfactory, and to his attorneys the alibi seemed water-tight and air-proof. From Alabama, his late wife's relatives, as well as Miss Adams's sister, had come to give even further support as to his whereabouts during his absence from Laurel.

After interminable suspense, Carter was called for his dreaded time in the witness chair. Marion Reily, rather than Watkins, was taking a position before the bench and would be questioning him. Carter intended to be robust and brisk, but as he struggled to rise, his chair scraped loudly when he braced to steady himself.

■ ■ ■

A bailiff approached with a Bible and asked Carter to take the oath. Carter heard his voice responding. To his own ears it sounded anxious and soft.

He watched his attorney approach.

"Mr. Carter, what are your initials?" Reily asked.

"W. M. Carter. W. M."

"Now, speak out so the jury can hear you. How old are you, Mr. Carter?"

"Sixty-eight."

"Your next birthday you will be sixty-nine?"

"Yes, sir."

"Where do you live now?"

"I live on Sixth Avenue."

"In the town of Laurel?"

"In the town of Laurel."

A series of friendly, preliminary questions was meant to set the witness at ease.

"Mr. Carter, where were you born?"

"Born in Georgia."

"When you came to Mississippi—how old were you when you came to Mississippi?"

"I came to Mississippi in '93, in 1893."

"Had you married at that time?"

"Yes, sir."

"Whom did you marry, Mr. Carter?"

"I married Nettie Newton."

Clearly Reily was asking him easy questions to acclimate him to the frightening procedures and to hostile faces in the audience.

"Where did you marry?"

"Married in Belleville, Belleville, Alabama."

"You married an Alabama girl?"

"Yes, sir."

"When you came here, had your union been blessed with children at that time?"

"One."

"One child. And when you came to Mississippi, what business did you go into?"

"I was in the sawmill business."

"What was the nature of that business?"

"Manufacturing lumber."

"What was the size of your mill at that time?"

"I had a small mill. Cut about six- or eight-thousand feet a day."

"What work did you do in that operation?"

"Well, I superintended it."

"Did you do any manual labor?"

"Yes, sir."

"How long did you remain in that business?"

"I remained in that business for fifteen or twenty years."

"With that one sawmill?"

"Yes, sir."

"Did you ever have any more?"

"Yes, sir."

"What other points did you have mills, Mr. Carter?"

"I had another mill at Haney, Mississippi."

"At any other points did you have mills?"

"Yes, sir, I had one down on the GM&N here at the creek."

"Did you have any other mills? You don't have to name all of them, just such as you remember, Mr. Carter."

"They grew to be larger."

"In 1920, where were you engaged in business? Do you remember?"

"Fifteen years ago? I was engaged here in Laurel. My office was at that time over here, I believe, on Magnolia Street, the one that runs right in front or comes up by the bank. I believe that is Magnolia."

"How many people were in your office at that time?"

"I had a couple."

"I want to ask you if you know Miss Ouida Keeton."

"Yes, sir."

"Under what circumstances did you become acquainted with her, Mr. Carter?"

"Well, I think she wrote me from New Orleans for a position."

"Tell the jury whether or not up to that time you had ever seen Miss Ouida Keeton."

"I hadn't that I know of."

"Did you know her mother up to that time?"

"No, sir."

"Do you remember the circumstances under which Miss Keeton came into your employ?"

"Well, I inquired of the school here. Mr. Decker, I believe, was the principal. Whether she would make a good office girl, and he told me he thought she would."

"At that time was Mr. Decker related to you by blood or by marriage in any way?"

"Yes."

"How?"

"Son-in-law."

"State whether or not he had taught school here and knew the young lady."

"Yes, sir."

"Tell the jury whether or not at that time you had ever seen her mother that you know of."

"Not that I know of, no."

"State whether or not the young lady thereafter came into your office."

"Yes, sir."

"Now, when she came in there, about how old was she?"

"I don't know. I think about nineteen, or somewhere in that—"

"Something like nineteen or twenty?"

"Yes, sir."

"Was there anything more than business between you and this young lady when she first came?"

"No, sir."

"After she had been in your office a number of years, tell the jury candidly what developed between you."

"Well, we began to be—to like one another, to be affectionate, and it grew to a love affair."

"Had a love affair with her, did you? Was Mrs. Carter living at that time?"

"Yes, sir."

"Did she know anything about the love affair with this young woman, the little lady in your office?"

"No, sir."

"How long did the affair continue, Mr. Carter?"

"Well, it continued—well, until recently."

"Tell the jury whether or not you ever had at any time any illicit relationship with that young lady."

"No, sir."

"You never did?"

"No, sir."

"Were you in New Orleans when she was there?"

"Yes, sir."

"On how many occasions?"

"One."

"Did any sexual relation, any sexual intercourse, take place between you and that young lady in New Orleans?"

"No, sir."

Judge Pack was noticeably responsive to this candid discussion. His eyes swept the courtroom, noting reactions.

"None whatever? Now, Mr. Carter, getting back to your association with her there in the office, at what salary did she start with you?"

He told that it had begun at $50 a month but that as she took on additional duties it rose to three times that amount. After the Depression hit, her salary dropped back to $50.

"Did she remain in your employ, or did she go out?"

"Well, she went out of my employ."

At this point in the interrogation, Judge Pack again sensed testimony about potentially troublesome topics too delicate for young ears. He spoke up.

"I hate to have this interruption, but we have to do it. Mr. Bailiff, take time and put every child out of the courtroom, every child under fifteen years of age, and don't permit anyone under fifteen years of age in the courtroom."

Shuffling and consternation resulted as several mothers with babies, tots, and adolescent children relinquished their seats. A number of adults leaning against the walls quickly claimed them, and when the back door was closed and all was settled, Judge Pack gave Reily a nod to resume.

"Now, the last question was—Did the young lady remain in your employ or go out?"

"She went out."

"Mr. Carter, what is the condition of your health?"

"Well, it is fairly good."

"Before this trouble, what was the condition of your health?"

The district attorney voiced an objection.

"Overruled," Judge Pack responded.

"What was the condition of your health with reference to your bladder or kidneys?"

This was a modest reference to the lapse of his sexual powers.

"Well, I have had trouble with my bladder and kidneys for a couple of years."

"Now getting back to the young lady of whom you testified, I want to ask you if during these years you have had a post-office box here."

"Yes, sir."

"Whose name was that post-office box in?"

"J. R. Sampey."

"Did this young lady ever write you letters addressed to that post-office box?"

"Yes, sir." Carter was candid, telling how he employed Sampey's identity for confidential correspondence.

"It's been testified here that you gave the young lady a thousand-dollar pin. Is that true or not?"

"No, sir."

"Did you ever give her a diamond of any kind?"

"No, sir."

"Did she ever have a pin, a diamond pin?"

"Yes, sir."

"Do you know where that pin came from?"

"Yes, sir."

"From whom?" Reily asked, in order to correct the mix-up of the name during Ouida's interrogation.

"Mr. *Price.*"

"Do you know whether or not she had a young gentleman friend by the name of Mr. Price?"

"Yes, sir."

"Do you know whether or not when she went to Hot Springs with her mother? Whether or not he visited her there?"

"Yes, sir."

"Do you know whether or not she was engaged to a young man by the name of Grace?"

"Yes, sir."

"Did you ever talk to her about being engaged to this young man by the name of Mr. Grace?"

"Yes, sir."

"Did you personally ever see Mr. Grace?"

"No, sir."

"When she went to Washington, how long did she remain there?"

"Three or four months, I think."

"When did this engagement with this man Mr. Grace that she told you about occur?"

"1930 to 1932."

"Was it before or after she went to Washington?"

"After."

"Now, Mr. Carter, on the night of January 19, 1935, when she claims she opened her window at two o'clock in the morning and let you in her room, tell the jury whether or not, according to her statements, she was engaged to another man."

"Yes, sir."

Reily asked about the two years Ouida was without a job and then about how Carter dealt with her absence when she went away for her management course.

"Did you write to her while she was in Washington?"

"Yes, sir."

"Did she write to you?"

"Yes, sir."

"After she returned from Washington, state whether or not you saw her."

"Yes, sir."

"Now, Mr. Carter, there has been some testimony here about your visiting in Mrs. Keeton's home. What relationship existed between you and Mrs. Keeton, as to whether you were enemies or friends?"

"We were friends, good friends."

"How often did you visit in her home?"

"I would visit her sometimes once a week and again sometimes two or maybe three times."

"Tell the jury the truth as to what would be the occasion of your going there?"

"Well, I collected her rents for her, and I carried and delivered her rents to her and also to visit her."

"Go visit with whom?"

"Visit with Miss Keeton."

"At that time about how old a girl was this young Miss Keeton in this home where you were going?"

"She is about thirty-three or thirty-four, I think."

"About what time of day or night would you go there?"

"Sometimes I would go in the day and sometimes at night."

"Tell the jury where you parked your car when you would go."

"I parked it in front of the house."

"Did members of your family know anything of your visits there?"

"No, sir, not that I know of."

"When you would go there, where would you be entertained, Mr. Carter?"

"Well, mostly in Mrs. Keeton's room."

"Did you ever go there and call on this young lady when her mother was not present?"

"No, sir."

"How long would you remain there at Mrs. Keeton's, Mr. Carter?"

"Sometimes an hour, sometimes two hours."

"I believe you had the misfortune to lose your wife?"

"Yes, sir."

"When did you lose her?"

"Something over two years ago, a little over two years ago."

"After you lost your wife, did you go and visit in that home?"

"Yes, sir."

"And you were doing it before she died?"

"Yes, sir."

"Did she know?"

"Well, I believe she did."

"Did she know how often you went?"

"No, sir."

"Did she ever go there with you?"

"Yes, sir."

"But she didn't go all the time?"

"No, sir."

"You would go around there at nights and she wouldn't know it, at times? Is that true?"

"Yes, sir."

"When you would go to see Mrs. Keeton, tell the jury how she received you, whether she received you politely or not."

"Politely as could be."

"Did she ever object to your coming and sitting and talking there?"

"No, sir."

"Did you ever have any row with her at all in any form?"

"No, sir."

"Now, Mr. Carter, I will ask you, Mr. Carter, whether or not on the night of January 19, 1935, you went to that house at two o'clock in the morning."

"No, sir."

"Tell the jury whether or not you went in that house through the window."

"No, sir."

"Tell the jury whether or not after you had gotten through the window and remained about ten minutes in Miss Keeton's room—"

"No, sir."

"—that you rushed in and shot Mrs. Keeton."

"No, sir."

"Did you have anything to do with the killing of Mrs. Keeton?"

"No, sir."

"Did you strike Mrs. Keeton with a poker?"

"No, sir."

"Directing your attention to that day, on Saturday, did you go to the Keeton home that day, on Saturday?"

"No, sir."

"When was the last time you had gone to that home, Mr. Carter?"

"The best of my recollection it was Friday night."

"That was Friday, before this Saturday?"

Carter told the court he had gone there about 6:30 on Friday, not on Saturday, to deliver ice cream. He handed it to Mrs. Keeton and then left.

Reily then asked him to examine the gasoline tickets he had signed at McRae's Service Station and asked from whom he purchased the gasoline.

"I purchased it from Miss Keeton, the best of my recollection."

"Do you recall who delivered that gasoline to you?"

"Well, the Negro delivered it to me, that is, drew it out."

"Do you recall whether or not Mr. McRae was there when you purchased it?"

"No, sir."

"Did you have a conversation with her?"

"No, sir, none that I can recall."

"Do you remember whether or not you got out of the car and went in the office or not?"

"No, I don't remember whether I did or not."

"How long had you been buying gas at the McRae filling station?"

"The best of my recollection, about six weeks or two months."

"What was the occasion for you starting to deal with Mr. McRae? Buying gas from him?"

"Well, Miss Keeton, when she went there, she asked me if I would come by and give them my business, and Mr. McRae owed me money, a little money."

"That's the truth about it? Now, Mr. Carter, on this particular evening that you went by there, tell the jury whether or not you discussed with Miss Keeton the question of killing her mother."

"No, sir."

"Was there any word spoken between you and she with reference to the killing of her mother?"

"No, sir."

"Or injuring her mother?"

"No, sir."

"Tell the jury whether or not previous to this you and she discussed at any time or any place the killing of her mother."

"No, sir."

"Did anything of that kind ever take place?"

"No, sir."

"Now, Mr. Carter, that the jury may understand, what was the relationship between Miss Keeton and her mother, so far as you know?"

"The relationship between them, so far as I know, was good."

"Did you ever see any trouble between them?"

"No, sir."

"Do you know of any trouble between them?"

"No, sir."

"Mr. Carter, do you remember the occasion some seven or eight years ago when a suit was brought against Mrs. Daisy Keeton for the alienation of affections by this man who married her young daughter?"

"Yes, sir."

"State whether or not you were sued jointly with her."

"Yes, sir."

"For how much were you sued?"

"$75,000, I believe."

"State whether or not that judgment was finally rendered against Mrs. Keeton."

"Yes, sir."

"Was it rendered against you?"

"No, sir."

"Do you know whether or not seven years had passed from the time of the rendition of that judgment and the death of Mrs. Keeton?"

"Yes, sir."

"Did you ever discuss with Miss Ouida Keeton the question of whether that judgment could be collected by the man in whose favor it was rendered after seven years?"

"Yes, sir."

"How many times did she mention it to you?"

"A couple of times."

"Did Miss Keeton, Ouida Keeton, discuss with you or question as to whether or not the judgment could ever be collected after seven years had expired?"

"Yes, sir."

"How long before this killing was it she discussed it with you last?"

"The latter part of the year."

"Now, how long had it been since the seven years passed—between the rendition of the judgment and the death of Mrs. Keeton?"

"The best of my recollection, it was about eight years."

"Between the rendition of the judgment and her death?"

"Yes."

"What was the length of time between the expiration of seven years and the time of Mrs. Keeton's death?"

"About, right around a year."

"Do you know whether or not Miss Keeton had money of her mother's?"

"Yes."

"She did have, and notwithstanding the fact that six months or a year had passed from the time that the judgment could be collected, this money was still in Miss Keeton's name and had not been transferred? Is that true or untrue?"

"That is true."

"Did Miss Keeton ever discuss with you whether or not her mother wanted her to deliver that money back to her?"

"She said her mother wanted the money so she could sign her own checks. She didn't feel like calling on her every time she needed a little money."

"How many times did she tell you about her mother wanting the money transferred to her?"

"I don't believe she mentioned but once."

"When was it she told you that?"

"During the latter part, during last year."

"Now, Mr. Carter, I want to direct your attention now to the day of January 19. Where were you on January 19?"

"Well, I was around my business here until late, until along about four o'clock in the evening, right about four o'clock in the evening. Then I went out to this mill, Lowery's Mill, C. S. Lowery, I believe, to place some orders with him and to line up on some stock I wanted to use for myself and also some stock for the retail trade."

"That was the nineteenth?"

"Yes, sir."

"Now, that night, the nineteenth of January, at six o'clock, about six o'clock, do you remember where you were?"

"Well, about six o'clock we closed up at six o'clock, and I was at the office."

"All right now. The cars you have—describe to the jury the cars you have."

"I have a Pontiac, a Buick, a Lincoln, and a small Whippet, but I don't use the Whippet."

Reily asked him to describe each automobile, to tell its age and color, and to comment on how each was used. Since the Carter vehicles had been mentioned so many times in the case, he wanted information to be clear in the jurors' minds. Reily then asked for a detailed summary of Carter's activities after leaving work on Saturday evening. Answering all his questions consumed half an hour.

"Well, the next morning about five-thirty," Carter concluded, "I waked up and got up and dressed and got out my car."

"Now, what time did you reach Mobile? Do you know?"

"I reached Mobile sometime between nine and nine-thirty, the best of my recollection."

"You have explained that you went on to Mobile. Where was the first place you went to when you arrived in Mobile?"

Carter told him of stopping by the St. Andrew's Hotel and washing up, although he had not registered at that time.

"After you washed up, where did you go?"

"I went out to see Miss Adams on Ann Street."

"When you went out there that day, Mr. Carter, what time did you reach her home?"

"Right about ten o'clock."

He told of driving her and her sister out to the cemetery to place flowers on their mother's grave. Then he and Miss Adams dropped the sister at home and drove downtown to the Metropolitan Café for lunch. Afterward they drove to the city park.

"Let's stop right there," Reily said. "This Miss Adams you were going to the park with and had lunch with, she is how old a lady?"

"About fifty, I think."

"How long had you known her?"

"Twenty-five or -six years, something like that."

"What time did you return from the park?"

"We returned to her home about between five and six."

He said they remained until seven or eight o'clock and then went for another drive around Mobile, again stopping at the park until ten or ten-thirty.

"Then what did you do?"

"We came back to her home."

"Then what did you do?"

"I put her out about eleven o'clock, and went on back to my hotel."

"When you went to the hotel, what did you do?"

"Registered."

Reily asked him to recall the attendant at the parking garage, for Carter had neglected to mention him in his alibi. Reily offered the parking receipt that had been stamped by the hotel desk clerk.

"Then what did you do?"

"I went to bed."

"I now present to you a sheet of paper which purports to be a record of the times you have registered in the St. Andrew's Hotel, January 20, 1935, appearing as Exhibit A, and call your attention to the handwriting on this sheet opposite, which there is marked a red cross, and ask you to look at the paper and tell the jury whose handwriting that is."

"W. M. Carter."

"I can't hear you."

"W. M. Carter."

"Who wrote that?"

"I did."

"Is that your signature?"

"Yes."

"Read that line."

"*W. M. Carter, Laurel, Mississippi.*"

"When did you write your name on that paper?"

"January 20."

"Does that record show what room you were in?"

"No. 223."

"After you went to bed in the hotel, did you arise any more that night?"

"No, sir."

"What time did you arise next morning?"

"Oh, about—between seven and seven-thirty or eight."

"Do you remember what you did that morning when you arose?"

"Yes, sir."

"What did you do?"

"I went from there to Evergreen, Alabama."

"How far is Evergreen from Mobile?"

"About 115 or 120 miles."

"What time did you leave Mobile for Evergreen?"

"Right around—between—right around eight o'clock. Between seven— right around eight o'clock."

"What was your business in going to Evergreen?"

"I have some land. My wife had an interest in some land over there."

"I can't hear you, Mr. Carter."

"My wife had an interest in some land over there, and we had been figuring on some leases, some of my brothers-in-law and I together, on getting up some leases, oil leases, on the land."

"State whether or not there was some enthusiasm around Evergreen, Alabama, at that time touching on or anticipating the discovery of oil in that section."

"Yes, sir."

Carter had been the overnight houseguest of Mrs. Newton, his wife's sister-in-law, while in Evergreen.

"And you spent Monday night there?"

"Spent Monday night there."

"Did you remain there all day Tuesday, Mr. Carter?"

"No, sir."

He stopped by Watson, Merrill & Company in Evergreen and sold an order of Masonite.

"What time did you leave Evergreen?"

"To the best of my knowledge around two o'clock."

"Where did you go from there?"

"Mobile."

Carter returned so that he could enjoy Miss Adams's company again. He arrived between five and six in the evening.

"I stayed out there until eleven. It was eleven or eleven-thirty when I left there."

"Did you remain at her house all the time?"

"No, sir, we drove out, drove down to the park."

After leaving Miss Adams, Carter registered a second time at the St. Andrew's Hotel.

"Now I place in your hands a sheet of paper which purports to be a record of registration in the St. Andrew's Hotel, January 22, 1935, said sheet of paper having been offered in evidence as Exhibit B, and direct your attention to an entry on that sheet which has marked just opposite it a red cross. Whose handwriting is that?"

"W. M. Carter's."

"What room?"

"223."

"Tell the court and jury when you wrote your name on that sheet of paper."

"On the night of the twenty-second."

"What day of the week? Do you recall?"

"Tuesday. Tuesday."

"Tuesday, the twenty-second. At about what hour?"

"Right around eleven-thirty."

"What time did you arise the next morning?"

"About—between seven-thirty and eight."

"And where did you go when you arose?"

"Why I went to breakfast first."

"You went to breakfast. Do you recall whether you had any trouble with your car? Getting it started or anything?"

"Let all the water out. The car was frozen the night before."

"I can't hear you, Mr. Carter."

"I say I let all the water out of it and had that refilled and checked over."

"Did you remain in Mobile that day, which was Wednesday?"

"No, sir, I left there about—best of my recollection—I left there right around nine o'clock."

"And what direction did you come home?"

"I came via Waynesboro."

"Now, Mr. Carter, on that trip, either going to Mobile or coming back from Mobile, did you transact any business?"

"I sold a small bill of Masonite on my way back."

"Do you remember to whom you sold it?"

"Andrews Hardware, at Citronelle."

"Where is Citronelle?"

"About thirty miles this side of Mobile. I came through Citronelle that week."

"Coming back?"

"Yes, sir."

"Now before we get any further with that trip, I will ask you if you purchased any article from anybody."

"Bought a pair of shoes."

On Tuesday, Carter had admired the shoes in the window of L. Hammel's Dry Goods Store and on impulse bought them for his daughter, Mrs. Bailey. He was not certain that they were the correct size, and as a safeguard, so that they could be returned if they did not fit, he had requested a receipt. Reily offered the receipt, in the amount of $6.75, as Exhibit B, and it was marked and placed upon the table.

"You got back to Laurel on Wednesday, the twenty-third?"

"Yes, sir."

"When you came back from Mobile, you say that in going to your place of business you passed by Miss Keeton's home?"

"Yes, sir."

"What did you do when you got to her home?"

"I went in on the piazza and knocked at the door, and there wasn't any response. So I started on out to my car and met Miss Keeton then coming out of the driveway, or alley. So I says—"

"Talk louder," lawyer Collins prompted from the defense table.

"I says, 'What are you doing going that way?' and she says, 'I'm staying over there at my aunts' while my mother is gone to New Orleans."

"Is there a filling station in that vicinity?"

"Yes, sir. Right in front of the house."

"How close did you stop your car to that filling station there in the broad open daylight?"

"I reckon fifty or sixty feet."

"When Miss Keeton came from that driveway, did you know where she had been?"

"No, sir."

"Did she have anything in her hand?"

"A bottle of milk."

"Now what was your reason for stopping there, Mr. Carter?"

"Well, Miss Adams had given me a message to deliver to her. Told me she was looking for her to come down whenever she wanted to come and had an opportunity."

"Miss Adams had sent that message to Miss Keeton?"

"Yes, sir."

"And you stopped to deliver it?"

"Yes, sir."

"When you saw her coming down the alley, what did you do?"

"I pitched a little snowball at her."

"Where was she when you threw the snowball at her?"

"Out near the sidewalk."

"Then what did you do? Did she remain out of your car, or what did she do?"

"No, we talked a few minutes. She remained out of my car, and we talked a few minutes, and then I asked her to get in my car. Asked her to get in, and we talked there maybe close around an hour."

"Around an hour? Tell the jury what you all talked about there in that car."

"She told me she had a letter from her boyfriend, and he was coming to see her the next week."

"What boyfriend was that?"

"Mr. Gray, no, I believe his name was Grace."

"Was that the man she was engaged to marry?"

"Yes, sir."

"Tell the jury whether or not you were infatuated with that girl."

"Well, I couldn't—"

"Tell them the truth about it. Tell them whether or not at that time you were infatuated with the girl that told you she was engaged to another man."

"Well, I will say yes."

"All right, Mr. Carter, the young lady told you what about the young man she was engaged to marry?"

"Told me that he was coming during the next week."

"And you sat there and talked to her in that car. Now tell the jury if she told—said anything to you then about having killed her mother."

"No, sir."

"Tell the jury if you then asked her for $10,000 to defend her with."

"No, sir."

"Tell the jury if you knew at that time her mother was dead."

"No, sir."

"Did you have any information that Mrs. Keeton was dead?"

"No, sir."

"When she told you her mother had gone to New Orleans, did you have any way to know whether it was true or not?"

"No, sir."

"Did she discuss the death of her mother with you at all?"

"No, sir."

"She did not? Did you tell her, sitting there in that car, that the other part of her mother's body had been buried as safely as though it were buried at sea?"

"No, sir."

"Mr. Carter, when you were sitting there talking to her, throughout that period, did she say anything about the circumstances under which her mother went to New Orleans?"

"No, sir, I just learned that her mother had gone to New Orleans to spend the week."

"When did she say her mother would be back?"

"Said she was looking for her back the next week."

"Did she make any statement with regard to how her mother got to the train?"

"Said she took her to the train."

Carter's version of the conversation with Ouida in the car was a striking contrast to hers.

Next, Reily asked Carter to answer questions about Ouida's burst water pipe and McLeod being brought to repair it and to drain her frozen radiator.

"What was the condition of Miss Keeton, so far as you could observe at that time?"

"Well, I didn't notice anything out of the way."

"State whether or not she was unconscious."

"No, sir."

"Did you see anything to indicate she didn't know what she was doing?"

"No, sir."

"How long did it take you, in your judgment, to fix the water pipe? About how long?"

"Well, best of my recollection, we were there about an hour fixing the pipe and cleaning out her car."

"Explain to the jury what you did to her car, if anything."

"Took the hood off of it and cleaned out the ice that was in it. It was frozen."

"Did you see any blood on that car at that time?"

"No, sir."

"Where was the car when that work was done? Do you know whether it was in the shed or outside?"

"In the shed."

"By the way, while I'm thinking about it, did you see the pistol that was introduced in evidence here?"

"No, sir."

"Did you see it the other day when it was introduced in the trial?"

"Yes, sir."

"Tell the jury the first time you ever saw that pistol."

"Here."

"Where?"

"Right here."

"Tell the jury whether or not you left that pistol on any hen nest or anywhere else on those premises."

"No, sir."

"Did you ever have that pistol in your possession?"

"No, sir."

"Mr. Carter, after the young man got through fixing the automobile and the pipe, what became of you and the young man?"

"We came on back to the warehouse."

"Where did you remain while he was fixing the automobile?"

"Right around where he was at work."

"Where was Miss Keeton?"

"She was right around him too."

"Does Miss Keeton own a dog?"

"Yes, sir."

"The dog was there in the yard?"

"Yes, sir."

"What kind of dog is it?"

"German Police."

"Large or small?"

"Large."

"Where was the dog at the time?"

"She had it chained."

"Where did she keep the dog chained at that time?"

"I don't remember whereabouts."

"When you left there with Mr. McLeod, where did you go?"

"Back to my business."

"Was there any payment made for that work that Mr. McLeod did there?"

"No, sir, not that I saw. She said she didn't have the proper change, and said she would pay him some other time."

"Before you reached Miss Keeton's home on this Wednesday evening, when you say she told you her mother had gone to New Orleans, had you observed in the paper any notice of the legs being found here?"

"Yes, sir, I think I had. At Mobile."

"It is your best judgment that you had?"

"Yes, sir."

"Had you any information that Mrs. Keeton had been killed at that time?"

"No, sir."

"When you came back to Laurel and stopped in front of her home in the way you have told the jury, at that time did you have any information that Mrs. Keeton had been killed or injured?"

"No, sir."

"When you sat there that afternoon in the car with Miss Keeton and talked to her, and she was telling your about this young man, Mr. Grace, she was engaged to, do you recall all that was said in that conversation?"

"No, sir, I do not."

"How long did she say it was before the young man was coming down?"

"Said he would be down the next week."

"Did she say anything to you about when they would be married?"

"During the year."

"Mr. Carter, you left Wednesday evening. About what time did you leave Miss Keeton's home?"

"About—right around four o'clock, I think. Four or four-thirty."

"Did you see her Wednesday night?"

"No, sir."

"Why was it you didn't go to see her, Mr. Carter?"

"Well, I didn't want to go to see her at her aunts'."

"She was stopping with her aunts?"

"Yes, sir."

"And you didn't want to go there and be seen with her there? Now Friday morning, what occurred, if anything unusual?"

"Friday? I don't know anything about Friday morning."

"Did anything occur Friday evening?"

"Friday evening I heard they were investigating Miss Keeton in connection with the legs."

"Was that the first information you heard that it was suspicioned that those legs were Mrs. Keeton's legs?"

"Yes, sir."

"Do you remember anything about what time you heard it?"

"No, sir, it was I think late. Somewhere after the middle of the evening."

"Did any officers come to see you Friday evening or Friday night?"

"Yes, sir."

"Who was that officer?"

"Mr. Hamilton and Mr. Jack—another policeman. I have forgotten his name. Mr. Hamilton and Jack Anderson, I believe it was."

"Mr. Carter, did you accompany those gentlemen any place?"

"Yes, sir."

"Tell the jury who you accompanied, who you went to see."

"I accompanied them to this place right here."

"The courthouse?"

"Courthouse, yes, sir."

"Tell the jury who you saw here in this courthouse on that Friday night."

"Well, I don't remember seeing anybody but Jack Anderson and Mr. Hamilton and Jack Deavours."

"Did you talk to Mr. Jack Deavours, the county attorney, that night?"

"Yes, sir."

"After you left the office where Mr. Deavours was, where did you go?"

"I went back home."

"Where did you go from there?"

"Went from there, after he examined me down here, why we went to Mobile."

"What was your purpose in going to Mobile? To investigate what?"

"Investigate where I had been Sunday night and Monday night."

"Who accompanied you to Mobile?"

"Mr. Hamilton and Mr. Anderson."

"Was that investigation made?"

"Yes, sir."

"Now after that investigation was made, what did you do then?"

Carter replied that they took him to his office and left him there.

"Now when you came back here with those officers, were you put in jail, released, or what happened to you?"

"I was released."

"Then where did you go?"

"I went back to Mobile."

"How long were you here before you went to Mobile?"

"I wasn't here but a few minutes."

"What was your reason for going back to Mobile?"

"I was uneasy for fear of Miss Keeton's brother or some of her relatives. I went back to the hotel and registered and then the next morning—"

"How about that night? Who was with you at the hotel, if anybody?"

"Earl McLeod."

"Did you remain in the hotel that night?"

"Yes, sir."

"What hotel?"

"St. Andrew's Hotel."

From his folder Reily took a page cut from the desk registry of St. Andrew's Hotel dated January 26, 1935. It was signed "W. M. Carter." It showed that he had been assigned to room 325. This was placed in evidence.

"Now, Mr. Carter, the next day where did you go?"

"Sunday. The next day was Sunday. I spent the morning with Miss Adams. We drove down to the park. Then we came back, and I delivered her at her house about one o'clock and started in for home."

"Came home?"

"How long after you got home was it before you were arrested and placed in jail in connection with this affair?"

"I was arrested the following Monday morning."

"Were you here in Laurel when you were arrested?"

"Yes, sir."

"Now, Mr. Carter, when you were arrested after you came from Mobile on Sunday, where were you taken, if any place?"

"I was taken to jail in Jackson."

"Did you come back before Miss Ouida Keeton's trial in this court or after her trial?"

"I came back for arraignment, and then I didn't come back until after her trial."

"And remained in the Jackson jail until when?"

"Until I was brought here about thirty days afterwards. I stayed there a total of about thirty-eight days."

"Was that before or after the trial of the case of the state of Mississippi against Miss Ouida Keeton, charged with the killing of her mother?"

"After."

"And then you made bond?"

"Yes, sir."

"Since that time you have been living where?"

"At home. Same place."

Reily next asked him to review the transfer of Mrs. Carter's Ellisville Boulevard property to Ouida.

"What was a fair value of that lot?"

"Well, at that time a fair value was $3,000 to $3,500."

"Who was that land conveyed to?"

"Conveyed to Miss Ouida Keeton."

"What did Miss Keeton pay for that land?"

"$2,750."

"In order that the jury may understand, tell them where that $2,750 went."

"It went into the office. Was paid out on bills and such as that."

"Went into the office of what?"

"W. M. Carter Lumber Company."

"The proceeds of your wife's property went into your business?"

"Yes, sir."

"Now what year was that?"

"I can't exactly say."

"What is your best recollection as to what year it was?"

"Well, I would say 1930, best of my recollection. About 1930 or '31."

"With respect to the Depression of this country, was that before the Depression, during the Depression, or after the Depression?"

"Well that was after the Depression started."

"Now after you so conveyed that property to Miss Keeton, was it rented?"

"Yes, sir."

"What rent did it draw a month?"

"Got down to, I believe, as low as $25 a month."

"When was it you collected that rent?"

"The last rent I collected was, I believe, in December."

"Did you attend to Miss Keeton's property?"

He replied that he collected the rents for her and gave her the money.

"Where did you deliver it to her?"

"Well, if I met her in passing the office or anything like that, I would deliver it to her, and if I didn't, I taken it over to the house."

"Now, Mr. Carter, I want to refer just briefly to the period during which the young lady was employed with you and the time she left you, and the state of your business. Did your business finally fail?"

"Our business practically failed."

"Did you have to compromise with your creditors?"

"No, sir, I didn't have to compromise with creditors. I managed to pay them all up but one or two who offered to release their claims if I wasn't able to pay them. I didn't have to pay them."

"What period was that? That's what I want to get at."

"That was in about 1930 and '31."

"What period did Miss Keeton leave your employ?"

"I think she left in '32."

"Who relieved Miss Keeton in your office?"

"Well, Miss Keeton was working in conjunction with my son's wife, and my son's wife took up the whole duty after she left."

Reily next shifted the interrogation back to Mrs. Keeton's death.

"I will ask you if you were present in Mrs. Keeton's home at a time when she fell against the mantelpiece and hurt her head."

"No, sir."

"I will ask you if you were present at any time in her home when you struck her with a poker."

"No, sir."

"And she fell to the floor, and after she was down you hit her again with the poker?"

"No, sir."

"Did anything like that take place?"

"No, sir."

"I will ask you if you ever placed her body, after she fell, in a wheelbarrow or any other conveyance and carried it to a car."

"No, sir."

"I will ask you if you ever carried any portion of Mrs. Keeton's body anywhere."

"No, sir."

"Did you ever bring part of her body, being her limbs, from the knees up above her waist? Did you ever bring it back in the house?"

"No, sir."

"Did you ever handle it?"

"No, sir."

"Did you ever have anything to do with that body at all?"

"No, sir."

"I will ask you this: What did you have to do, if anything, with the killing of Mrs. Keeton?"

"Nothing whatever."

"Did you know it was going to take place?"

"No, sir."

"Had you ever conspired or discussed it with anybody?"

"No, sir."

"Did you dispose of any part of the body?"

"No, sir."

"Or have anything to do with it?"

"No, sir."

"What knowledge or information did you have as to the death of Mrs. Keeton until the officers questioned you about it?"

"I didn't have any."

"Didn't have any until the body was discovered by the officers?"

"No, sir."

"I will ask you this: On January 19, when you say that you spent the night at your son's house, that is, Saturday night, after you retired there that night, did you ever get up until you arose at five-thirty next morning?"

"No, sir, I got—"

"How was that?"

"I got up to the chamber."

"You say you got up to the chamber?"

"Yes, sir."

"Explain that to the jury now."

"I was just bothered. I was bothered with kidney trouble, and some nights I get up two or three times or more."

"What sort of chamber have you, Mr. Carter?"

"An iron one."

"Iron chamber?"

"Yes, sir."

"Where is it kept?"

"Under the bed."

"In order to get the chamber, what do you do?"

"Pull it out."

"Well, how often? Do you remember whether you got up that particular night or not?"

"Well, I think I got up a couple of times."

"During the night?"

"Yes, sir."

"After you used the chamber, what did you do?"

"Went back to bed."

"Did you ever leave that house after you went to bed?"

"No, sir."

"Until you got up next morning?"

"No, sir."

"After you went to that house from Mrs. Bailey's—from the time you left the Bailey home and went to Mr. Carter's house, your son's house, did you ever leave your son's house until Sunday morning when you went to Mobile?"

"No, sir."

"Was your car parked in front of Mrs. Keeton's residence—your Pontiac—at two o'clock on the night of January 19, 1935?"

"No, sir."

"Where was your car parked at that time?"

"It was parked in the garage at home."

"Did you have it parked in front of Mrs. Keeton's home at any time Saturday night, that Saturday night?"

"No, sir."

"Or Sunday night?"

"No, sir."

"Now your place of business is on what street?"

"Front Street."

"State whether or not the general line of travel is in front of your place of business."

"Yes, sir."

"Your place of business is how many blocks from this courthouse?"

"About two blocks."

"Would you say there is little travel or much travel on that street?"

"Much travel."

"I will ask you if on Saturday night after midnight, of the nineteenth or any time after six o'clock that evening you were on that Front Street talking to two Negroes or anybody else, late at night."

"No, sir."

"Mr. Carter, is there a Negro doctor who has got an office on Front Street?"

"Yes, sir."

"Now tell the jury where that office is."

"Well, his office is upstairs, but I don't know where it is, don't know where it is located. I never have been up there."

"Well, it is on Front Street?"

"It is on Front Street, yes, sir." -

"Has the Negro doctor got an automobile?"

"Yes, sir."

"What color is that automobile?"

"I think it is a dark—oh, a kind of green, the darkest kind of green."

"Mr. Carter, I ask you to inspect these and say what they are please."

Continuing to establish Carter's alibi, he handed him two sheets of an invoice.

"A shipment that went—a shipment of Masonite that went to Citronelle to the Andrews Hardware Company."

"What date was that shipment made, please sir?"

"1st and 24th."

"That was a shipment over the Gulf, Mobile & Northern Railroad from the W. M. Carter Lumber Company, Laurel, Mississippi, to the Andrews Hardware Company, Citronelle, Alabama?"

"Yes, sir."

"State whether or not that is a shipment of the stuff about which you testified this morning, as having been sold by you on this trip to Evergreen."

"Yes, sir."

Reily introduced these papers as Exhibit C.

"Has your life been devoted to that work?"

"Well, that and the lumber interest."

"That's all."

District Attorney Currie stepped forward for the cross-examination. From the start, his manner would be adversarial. He confronted Carter with questions about his Jasper County history. Pressing him for exact locations, he established that Carter's earliest sawmill, at Haney, had been within a few miles of Corinth Church, the old McKinstry home place, and Andrews Mill Pond. The proximity of the sawmill implied that Carter may have had an acquaintance with Daisy Keeton before Ouida become his secretary. Carter claimed this was not so. He testified that he had met Mrs. Keeton only after Ouida came to work for him.

Next, Currie shamed him for his seduction of a young woman the age of his own daughters and for leering at the young Ouida during church.

"And I will ask you if you didn't know Ouida Keeton when she was a young girl and attended the Presbyterian Church over here."

The church was diagonally across the street from the courthouse.

"No, sir."

"And if Daisy Keeton wasn't likewise an attendant of that church."

"I don't remember."

"Don't you know it was there where you first knew the girl?"

"No, sir."

"Wasn't it in the church through the window here and now being seen from the courtroom where you are now being tried that you first knew her?"

"No, sir."

"You say you didn't know? That you have known Daisy Keeton about the same time you have known Ouida?"

"About the same time is my best recollection."

"So you deny having known Mrs. Daisy Keeton, mother of Ouida Keeton, until about the time she went to work for you?"

"Yes, sir."

"And she was a single girl at that time?"

"Yes, sir."

"You knew she was a single girl?"

"Yes, sir."

"You were a man of family?"

"Yes, sir."

"And your home had been blessed with children?"

"Yes, sir."

"And so you hired this girl to work for you?"

"Yes, sir."

"She was a bright, intelligent girl?"

"Yes, sir."

"Capable of and did do good work?"

"Yes, sir."

"And you found no fault with the quality of her work?"

"No, sir."

"And she continued in your employ throughout a long period of years?"

"Yes, sir."

"And during that time her salary rose to $150 a month?"

"Yes, sir."

"Now you began, you told your counsel this morning, that after your co-defendant, this girl, began working for you that you became infatuated with her?"

"Yes, sir."

"That you began paying attention to her?"

"Yes, sir."

"Tell the jury when you began paying attention to Ouida."

"Been seven or eight years ago."

"You began paying attention to her, so much so that you painted the window of your office to keep people from being able to see the manner of your treatment of her in your office, didn't you?"

"No, sir."

"Why, tell the jury then why you painted the window to the office in which the two of you worked. Tell the jury why you painted that window after she went to work for you."

"Painted it to keep out the view from the other side."

"To keep out the view from the other side! So you said you began to have an infatuation for her?"

"Yes, sir."

"She didn't have any sweethearts at that time, did she?"

"None that I know of."

"You were a married man?"

"Yes, sir."

"Your wife resided in Laurel?"

"Yes, sir."

"You were living with your wife and children?"

"Yes, sir."

"You had one just about her age, didn't you?"

"Yes, sir."

"Then you began going to her home, didn't you?"

"Yes, sir."

"Did you have any infatuation for Mrs. Daisy Keeton?"

"No, sir."

"Did you ever have an affair with Mrs. Daisy Keeton?"

"No, sir."

"Then you had no interest in her personally of that character?"

"No, sir."

"Miss Ouida Keeton has all through these years lived in the home with her mother, hasn't she?"

"Yes, sir."

"Now you said this morning in response to your lawyer's question, that these visits by you continued until recently?"

"Yes, sir."

"Something happened to terminate those visits, didn't there?"

"Well, I reckon so."

"You have testified that you were in the home on Friday night, January 18th?"

"Yes, sir."

"You said you carried ice cream over there?"

"Yes, sir."

"Well, you said that after this co-defendant began working for you that there grew up between you an infatuation?"

"Yes, sir."

"Then was it a mutual affair between you?"

"Yes, sir, so I thought."

"That was your understanding?"

"Yes, sir."

"You knew she was a young girl working under you? You had the power to control her hours of work and the work she performed? You had the power to fix her salary? And you had the power to say when she should come and go, so far as her employment was concerned?"

"Well, I judge so."

"You were then how many years of age?"

"I believe I was fifty."

"You were then in the zenith of your physical being, weren't you?"

"Yes, sir."

"You were at the height of your financial and earning capacity as a man, weren't you?"

"I judge so."

"You were recognized as a man of great ability in all respects of life, weren't you?"

"Well, I don't know about that."

"Tell the jury when you first began to go to her home. I want you to fix the date."

"I couldn't fix the date."

"You have records to show that, haven't you?"

"To show when I first went to her home? No, sir, not that I know of."

"You know you began writing her letters, don't you?"

"Yes, sir."

"Why did you begin to write her letters?"

"Well, just to express my feeling."

Carter's voice began to fail, and he spoke in a tone just above a whisper, his hand against his chin. One of the jurors shouted, "Talk out!"

"You don't mind talking out, do you?" Currie remarked in a shaming manner. "Take your hand down. Why did you begin to write her letters?"

"To express my feeling."

"And what feeling was it you were expressing?"

"Feeling of love."

"So then you were back there in the early stages of this girl's employment with you, expressing your feeling of love for her?"

"Yes, sir."

"State whether or not you followed that written expression of love and affection for her with personal visits to her home."

"Yes, sir."

"Now you have said that continued until recently. When was the last time that you wrote her?"

"I don't remember whether I have written Miss Keeton this year or not."

"You did write her while she was in Washington, didn't you?"

"Yes, sir."

"At that time you wrote her letters so they would reach her every Sunday morning, didn't you?"

"Did what?"

"While she was in Washington, you wrote her so that a letter would reach her from you every Sunday morning, didn't you?"

"Well, I don't know that I wrote them so they would reach Miss Keeton every Sunday morning. I wrote regularly."

"Your wife was then living?"

"Yes, sir."

"You said that it continued up to the present, didn't you?"

"Well, until recently. I don't know just when."

"Did your children know about it?"

"Not that I know of."

"Now you are calling her 'Miss Keeton.' Have you always called her 'Miss Keeton,' or are you just doing that today?"

"I have always called her 'Miss Keeton.'"

The district attorney next quizzed him about the floor plan of the Keeton home and made him detail the location of each room and who occupied it. He asked about the situation of the three fireplaces and whether each fed smoke through a single flue. The one in the living room, having been renovated, had only the mantelpiece and was heated by the Heatrola.

"There isn't a fireplace in the living room now," Carter explained. "There was one there a number of years ago, but it has been taken out."

"Who took it out?"

"We had it done."

"Then there were three fireplaces accommodated by one common stack, but the one in the living room was taken out, and that left Miss Ouida Keeton's fireplace and Mrs. Keeton's fireplace accommodated by one smokestack?"

"Yes, sir."

"Now how would one get from Miss Ouida's room into her mother's room?"

"Well, there was a door between the two rooms, a door leading right between the two rooms."

"You were never entertained in the living room, were you?"

"Yes, sir."

"You were generally entertained in Mrs. Keeton's room, weren't you?"

"Yes, sir."

"And Mrs. Keeton was generally, if not always, present?"

"Yes, sir."

"And when you would go there, you very frequently carried letters you had written and, when you were arriving or leaving, dropped them on the sofa in the living room, didn't you?"

"Yes, sir."

"So you actually delivered many messages to Miss Ouida Keeton, the co-defendant, that her mother never knew of?"

"Yes, sir."

"And continued it up until the death of Mrs. Keeton, didn't you?"

"Well, continued it up until recently."

"So you would go there and you would be ushered into Mrs. Keeton's room and the three of you would sit and talk."

"Yes, sir."

"And when you would go, you would deposit a letter which you had written to Miss Keeton on the sofa in the living room?"

"Yes, sir."

"And as I said, you did that when you were both a married man and a widower?"

"Yes, sir."

Currie, tightening his lock on Carter, kept probing into intimacies. Broaching an embarrassing liaison, he asked about a trip to New Orleans. The courtroom crowd was bristling with interest.

"When did you see her there?"

"Well, I reckon over two years ago."

"Where did you see her there?"

"Saw her at the Jung Hotel."

"Now I will ask you if this isn't true: That your co-defendant, Miss Ouida Keeton, and yourself didn't have an understanding whereby she would go down there and get on No. 43 and you would stand on the opposite side of the train, that is the side from which persons boarded the train, and see that she got on the train, and you would follow on the next train, No. 41?"

"No, sir."

"Don't you know that this is true!"

"No, sir."

"Then how did you learn that she was in New Orleans?"

"Well, I had an understanding with her before she left."

"When was the first time that you had an understanding with her that she would go there and you would follow?"

"That was the only time."

"Was it while she was employed by you?"

"I don't believe it was."

"Her mother didn't know it, did she?"

"No, sir."

"Her mother would not have consented to it, would she?"

"I do not know."

"Why were you in New Orleans?"

"I was down there on some business matter and also to meet her."

"Were you ever with her in the city of Mobile?"

"No, sir."

"Don't you know that at the time of the death of Mrs. Daisy Keeton that there was a train ticket on the GM&N Railway, a passenger ticket from Laurel to Mobile? You knew that, didn't you?"

"I had furnished Miss Keeton one quite a number of months ago."

"Why were you furnishing her a ticket to Mobile?"

"I just gave her a ticket because she had worked a few days for me and didn't charge me for it."

"Why didn't you just give her the money rather than furnish her a ticket to go to Mobile?"

"Well, she had been talking about going to Mobile."

"She didn't go to Mobile though on that ticket, did she?"

"No, sir."

"Her mother wasn't willing for her to go to Mobile, was she?"

"I don't know. I never did hear her say."

"Do you own, or have you procured another mail box than the one used by W. M. Carter Lumber Company?"

Carter replied that it was the J. R. Sampey box, No. 74, that he already had referred to and on which he still paid the rent. Joe Sampey, his employee for twenty-five years, had bought a house from Carter's sister and left Carter's employ. Carter told again that this secret mailbox was the one to which Ouida sent him letters from Washington. He stated that Harriet Adams also had addressed her letters to No. 74.

"For how long have you been receiving letters from Miss Adams of Mobile?"

"Something over twenty years, I reckon."

"Is this the woman you went out to see on January 20 of this year? The woman you testified you saw on January 22 and January 26?"

"Yes, sir."

"Now you said that you knew that Miss Ouida was engaged to a Mr. Grace?"

"Yes, sir."

"Who advised you of that?"

"She did."

"You understood that they had contemplated matrimony for some time?"

"Yes, sir."

"You continued to visit with her in her home after you knew that, didn't you?"

"Yes, sir."

"And that you were still infatuated with her?"

"Yes, sir."

"Before her sister Eloise's elopement, you had been business adviser of Mrs. Keeton, hadn't you?"

"Well, I don't know whether I was or not. There were some things she would take up with me, but I was not a regular business adviser."

"She discussed her affairs with you?"

"Yes, sir."

"You knew about her property interests, didn't you?"

Currie was laying the precedent to show Carter as a financially stressed schemer out to take control of Mrs. Keeton's money.

"Yes, sir."

"You had talked about it with her?"

"Well, about nothing except buying this land for the city when they bought this underpass."

"All right, you advised her about that?"

"Yes, sir."

"You played in dual capacity? The city was willing to trust your judgment?"

"Yes, sir."

"Mrs. Keeton was willing to trust your judgment?"

"Yes, sir."

"And when Miss Ouida began working for you, that further united your knowledge and business interest, didn't it?"

"Well, I guess so."

"Miss Ouida talked to you about it, didn't she? You counseled with her about it, didn't you?"

"Yes, sir."

"You knew that Mrs. Keeton had, and Miss Ouida had, a considerable sum of money, didn't you?"

"I knew that when that case was sued out on account of that runaway." He was referring to Eloise's ill-fated elopement. "I knew they transferred some money from here, bonds or something, from here to Mobile, Alabama."

"And that's what you knew."

"No, I didn't know, except from hearsay."

"You and Miss Ouida have discussed that, or had discussed it, since that judgment expired, hadn't you?"

"Yes, sir."

"During the latter part of 1934?"

"Yes, sir."

"And you all discussed Miss Ouida's business affairs, and her mother's?"

"Yes, sir."

Carter had grown quieter in his answers. His voice was so low that it was only a mutter. He seemed to realize that with each response he was helping the prosecution establish a money motive for Mrs. Keeton's death.

"Wasn't your car, the black Pontiac, parked on the left side of Cross Street—that is, on the same side the Keeton house is on—about eleven o'clock on Saturday night, the nineteenth of January?"

"No, sir."

■ ■ ■

Although the defense had constructed a timetable of Carter's stay in Mobile, Currie forced him again to recall it. At the relentless demand of his prosecutor, he again accounted, hour by hour, for his arrival, his squiring Miss Adams around town, his bedtime, his arising on Monday. Carter realized that Currie's intention was not only to make him repeat his testimony but also to frazzle his concentration so that he would appear at a disadvantage to the jury. Carter's voice continued drifting away, and he slipped into errors. Currie, twenty years younger than he, pounced each time Carter faltered.

He asked him to recount again his trips to the bathroom on the night of the murder. Carter began to stammer. The room seemed to go round and round.

"But you do remember distinctly being up twice and using the bedroom chamber twice during the night of the *nineteenth*?"

Carter spoke objectively of his troubled sleep and of his rising a couple of times to use the chamber pot. Then Currie pressed him to state the number of his bathroom visits on January 18 and on January 20. Here was a contradiction. If Carter could recall the number of times he urinated during the night of January 19, why wasn't he able to recall his use of the chamber pot on the other nights? Currie asked the court, furthermore, to take note that Carter had requested no restroom breaks during the four hours of his giving testimony. He implied that the "bladder trouble" was less acute than had been professed.

Carter was so muddled from the hammering questions that his voice grew weaker. He was aware that his answers were becoming vague. When Currie began badgering him to recall minutiae of events at McRae's filling station, about the frequency of his going there and about his failure to write the date on one of the invoices that would prove he had taken a sales order while in Evergreen or on the road home, he tried to give pertinent answers, but Currie kept casting doubt on his alibi. He made him tell again about stopping by to see Ouida Keeton on Wednesday and asked him why he made her get into the car.

"Well, she was just standing by the side of the car and it was cool. Cold weather." He began to meander. "She was standing by the car, stooped down, and I just moved out from under the wheel and said 'Get in and sit down.' I don't know of anything special we talked about. She said her friend was coming the next week, her boyfriend, and I said 'Who?' and she said 'Mr. Gray,' no 'Mr. Grace,' and she said 'I want you to meet him when he comes,' and I said 'I don't know whether I care anything about bothering you,' and she says 'I will phone you when he comes. Come on over and meet him.' and I said 'All right, if you want me to.'"

"You told your lawyer that when you were there talking to that girl in that automobile that you were in love with her still. Is that true?"

"Yes, sir."

"And that girl appeared very nervous, didn't she?"

"No, sir, not that I noticed."

"And didn't you know then and there told her that she had acted very foolish in the matter of the disposition of those limbs?"

"No, sir."

"Didn't you then and there tell her the story of how to undertake to conceal the crime for which you are both now charged?"

"No, sir."

"Now have you ever brought an invitation from Miss Adams to the co-defendant to visit her before this time?"

"Yes, sir, I think I have."

"When?"

"During the last year."

"And she didn't go, did she?"

"No, sir."

"Now, Mr. Carter, you were asked the question this morning, by your lawyer, whether or not you had ever had any intimate relationship with Ouida Keeton. What was your answer?"

"I said no."

"Then tell the jury why you secretly arranged for her to meet you in New Orleans."

"Well, just to be with her."

"Didn't you know back in the beginning of this girl's employment with you that you are the first man that ever had sexual relations with that girl and that you are the only man?"

"No, sir, I don't know that."

"Don't you know that her virtue, her chastity, was taken by you as her employer?"

"No, sir."

"Don't you know that you took that girl as an orphan seventeen years of age and that today her virtue is chargeable to your account?"

"No, sir."

"And that you had her in the city of New Orleans for the sole purpose of satisfying your lust for her. Don't you know that is the truth, Mr. Carter?"

"No, sir."

"Don't you know that as a girl you went into her mother's home and there betrayed the confidence of Daisy Keeton by taking the virtue of her orphan daughter? Don't you know that is true?"

"No, sir, I don't know it."

"Mr. Carter, don't you know that the reason for the death of Daisy Keeton today is because of this clandestine and unholy love affair that you caused to be generated between you and your co-defendant?"

"No, sir.

"And that Daisy Keeton, a good woman, fought to protect the virtue of her orphan girl, back yonder years ago, when you were in the zenith of your manhood, physically and financially, and when you were a power of this city and this county? That Daisy Keeton, a widow woman, then and there registered with you her objection to your attentions to her daughter and begged you not to spoil her?"

"I never did have any words with her about that. There never was any mention along that line by Mrs. Keeton," Carter sputtered.

"But you were delivering letters secretly to her daughter?"

"Yes, sir."

"And at a time when you were trying to rear and were rearing children in Laurel?"

"Yes, sir," he mumbled, mortified.

"Mr. Carter, can you speak out louder?"

"Yes, sir."

"I will ask you to speak out so the jury can hear you. Tell the jury if Daisy Keeton, the mother of Ouida Keeton, hadn't on many occasions begged you and reminded you that you were a married man and a man of family and begged you to leave her daughter alone?"

"No, sir, there never has been anything said about it."

"Don't you know that Ouida Keeton then and there undertook to lay aside the life of shame that the two of you had lived together secretly in Laurel and that she then and there made known to you that she wanted to have a clean and wholesome life hereafter?"

"No, sir, that wasn't mentioned to me."

"And don't you know that was the culmination of that unholy life you and your co-defendant had been living? That through your influence, on January 19, you went down here to the filling station and there bought gasoline as a pretext that you might come in vital, personal contact with this girl and that the two of you acted as conspirators? And don't you know you then and there agreed that was the night Daisy Keeton must pay with her life for the obstruction she was putting in your way?"

"No, sir, there was no talk, no agreement."

"Don't you know that night in Laurel, if indeed you did go by and tell the different members of your family good-bye, your sisters and your brothers and your daughters and your sons-in-law and your grandchildren, if you went by and told them all good-bye on that eventful Saturday night, don't you know it was because your conscience was knocking at your door and lashing you because you realized that Daisy Keeton would soon be in eternity?"

"No, sir."

After this barrage, Carter appeared so weak that he could hardly speak. For the redirect examination Reily came forward, hoping to repair possible damage.

"Mr. Carter, at your place of business have you an upstairs there?"

Reily was alluding to insinuations the prosecution made about the secret deeds behind the painted window.

"No, sir, nothing but just a loft and just trash and such as that in there."

"Is there a stairway leading up there?"

"No, sir, no way to get up there except to get on a ladder."

"Did you have another place of business before you moved to Front Street?"

Carter replied that it was located on Magnolia Street and that twelve or fifteen rooms were in the building.

"Were those rooms occupied?"

"Part of them were, and part of them weren't."

"Did any improper relations take place between you and Miss Keeton in any of those rooms?"

"No, sir."

"He asked you about your coming home from Mobile and sitting in front of the house for an hour. Why didn't you go in the house?"

"Well, I knocked at the door, and there wasn't anybody in the house, and she came on out from the alley, as I told you."

"When she came out and told you her mother was gone, state whether or not you then knew there was no one in the house."

"Yes, sir."

He asked him to clarify the matter of his purchasing a pair of shoes for his daughter while in Mobile.

"Just why did you get a receipt for the shoes when you didn't get a receipt for anything else while you were on that trip?"

He explained again that he thought he might need to request a refund and return the shoes if they were the wrong size.

"When Miss Ouida was first arrested and first taken by the officers, did you then know she was accused of her mother's murder?"

"No, sir."

"Did you have any reason or know why she would be accused of her mother's murder?"

"No, sir, I never thought of such a thing."

"Did you know her mother was dead at that time?"

"No, sir."

"When you had talked to her, she had told you she had gone to New Orleans?"

"Yes, sir."

"When you stopped there on Wednesday and talked with her, was the question of the disposal of the limbs mentioned at all?"

"No, sir."

"Well, now, Mr. Carter, you were asked about when you were leaving here you were telling people you were going to Evergreen. Tell the jury why you didn't want them to know you were going to Mobile."

"Well, I just didn't want them to know."

"Did your daughters know that while their mother was living you were corresponding with this lady in Mobile?"

"Not that I know of."

"When you saw Miss Keeton at the Jung Hotel in New Orleans, was anybody else present when you saw her?"

"She, Miss Adams, and myself."

"You were together in the hotel in New Orleans?"

"Yes, sir."

"Who was in the room where you were when you saw and were with her?"

"All three of us."

"Tell the jury whether or not you were guilty of having sexual intercourse with that woman, Miss Keeton, in New Orleans."

"No, sir."

"Counsel has asked you about the money of Mrs. Keeton. I want you to tell the jury if you ever received or ever attempted to receive any of the money, bonds, or property of Mrs. Daisy Keeton."

"No, sir."

"Counsel has asked you if Mrs. Daisy Keeton wasn't complaining to you throughout the years and entreating you with regard to her daughter. Tell the jury if Mrs. Keeton ever mentioned at any time, any where, any objection to any conduct of yours, real or imaginary, towards her daughter."

"No, sir, she never did say a word to me."

When Carter stepped down, he was a broken man.

Closing arguments were impassioned in rhetoric and adroit in manipulating the facts. The defense put the murder entirely on Ouida. Demonstrating that she was in control of the family money as well as her own savings, Reily played her up as a woman whose mind was out of balance.

"Naturally she put it on somebody else. She couldn't admit it to her own family. It was easy to lay it off on this old man who had been hanging around there." Reily clinched the positive image of his client as a practical and savvy fellow. "Do you think Mr. Carter would have gone to Mobile and left part of the body to be disposed of? Why he's a hardheaded businessman! You haven't got the truth about this killing. The chances are if you did get the truth about it, you would hang somebody else."

District Attorney Currie had the last word. He pronounced the butcher slaying to be the crime of the century and Ouida to be a girl who had sacrificed "the jewel of her womanhood" to her lecherous boss. He pictured Carter frolicking in adultery while his good wife was at home gathering their children at her knee for evening prayers. Blaming Carter for involving Ouida in the crime, Currie heightened thoughts of murderous conspiracy and cover-up. "There is no escape for this man," he declared, facing the twelve men in the jury box. "It is a question of whether you are men of courage, if you have the backbone to convict him." As Currie spoke, the eldest juror, W. H. Ponder, sixty-eight, openly wept.

The court's instructions stated that if Carter should be found guilty, the jury was required to consider one of three verdicts: guilty as charged, with the sentence of death; guilty, with life imprisonment; guilty, with the jury not able to agree on the sentence, thereby giving the court the duty of imposing it.

At half past noon on Wednesday, June 5, the jury retired, and after twenty hours of deliberation and three ballots, Carter's fate was decided. Their bailiff rang Judge Pack and the prosecuting attorneys at 7:00 a.m. on Thursday, and by 8:00 they, along with Carter, his lawyers, and his family, were in the courtroom. Anxiously, all watched the jurymen taking their seats again. On this sultry morning the courthouse windows left open to admit any breeze admitted instead the racket of untuned jalopies passing by. Sitting high at his bench and suffering in his hot robe, Judge Pack had calmed the eager spectators ready to hear the outcome of Carter's turbulent ordeal. At the rapping of the gavel, they stifled chitchat and a few self-conscious coughs. With perspiration trickling down his spine, Carter braced himself and watched the foreman hand a folded paper to the bailiff. The Carter children held their breaths as Judge Pack nodded, and the paper was transferred officiously to the hand of the court clerk.

In a flat tone he read the verdict.

We the jury find the defendant guilty as charged and fix his punishment as life imprisonment.

It was not to be believed! Carter was badly shaken, although the city newspaper would describe him as "flushed but otherwise apparently unmoved." Then came a long moment of silence, as though the room were allowing roiled waters to become clear again. In this instant the globe seemed to pause and hold in abeyance every annoying triviality attempting to intrude. But the moment passed, the earth reawakened. Ouida Keeton was not present to exult but at home waiting to learn the verdict.

Carter's cheeks burned, and even while maintaining a gentlemanly demeanor, he seemed to crack. He could not help wondering that this conviction, rather than retribution for murder, was punishment for his breaking the seventh Commandment. His family lowered their heads.

The *Leader-Call* described the scene: "Carter, seated with his counsel and members of his family, maintained the cool, calm attitude he had exhibited throughout the trial, except for the first few days when he was visibly nervous."

Lawyer Reily, fuming in defeat, protested in Carter's ear.

"I'll bet my old striped dog Trouble that we reverse this case!"

But an hour later Carter had every reason to be downcast. He was back behind bars, haunted by what had happened to him. Few sounds could be more dispiriting for a newly convicted prisoner than the clang of the iron door. Carter was horribly alone. He was incarcerated, not in Hinds County this time, but in the Jones County jail. In the sudden gloom of the lockup, like many other prisoners rightfully or wrongfully convicted, he sat in the valley of the shadow, pondering the unreasonableness of the verdict. Sickened by the thought of being bound to the penitentiary for life, he not only faced the cold reality of being in jail but also agonized in rehashing every

testimony to discover what had gone wrong in the defense. He was no different from thousands of others thrust suddenly into their penitential cells
and reliving their trials. His mind would not be still. Courtroom scenes
remained continuously in play. His sentence, haunting and awful, reverberated in his head.

Judge Pack had ordered him to rise and then asked if he had any words to
say.

"Nothing."

It was the sound of a fractured voice reduced to a bleat.

The judge looked into the face of a colleague with whom he had served on
the boards of the bank and the building-and-loan association, an old friend
with whom he had enjoyed jovial affiliation. Following the dictates of the
jury, he spoke.

"I have no choice but to sentence you to life imprisonment."

Watkins, flustered but professional, rose immediately to announce that
he would enter a motion for a retrial. Should it be denied, he said an appeal
would be made to the supreme court. His protest sounded procedural and
hopeless.

Carter was impatient for this first day and night to pass. The tumult of
prosecution and the degradation of conviction had swept his soul clean of
lustful cravings. The once-dear images of both Miss Adams and Miss Keeton went away, as though their fading photographs had vanished from two
golden picture frames.

Already the June weather was hot. Prisoners were meant to suffer. Without electric fans, the cells would become as stifling as ovens. The concrete
walls and iron bars would retain heat throughout the coming summer. The
one high, unscreened window above his bed gave limited ventilation. In the
dim corner behind the stinking toilet he detected ominous movement. Mosquitoes floated upward in search of blood. Throughout tormenting nights
of insomnia he would be hearing their menacing whines and feeling their
smarting stings.

Since he objected to the smell of the toilet at the other end of the bed, he
lay down for a while with the top of his head nearly touching the bars. He
wished to stop himself from thinking. He needed to lose himself, to escape
from the turmoil in his tired brain. Although he had done no physical work
in a long time, he was dog-tired. He wished for a cool breeze, a sound nap,
and serenity. But recollection of the courtroom voices would not leave him.
Images from his trial marched through his brain like a thundering army.

He recalled being so eager to see Miss Adams on that Sunday after Mrs. Keeton was killed that he had sneaked immediately to Mobile. Evergreen and the duty of checking on the oil drilling near his wife's land were shoved to the background while he satisfied his yearnings for Miss Adams. After the three-hour drive from Laurel, he had stopped first at the St. Andrew's Hotel to freshen up. In his haste to see her, he delayed signing the registry, saying he would do so when he returned late that night. He rushed to her house, put her in the Pontiac, and they rambled around Mobile for the rest of the day and evening. On Monday he left her, promising to return after checking on the family matter in Evergreen. On the outskirts of Mobile he picked up a hitchhiker and gave him a ride as far as Evergreen and then stopped there at the Newtons' as the overnight guest. His son phoned from Laurel to say that business was especially slow because of the bad weather. He told his father to take care on the highway and not hasten home. Carter reported on oil drilling in Conecuh County and gave him the disappointing news that Mrs. Carter's property was too remote from the drill site for the Carters to expect a strike. After short visits with in-laws, Carter said farewell and hurried back to Miss Adams for another night of romance. After a good-bye kiss, he drove home through Citronelle and stopped there to take an order for a load of Masonite. Then, with yearnings for Ouida, he drove on to Laurel and knocked at her door.

Why didn't the jurors believe him? Couldn't they believe his little grand-daughter? In closing arguments Reily had played her up as "that little curly-haired girl on the witness stand. Do you think she lied?"

Carter had been obliged to divulge his long-held secrets, and the love affair with Miss Adams had substantiated his alibi. Was it credible? How could he be convicted when the evidence told that he was snug in his bed on Saturday night and far from Laurel on Sunday? To save his life he had sacrificed his name and his reputation.

After hearing the clang of the iron door, Carter had awakened to the repugnance of his condition. Emotionally wrenched, he sat upright next to the reeking toilet, reflecting over every jarring word of the testimonies. He had to bend forward because the upper bunk was so low. He was too confused to notice that a man was lying on the pad above him. The sordid conditions mocked the few weeks he'd spent sleeping comfortably at home, eating meals at his own table, and planning his defense. While awaiting his own day in court, he had followed timely reports of Ouida's trial, and, looking for pitfalls to sidestep, he painstakingly had read news coverage in the *Leader-Call* and the *Clarion-Ledger*.

Since he was under conviction of murder, Mississippi statute allowed bail only if imprisonment threatened the felon's health. Carter kept spinning thoughts of where his defense strategies perhaps could have been strengthened if given a slightly different turn. There was absolutely nothing to do except to sit and think. As the afternoon passed, a buzzing greenfly kept freely circling the cell and alighting on the stained rim of the toilet.

Carter was trembling. Beyond the dirty smears on the wall and the rectangle of sky in the small window, his eyes settled on a point far away. His thoughts continued to levitate over the many testimonies, assessing which were most damaging. He had lost count of so many witnesses coming and going, ranging from virtual nobodies to major figures in the case. He kept questioning whether it was Ouida Keeton's or his own testimony that most swayed the jury to convict. She had been decidedly chic and seductive. Except for one or two slips, her speech had been as articulate as a schoolteacher's. Exposing no intimate feelings she once may have held for him, she had denounced him as a friend who had betrayed her. The broken doll had come back to life, but in the glare of this distress, she lost her sexual magic. Rehearsed and well tuned by the prosecution, her tricky performance had been painful both for her and for Carter.

After replaying this scene, he realized how everything had gone wrong. His family was under stress. His health was breaking. His money was going down the drain. Not only had he been convicted, but also, with the appeal, this torment would be protracted even further. At best, the appeals court would not bring a decision for a full year. Without bail, he could suffer for at least twelve months in the Jones County jail, and if the appeal should fail, he would have to work out the life sentence on the Parchman prison farm. As he wondered about how many years he must serve before being considered for parole, the shadow of despair fell upon him. Never had he passed through a darker hour. His suffering soul was so full that if he had not been firm and disciplined, the mist in the corners of his eyes might have flooded down the crevices of his cheeks.

He had sat at the defense table stupefied, the verdict still ringing in the courtroom. Everything that followed seemed to be a nightmare: the hastily whispered advice and consolation from his attorneys as Sheriff Jordan's men surrounded him and clamped him in handcuffs, his horrified family and friends looking on.

Of course, his attorneys were taking his case through the usual procedure, a motion for retrial. This was sure to be denied unless they could perform a miracle. Watkins, Reily, Collins, and Ross would be drafting the motion and the appeal. Like almost every other convicted man, Carter put his faith in hope and rationalizing. Since Sheriff Jordan had released Ouida on bond, Carter, a man with diagnosed ailments, thought he likewise would be at liberty if he could raise the bail money, but he dreaded a lengthy wait.

He couldn't recall eating any lunch. At first dark when the guard asked him if he was ready for supper, he said he wasn't hungry. A plate of food and a cup of coffee were left anyway. As flies came to settle upon the beans and the biscuit, Carter, indifferent to eating, stretched out on the lumpy bed. Its filthy ticking was an offense he must disregard and get used to. His feet touched the side of the toilet when he lay down again. A prickling of sweat spread over his forehead and upper lip. He needed air. The high window he faced, with its closely spaced bars, exposed the faint glow of evening. Over at the bank he imagined how each slow minute was passing as the pointed hand on the big clock gave a jerk and approached the next black numeral. He remembered how it seemed not to move if you watched it. The twilight was short. The hour hung in transition, telling him that he was about to spend his strange first night as a convict. He was certain, although it was suppertime, that his children would have no appetite for food. They would be grieving. Like him, his daughters would be lying down. They would be weeping and wondering how Papa was bearing up under his ordeal and persecution.

Carter watched the darkness fill the space that was his window. Flitting moths were batting against the hot lightbulb hanging outside his cell. He was so absorbed in his reverie of pain that, until he saw smoke from a cigarette, he did not notice the fellow prisoner the guard addressed as Welborn lying on the upper bunk. Getting acquainted would come at another time.

Carter's busy brain would not slow down. A sleeping powder he had taken gave no relief. The hours dragged on. Time was hanging, without breath or motion. Welborn was snoring. If the bank clock continued chiming, it could not be heard here. At dark the flies had gone to sleep, but mosquitoes began to strike. The cell was heavy with the odor of the pot. Down the way, men were cracking jokes.

Carter recalled the warmish Saturday evening of Daisy Keeton's murder, just before the sudden cold spell. At six o'clock, closing time, he had locked the door of his business and headed around his building toward his car, the dark Pontiac coupe. Above the main counter a feeble light was left burning as a safeguard. Newton and Carolyn had gone home a few minutes earlier.

Up and down Front Street almost all commerce had shut down. In the winter evening the wide glass panes on Marcus Furniture Store, Freeman's Hardware, and the New York Bargain Shoe Store were reflecting tired, gray shadows. Over the gritty sidewalk a rising gust stirred the candy wrappers, newspapers, rattling bottle caps, cigarette stubs, and spilled picture-show popcorn. Across from Carter's business the drugstore and the dentist's office operated by blacks already were shut tight, and the earlier Saturday throngs of dressed-up blacks milling the littered pavements but buying little besides ice-cream cones and penny drink had migrated homeward or to juke joints in the quarters. Carter was one of the last merchants to lock up and head home. Since the national economy was in depression and the construction business in hard times, Carter, although still well-to-do, was feeling the pinch. He knew how some joked that he would keep his door open for as long as he could draw in one more customer's dime. The lights had been turned on over at the Good Eats Place, and at the end of Front just north of Carter's firm, Winn's Garage was still in operation, though dark was settling fast. He could hear tire irons dropped on oily concrete.

■ ■ ■

During the early summer of 1935 W. M. Carter was, without question, the most socially prominent prisoner in the Jones County jail, and at least the jail was close to home and not in Jackson. He sensed his fellow inmates eyeing him with envy as his daughters delivered home-cooked meals to him each day.

He overheard one prisoner offering the notion that he, like one of the boys, was adjusting to the jailhouse routine, but Carter knew this was not so. He was just not one to whine or protest. Welborn claimed Carter was "very well, so far as I know" but "not as fleshy as he was when he went in." He was locked up with two talkative, down-and-out Jones Countians who had followed his case and did not hesitate to discuss it. One, a familiar face to the court, was R. C. Buckalew, back behind bars, this time for gambling. He had been the prosecution's opinionated witness who, while on furlough from the prison farm, claimed to have passed Carter outside his place of business a few hours after Daisy Keeton was murdered. Bowled over by such a report, Carter had protested to his attorneys that the testimony was corrupt and false, a complete fabrication. Buckalew's manner had impressed some in the courtroom as a clash of haves with have-nots, with Buckalew eager to topple a bigwig. For unknown reasons the governor had granted Buckalew a mysterious pardon for the earlier crime of whiskey possession, but here he was, again in the lockup. Maybe Carter was having the last laugh.

The other was Welborn. When they finally broke their silence and got to talking, Welborn volunteered a piece of valuable inside information. Like Buckalew, he enjoyed sharing scuttlebutt about the Legs Murder case. From his window Welborn had watched the Carter daughters coming to leave their father's meals with the jailer. He was serving time for bastardy and for refusing to support the child said to be his. He told of being acquainted with A. W. Pryor, one of Carter's jurors, and claimed that before the trial Pryor had expressed a bias that should have disqualified him from serving. In an encounter outside Fine Bros.-Matison Company, Welborn and Pryor had exchanged opinions about the Legs Murder case and Carter's indictment. He quoted what he claimed Pryor had said: "I don't know so much about you,

Welborn, but Mr. Carter's guilty of that. Mr. Carter, you know, ain't nothing but a sonofabitch."

A contaminated jury? Here was a ray of hope. Carter quickly notified his attorneys of this new information. Already they had found four witnesses who would testify that W. H. Ponder, Carter's weeping juror, also had expressed pretrial bias. Watkins, Reily, Collins, and Ross petitioned the court for a hearing to argue that errors were made by seating jurors with fixed opinions.

These two alleged pieces of mischief were added to the other evidence Carter's counsel and his children were accumulating. Earlier they had located a "strange young white boy" Carter had picked up on Cochran Bridge near Mobile but had failed to mention when giving his attorneys a timetable of his activities in Alabama. This hitchhiker was Roy Newton. Though the name was the same, he was not kin to the late Nettie Carter's people, the Newtons of Evergreen. He had been brought to the Jones County jail to identify Carter and to confirm the alibi. He signed a deposition affirming that Carter was more than a hundred miles away from Laurel on Monday, January 21.

These late developments stirred optimism. Along with the motion for a new trial, Carter's attorneys would plead for the court to permit him to post bail for reasons of declining health. Being locked behind bars in Jones County was not the hellish brutality he had feared, but despite fellow prisoners' claim that Carter was fitting in as one of the boys, Carter was not well. Jailhouse conditions were exacerbating all his ailments. He sensed a piercing ache in his kidneys, his stinging bladder always seemed painfully full, and he was getting no relief through restful sleep. Already it had been established that even in the comfort of his own home he had difficulty sleeping. Now his eyelids were red and sore, and his flesh was inflamed by mosquito stings and by greenfly bites near his face. His attorneys petitioned for a medical examination, and the county complied by summoning Dr. J. S. Gatlin, Carter's own physician. Dr. Gatlin's deposition reported Carter's exacerbated kidney and bladder ailments.

On June 29, after passing twenty-three onerous nights in the hot, mosquito-infested cell, Carter was taken back to the courtroom for a hearing. Pallid and frail, he looked like some gaunt, hollow-eyed dog after a whipping. Even though attired in his good summer suit, he knew he was not dapper or distinguished. He attempted a lively gait to impress the few of his friends in the courtroom, but after climbing the marble staircase to the second floor, he was so fatigued that he doddered to the chair assigned him at his attorneys' table.

At the bench, Judge Pack was studying the medical declarations. First was the plea of Carter's four attorneys. It claimed that his health was deteriorating and that his cell was infested and unsanitary. "A toilet which will not flush is situated at the end of his bed. It is almost impossible for him to take or retain food, and such surroundings, combined with his present physical condition, would greatly impair his health."

This writ was supported by the notarized deposition of the highly respected Dr. Gatlin. In the same stack of papers was a plea from Carter's family. Despite his murder conviction they were unified in his staunch support. It was signed by Walter Bailey, Carter's son-in-law, who with his wife and her sister had visited their father at the jail. Their horror was no less extreme than Eloise Keeton's and Miss Laurendine's when they had visited Ouida in her deplorable confinement.

Carter wasn't asking to be mollycoddled. He wanted a reprieve only to regain his stamina. He had given his son-in-law's petition a preliminary examination to be assured it did not exaggerate. Whiners, he had observed as a prisoner, sometimes were subjected to subtle punishments for pointing fingers at jailhouse offenses. So he had taken a pen and added a postscript, advising any authority studying the petition that he was not making the complaint himself and that he had not suffered any abuse during incarceration.

Judge Pack listened to the testimonies. Over his spectacles he regarded his former colleague, indeed a sick man likely to be harmed by extended imprisonment

On the desk lay the attorneys' motion for the court to quash the conviction and grant Carter a new trial. Watkins, Reily, Collins, and Ross were basing their plea on fifteen grounds, mainly on a claim of court errors, prejudiced jurors, the exclusion of qualified jurors, and "willful, felonious, and corrupt testimony" by the state's witnesses.

After further pondering, the judge again looked down at his old friend now broken and shamed by conviction and by nearly a month behind bars. Keeping his feelings separate from judicial reserve, he announced his decision. Carter heard him deny a retrial, but bail was granted, for reasons of health. As his family emitted pleased sighs of relief, Carter himself remained stoic and silent. Judge Pack set bond at $25,000. Although Carter's attorneys pleaded that the figure be reduced by $10,000, the court remained firm. If

IN THE CIRCUIT COURT OF THE SECOND JUDICIAL DISTRICT OF JONES COUNTY,
MISSISSIPPI.

STATE OF MISSISSIPPI

      V.   NO._____

W. M. CARTER.

      Comes W. M. Carter, defendant in the above-entitled cause, and
shows unto the Court that at the last preceding term of the Circuit
Court of Jones County, Mississippi, he was convicted of murder and
sentenced for life in the state penitentiary; that the said defendant
filed a motion for new trial, which was, upon June 29th, 1935, overruled by the Circuit Judge; that he desires to appeal said case to the
Supreme Court of the State of Mississippi, and for such purpose, files
this petition. The said defendant states that he is without means of
any kind, and is therefore unable to give bond for costs to accrue in
said cause or to make a deposit in cash to cover the costs of said
appeal. Wherefore, he prays an appeal with supersedeas, in accordance
with the statutes of the State of Mississippi.

Facsimile of W. M. Carter's petition for an appeal of his conviction. (Crime file,
Jones County courthouse)

their client could raise $15,000, he could raise $25,000. Being short of money
and having massive legal expenses, Carter declared that he could not meet
it. His son, sons-in-law, brothers, a cousin, and friends came to his rescue
with a collection of contributions. To the echoing congratulations of well-
wishers, his family gathered around him and led him to the staircase.

Since the opinion even of supportive friends was shaded by doubt, Carter's happiness was clouded. In a small town, once adultery and a claim of
treachery have been exposed, it is nearly impossible to make them vanish or
to restore the accused to grace and former standing. Though some avoided
looking him in the eye, they were glad Carter's children were getting a spell
of ease.

In Laurel, Mississippi, a father, deacon, and business leader who carried
the scarlet A on his breast and the heavy weight of felony on his back was
made to sense irreparable change in relationships with his fellow townspeople

and with his children. Even the momentary rapture of homecoming was impaired. Knowing that sexual misconduct garners dark thoughts in righteous minds and that murder and mutilation dwell forever beyond the pale of Christian ways, Carter sank into depression.

As he lay suffering on his familiar bed at home, all thoughts about his plight were painful. But the spirit of Mary Lou, dead for twenty-five years, came forward to sit beside his bed as he had sat beside hers during the long nights of her lingering sickness. He remembered her last bedridden years, when she required home care by a young nurse from Mobile. In 1906, when this resourceful young woman arrived to occupy a bedroom in their house, the fetching creature in white inspired hovering notions and naughty overtures. At first, Carter had joked and bantered with her and occasionally took an employer's liberties of giving her an affectionate pinch or pat. Kissing came next. During four years of Mary Lou's last illness, Nurse Adams was present to gratify his excited backstairs urges. Rationalizing that his turpitude was harmless indiscretion, he yielded to the sweet craving. He was, he mused, no different from many other men. Mary Lou was too sick to notice the division of his attentions. With her death he thought he could bear no greater grief. To relieve it, he installed a lavish tombstone on her grave.

Seeking escape from these morbid reflections and the dreariness of his room, he rose and planned a trip to the office. The little Pontiac was awaiting him in the garage, but its covering of dust was like the black cloud haunting him. When he appeared in public, he was troubled by humiliating jokes circulating around town, that Old Man Carter, Ouida's dashing beau, was suffering from prostatitis, insomnia, incipient diabetes, bladder pain, and pus on his kidneys. When he was released, the newspaper had broadcast the complete list of his medical ailments. So everyone knew. Canceling the outing, he returned to his bed downhearted and sank again into depressing meditation. He saw the world's ludicrous picture of him: a foolish man of some years panting for a young woman of fatal charms.

He confronted not only the disintegration of his reputation but also the death of his ardor for Miss Adams. For so many years she had been his dark secret, but now she no longer mattered. There would be no more trips to Mobile, no more hand-holding strolls past Admiral Semmes's statue on Government Street. Whenever Miss Adams's image flickered across his mind, it was revolting. She had closed the door on their long romance. Although her brother and sister had come to the courtroom to give testimonies in support of his alibi, she had refused to participate in the trial. As though to protect her good name with the school system, she had betrayed him and shied away from contamination.

And so both of his secret loves faded from his heart.

Though bail bond gave only temporary reprieve and a dread of what might come, he was thankful for his own clean bed and for the privacy of his bedroom. He realized that his association with his children was irreparably changed. Someone else now held the reins. All together, they continued to live in the close community of Laurel's richest avenues. Like some dying man in a hospice, Carter received his son and daughters, his brothers and sisters, and his grandchildren as they would come and go, delivering little mementoes and expressing concern about his illness. They appeared tolerant of his new presence, his changed status. Though the unquestioned respect he had commanded was not entirely gone, it was different. They were like adults with an errant child deserving of correction and quiet isolation. For them, the horror of the murder and the trial refused to die away. Whether guilty or not, their father and brother's appalling involvement with the Keeton woman was the source of this reverberating shame. Theirs was a family in distress, a family that through the benevolence of time could be healed. During long hours that Carter lay alone in his room trying to make sense of the turmoil, he heard the footsteps along the hallway. He heard the closing of doors, the cranking of the automobiles, the running of water through the plumbing, the happy voices of the grandchildren. But then he heard the youngsters restricting their own noisiness and falling into unnatural and deferential quietness so that he might rest. J. B. Price, as silent and respectful as a tolerated mouse, continued to rise at 3:30 and go on his rounds of delivering the morning newspaper. Carter kept out of the way until an appropriate moment to emerge from his room. He suffered his insomnia and incontinence alone and waited for the family to rise, establish the household order, and then summon him. When called to breakfast, he nibbled at his toast and drank his hot coffee. The unnatural absence of childlike boisterousness in the grandchildren gave him a troubling unease.

With his problems came a new vision, a perception that the motion of life cannot be stalled or delayed. Although one whining individual might hope time will stop ticking, the world continues to turn. Births and deaths occur on timetables a suffering old man does not set. As Carter tried to move to the unfamiliar new rhythms, his step was slower, his burden heavier, his physical system strangely out of kilter.

The sum of these changes brought him vivid awareness of sin and his own mortality. For more than three-score years he had lived in the harmony of familial love and fellowship. Now uncertainty plagued him. He seemed alone in a vast haunted cavern, pursued by devils. For how long, he wondered, would he remain alive in these changed conditions? Like Job, would he be restored? Or would he pass a few months in the lenient household and then be thrust back into prison to die? What was the plan?

And so, in a plea for religious blessing and public understanding, he drifted to God and cast his burden upon the Lord. On Easter Sunday of 1936 the humbled penitent made a profession of faith at First Presbyterian Church. Then with a heavy heart he waited almost a full year for the appeals court's judgment.

■ ■ ■

On March 6, 1936, while Ouida was awaiting the decision on her appeal, the high court released its decision on Carter's. In the house on Cross Street the announcement was shocking:

"We reverse and remand this case for a new trial," the decree stated, "upon the ground that the testimony of Ouida Keeton, upon whose evidence alone the conviction was had, is so unreasonable as to be utterly unworthy of belief."

Ouida's statements "out of court under oath and otherwise" were deemed to be contradictory. The court further declared that Carter, "by apparently credible witnesses, showed a complete alibi covering the whole period during which, under the testimony of Miss Keeton, the homicide took place and the body disposed of." The judges pronounced that the Jones County court had "erred in giving the conspiracy instructions for the state. There was no substantial evidence tending to show a conspiracy between appellant and Miss Keeton to take the life of Mrs. Keeton. The statements Miss Keeton made out of court tending to show a conspiracy were not competent for this purpose; they were purely hearsay evidence and only competent to discredit her as a witness. . . . Reversed and remanded."

Since Carter was not clean as a whistle, Jones County would try him a second time. For Ouida, the high court decision was a hard slap in the face. She was discredited. For Carter, it was a mixed blessing: temporarily he was officially not guilty, but he must be dragged again through the mire of humiliating exposure and suffer the additional expense of litigation.

The Keetons were hurting too. The confused sister at the center of their lives seemed to be grieving only for herself, not for them and their mother. She kept shaking her head and crying that her persecutors were laying all the blame on her. Carter's interim reprieve boded the probability that her appeal would be rejected by the same judges who had affirmed his. Ouida's rambling explanations made little sense. Her psychic retreats and disruptive outbursts were beyond her sisters' and her aunts' control. They began to see the devious side of her character and to wonder if her self-justifications were in fact inventions of a disordered mind. The persistent ringing of the telephone shattered everyone's nerves as bullies, cranks, and mischief makers kept calling 209-W, the Keetons' number listed in the public telephone directory, making taunts and scary accusations. Ouida complained to Chief Brown, but he could do nothing. Earl was often drunk and unruly, and the sisters were at one another's throats. Giving all the support he could muster, David McRae was stressed to the limit.

The bickering siblings accepted the truth that their beautiful sister was mentally ill and that the turbulent Keeton family was in wreckage. Eloise's and Earl's marriages had failed. On September 20, 1935, after her third try at matrimony, Eloise had parted from the handsome Jack Anderson, and Jewel, fed up and defiant, had left Earl. She filed papers for divorce with alimony, and the decree was made final on May 1, 1936. She and her little daughter moved in with Jewel's mother in northeast Laurel. Eloise asserted herself and became the owner and occupant of 539 Cross Street.

Cooper and Welch had been vindicated in having proposed to defend the troubled client with a plea of insanity. The family's outraged objection had been a mistake. Eloise took charge by consulting Dr. Jarvis and Ouida's former attorney, Ellis Cooper. Dr. Jarvis felt secure in the earlier diagnosis. All along, he had known Ouida was insane. Even if the conviction should be overturned, he was certain that she was too ill to remain unsupervised. She must be institutionalized at the new state hospital at Whitfield.

They hustled to gather the documentation for her possible commitment. On April 6, 1936, however, this contingent plan was thwarted. A month after Carter's conviction was reversed and remanded, the court issued its judgment on Ouida. Though two of the six appellate judges dissented, the majority confirmed the verdict of the Jones County jury.

By the conditions of her bond Ouida was required to surrender to the Jones County sheriff within one week. As Eloise and Maude agonized in preparing her for the inevitable trip to the Parchman prison, they also held to their hopeful plans for committing Ouida to Whitfield. But it was not to be.

On Monday, April 13, the felon turned herself in. Her sisters took her to the courthouse. Chief Brown and the new sheriff, Charlie Thompson the undertaker, were waiting to administer the formalities of incarceration. Terrified by the ordeal, Ouida was handcuffed and then confined in the sheriff's car for transport to the state prison. Too feeble to fight against her restraints, she sank onto the backseat in a pitiful heap. A gathering of onlookers standing close by noted that Sheriff Thompson had retained Miss Laurendine to accompany Ouida. The two women sat together behind the officers. Miss

Laurendine's services would be required until the Parchman hospital staff could take over. En route, the car would stop briefly in Jackson so that the sheriff could pick up the commitment papers from the supreme court offices.

Parchman, in the Mississippi Delta, was more than two hundred miles from Laurel. After the quick layover in Jackson, they traveled northwest to Yazoo City, then, turning north, descended from Mississippi hill country into the deep flatland of the Delta and headed to Sunflower County. The long, tedious trip took them over gravel roads and upgraded stretches of concrete highway the Works Progress Administration (WPA) crews were paving and across rich cotton lands and plantations. Manacled and teary, Ouida wept and whimpered all the way. Miss Laurendine soothed her with murmurs and comforting strokes.

When the four reached the vast detention farm, Ouida was too ill to undergo the procedures of processing, the required "dressing in" to which each newcomer was subjected. In her terror of the harsh and unforgiving setting she began vomiting, and Miss Laurendine informed officers that Ouida suffered from nervous nausea. To the stern custodians she was no more and no less than any other new inmate, not the pampered Laurel young woman who wore pretty frocks and a sapphire ring and drove about town in her Willis Knight, but they agreed to be temporarily tolerant and during the delay locked her in the women's ward of the prison hospital. Before returning to Laurel, Sheriff Thompson gave the order for Miss Laurendine to remain with her.

On the third day the transition and the coddling were over. When guards appeared at her bedside to seize her, Ouida, resisting and protesting, turned her face to the gray wall and went rigid, but the authoritarian handlers held to directives on the official paperwork and brooked no further delay from the delicate prisoner. They pulled Ouida from the sickbed and wheeled her to the receiving unit to be physically examined, photographed, fingerprinted, and entered in the admissions book as Convict Number X-10424.

In Laurel, the Keetons had not given up. They had petitioned the court to transfer Ouida to the state hospital. Eloise had met with Dr. Jarvis to prepare the medical paperwork. Already, the family's lawyers had filed a writ in Jackson arguing that the high court had made an error in its four-to-two decision to uphold the conviction.

The Parchman admission record completed during the invasive processing lists Ouida's age as thirty-three, her weight as 111½ pounds, her height as five feet four inches, her build as "slender," her hair "Dk. Br.," her eyes "br," complexion "Pale Brunette," face "Angular," mouth "Med," teeth "poor," nose "Long st.," eyebrows "Med st.," education "H.S., Business," read and write "yes," relatives "Miss Eloise Keeton–Sister–Laurel, Miss.," criminal history "None," marks, scars, etc. "Vac scar and lump scar on left upper arm," county of conviction "Jones," crime "Murder," terms "Life," expiration of sentence "Life," nativity "Miss.," race "White," occupation "Secretary," religion "None."

Afterward, lying helpless on her hospital bed, Ouida seemed like a fragile doll stripped of lace and violated by dirty hands. She kept her face turned toward the dull-gray wall. When her condition improved, the plans called for placing her in the women's camp. She was enumerated as the seventh white woman in the Mississippi penitentiary.

"It is always a problem to know what to do with a prisoner like that," the superintendent remarked to newsmen. "There is not much they can do, just some sewing or just piddle around."

Many inmates worked in prison factories, but most males not in maximum security or on death row toiled in the fields, watched over by menacing armed guards on horseback. The superintendent expressed strong feelings against imprisoning well-to-do white women. The few who were serving their time there were idle and bored.

But on the very day she was processed Ouida's destiny took a surprising turn. The final entry on the admissions form signals that she was not fated to sit around sewing and whiling away her sentence. Dr. James D. Biles Jr., the examining physician, decided that Ouida was unsuited for incarceration at the penitentiary. Without explanation he wrote beneath the heading *Remarks*, "Transferred to Hospital." As her sisters had hoped, Ouida's future residence was to be the Mississippi institution for the insane.

April 17 was a Thursday, and an ambulance ordered from Wright & Ferguson Funeral Home in Jackson arrived to carry Ouida across the state to the asylum. Miss Laurendine rode as far as Whitfield with her. On arrival, Ouida was self-absorbed, paying no attention to her surroundings. She stared into space and answered the strangers' questions with flat monosyllables. Of the faces poring over her, she recognized only Miss Laurendine's. She complained of backache and tiredness and expressed a wish to go to sleep. Attendants examining her detected no evidence of hallucinations or delusion, but as they asked her question after question, Ouida was not able to give dates or to recall events just prior to her admission to the hospital. Her memory was blank.

The time had come for a final separation, and Miss Laurendine said her farewell and departed for Laurel. Ouida was forlorn. She lay on her bed, kept her face to the wall, and lost herself in dreams.

By her third day Ouida had been assigned to the hydrotherapy department. In one of her treatments, a soaking in a steaming-hot bath, the supine patient was confined in a flat tub covered by thick canvas tent. Only her head was exposed. An alternative was a shower administered in a stall with multiple spigots that sprayed her simultaneously with jets of hot and cold water. At a console across the room an attendant monitored the controls and the water pressure.

Ouida was given hydrotherapy each day, but mentally she lived in a world apart. After her treatments she kept herself isolated from other patients. She lay quietly on her bed, seemingly lost in hallucinations. When questioned, she expressed her confusion and her inability to remember things correctly. Free now of nervous nausea, she had begun eating semisolid food.

Into the eighth day she remained quiet and attempted to cooperate. In the first week she gained two pounds, but after a frightening interview with an assembly of staff physicians she had a spell of nausea. Besides this, she complained of only one problem, pain in her lower spine. She continued to show mental confusion and to engage in fixed staring, and she did not mix with other patients. In replying to her doctors' questions about her dream states, she told of seeming to be in the company of her mother and of having conversations with her.

Ouida was absorbed by the rituals of the asylum. Although recalcitrant and deeply in denial, she acquiesced to procedural demands but deviously bent rules. In her delusion, she believed her incarceration was some authority's dreadful mistake.

About ten days after her admission, she was required to complete a questionnaire. It was headed *To Be Filled Out by the Patient*. Part one addressed "Consciousness and Orientation." The responses Ouida gave to the grade-school questions seem perfunctory. The first asks, What is your name? Ouida wrote "Ouida Keeton." What is your occupation? "Bookkeeper, typist." Where do you come from? "Laurel, Mississippi." How old are you? "32." What year is this? "1936." What month is this? "April." What day of the month? Ouida did not know, so she left this blank. What day of the week is this? "Tuesday." In what town are you? "Whitfield, Miss." How long have you been here? "Little over a week." In what sort of a place are you? "Miss. State

Facsimile of Ouida's signature on her admissions examination at Whitfield. (Permission of Judge John S. Grant III, Rankin County, Mississippi, Chancery Court)

Hosp." Who am I? "Ouida Keeton." What is the matter with you? No answer. Where were you a month ago? "Laurel."

The next section covered "School Knowledge." Ouida wrote "High School, Soule Business College." The questionnaire asked the patient to write the letters of the alphabet, to count from one to twenty, and to name the months of the year. Ouida provided the correct responses. She left blank the name of the largest river in America but named the U.S. capitol as "Washington," the largest city in the world as "New York," the capital of Mississippi as "Jackson," and the states bounding Mississippi as "La., Tenn., Ala., Ark." She counted backward from twenty-five to one but left the next three questions unanswered: What was the war of the American Revolution? What was the World War? and Name Some Important Happening in the World. She filled in the rest of the answers: Who is the Governor of Mississippi? "Gov. Hugh White"; Who is President of the United States? "Franklin D. Roosevelt"; Who is the Ruler of England? "King Edward VIII"; and What is the population of your city? "Approx. 19,000."

The rest covered twelve problems in basic arithmetic. All of these she calculated correctly. Then she was asked to write her name and "God Save the State of Mississippi," and she did so. The problems required her to add 2937 + 9365 and to multiply 492 by 93. Both her answers were correct. Last, she filled in responses to height: "Five feet four inches" and weight: "One hundred eighteen pounds."

At the hospital Ouida was identified as Case Number 14,806 and as a "white female, age 32 years, Mississippian, no occupation, single, high school education, 3 ½ months business college."

Her family history, perhaps taken from Dr. Jarvis's report, was studied by the medical staff: "Patient has one brother who is strongly addicted to alcohol; brother [served time] in jail charged with rape, murder and drunkenness. Entire family has been high-tempered and of a nervous makeup. Three aunts are described as being nervous and very peculiar. Father [thought to be a suicide] is described as irritable and very high-tempered. Mother described as very stubborn and very high-tempered. Has two sisters and one brother living, and one brother dead. Since patient's admission to the hospital one brother has been divorced from his wife and her sister has gotten an annulment of her marriage."

At Whitfield, the admissions report on Ouida's personal history, perhaps furnished by her sister, states incorrectly that she was born October 6, 1903, but, although pocked with several small misstatements of fact, it provides a good deal about Ouida's early years:

> Began talking at age 15 months; walked at age 2 years. She was fearful of dark as a child and was addicted to fingernail biting. Had severe temper tantrums and then pouted for weeks. As a child had ear trouble, throat trouble and some injury of the spine. At age 15 had mumps and her left ear gave her trouble at this time, and she apparently has total deafness of the left ear which dates from the time she had mumps. Began school age 5 and stopped at age 19. Graduated from high school and had 3 ½ months business college. Was never left back in any grade. Began work at age 21 and continued in the same position until about 1933. Her makeup before the onset of psychosis is given as shy, bashful, unsocial, given to daydreaming. She has been suspicious, jealous and sensitive, was quite changeable from cheerful to blue, easily discouraged and at times gloomy. She is very high-tempered and following temper tantrums would pout for weeks, being very irritable and displaying ugly moods.

If given the choice of incarceration at the Parchman penal farm in Sunflower County or at the Mississippi State Hospital at Whitfield, Ouida would have preferred neither. Truly, she wished to be back home. If she was pressed with no other option on where she was to spend the rest of her life, the institution at Whitfield was preferable.

Parchman was a work farm, notorious for harsh punishment and injustice. However, the asylum, of lesser objection, was located on the site of an old penal colony between the capital city of Jackson and the nearby town of Brandon. The country setting of woodlands, fields, and meadows made the facility look more like an estate than a prison. The vast complex of handsome Mount Vernon–style buildings and landscaped grounds housed a few thousand patients and encompassed thirty-five hundred acres of farmland, fifteen hundred in cultivation. A serene lake had been dug down a slope in front of the main structures. The complex was a self-contained, self-sufficient institution, having a post office, a bakery, a dairy, a laundry, water wells, a power plant, a fruit orchard, a truck farm, and a tuberculosis hospital. The dairy produced five hundred gallons of milk per day. The farm provided all the food for the dining halls. The staff and all employees lived on the campus.

At almost the same time Daisy Keeton was murdered, the state hospital for the mentally ill, called the Mississippi State Insane Asylum, was being relocated from its nineteenth-century buildings on the northern outskirts of Jackson to this new campus. The wards quickly became so overcrowded with beds that attendants had to walk over them to reach patients. Over time, the Whitfield institution became a lifetime holding pen teeming not only with the insane but also with problematic family members suffering from alcoholism, depression, menopause, and assorted maladjustments that in the coming decades would be addressed with medication and counseling. Though new regimens and strategies would diminish the population, the hospital became the largest facility in the United States for the treatment of mental health problems. For a generation or two after moving to Whitfield, it carried its forbidding name, Mississippi Hospital for the Insane. Most would refer to it as "Whitfield," the community in which it is situated, but officially it became the Mississippi State Hospital.

In 1935 Whitfield had a staff of 475 employees and three thousand patients. Serving them were eleven doctors, one dentist, one pharmacist, and two lab and X-ray technicians, as well as registered nurses and attendants. No full-time psychiatrists were employed. The campus was racially segregated, with whites to the right side of the campus and blacks to the left, with separate dining halls, recreation areas, and chapels for each.

In this day such pharmacological controls as Thorozine, Haldol, and Risperdal were inaccessible. Maniacal patients were subdued with narcotics or straitjackets. The prevailing treatment modalities included EST (electro-shock), which was administered on the floor without anesthesia, lest the patient fall from a bed during seizures and break bones; chemical shock, induced by overdoses of such medications as insulin; psychotherapy; hydro-therapy; restraint; and seclusion. Dr. C. H. Mitchell, who became the director of the hospital shortly before Ouida was admitted, was a steadfast proponent of electroshock.

Most patients were put to work while at Whitfield, and occupational therapy was a planned part of treatment. Patients made sheets, wove blankets and rugs, and manufactured brooms and mops. Some performed office tasks or janitorial services. Few were left idle.

On Ouida's admission, her attending physician was Dr. Donaldson. Nearly a month after she arrived, Dr. Mitchell, recently put in charge of the hospital, reviewed her history at a meeting of the medical staff. He knew Ouida's case well.

"I would like to make a few statements in regard to Miss Keeton," he told his colleagues seated around the conference table, "as I saw her before she went on trial for the murder of her mother. I was in Laurel some time before the trial and went to see Miss Keeton. At this time she appeared to be in a stuporous state. She wouldn't speak to anyone, would just lie and stare at the wall. Then I saw her again just about a week before the trial, and she was in the same condition. Then during the trial she was rolled into the courtroom in a chair. She just lay there with a stare looking up to the ceiling and paying no attention to anything. I sat there and watched her every day, and she would never bat an eye, keeping her lips closed tightly, never moving them even to moisten them."

He told of testing her. He had raised her hands and arms to various positions. Mindlessly, she had held her limbs thus until someone moved them. He went on to say that a family physician who took the witness stand testified that once he almost had run over Ouida. She was standing in a downtown street as though in a dream state. He sounded the horn, but she did not respond. He swerved to avoid hitting her.

Dr. Donaldson acknowledged that her fixed staring had been evident since her admission. In the hydrotherapy department she stared at the wall. When he spoke to her, however, she emerged from the dream state and tried to cooperate. Dr. Dearman reviewed her background. He reported it to be characterized by emotional instability and peculiarities. Her father's brother was thought to have committed suicide. Dr. Donaldson discussed the history of Ouida's "unhappy environment in childhood" and "the abnormal devotion" to her mother. Dr. Mitchell told of her lack of interest in playmates and her rushing home to her mother after school. During graduation she shied from parties so that she could be with her mother.

Dr. Clark offered his diagnosis.

"I would call her a catatonic praecox."

"That was my opinion during the trial," Dr. Mitchell agreed, "and it is now."

All physicians pronounced the same diagnosis, and Ouida's illness was entered in the record as "dementia praecox: catatonic type—profound."

She was kept under close observation. She was assigned to a ward, but Ouida kept herself apart from others. Much of the time she lay on her bed, evidently awake. She passed long hours by staring into space and showing no contact with her surroundings. When she was summoned for an interview, she was nervous and fearful. The doctors found her to be neat and quite agreeable, although confused when trying to answer them.

"Her replies to questions," their report states,

are given in a relevant, coherent manner. She attempts to cooperate to the best of her ability. However, questions are frequently misunderstood, and she frequently states that she cannot describe how she feels, that it seems as if she has lost control of herself. She cannot give a relevant account of the development of [her] psychosis. States that her memory since 1933 is all confused and that she cannot definitely date any of her actions or her behavior during this period. States, however, that she began to get nervous some time about the early part of 1934, that she began to notice a change in her eyes. States that she would look into the mirror and that her eyes did not look normal to her. She could not give a description of this change, merely stating that they were different. She states she had been told that she would sit and stare for long periods of time and would not speak to people; however, states that she could not definitely say that she remembers this herself and that it might be that she remembers this simply because she had been told this so many times.

Says that during her early childhood she was high-strung, had always been nervous and that she had an abnormal attachment for her mother and that she had known this for quite some time. States that she could not make a statement as to whether she remembers her mother's death or not, that she has had so much stuff pumped into her about this. States that it is all quite confusing to her, and that she could not even attempt to make a statement on this. States that she doesn't remember the happenings after the trial until she came to at her sister Maude's house. States that it is not quite clear as to when she first remembered things due to the fact that she had been told so much of her actions during this time that she could not clearly differentiate between the memory of things told her and her actual memory of things. Her productions are limited to answering questions. She shows no spontaneity, no flight of ideas, and no speech defect, except that she is somewhat hesitant in answering questions. She attributes this to the fact that she is still some-what confused and that she cannot think clearly and that it takes her a little time to straighten out her thoughts. Shows no attention disorders at this time. Shows no mannerisms except that she continuously wrings a handkerchief in her hands throughout the interview.

The report notes that her mood did not change while the physicians were questioning her, although she was apprehensive, anxious, and somewhat agitated. When she spoke of Daisy Keeton, Ouida became sad but not tear-ful. She remarked that at times she felt her mother was beside her, advising and talking with her. She was aware also of moments when she was not in control of herself, when she seemed to be two persons, and when another's influence was possessing her.

Despite her psychosis, slight anemia, and pains in her spine, Ouida's physical health was classified as generally normal. The initial examination found discoloration around the eyes, a "blowing systolic murmur" in her chest, and partial deafness. When a watch was held against her left ear, Ouida could hear nothing. Her teeth were broken and decayed, and her dark hair was streaked with gray. Ouida's beauty had been devastated.

After three months at Whitfield she was still assigned to the hydrotherapy department. She was noticeably quiet and agreeable, although antisocial. She took nourishment and slept well. She passed time by writing rambling, incoherent letters.

When a full year had passed, she was in a state of calm and seemed close to normal. At times, however, she held a wild stare and appeared to be hallucinating. She told of hearing her mother's voice. During this period Ouida gave the staff no trouble of any kind, and because she showed signs of improvement, she was assigned to work in the hospital library, one of the nicer duties.

■ ■ ■

In the general election of November 1935, Ouida's scourge Jack Deavours defeated two opponents and won his race to become district attorney, and since the first of January 1936 he had been serving Forrest, Jones, and Perry counties in his new position. Dead set to be thorough, he intended to place Carter's second trial on the earliest docket. Deavours's star witness, now confined at Whitfield, would be required to take the stand again. Carter was driving his Pontiac around town free as you please, and the thought of Ouida comfortably ensconced free of charge at the asylum rankled her persecutors. For the public good, it was time to check the insulting liberties of these felons. Prodded by Deavours, Judge Pack signed the order for Ouida's subpoena.

The writ was mailed to the sheriff of Rankin County and was served at Whitfield on Thursday, May 21. Dr. Mitchell immediately refused to honor it. His terse response to the subpoena was a notation he wrote across it: "Incompetent to answer process by reason of insanity." It was returned to Deavours. The physician's action was approved by Attorney General Greek L. Rice, who decreed that if Ouida Keeton should be compelled to appear in court, Jones County must issue a writ of habeas corpus. "Even then," he said, "she would be incompetent as a witness since she had been declared insane."

Steaming over being blocked in his plans for prosecution, Deavours blustered.

"It is the first time I ever heard of a court official being required to get out a writ of habeas corpus to obtain the presence of a state witness who is a prisoner of the state and confined in a state institution." He declared himself to be undecided on his next move. "I'm going to wait until Monday and see what they do with the girl."

Reporters questioned whether the case against Carter would be moot if Ouida was withdrawn as the star witness.

"I can't tell," he replied. "We will wait and see if we can get her."

Was it was possible that Carter's case be declared nolle prosequi, and if so, would the prosecution be blocked by the absence of Ouida Keeton's testimony?

"I'm going to wait and see what kind of returns we get on that subpoena," Deavours replied. "She may show up."

Attorney General Rice called Deavours's attention to Section 2983 of the Mississippi legal code. It states that a person "judiciously declared insane" is incapable of testifying. The attorney general advised Deavours that Dr. Mitchell was acting within the law. Even if Jones County should take the case through habeas corpus proceedings, Rice said, "it would place the circuit court in contradiction with other judicial processes in which Miss Keeton has been declared insane and incompetent as a witness."

Throughout 1936 Carter, an anxious man in legal suspension, remained on bail with his contentious case debated by the public. Intending to bring the matter to a close, Deavours placed it on the February docket of 1937. Ouida Keeton again was named as the key witness for the prosecution. After the passing of nine months, the moment had come for her to give her testimony. Deavours's resentment that Ouida was incarcerated at Whitfield rather than at Parchman was obvious. He had been lenient, relaxing his demands so that she could receive medical treatment, but after more than a year it was time for her to emerge from the hospital.

He subpoenaed Ouida and commanded that Dr. Mitchell send her to Laurel for the hearing. Dr. Mitchell did not comply. Deavours's next move was to petition Judge Pack to issue a writ of *habeas corpus testificandum*. The petition stated

> that although the said Ouida Keeton was incarcerated in the state peni-
> tentiary, in accordance with her sentence, in some way and in some
> manner and by some procedure, the exact type and form of which is not
> known to this petitioner, she is now an inmate of the Mississippi State
> Insane Asylum, at Whitfield, Mississippi, where he is advised and upon
> information and belief, alleges that she is acting as Assistant Librarian of
> said institution.
>
> That a previous summons issued from this court and served upon her
> was returned by the certificate of the superintendent of said insane asy-
> lum, one Doctor Mitchell, to the effect that the said Ouida Keeton was
> insane and unable physically or mentally to attend court. . . . That the
> superintendent of said hospital has refused and still refuses to deliver

the said Ouida Keeton before the Circuit Court of this county upon
an ordinary summons, although she is a material witness in the cause
above named, and her evidence is material and necessary to the trial of
said cause.

Wherefore petitioner prays that a writ of habeas corpus testificandum issue from the court directed to the superintendent of said penitentiary to produce the said Ouida Keeton before this court on the 19th
day of February 1937 as a witness in the case of the State of Mississippi
vs. W. M. Carter.

Judge Pack signed Deavours's petition for the preliminary hearing and
then demanded that Dr. Mitchell deliver Ouida to the Jones County courthouse on the amended date of February 24, and "after she shall have given
her testimony in said cause, that you return her to the said asylum. Herein
fail not, under penalty of law."

The Rankin County sheriff served the papers, Dr. Mitchell complied, and
on Tuesday, February 23, Ouida arrived in Laurel. She was guarded by two
female administrators from the hospital, and the three women registered at
the Pinehurst Hotel for an overnight stay.

Facing Judge Pack the next morning, Ouida sat placidly between her two
attendants. Intrigued by her presence, the audience ogled her frock, black
trimmed with white. Warming her shoulders was a gray raincoat. It was
whispered that her pretty face had withered since her previous day in court.
Her mouth seemed different. With new false teeth, she was a startling contrast to the dazzling woman in white showcased at Carter's trial.

Earl, the only other member of the Keeton family present, had shuffled in
with the rest of the jostling crowd of several hundred. No one spotted Eloise
or Maude in the courtroom, for, indeed, they were not there. Even David
McRae, the family anchor, was absent. A sick man suffering from high blood
pressure, he was kept away from the stress of the controversy.

It was afternoon before Ouida was called to the stand. During the lunch
hour she had replaced her raincoat with a garment a *Leader-Call* reporter
described as "a swagger coat." Although frail and certifiably insane, and
although the reporter mentioned Ouida's age as the early thirties but she
"appears several years older," she still maintained a certain flair. "Ouida Keeton" had become a highly charged household name throughout the city, and
in the courtroom many an eye studied her suspiciously as a murderous felon
cosseted in the state insane asylum, as a madwoman who had deceived her

mother and masqueraded as a wronged virgin. She walked gracefully to the front and took a seat in the witness's chair.

Deavours moved forward to begin his interrogation.

"Miss Ouida, we are trying to investigate this case against W. M. Carter, in which you were the principal witness. I want to know what you can tell us about it."

Ouida turned her good ear toward his voice, absorbing his question.

"After my trial, and then after Mr. Carter's trial, and both cases had been carried to the supreme court," she responded, "my mental condition was good enough that I realized that I did not know whether what I said was true or untrue. So I told Mr. Deavours, and I gave the same things to Chief Brown in writing, because I wanted something done before decisions were made in the case."

It was the soft contralto they had heard at Carter's trial. But, rambling off the mark, she seemed a touch haywire, for "Mr. Deavours," about whom she spoke, was not absent but standing in front of her. Some thought her straying from focus was a sign of derangement. Others thought the gray in Ouida's hair was in need of a touch-up.

"Well of course, nothing, I don't imagine, was done," she continued, "because both cases were decided, and then I was sick for quite a little while, and then, as I said way back yonder, and as I said today over here, I haven't changed any opinion. I am still of the same mind. I don't know whether what I said was true or untrue. I wish I did."

She was closely focused on herself.

"Of course, Miss Ouida," Deavours answered gingerly, hoping to guide her into making better sense, "nobody wants you to tell anything that is untrue. I am not trying to over-persuade you. I don't want you to tell anything that isn't true."

He appeared to be speaking simply and deliberately, as though to a child.

"Of course, the only thing any of us are interested in is just seeing that justice is done. Your mother is dead, and—"

"Of course," Ouida interrupted, "as I explained to you over a year ago, I really need to know things, and I don't know. I don't know the circumstances involving my mother's death and all that has been done. I want you to believe me when I tell you my mental condition was such that I did not know, and as soon as I got to where I realized—my own self—that I didn't know whether the things I told were true or not true, I went immediately and told Mr. Deavours over there, and I told Chief Brown. I told them that I didn't know then, and that I wished for something to be done."

She was confused and rambling. She had spoken of Deavours a second time as though he were not standing there as her interrogator.

"In other words," Deavours asked gently, "what you are telling is that if Mr. Carter had anything to do with it, you don't know it?"

"As I said, I don't know whether the statements I made—I don't know whether they are true or untrue."

"And you can't say he did have anything to do with it, and can't say he didn't have anything to do with it?"

"That's right. I can't say."

"In other words, if the case is brought to trial and you are put on the witness stand, you will just have to tell the petit jury that you don't know whether Mr. Carter had anything to do with it or not? Is that correct?"

"That would be right. I would have to tell them, as I said, that I don't know whether the things I said were true or untrue."

Deavours tried to approach her from another direction.

"Miss Ouida, is there anything else, any facts or circumstances, that you haven't told us, that you can tell me that might have some bearing on it?"

"Well, there were," she replied, and again she took an oblique sidetrack. "After I went back over to the house to stay with my sister, I turned over those little messages, those anonymous messages, and I didn't think you would pay much attention to that because they were anonymous, but there were threatening phone calls. I told Chief Brown about these people implying first one thing and another, but as for knowing about that—"

"Well," Deavours snapped, changing the subject and dodging this belabored digression about pestering attacks on her by local nuisances, "do you know where the rest of your mother's body is?"

"I don't know anything about my mother's death."

"Well, the situation, Miss Ouida, is this—Mr. Carter is indicted for murder and indicted principally on your statement. I didn't have any other reason to disbelieve you, and nobody else did. Of course, the supreme court reversed his case, and it has got to be tried again. And it has got to be disposed of. And the only way we can possibly try it would be through your testimony. If you can't testify, of course, we can't try it. But now if you can testify, we want you to do it. We don't want you to protect anybody in the thing, because it isn't fair to you to take the whole blame on yourself if somebody else is involved."

"Well, as I said, he was convicted of murder," Ouida responded, "and he has a case, of course, pending, but just as I told you and just as I told Chief Brown the minute I realized—where I think a whole lot of the trouble is, the average person probably just can't understand all the stages I went through and everything. I can't explain it to you because I don't understand it myself, but as I explained to you over a year ago, that if it was possible, if I knew, if I knew what I said was true, all right, but I don't know it, and the only honest thing I could do is tell you that I don't know. You have everything, and you should know."

"Of course, Miss Ouida, the only way I know it is true is that you told me. Of course, if you don't know that it is true, why certainly I don't know."

"I don't know that it is true. I don't know anything about my mother's death, and—"

"I don't want you, and no one else wants you to tell—"

"No, I didn't feel that you all did. That was the reason why I explained it to you over a year ago, while the cases were still pending."

"That was after the trial here?"

"That was after both cases had been carried to the supreme court. Chief Brown said he remembered about the time I called him. I don't exactly."

"Of course, nobody wants you to tell anything you don't know is true. That wouldn't be fair to you and wouldn't be fair to Mr. Carter, and wouldn't be fair to the people, but on the other hand, if you do know anything you can tell us that throws any light on it, with reference to him or anybody else, we want you to tell it. I think you owe it to yourself, owe it to your mother and your own people, if you don't owe it to the people, to tell us everything you can."

"As I explained before, I want to know and wish I did know, and I have begged for information and anything that would help clear it up, because you know it is really frightful to love anybody as I loved my mother and go day in and day out with this pending, and really not knowing whether it is true or not true."

Deavours had done his utmost. Defeated, he asked Ouida to step down. All eyes watched her walk to her chair, and just as she was taking her seat, the judge nodded to her attendants. Each took hold of the felon and quickly steered her toward the back door. Not allowing her to pause or look back, they rushed her onward, her high heels clicking on the marble steps her wheelchair had negotiated day after day two years earlier. Outside, they led her to the official car and shut her inside. No observer intruded to whisper a hello or good-bye. Most of Laurel was fed up. The day's exposure of the bro-ken beauty had slaked the blood thirst for sensation. The sorry case boiled down to one proven killer who had lost her charm and her good looks. She alone must bear the brunt of the murder while Carter remained at large. She was oblivious to the dreadful life that lay ahead.

Without delay, the state auto left Laurel and headed toward Whitfield. The sated city had seen the last of Ouida Keeton, and with her departure Jack Deavours saw his case against W. M. Carter fizzle and fall apart. Without Ouida's testimony he could not carry the prosecution forward. The next day he petitioned that the cause be passed to the court files and be left pend-ing. Countering him, Will Watkins and Jeff Collins entered a plea that it be declared nolle prosequi so that there could be no further prosecution of their client. Rather than debate a fine point, Deavours conceded, claim-ing little difference in passing a suit to the files and classifying it a nolle prosequi.

In the absence of ailing Judge Pack, Judge George Currie of Hattiesburg presided at the termination. After guiding the two cases through the laby-rinthine trials, Pack was not present for the ending. His proxy declared Case Number 577, the *State of Mississippi v. William Madison Carter*, to be nolle prosequi. For this decisive event the defendant himself was absent, although his son and both his sons-in-law were in the courtroom to hear him declared a free man. And thus the long-running courtroom carnival ended.

But this triangular tragedy could never be truly over. People had flaws that caused lasting reverberations. Daisy Keeton's grasp on money, Ouida's frail hold on sanity, and Carter's undaunted urge to possess her had caused family injury and personal ruin. The unnerving setback for Carter tested his familial authority. Always he had been the dominant figure in the business and in the home. Formerly, no one doubted his self-assurance, the authority in his manner, the dignity in his bearing, and the propriety in his stance of command. Now he seemed in his sorrow to lie toppled low.

Though Carter was freed from the worry of a second trial and of more money flooding from his bank account, the facts were not settled. The smell of scandal refused to dissipate and vanish. With the case at a stalemate, he was not genuinely exonerated. Public suspicion would never go away, nor would the seaminess of his back-street adultery with at least two young women. Released from further legal prosecution, yet carrying the deep-dyed stain, he was a gentleman at large. In the better circles he was politely received, although no longer among the town worthies or his church's deacons. His name was erased from the roster of bank directors and from the session of the Presbyterian church. In his own firm he was resigned to accepting his disgrace so that Carter Building and Supply Company could survive. His son had become president, Pauline vice president, and Helen secretary-treasurer. The 1936 city directory lists the children as officers, W. M. Carter as "clerk." As the public showed its weariness of the ubiquitous Legs Murder case, Carter was appreciative of at least one courtesy, that the brutal story was not continually thrown in his face. As mention of the case became taboo among the select of Laurel, Carter quietly carried his burden, seldom mentioning it, seldom reviewing or trying to explain away the old hurt. Yet wherever he was seen in his rambles, he was regarded as a shameful sinner and a possible murderer. Innocent? Guilty? How could anyone ever know the answer, not even Ouida, who claimed that the heinous act had impaired her memory?

If Ouida learned the outcome of the wearisome case against her onetime fatherly friend, she never acknowledged it in any public way. She was enveloped in a confounding world at Whitfield, a life altogether separate from Laurel. Maude, nursing David, seldom if ever visited Whitfield. Possibly Ouida was not informed of her brother-in-law's death. On November 26, 1937, David McRae died at home of a heart attack brought on by hypertension. He was forty-seven. The wreckage of the Keeton family no doubt contributed to his own.

As two years passed, Ouida adapted herself to a routine of treatment and work. She was observed to be a loner and a chain smoker. In 1939 the hospital library was placed in her charge, and she gave evidence that she enjoyed her assignment. Moreover, having privileges in the kitchen of her building, she was preparing her own food, and she was sleeping fairly well. Her doctors pronounced that her physical health was good. They characterized her as agreeable and cooperative, although still seclusive from other patients. Her emotional states alternated between cheer and depression, and since the extraction of her remaining teeth and the fitting of dental plates in 1936, she no longer was suffering from severe headaches. Each day she was treated with hydrotherapy. Though she could never be cured, her physical health improved.

In 1940 as Ouida was being examined for a bad cold and respiratory infection, her doctor discovered a large mass the size of a grapefruit in her uterus. Immediately he suspected pregnancy, but after closer examination, the growth was diagnosed as a fibroid tumor. However, it was not obstructing bodily functions. Displaying her streak of obstinacy, Ouida bitterly objected to surgery. She would rather be killed by the tumor than to go through an operation.

She recovered from her cold and returned to her duties. Three weeks later, Ouida was reminded that she was a felon with a life sentence. Her case report for July 31, 1940, marked what was to become an alarming reversal of her accustomed routine: "A traveling agent from Parchman Penitentiary came with the order from Governor Paul B. Johnson to remove this patient from the insane hospital at Whitfield to the White Female Camp, Parchman."

Ouida had been in treatment for four years. The governor's envoy seized her at 1:30 p.m.

"With the exception of the tumorous mass that involves the entire pelvis," the medical report continues, "she is considered to be in good health. She was in a state of mental remission when she left."

Some force in Laurel intended to transform what was supposed as her soft life at the mental institution into hard time at the penitentiary. The Jones County courthouse has no record of habeas corpus paperwork to relocate Ouida. The move came suddenly. In neither Governor Johnson's personal files nor his official papers archived at the University of Southern Mississippi can such a document be found, nor indeed any mention of transferring Ouida Keeton back to the prison. Dr. Mitchell was angered that the governor and the people of Jones County had demanded the extradition. He knew his patient would not fare well at Parchman.

"There was quite a little bitterness and feeling about this case," his colleague Dr. Schmid recalled in a later year. "And a lot of politics too."

In her previous experience with penal life, Ouida had passed only three days at Parchman. As she approached the gates this time, in all likelihood she would spend the rest of her life there. The state prison, a farm of more than fifteen thousand acres, was planted in cotton and other crops, but mostly cotton. In the 1930s it was, like Whitfield, a self-sustaining operation. Its gin, machine shop, brickyard, and factories were sometimes profit-making for the state. The male prisoners toiled in backbreaking labor and lived in various camps supervised by authoritarian bosses and their convict aides, called "trusties." The women's camp, largely populated by black inmates, was a venue for manufacturing utilitarian cloth goods. Through the day they sat at sewing machines, making striped uniforms, bedding, and curtains for use at Parchman. During lulls in this sweatshop regimentation, they were sent to the fields to chop cotton.

The female population at Parchman remained small and segregated. Within the women's camp was an enclave exclusively for white inmates, and Ouida again was confined there. As Dr. Mitchell had predicted, her mental illness worsened. Adjustment to the new restrictions was difficult, and Ouida was not able to respond to ordinary demands.

One of these was a family matter. On November 4, 1935, for a payment of $1,800, she had deeded the Cross Street house and lot to Eloise, but five years later Eloise discovered that the title to the property remained in Ouida's name. She petitioned for Ouida, officially now a resident of Sunflower County, to relinquish any claim. To do so required Ouida's signature, and on October 18 the writ was submitted to her at Parchman. She was too ill to comply. Since she did not respond, on November 4, 1940, Chancellor A. B. Amis Sr. of the district court sustained Eloise's claim and awarded her full title. The petitioner was designated as Mrs. Eloise Keeton Flowers. Eloise had married yet again. Her fourth and final husband was J. M. Flowers.

Earl also had remarried. His second wife was Annie McVey Cameron, a widow with two sons and a daughter. At 216 Central Avenue she operated the Cameron Café and a rooming house above it. The business, in her previous husband's name, was situated in a sector of old Laurel that was now rundown and commercial. From the doorway, one could gaze west beyond the tracks to the bustle of Front Street and see the Coca-Cola bottling plant and Fine Bros.-Matison Company, Laurel's flush department store. A block to the north was the train station and three blocks farther the Keeton house. On the social ladder of neighborhoods, this one on the wrong side of the tracks was a few rungs below Cross Street. Gossips were of the opinion that this time Earl indeed had married down. The family lived upstairs among their clientele of blue-collar workmen and travelers. After the marriage Earl, no longer employed at the bakery, became the proprietor, and the name of the business was changed to Keeton Café.

Life with Earl could not have been a happy circumstance for any wife. His fiery temper, drinking, and reckless conduct kept him in trouble. In February 1940 he was indicted for "assault and battery with intent." At his arraignment he pleaded not guilty. The circuit judge reduced the charge to simple assault, but Earl was convicted, fined $25, and billed for court costs. Still wild as a buck, he never did settle down, and, finally, after 1941 Annie had to carry on without him. On Sunday, November 23, at 3:00 a.m., Earl's long streak of luck ran out. After a wild Saturday night, he was headed home on Highway

15, and in the pitch-black dark one mile north of Richton, his car flipped over. He was instantly killed.

Though evidence is thin, Ouida, an inmate in the penitentiary, may have been notified of his death, since precise information about his birth and parentage, to be recorded and certified by the state registrar, was supplied from her Whitfield records. John Earl Cotton Keeton was thirty-nine. His death certificate states that he was born on March 11, 1902. In Hickory Grove Cemetery, his solitary grave near the entrance on Old Bay Springs Road is surrounded by an expanse of grass. It shows him to be at rest remarkably alone. W. M. Carter need never fear violent Earl Keeton again.

Ouida lasted only four years at Parchman. She was a problem the prison system could not control. Periods of confinement in the sweatbox produced no satisfactory solution to the authorities' bouts with her aberrations. By 1944 she had become so delusional that the superintendent chose to transfer her back to Whitfield. Her last two weeks at the penitentiary she spent on her bed in paranoid whining. She was in her forties. Emaciated and malnourished, she weighed only ninety-one pounds. She was still menstruating regularly, her hair had gone almost entirely gray, and her skin was pale and dehydrated. The tumor in her lower abdomen was ever more pronounced. Although she disliked Parchman, she was distressed on learning that she was being returned to the asylum. Yearning for her former life on the other side of the divide, she was homesick for Laurel, her private bedroom, her car, her pretty things. She pleaded to go home.

In the heat of late August she arrived at Whitfield by ambulance. It pulled up at the admissions entrance, and the guard accompanying her opened the door and asked her to get out. Ouida held to the chrome-plated handles and refused to let go. In a noisy altercation, he dragged her loose and steered her to the porch. As he pulled her up the steps toward the doorway, she balked and lay down on the hot concrete. No matter how he coaxed, she refused to go inside. She wanted to go to Laurel. Dr. McDonald came to assist, and the two lifted her and carried her indoors for processing.

On September 5 Dr. Carr examined her and made a brief report: "She was a patient here from April 17, 1936, to July 31, 1940. At that time the patient was returned to the penitentiary in fair mental condition. She now returns to this hospital in a delusional and somewhat excited state."

On September 14 the four staff physicians—Drs. Mitchell, Denser, Schmid, and Thorpe—and two social workers were present for Ouida's first group interview. Such confrontations always frightened her, and on this occasion she was a touch belligerent.

"Miss Keeton, these are your doctors of the staff and the social workers," Dr. Carr advised. "They are pretty well acquainted with your past, but they want you to tell them why you were sent here this time."

"Well, doctors, about all I feel like I want to say after making that protest about being sent here is I tried to give all the cooperation I could and gave Dr. Carr's secretary a history, but I think it is necessary that I talk to Governor Bailey and Superintendent Love. And that is all I want to say. It is necessary that I see these two."

There was no sweetness in her voice. She was confrontational and delusional.

"Do you still want to see Mr. Love? He is not the superintendent any more."

"Yes, sir, I still want to see these two."

"You are looking much better than when you came here," Dr. Mitchell said, guiding her away from the impossible demand.

"Well, as I explained, certain conditions brought on this weakness."

"What were those conditions?"

"I cannot discuss them until I talk to these two men."

"You don't seem to understand that these two men cannot come here."

"Well, we will put it this way. I have been waiting ten years, almost, for governors and superintendents, and maybe we can wait a little longer."

"For what are you waiting?"

She looked at him with an expression of wild surprise.

"Doctor, for exoneration and permission to go home."

"Miss Keeton, do you feel that you have been treated unjustly in the past?"

"Well, naturally."

"And you feel this information might clear up something for you?"

"Well, I cannot divulge anything, and this is quite different from what you people would expect."

"Tell us about that treatment in the sweatbox. Was it a pack or diathermy?"

"Well, you see that was in the penitentiary, not a hospital."

"And you feel that you cannot tell this?"

"Not until I talk to these two gentlemen."

After Ouida was dismissed, the physicians conferred about her history.

"This family has always been peculiar," Dr. Schmid recalled from his experience with Ouida's case in 1935. "And she has been the mainstay of the family. Her brother was suspected of killing the brother of the district attorney, and her father was killed on the railroad, and finally double indemnity was collected and Ouida was put in control of this fund. This man who was involved in the murder of her mother was a big lumber contractor, and this girl was his secretary and very capable. He would make a trip, and she would be left in charge and would draw up big contracts. Very efficient. Then all this came up, and he closed his business, and she worked for a while at a filling station."

His recounting of Ouida's story was succinct and not in every point correct.

Dr. Schmid summarized his examination of Ouida before her trial nine years previously. In her room at Laurel General Hospital he had tested her reflexes by holding a threatening pin near her open eye. "She never batted." He stuck her tongue with a pin, and she did not flinch. "I saw her after Dr. Mitchell had examined her," he continued. "She only answered one question at the trial, and that was when I asked her 'What is the last thing you remember?' And she wrote the answer and stated that in a dream she saw her injured mother carried out of a room, and that was the last."

Dr. Carr was of the opinion that she would be considered paranoid now.

"Don't prisoners very often develop a paranoid state?" Dr. Schmid responded.

"Well, yes. I believe if one of you would talk to her alone, she might talk to you, but she will not open up before a crowd."

Dr. Denser recalled that she had been a troublemaker.

"When she was here before, there were a lot of activities here on the ward and in the doctor's office. And every once in a while the records would be tampered with. I don't know whether it was destructiveness or just things missing, but every once in a while something would take place in regard to the records, and some notes were left around, but I do not know all the particulars. But in some way they thought she was connected with it, and they were afraid she might [make an] attempt [on] someone's life. This is more or less scattered and fragmentary information that I am piecing together, and I don't know the whole reason that she was sent back to Parchman."

"She is schizophrenic, without a doubt," Dr. Carr said.

Dr. Schmid recalled the politics and the hometown resentment behind her being shipped to Parchman in 1940.

"She told me on a later date," he added, "that her employer had nothing to do with it. When he was coming to their house, as he often did, it was to see her mother. The patient was quite stingy with these funds of her father's and wouldn't give anything to anybody. It was said that when the girl was at home, her mother would follow her every move. If she went on the porch, her mother went too and would not let her out of her sight. Two doctors testified at the trial that Ouida [had] wanted to talk to them, but her mother came to the office and took her away. When I saw her [in Laurel], she was a typical catatonic."

All nodded in agreement. Ouida's previous diagnosis should be retained: "dementia praecox, catatonic type."

She was placed again in the hydrotherapy ward and treated by a routine of hot baths. In addition, each day she was given intravenous drips, vitamins, and liver and iron supplements. It was observed that she slept a great deal and seemed weak. She recognized patients she had known previously and greeted some of them as friends, yet she took little interest in anything except herself. She kept repeating a need to "study and figure things out."

In November a staff evaluation gauged whatever degree of progress she had made after three months. She was adjusting to her new circumstances. "She is rather quiet and prefers to go her own way, not associating any more than is necessary with the other patients. She talks but little and converses with the attendants and her physician only when necessary. However, she is usually pleasant and cooperative. There have been no signs of any mental storm since admission. Patient is in good physical health and enjoys ground privileges."

Suspicious and withdrawn, she expressed a devious wish to make productive use of her time, and on September 19, 1945, she let her Whitfield staff physician know that the superintendent had approved her request to work in the White Employees' Dining Room. Likely this was a delusion, for her monitor responded negatively. "It appears that the patient is definitely desirous of employment in order that she might be on the payroll more than in order to engage in any helpful therapeutic pursuit. It is deemed inadvisable for this patient to engage in such employment."

And what was happening to Ouida's former boss since his exoneration? Like Ouida, he was down and out and drifting. The flawed and tragic figure was merely a shadow in his place of business, controlled by his son. Customers regarded him with the mistrustful air of people who don't know how to mingle with an accused butcher-murderer. Watching others take over, he clerked in the store sporadically and bestirred himself about town, always eyed as a subject of suspicion and as a questionable citizen in shame. How ever could he resuscitate his former reputation? At home the family stuck together, putting their feet under the table at supper time and by the daily act of living were on the surface like all other families on their street. In the mid-1940s Carter's health began to fail, and those various ailments reported to the court in securing bail became pronounced and dangerous.

Snide citizens of the rougher variety snickered about him as the old jail-bird, but his attractive family held their heads high and, despite the lingering notoriety of the Legs Murder case, remained popular and admired. Carter's dignified daughters were regarded as lovely assets to Laurel society. Polite-ness governed conversations around bridge tables and golf tees, and lest feel-ings be injured, discussion of the case was carefully avoided. If it happened to come to the surface, inevitably the presence of some relative of the fam-ily or someone unpleasantly entangled in the story would cause embarrass-ment, for Laurel was a small town, and the tree of kinship was intricately ramified.

The death of Carter's brother Eugene in 1935 and his sister Ida in 1942 jolted him. He, Charles, and Rosa were left as the last Carter siblings. The demise of family members was like the tocsin only elders hear, tolling news that they too are fading and that the unstoppable sand in the hourglass is running out fast. With his own end in sight, W. M. Carter resigned from his company in 1945, and on Christmas Eve 1946 he put his signature on his will. He made his bequest simple, clear, and unencumbered.

"I do hereby give, devise and bequeath all of my property of whatever kind, nature and description and wherever situated, share and share alike, to my son . . . and my daughters. . . . I make this gift of all of my property to my children and free of any charge, but with full confidence nevertheless that they will care for my sister, Rosa Carter. I admonish my children to contrib-ute equally for the necessary support and maintenance of my said sister, but this is to be without any charge on my property and so as to enable my said children to dispose of their interest therein without restriction, and is an admonition only." He named his son as executor.

Charles, the youngest brother and his occasional business partner in early years, died in Laurel in 1947. The tocsin was tolling yet again.

Increasingly enfeebled by bad health, Carter lived for three years after signing the will. Like every long-dying life, his cycled toward the end in wounded reflection. The resonant words of the old prophet echoed in memories of Presbyterian sermons: "And what doth the Lord require of thee, but to do justly, and to love mercy, and to walk humbly with thy God?"

Carter lay on his sickbed, curtailed by his many ailments. He'd had fine and loyal children, a good wife, a prosperous business, a long span of eight decades, a fair share of success, pain, bad luck, and a frightening phantom. How sad it was that a man's good deeds were so overclouded by his slips into sin and wickedness. Despite prayer and repentance, the deep stains marred life's record. As the end approached, the sum of suffering revealed its meaning: "Truly this is grief, and I must bear it." It offered the sad serenity that comes to the dying, of knowing that millions of men and women are foolish, most of them harboring a secret existence in a world of never-ending troubles. Suffering was a way of comprehending the import of grief and prayer, of sin and forgiveness, and of a precious particle of goodness and mercy in every life. In his last days the terrible tocsin's peal told that all on the earth are dying, that all are destined for the same end, death by vicious mischief, disease, disaster, or a broken heart.

William Madison Carter had endured long enough to be a valid witness to folly and loss. In the failing light the shades of good and bad were present in a motley mixture—Mary Lou and Nettie, his brothers Eugene and Charles, his sisters Dorothy and Ida, David McRae and Judge Pack, Earl Keeton and his imperious mother. Still absent from the ranks was the triumphant, artful Miss Keeton, the fairest and meanest phantom of all.

On January 21, 1949, at the age of eighty-one and one day past the fourteenth anniversary of Daisy Keeton's murder, Carter died. The cause of his death was recorded as "complete heart block due to myocarditia" aggravated by diabetes. In a front-page story the afternoon paper took note of his death.

The lead to the obituary reads, "W. M. Carter (William Madison) since 1907 a prominent lumberman and building material merchant here died at his home on Sixth Avenue at 2:20 Friday morning, after three years of failing health. A devoted family was with him to the end, which came after two days of gradually diminishing strength."

The hometown paper acknowledged his prominence. "The deceased was actively engaged in lumber and the building supply business that bears his name until 1945, when he retired because of ill health. . . . Styled as the W. M. Carter Lumber Company, his business grew to large proportions in Laurel and was expanded in late years, to include Carter Building and Supply Company." In the six paragraphs there is no mention whatsoever of the most salient event in his life or of his previous page-one exposure.

The at-home funeral was quiet and intimate, with friends and relatives serving as his pallbearers. Among them were the McLeod brothers, Sid and Earl, Carter's loyal employees. Some would remember Sid as his guard and companion during the flight to Mobile before Carter was arrested and would remember Earl as the plumber who came to clear Ouida's blocked water pipes the Wednesday Carter returned from Alabama.

On the brick pavement before the Carter residence the black Thompson Funeral Home hearse whispered to a halt beneath arching oaks. Between funerary sprays, the Reverend Grayson L. Tucker awaited inside before the mantelpiece, ready to commit the weary Presbyterian to his deserts. A half an hour later, after the pallbearers had lifted the casket, carried it through the front door, and slid it into the hearse, the cortege crept toward Hickory Grove Cemetery.

Facing the wintry sunrise, the tired old man was buried next to his wife, dead for fifteen years. When the earth had warmed and settled, his family laid his marker. The unadorned gravestones of Matt and Nettie Carter are identically matched in simplicity.

Did anyone inform Ouida that her fatherly friend and convicted partner in crime had died? At Whitfield, her treatment with electroshock may have erased her memories of three decades past, when she was a delectable secretary looking for a job and this bored family man of fifty was looking for refreshment and rejuvenation. Laurel would never know the real story. The complexities were too confusing to consider. Even if she had not been so deranged and had any thoughts of Carter, possibly his dying would not have mattered to Ouida. She was wholly focused on herself, a soul in limbo, yearning to go home.

■ ■ ■

An inventory of Ouida's property listed valuable assets: four Series E bonds, three with maturity values of $100 and one of $25; vacant land in Pearl River County, described as "Blocks 37 and 43, and Lots 2 and 3 in Block 38, of the D. O. Summer's Plat West, located in the town of McNeill"; a fancy ring with one crystal-white diamond of about 1½ carats in a platinum mounting set with eight small and full-cut diamonds and six small marquise diamonds; a fancy ring with a flawless central sapphire weighing about 75/100 carat, with two side diamonds weighing about 30/100 carat and twelve small full-cut diamonds in a platinum setting; a fancy ring with a sapphire-caliber center diamond weighing about one-half carat, very slightly flawed, with eighteen small diamonds (one missing); one brooch (one small diamond missing) containing one marquise diamond weighing about 38/100 carat and seventy-nine small diamonds set in platinum (the "thousand-dollar pin" she claimed Carter had given her).

Ouida's jewelry had been left in the care of one Armand L. Haynes of Oxford, Mississippi, and kept in his safety deposit box in a Jackson bank. The records are silent about why Ouida had entrusted these valuables to him. Upon Haynes's death, O. O. Robbins, administrator of his estate, refused to transfer them to Ouida, since she was legally non compos mentis. He delivered the jewelry to J. B. Howell, the chancery clerk of Lafayette County, Mississippi, for safekeeping. Howell instituted a lien of $25 for actual expenses, a fee of $25 for services, a sum of $300 in attorney's fees, and a fee of $27.80 as the cost of the chancery court proceeding. To reclaim the jewelry, Ouida's guardian, "Mrs. Eloise Flowers," was required to pay the Lafayette County court $377.80. In addition, Eloise paid her attorneys Collins & Collins of Laurel $350. The writ was filed and processed in Jones County on January 22, 1953, and Eloise placed the jewelry in a safety deposit box in Laurel.

Since the 1930s when she was page-one news, Ouida's notoriety had waned. The later reports of her admission to Parchman and of her transfer back to Whitfield were relegated to less noticeable spots in the state papers. Afterward, her case had gone to sleep as the world moved onward to new sensations. However, on July 12, 1953, with the leak about her alluring cache of diamonds and sapphires, the story of Ouida Keeton was reawakened. A dreamy reporter at the *Jackson Daily News* who got wind of the jewelry thought it merited a feature article and conceived the erroneous thought that the owner of such precious gems, actually a reticent girl who never dated or attended parties, had been a lumbertown socialite.

> The scintillating jewelry Miss Ouida Keeton wore at brilliant society balls in Laurel before she was convicted in 1935 for the murder of her mother was included recently in the corpus of the estate when the courts established a trust fund of $5,000 for her benefit.
>
> Ouida is hopelessly insane today at the State Mental Hospital at Whitfield, and the court decreed that her guardian can draw for her $100 "for necessary expenditures including special food, clothing and other necessities."
>
> She has no use for the jewels.
>
> The then young society belle . . . is in a deteriorating state.

At Whitfield, the mystery of the jewelry had been addressed in an interview Dr. W. Lawson Shackelford conducted with Ouida on October 20, 1947. Through a crack in her muddled discussion the truth of how they chanced to be in Oxford came to light.

"When you first came to this institution, do you remember whether or not you turned over to any particular party a key to a lockbox that contained your valuables?"

"Do you mean way back in '41, May '41, when Governor White was in office?"

"It was when you first came here."

"Can you give me any reason for asking me this?"

"Yes, it is because we want to protect your interests."

"Well, possibly you are talking about in the past year or so. You are not talking about way back."

"Well, I was just letting you talk, just letting you do the talking."

"Well, you see in my lifetime I have had several lock boxes."

"Now, what we are trying to establish is whether or not you know where your jewels are."

"Well, I wanted Mr. Armand L. Haynes of Oxford, Mississippi, and at that time they had a Dr. Smith, a son-in-law of Senator Bilbo's, and they were to bring my things to Parchman. Dr. Smith said, 'I will drive down there and see that they get there safe?' I had kept my jewels all the time, and I didn't know anything about going to the penitentiary. That was a surprise to me, and I didn't want to go. But Dr. Smith said, 'Don't worry about this, and I will see that you get down there safely.'"

Pleased to be out of the shadow for the moment, Ouida sparkled in the sudden spotlight of attention. She answered pertly as though to remind how she was privileged and special among the multitude of gray individuals at Whitfield. As she explained the history of her jewelry, extraneous subjects fragmented her discussion.

"They were to be delivered to you at Parchman from Oxford?"

"No, Dr. Smith was here then, and when the time came for them to come, they didn't come. A short time after that Dr. Smith was replaced. I got a letter from Dr. Smith and Mr. Haynes. They both wrote the letter together and said they were afraid to do anything at that time and that was the first time that word *opposition* was used, and they did not make the trip and did not bring my jewels, and things just rocked along, and, you know, I just thought every week they would bring them down. And, Dr. Shackelford, I have always thought that you should live your life so that you could do what should be done with courage and not be cowardly about it. And the next thing, I had a receipt from the Jackson State Bank in Jackson, and they sent me a box number, either 84 or 89. I am not sure which. But if you want to be accurate, I can look it up, for I have my receipts."

"This box was in your name?"

"No, it was in the name of Armand L. Haynes, and he kept that box with jewels in it during the entire time I was at Parchman, and when I was back here, I had a letter from him wanting to deliver me the jewels, but I didn't want him running a risk like that. In other words, I didn't like that plan of handling them, and that closed the incident of the jewels until he passed away a year ago last October in the Veterans Hospital, for in the meantime he had developed TB. And being a veteran was there. After his death, the Veterans Administration sent two of their representatives from Jackson out here to see me, and at that time I was doing some special work in Dr. McDonald's office, as his wife was sick, and they wanted to know what disposition I wanted to make of the jewels. And I told them I wanted to take them and had wanted to take them for five years. Their lawyer is Smallwood of Oxford, Mississippi, and Mr. Turnbow was with him."

"Guy Turnbow?"

"Yes, I believe it is. And Mr. Smallwood brought me my jewels and asked me if I would object to signing papers in the presence of Dr. Mitchell that I did receive the jewels, and I said 'None whatsoever.' And I told him I would come down to the office, and he was very nice about it, and we went on down there. After we got down there, we could not do a thing with Dr. Mitchell."

"What do you mean by not being able to do anything with him?"

"Well, you see Dr. Mitchell had said he was going to clear this thing up about his father, but anyway he just didn't do anything."

"Well, we seem about to get off the subject," Dr. Shakelford responded, noting symptoms of her schizophrenia in the meandering discourse.

"Well, you see, that afternoon Dr. Mitchell didn't do anything, and he said he wanted to clear up this thing about his father, and he said he felt that he was sitting in his father's chair, and he talked and talked."

"But did he witness your acceptance of the jewels?"

"I did not accept the jewels, and I said, 'I wish your father were sitting in that chair.' And we didn't arrive at anything that afternoon. I told Mr. Small-wood, for the time being, to take the jewels back, as I think he was appointed Mr. Haynes's guardian. I imagine that is what you want to know."

"Are the jewels in Oxford or in Jackson?"

"The box in Jackson was closed out, and the bank in Oxford has them."

"So far as you know, then, the jewels are in Oxford?"

"Yes, Mr. Smallwood has them. All my records are to that effect, and I feel that they are perfectly safe."

"We are just trying to protect your interests and not standing idly by and letting anything happen."

"Well, I have not worried. The time is not long, and I was just content to stay here and fulfill my mission."

■ ■ ■

A diagnostic summary of Ouida's case, entered by Dr. Peterson in September 1951, recounted all too briefly and inadequately her eleven-year history at the asylum: "This is a white female patient born in 1903 [sic], and admitted to this hospital August 29, 1944, with a history that she would stare into space and at times enter into a silly conversation. This continued until 1935 at which time it is stated that she killed her mother. She has lost approximately 50 pounds in weight and has been eating poorly, has nervous nausea and vomiting. She would have temper tantrums, pout for weeks, suspicious, sensitive, and jealous."

In this precarious mental state Ouida may not have taken note of her younger sister's death. The fetching Eloise died on Halloween 1953. For six days she had been a patient in Providence Hospital in Mobile, being treated for uremia caused by malignant hypertension. Her fourth husband and their two daughters buried her in Pine Crest Cemetery. Her age, always equivocal, was reported as forty-six. For one year Eloise had been Ouida's guardian. At her death this onus passed to Maude, but she was far removed from the immediate harm her mad sister could inflict. After ridding themselves of the Keeton house, the two survivors had fled in separate directions from the corruptive horrors of Laurel. Maude had moved to Los Angeles.

A "ward note" Dr. Pennington wrote in January 1954 states that "this patient still feels that she has lost twenty years of her life due to the mistakes of other people. She admits nothing, gets along fairly well on the ward, assists with some of the lighter ward duties, has a marked-like pigmentation over her arms, left side of her chest, and this has been coming on for about ten years. Her hair is white, but she dyes it black. Artificial dentures upper and lower. She is a patient in Cottage Two. Her weight is 114 pounds."

In 1955 she was being treated for anemia. After an interview with Ouida, Dr. Peterson reported: "This patient seems to be her usual self. She is calm, friendly, and cooperative and has thanked the ward doctor many times for restoring the privilege of having her furniture and a private room to her. The patient keeps herself well groomed and keeps a clean and orderly room. The ward doctor sees no reason why a patient in as good a condition as she is should not have as much pleasure as possible, especially since she is to spend the remainder of her days in this hospital. It also makes it easier on the attendants for the patients who are able to do so to attend to their own clothing."

By the end of the year Ouida was taking tranquilizers, identified as "Medicine 5" and "Medicine 6." She saw no difference in them. In January 1956 Dr. Pennington wrote: "This patient is getting along nicely. She says she feels relaxed since taking all of these ataraxics, but she can notice no difference in the one that she is taking at the present time." By May she was taking "Medicine 2" and was "getting along satisfactorily."

By November there was a change.

This patient was going to the dining room for the noon meal about twelve o'clock Thanksgiving Day. She suddenly felt faint and told the attendant that she was going to fall. She fell to the ground and had a hard seizure lasting about five minutes, with tonic and clonic movements of the extremities. She urinated and defecated in her clothing and became markedly discolored. When she returned to the ward, her temperature was normal, blood pressure was 100/70. This morning, 11/23/56, it was 120/70, her pulse was regular in rate and rhythm, of good quality. It is considered that this was epileptic seizure, which is common to catatonic schizophrenics. The patient says that she has had several blackout spells previous to this time. Since these spells are far apart, it was thought best not to begin any continuous anticonvulsive medication.

In January 1957 Ouida was described as having been "nervous and upset for a considerable period of time. She doesn't like to take medication." She had a red rash on her forehead, treated with Benedryl capsules and cream. An eye infection caused swelling and redness. It spread to her entire face. She became nervous and demanding, and when hospitalization was suggested, she was admitted despite her protest. "She wanted to be sent with the ambulance driver alone without a nurse. She apparently dislikes the idea of an attendant taking her any place; however, this privilege was denied since a woman should always accompany a female patient in any vehicle. She talks in a rather loud, nervous manner and is quite excitable."

She entered the general hospital on February 7 with

evidence of contact dermatitis about the face, areas of the dorsal of the hand and dorsal of the foot. It was thought this was probably due to hair dye which the patient admittedly used. However, the story is distorted. She says it has been a period of six months. This is denied by the ward personnel. Because this disease did not respond to routine supportive treatment, the patient was treated with cortisone. Her psychosis was aggravated, but soon she returned to her normal state. The lesions disappeared, and she was returned to Cottage 2.

In mid-December Ouida

had a running convulsion and ran down the hall and fell. Then she got up and went to her bedroom and fell again when she got inside of the door. She hit the wall, and there was a marked discoloration about the left eye and also a cut place on the lid. This was minor and was immediately painted with Merthiolate. The patient had difficulty for a couple of days in chewing, although there seemed to be no fracture of the jaw. The patient was unconscious, and she urinated and defecated all over her clothing. Ouida interpreted this incident to me the following morning, saying, "I slipped on a little piece of paper that was lying on the floor and struck the wall and hit my eye." She is always anxious to have her convulsive seizures attributed to something else. She denies having no insight into her general condition. She is unusually nervous several days before having a seizure, and this was true this time.

Ouida continued to reside in Cottage 2. In 1959 she was described as a "patient, aged fifty-six years, who carries the diagnosis of Dementia Praecox, Catatonic Type. . . . Patient has adjusted well to the hospital routine. She is a good worker. She helps with other patients. Physical condition is satisfactory. She is on no medication."

In September 1960 she showed "no change in her mental or physical condition during the past year. Patient does not appear to be psychotic. She is helpful with the ward work and with errands. Patient's physical condition is satisfactory. She is well nourished. Blood pressure is 120/60. She has a fibroid tumor of the uterus which does not give her any trouble. She is on no medication."

Her reports for 1961 through 1963 show little change in her behavior or treatment. She still refused to have surgery on her tumor. She was described as thin and slightly stooped. Her weight had risen to 120 pounds.

In 1965 Ouida's age was given as sixty-five. "There is a history," Dr. Nail reported,

that she brutally murdered her mother, and she apparently spent time in prison prior to coming to this hospital. She makes a good hospital adjustment, is helpful on the ward, making beds and helping with other patients. At interview today she is alert and oriented. She has apparently developed a satisfactory way of handling the guilt about her mother's death in that she completely denies it, stating that she was not guilty and it was done by some strangers. She says that she could not accept a pardon because she was not guilty of the crime. She goes on in a similar grandiose, delusional manner. She says, "It is all a big mess, and there is a lot involved." She talks about getting letters from J. Edgar Hoover and in the past having asked the F.B.I. to check over the whole case, etc. She will most likely require indefinite institutional care.

In 1968 Ouida was transferred to Cottage 3 "for administrative convenience. We are placing older patients in Cottage 3 and younger patients that we can work with more intensively in Cottage 2."

In January 1969 Ouida lost control and had "a confusional episode." She either fell or jumped into the lake in front of the administration building. She was placed in Cottage 1 for treatment. "She is now much improved and is being transferred back to her usual cottage." By the middle of the month, however, she again was "disturbed. She is being transferred to Cottage 1 for closer observation and possible shock treatments." On January 10 "this patient had an episode of extreme confusion and agitation this morning. She was seen to have fallen in a ditch near Cottage 5 and was brought to that building. She was found to be wet and very cold. She was unable to give any reliable history or reason for her behavior because of her disturbed state. She will be allowed to remain in Cottage 5 in the sick room under observation for the present time."

On October 7, 1970, Ouida was transferred from Cottage 3 to the general hospital. She had abnormal respiratory sounds in both lungs. The pelvic tumor had grown to the size of a man's head, and she had lost twelve pounds in the past sixty-five days. In the past ten she had spells of listlessness. Dr. East, new to her case, recorded that "she has a loose, productive cough, and I suspect that she is quite a heavy smoker. She does sell cigarettes to other

patients, and keeps a good supply on hand at all times in her locker." He
noted that Ouida complained of a localized pain in her back. She pointed
to the spot, the center of the thoracic spine. "I note with interest, in a brief
scanning of her record, that she had this symptom, or a similar complaint
about this pain in her back, thirty years ago. She did remark that she has
had this growth in her abdomen for the past thirty years. I very strongly
suspected that this was malignant, since she had a loss of energy, a loss of
weight, and a washed-out look, and was much paler than she ordinarily is,
but on reading the record, I find that she had a fibroid, for which she refused
operation a long time ago."

Dr. East remarked further: "The communication with this patient is not
as easy as one might expect, because she has always been a pleasant, outgo-
ing type of individual, but I find it quite difficult to get her to commit herself
in a clear, distinct manner or to give an accurate history about her recent illness. She was on no medication at the time of her transfer. She has not been
in close contact with any of her relatives." He named two nieces. "But as far
as I know, she has not been visited by these nieces in a long time."

One of Ouida's diversions was a class in ceramics. In an evaluation her
teacher remarked that Ouida was "a lovely lady who liked to make pretty
things."

When Ouida was reportedly sixty-one, the tumor, by then classified as "a
calcified uterine fibroid," had begun to obstruct her ureter. A sharp pain in
her side was debilitating her normal habits, although she was able to go the
dining hall for meals. Finally, she agreed to have surgery. At long last, on
November 20, 1970, the tumor that had troubled her for more than thirty-
five years was removed. Her surgeon thought it advisable also to perform
a hysterectomy and an appendectomy. The obstructive tumor had exacerbated a kidney problem. The diagnosis showed chronic inflammation
of the pelvic lining and the kidneys, yet her recovery from the operation
was relatively easy. Then shortly before she was discharged, she suffered
an episode of psychosis, fell mute and stubborn, and refused to eat. On
the day she was discharged she was given the antidepressant Vivactel and
electroshock.

Ouida continued to deteriorate both mentally and physically. The following March she fell and broke her leg. Both the tibia and fibula were shattered,
and after a painful and prolonged convalescence, she was fitted with a leg
brace. Although she was ambulatory, she was not able to walk the distance to
the dining hall for meals. Through 1972 Ouida's diseased kidneys worsened.

After the storm. (Photo by Hunter Cole)

On October 30, 1973, she was admitted to the general hospital with severe uremia. It was to be her last illness.

On November 11, at 2:00 in the afternoon, Ouida Keeton died of pneumonia. If news of her death was whispered around Laurel, it caused scarcely a ripple. In death Ouida could claim at least one victory. She had outlived her adversary and former schoolmate Jack Deavours by fifteen years. He died in 1958.

Four of the attorneys from the two trials became in turn president of the Mississippi Bar Association—Marion W. Reily (1937), W. H. Watkins (1939), Alexander Currie (1941), and Quitman Ross (1951). The deserving Deavours never made the list. Nor did F. Burkitt Collins, although he succeeded W. J. Pack as circuit judge. Facing the bench in their courtroom, photographs of the two jurists hang together on the south wall.

In 1969, three years before Ouida lay dying at Whitfield, a dark-of-night windstorm had blown through downtown Laurel and toppled a huge water oak in front of the courthouse. Falling against the Confederate temple, it cracked the cornice and shoved the stalwart soldier off his high perch. He struck the ground and was dashed to pieces, his rifle to smithereens. His head lay in sad profile, still facing west. His feet and lower legs, stuck to their pedestal, landed upright. Lying beside them, the shocking hips and thighs were remarkably like the images of Daisy Keeton's pale limbs in the lurid crime photos. The winds had blown through the columns, and in her sanctuary room the beautiful marble lady was shielded from the chaos. Wan and mysterious, she was unfazed by the disorder, being exactly as she always had been. On the roof above her asylum lay the wreckage of the old tree.

Laurel's other downtown emblem, the iron clock once hanging high on the corner of the bank and near a window of Jack Deavours's office, was missing. Before the old bank building was demolished, the city's sentinel timepiece was brought down and dragged to the gutted Carter building a block north on Magnolia Street. Thereafter it vanished.

Even though the furor of the Legs Murder scandal died down, like a chronic, hurtful wound its memory still causes anguish. As Laurel moved forward, a number of citizens hoped the case would drift away and be let to lie, like sleeping dogs in the adage. But it did not. Ouida's gothic story, crudely and unfairly distorted, has flared every once in a while, and today it continues to haunt excitable imaginations. Macabre thoughts and stirring images still abound—of sizzling gobbets on the fireplace grate; of Ouida's frantic, early-morning drive with her mother's severed thighs resting on sheets of the *New York Times*; of the stuporous defendant displayed in her wheelchair; of embalmed body parts paraded through the courtroom; of the horrific union of beauty, adultery, money, mutilation, and insanity. These are grotesque substances for a fearsome ghost tale.

AFTERWORD

But this is not really a ghost tale. Ouida, W. M. Carter, and Daisy Keeton were not characters in fiction, but actual, living beings well known in a little southern town and vividly reported in its history. The Legs Murder case is a story of revenge, of payback, of a willing young beauty in the grip of her predator, and of the predator in the constricting coils of a madwoman. Most of the facts about them can be found in public records scattered in Laurel and Jackson. When connected with the medical reports, they recount the biography of Mississippi's own Lizzie Borden and expose lives rocked or ruined as the two cases were prosecuted. Although we know the outcome for the three principal figures, what we are most curious to learn is what really happened during the mad scene on that dreary January 20. Since Ouida was paranoid and her fanciful admissions were a jumble, no one knows for certain. But here is a possible scenario:

That night, the long-festering trouble between Daisy and her daughter came to a head and burst. There was a violent argument. In a flash of insane rage that broke the parental stranglehold, Ouida struck her bossy mother with the fire poker. Though a mortal blow, it did not kill her instantly. After helping Daisy to her bed, Ouida put her out of her misery with three gunshots. As shock and panic surged over her, she tried to erase the deed by making the corpse disappear. In a trance she dragged her heavyset victim to the bathroom and went to work with kitchen knives. When the flushing toilet and the bathtub drain proved inadequate for the disposal, she stoked the fireplace. The chunky leftovers she dumped here and there in Jones County. Afterward, she tidied up the crime scene and attempted a cover-up. Somehow she had summoned terrific energy, and after its peak she was left a total wreck.

In her many statements, the clashing accounts she gave only intensified public confusion. On the night of the murder had Carter actually entered the house through Ouida's bedroom window? Her signed confession, on which Deavours built his case, reported instead that Carter had come to sit with her and her mother before the fireplace and had struck Mrs. Keeton then.

In his credible testimony, the night watchman told of overhearing two women's tetchy outbursts as he was walking past 539 Cross Street. That was Saturday, a few hours before Daisy Keeton was killed. The next evening as he made his way to work, he again heard female voices. Yet by dusk on Sunday Mrs. Keeton was dead, and Ouida, alone in the house, was cleaning up the mess, burning bloody residue, and painting the fireplace. Although only she was at home, the watchman held to his story of the two female voices. Where was the second voice coming from? Against whom was Ouida raging? The testimony provokes a perturbing reaction. As Ouida labored, she may have been conversing with her mother's taunting voice within herself. Hearing mystery voices is a symptom of paranoid schizophrenia, and while she was confined in the Laurel hospital, at the penitentiary, and at the asylum, Ouida told her doctors she continued to commune with her mother.

This delicate young woman was crushed between a demanding parent and a pestering boss. Evidently love turned to hate, and in a mad moment she lashed out. Any daughter who slays and then dismembers her own mother is, without question, insane. In effacing the violent act, Ouida burned portions of the corpse and, in creating the illusion that Mrs. Keeton was away on a trip, tossed her mother's traveling clothes, hat, and corset into the flames. But was Daisy Keeton's death calculated? If not, why then had Ouida stolen her brother-in-law's Spanish pistol, presumed to be the fatal weapon? Was Mrs. Keeton's death murder? Was it manslaughter? In taking Ouida Keeton to trial, was justice served? The opposing psychiatrists who examined Ouida in her hospital room brought no immediate resolution to stymie the prosecution, and the case went forward. When Ouida's family came around to realizing the degree of their sister's dreadful pathology, they must have regretted blocking the initial insanity plea. Although mentally and physically frail, Ouida had a will of iron. Jack Deavours's son Bill recalls his father's comments about her savvy manipulation of facts. She was astute and quick, usually a step ahead of him in the interrogations. Though the community clamored and the state's attorneys postured, this insane woman was incompetent to stand trial. After she was confined at Whitfield, Drs. Mitchell, Schmid, and McCool had satisfaction in confirming that their original diagnosis had been correct and that Ouida was incarcerated appropriately in the care of physicians. Like the tragedy of another notable beauty from Laurel, the fragile Blanche DuBois of Tennessee Williams's *A Streetcar Named Desire*, Ouida's turbulent story ended in the asylum.

The Keeton home became an exciting landmark in local folklore, but anyone looking for the murder house today will be foiled. The entire neighborhood and its knoll are gone. Bulldozed flat and occupied by a parking lot and prefabs for small businesses, it has lost all semblance of family life. The site is approached after a drive through the viaduct beneath the railroad tracks and turning to the left as though en route to Waynesboro or Meridian. The residence, originally brown but painted white after Ouida departed, was the first house on the right just after the turn. Passing by while en route to Lake Waukaway two generations ago, teenagers would point their fingers and recall hearing the legend of a heinous murder. In that house something horrendous had happened, some debacle that changed the town. Although curious, they didn't know the exact story. It was so interconnected with living people that few parents were willing to discuss it. "You can't talk about them around here," many folks agreed, when the names of the families came up. "Everybody's kin." In the 1960s the Cross Street neighborhood was becoming run-down, and the sick oaks along the street had been removed. The Keeton house, turning into an eyesore, remained evocative of mystery and crime.

The original Carter home on Seventh Avenue was razed in the 1960s and replaced by the Kalmia Apartments. His home on Sixth, extensively remodeled, still graces the neighborhood.

The euphonious name Ouida Keeton arouses sinister associations and sometimes confusion. In my research I have found documents in which office clerks distorted the spelling of "Ouida" as "Quida" and "Weda." My earliest recollection of hearing the name dates from 1951. At the supper table one evening my elder sister reported that high school students on a field trip to Whitfield had glimpsed Ouida. "They said she is the librarian, and she has white hair." My sister's study of shorthand was mentioned within earshot of a neighbor, Lelia Mae Martin, who showed us her steno pads from years past and explained their significance. These were her original notes taken during the hours Ouida was grilled, the records Deavours claimed to have been destroyed. I was too callow to comprehend that the discerning and articulate Mrs. Martin, now deceased, had been the deputy circuit clerk who took Ouida's statements in shorthand. It was a surprise to discover in the trial transcripts the importance of Mrs. Martin's role.

In the 1960s the hush-hush of the crime stimulated my inquiries. Lavon Boyles, a family friend, was the first to mention W. M. Carter to me. "Well, of course you know who the man was!" he said, pointing in the direction of the Carter home, two blocks east. Even after thirty years, since the Legs Murder case remained a reverberating Laurel scandal, Boyles was astonished that I was naive and uninformed. When he said the name, it meant nothing to me. The phone book was chock-full of Carters.

If ever I saw W. M. Carter, I was not aware of who he was. Possibly at some moment we were within one large crowd, I a child and he an elderly man. Along with many others in our small town, we drifted anonymously through the same square mile like cars crisscrossing Laurel in the dark of night. His downtown place of business was obliterated some thirty years ago by urban renewal, but with my mind's eye I can recall his plate-glass storefront and a night light burning from the interior. The picturesque street on which he lived was a familiar scene from an automobile window. So, except from the public records and from the rumors stirred during the aftermath of his trial, I did not know him when I started writing this book. The technique by which I express my empathy for him may draw criticism. In the scene that plays back his recollection of his trial, my imagination took charge of details mentioned in the records—the flies, the mosquitoes, the heat, the foul latrine, the low-hanging upper bunk, Mr. Welborn, the jailhouse conversations—and I offered my interpretation of Mr. Carter's tragedy and filled in the blanks with plausible inferences. Like Ouida, he had crossed the divide and could never go back to the other side. I know that except in fiction a writer should not appropriate the point of view or relate the mental processes of an actual person, but for me the best way to tell Mr. Carter's story was to show him in his cell and in his bedroom as he was suffering his own ruin. In surmising his stunned reactions after the conviction and lockup, I wanted to understand him as not only as a flawed human being experiencing his first moments behind the iron door but also as an uppercrust figure in a sordid situation. One reader who critiqued the manuscript for the publisher remarked that my depiction is "completely believable and probably dead-on certainly accurate."

As the Legs Murder case evolved into legend, the public has harbored several misconceptions. One is that the white-haired Daisy Keeton was elderly. In his jailhouse interview in Jackson, Carter commented that "the old woman made good wine." Old? Not so. She was fifty-six, postmenopausal rather than geriatric, and only twenty years older than her daughter.

By mistake, the youngsters of my generation assumed the Legs victim was "Maw Keeton," notoriously known since the 1940s for her conviction of operating a house of ill repute. By no means was this person Daisy Keeton. The murdered woman had been proud and respectable.

Even with Ouida out of the limelight and put away for good, the Keetons of Laurel were not free from further scandal. Once again, in the 1940s any trace of good reputation the family might still claim was sullied. This time the malefactor was an in-law, Earl's widow. Since his death she had been sole proprietor of the Keeton Café and the rooming house. It was wartime, and south of town a base called Laurel Army Air Field united a small population of airmen and military officers. Laurel suffered a serious shortage of housing and, for lively outsiders, an absence of rousing entertainment during free hours. Annie Keeton's café across the tracks became a lure to men looking for a good time. Some of the airmen lingered there. The waitresses and the rental rooms upstairs became known for accommodation.

As a result, the city attorney instituted a charge against Annie Keeton and filed it with the Jones County circuit court. It read: "Before me, the undersigned Clerk of said City of Laurel, I, Paul G. [Polly] Swartzfager who makes oath on information and behalf that Mrs. Earl Keeton on or about 26 day of April 1943 in the City of Laurel, in said county, did unlawfully rent a room knowing or with good reason to know that it was to be used for prostitution and did unlawfully aid and abet the act of prostitution by renting said room or having reason to know that said room was to be used for the purpose of prostitution in violation of Senate bill No. 220."

Pleading not guilty, Earl's widow was tried and convicted first in justice-of-the-peace court, then in county court, and last in circuit court. After each trial she appealed. Four of her waitresses testified for the prosecution. They told of working in the café for no pay in exchange for access to rooms upstairs. In fact, they paid the proprietress a fee of one dollar each time a room was used. In her defense a former tenant served as a character witness. He testified that he had lived at the rooming house for five months before Earl was killed and had not known of any misbehavior.

Annie Keeton's conviction in circuit court on May 22, 1945, states that she

> did unlawfully keep and maintain a certain house of ill-fame there
> situate open to the public night and day for common bawdry, enticing
> thereto and harboring therein lewd women and common prostitutes

and lascivious men attracted thereto by said women. . . . It is therefore ordered by the Court that the defendant, Mrs. Earl Keeton, for such her offense be and she is hereby sentenced to serve a term of three months or ninety days in the county jail and to pay a fine of two hundred dollars and all costs of court. It is further ordered that she stand committed until said fine and costs are paid and said jail sentence served in full.

W. Joseph Pack was not present in the courtroom as her judge. In Hattiesburg, on November 13, 1939, while on the bench for the regular term of district court, Judge Pack had been felled by a stroke. He died at the age of sixty-four. Presiding at Annie Keeton's third trial in Laurel was Ouida's former attorney F. Burkitt Collins, Pack's successor.

In a last resort Annie continued to protest her conviction by petitioning the state supreme court. Her appeal was dismissed because "no constitutional question was presented to the circuit court." She stood convicted. A seamy renown was inescapable, and as the city joked about "Maw Keeton," Annie was no less fixed in Laurel history as a whorehouse madam than Ouida was stigmatized as a mad murderess.

At Whitfield, Ouida possibly had no knowledge of her sister-in-law's controversial case. It is unlikely that someone of Ouida's station had been acquainted with Annie Keeton. Because the outside world revolved far beyond the penitentiary and the asylum gates, Ouida's Parchman and Whitfield records give no indication that during the years of World War II she was fazed in any respect by reports of military combat, ration books, or shortages. Her turmoil was personal and entrenched in scheming. She was so absorbed in herself and in her rambling rationalizations that all else seemed of lesser consequence. Protesting that her conviction and sentence were all a terrible mistake, she sank ever more deeply into paranoia and denial.

There is no evidence to support another popular theory circulated around Laurel. It claimed that Carter evaded the prison sentence and let Ouida take the rap because he was powerful, influential, and upper class. Some continued to insist that he induced Ouida to kill her mother, knowing he could extort money from his protégée. His story remains haunted by this unproven rumor.

One wonders how young Ouida responded to Carter's first overtures. Was he a pincher, a fanny patter, or just a toucher? How intimate was their sex act? Two times in the courtroom he denied having had sexual intercourse with her in a New Orleans hotel. After he was released in shame, his hang-dog demeanor provoked cruel generalizations: "He was badly stung and learned a hard lesson. I'll bet he never went near another woman!" The community debated whether Ouida was a cowed and submissive employee, an elated pet, or a questing daughter who had found the arms of a long-lost father. But the ardor cooled. One wonders what killed such devotion. Possibly Ouida entertained expectations of wedlock and not just gifts and stroking. She passed a dozen years as the philanderer's confidential Girl Friday, but after she left his employ and after his wife's death in 1933, he continued to tempt her. The removal of Mrs. Carter from the story marked the approximate time Ouida's first episodes with psychosis were noticed. Perhaps jealousy over Miss Adams ignited the charge that exploded in anger, delusion, and mayhem. Because of self-destructive flaws and concealed urges, two lives went terribly wrong.

News of this local cause célèbre spread instantly via wire services. While Ouida was waiting on Cross Street to hear the appeals court's decision on her conviction, her hometown Mississippi murder story was showcased in England. In *Corpus Delicti: An Enquiry into the Various Methods by Which Famous Murderers Have Disposed of the Bodies of Their Victims* (Geoffrey Bles, 1936), David Whitelaw explained the crime as "one of the most curious cases of dismemberment. . . . There is no doubt that here was a case of a species of sex repression, for it was proved in evidence that Ouida had in her wardrobe a complete set of baby garments, also that she would at times suffer from fits of depression for weeks on end and would gaze at her own reflection in the mirror for hours together. It was proved, too, that although the girl was for ever receiving love-letters and huge boxes of expensive flowers and sweets, she herself had been the sender." Whitelaw's anthology includes not only an account Legs Murder case but also, as the frontispiece, L. M. Jones's photograph of Ouida in her wheelchair.

In August 1939, while Ouida was in treatment at Whitfield, a full-page feature by Fred Menagh, replete with a history of the crime and punishment, the photo of Ouida in her wheelchair, L. M. Jones's photo of the Keeton home, and doctored mug shots of Ouida and Mr. Carter, was syndicated in a number of newspapers across America. It told that Ouida's clouded mind blocked her memory of why she was in the asylum. "And still no one can say whether the beautiful southern matricide, who wants one last look at home, is sane or crazy." The wildly popular film version of *Gone with the Wind*, forthcoming at the time this was published, gave Menagh his hook. He titled his story "It's a Living Nightmare for the Modern Scarlett!" and asked, "Is she in real life experiencing the nightmare that Scarlett O'Hara knew only in her sleep? Scarlett, you remember, would search desperately through fog and mist for something in her dreams and awake sobbing."

In Laurel, the Legs Murder case remained a touchy subject and a painful memory, since prominent persons were involved and disgraced. In the 1960s, thirty years after the trials, I requested permission to browse coverage of the case in old city newspapers. With a frown Nell Davis, the head librarian, shamed me by saying, "We just never bring those out." In tracing the chronicle of the lumber town (*The Laurel Story*, Diamond Jubilee Souvenir Program, 1957), the local historian Walter Watkins also dodged the notorious event. He gave it two glancing sentences: "The thirties crime was a tragic case of matricide involving insanity; its lurid details made headlines all over the United States." Most recently, Anne Maddox Sanders's *Off the Record* (Author House, 2004) summarized the Legs Murder case in a roundup of exciting news covered by the *Laurel Leader-Call*.

Having been so widely reported by the Associated Press, Ouida's story popped up occasionally in pulp magazines and in syndicated articles. One of these renderings, titled "Case of the Fiery Passion" (King Features Syndicate, 1952), is a melodramatic dramatization that deviates far from fact. "Both Carter and Ouida Keeton," the narrative misstates, "viewed the severed feet, and the girl fainted. But they could not say for certain that they had belonged to Daisy Keeton. . . . The 23-year-old girl and the 60-year-old businessman had carried on a passionate love affair for months until discovered by Mrs. Keeton. When she flew into a rage and insisted that it be ended, Ouida explained, Carter had slain the mother and the two had spent days burning the body."

Wyatt Cooper's impressionistic account of the murder in *Families* (Harper and Row, 1975) is larky reminiscence. Cooper, Gloria Vanderbilt's husband and Earl Keeton's nephew by marriage, presents Ouida as "well born and enchanting." His facts, although entertaining, are off the mark:

> My mother's sister was married to Ouida's brother. The Keetons were people of substantial means, and there, I believe, the trouble began. Ouida, who was, in my judgment, extremely pretty, charming, and friendly, got into a dispute with her mother over a large sum of money and the whole matter was about to become public knowledge. Mrs. Keeton, in any case, had never been easy to get along with, so Ouida (with the assistance of another person who was never named) shot her mother

one night, sawed her up into sections, and disposed of the body—Mrs.
Keeton was not a small woman—in several imaginative ways. . . . It was
all very shocking and hard to believe and it stayed in the newspapers
for a long time. . . . The trial was sensational, and it was decided that
the best thing to do—Southerners don't like to execute ladies if they
can possibly avoid it, especially not ladies of Ouida's class—was just to
declare her insane and send her to Whitfield.

Aside from these and the extensive newspaper reportage, very little discussion of the case has been published. The public records remain the best
accessible resource for research and snooping. In the circuit clerk's office of
the Jones County courthouse, the minutes and the docket books document
the progression of the case through the courts. The evidence files, brim-
ming with subpoenas, hotel records, Carter's sales pad and invoices, plats
of floor plans, receipts of Carter's purchases of gasoline at McRae's Service
Station, depositions, a photostat of "Learn Hotel Business," and photographs
of body parts, remain enticing, despite having been pilfered. The transcripts
of the two trials, meticulously prepared by Hattie Belle Stevens, are generally intact, though approximately one-third of the Keeton pages are missing.
However, the events detailed in the lost section can be reconstructed from
the coverage in the Laurel newspaper, whose reporters and shorthand stenographer were present at the trials. Mrs. Stevens's immense assignment of
preparing the transcripts was so onerous that the court extended her deadline. She prepared multiple copies, one for the circuit court and duplicates
for the appeals court judges. The total pages in each trial's transcript ran
to nearly two thousand 8½-by-14-inch sheets of paper. After the appeals
court's decisions were announced, its copies were shelved for reference in
the state law library and some years thereafter deposited at the Mississippi
Department of Archives and History. The court's Keeton transcript has been
lost, but Carter's is complete and accessible. Mrs. Stevens ploughed straight
through the trials and showed no breaks except as indicated by dialogue or
by the court's instruction. Although Carter suffered from incontinence, her
record does not signal recesses for restroom breaks. In bringing attention to
his remarkable stamina, the prosecuting attorneys cast doubt on the grave-
ness of his ailment.

Since the transcripts are voluminous in pagination and in legal palaver,
and since the same witnesses, for the most part, took the stand in both trials, I compressed testimonies and attempted to reduce repetition without

blocking the flow or erasing entertaining drama. The bustle in the teeming courtroom and the grandstanding of eager witnesses lifted the theatrics of the scandal to a higher pitch. As Carter's trial was winding down, a trio of late bloomers—carpenters constructing a lunchroom in a schoolhouse beside the road to Corinth Church—surfaced for the prosecution. The district attorney brought them in testify to having seen Carter passing them in his coupe at the very hour Ouida was depositing the bundle on the lonely trail a few miles away. Seated beside Carter, they claimed, was an unknown woman. Carter, of course, was in Alabama that morning, but Currie's closing argument pointed out that Mobile was only three hours away and that Carter's companion possibly had been Miss Adams.

At the courthouse in Laurel bound issues of the *Laurel Leader-Call* are shelved in the basement of the chancery clerk's offices, but the brittle, much-read pages reporting the Legs Murder case have been torn and vandalized. The state archives preserves the Laurel newspaper on microfilm, but the issues reporting the Keeton trial are omitted. Strange to say, these exact pages surface in the historical newspaper collection on the Web site Ancestry.com, which also publishes W. M. Carter's genealogy.

I mined all these materials, but without human help and advice I would have been a much less successful sleuth. I am grateful to all who assisted me in amassing the facts of this tragic story. I spent more than a year of research in Laurel, Jackson, and Hattiesburg. In Laurel, I rambled alone and unobserved to the key sites associated with the crime, now much denatured by time and renovation. Because she helped me get started, I first must thank Concetta Scott Brooks, who has a deep interest in the case. She guided me through the maze of Jones County records in the offices of the circuit clerk and the chancery clerk and gave me a tour of the courtroom in which the trials were conducted more than seventy years ago. It has been remodeled, the balcony has been removed, and the blocked skylight no longer admits sunshine and is now mere decoration. Together we counted the marble steps of the staircase that Ouida and her wheelchair traveled up and down for her long days in court.

I am grateful to the Honorable John S. Grant III, judge of the chancery court, Rankin County, Mississippi, for opening Ouida Keeton's files at the Mississippi State Hospital to me and for encouraging my research; to W. Welborn Johnson, special assistant attorney general, Mississippi Department of Mental Health, for coming to chambers to advise Chancellor Grant that the Department of Mental Health had no objections to releasing the Keeton records to me and for offering to deliver the court order to Whitfield; and to Mary Crossman, director of the Health Records Management Department at the Mississippi State Hospital, for providing photocopies of Ouida Keeton's file. I thank also my attorney Clay Pedigo, who advised and instructed me in legal matters.

I give thanks to Clara Joorfetz at the Mississippi State Law Library for locating Keeton and Carter supreme court records and for her infectious interest; to Ann Webster, D'Niecechsi Layton, Nancy Bounds, Grady Howell, Clinton Bagley, Susan Johnson, Joyce Dixon-Lawton, and Jean Hudspeth at the Mississippi Department of Archives and History for helping me find death certificates, marriage licenses, trial transcripts, maps of 1930s highways, and significant Parchman and Whitfield records; to Susan Blakeney, genealogy librarian, Laurel Jones County Library, for opening her collection of Legs Murder case documents to me and for use of Laurel's city and cemetery directories; to Barbara Odom for assistance in locating Ouida Keeton's school records; to Barbara Goff, M.D., for information about paranoid schizophrenia and its treatment; to Kathy Denton, community affairs coordinator, Public Relations Department at the Mississippi State Hospital at Whitfield, who gave me a tour of the museum and old treatment rooms and provided historical facts about the hospital during the years Ouida Keeton was a patient there; to Joan and Jim Sentilles for their lasting encouragement and for photographs of the Keeton graves in McNeill, Mississippi; to Tracy Carr of the Mississippi State Library Commission for discussing the case with me and for sharing her keen insights; to Bill Pitts for preparing the map of old Laurel and the diagrams of floor plans of the Keeton and Carter homes; to JoAnne Prichard Morris, Alfreda Spell, Chrissy Wilson, Anne Stascavage, Virginia Spencer Carr, Leila Salisbury, Noel Polk, Will Lippincott, and the attorney Larry Schimmell for critical readings of the manuscript; and, for motivation and inspiration, to Sarah Portis, Martha Rester, Seetha Srinivasan, Johanna Grimes, Louis J. Lyell, Steve Yates, Peggy Whitman Prenshaw, Jimmy Bass, Carol Caver, Sandra Harpole, Virginia Turman Newman, John Eudy, Nancy Ellzey Eudy, Dean Faulkner Wells, Lawrence Wells, Lucius Lampton, Mary Carol Burnett, Susan K. Garrett, Tommy Goza, Linda Goza, Gwen Burton, Max R. Evans, John Ferrone, Brenda Currin, Eudora Welty, Elizabeth Spencer, Charles East, and Martha Evelyn Walters.

I thank Bill Deavours for the photograph of his father; Chris Zimmerman, publisher of the *Laurel Leader-Call,* for permission to include the newspaper's Legs Murder case images in this book; Dan Davis, managing editor of the *Hattiesburg American* for permission to include the photograph of Alexander Currie; Ronnie Agnew, executive editor of the *Jackson Clarion-Ledger* for permission to include the photo of Ouida Keeton being taken into the Laurel courthouse; and to Tammy Yates of the *Clarion-Ledger* for advice and assistance.

I am grateful to the late Mark Therrell, the father of a friend in Laurel. In 1967, even though I was aware of risks in my broaching the subject of Ouida Keeton, he and I fell into long conversations about her. Only when reading the trial transcripts did I discover that his brother was Walton Therrell, the Keetons' neighbor across the driveway. Mark Therrell, a quiet gentleman who did not gossip, answered my questions and shaded them with reserve. Was Ouida red-headed? "Oh, no, a brunette." Was she beautiful? "She was." He recalled that admiring men were easily smitten by her good looks. He recounted a little event that I think is a crystallized vignette of what has gone before in this book: Ouida came into the car agency where Mr. Therrell was employed. A Willis Knight automobile struck her eye. She was alone, and a few salesmen began to flirt with her. "Then Old Man Carter arrived, and everything quietened down." Mr. Therrell described Carter as being highly protective of Ouida and told of his brooking no interference from attentive males. His answers to my questions conveyed Carter's aura of prominence and influence, and he shook his head over Carter's deep stain and downfall.

Many a moralist has pronounced that a fallen man himself has sown the seeds of his destruction and that innate flaws of character bring him down. Unpunished peccadilloes are easy for the sinner to repeat, amplify, and forgive. Yet who can see such errors clearly until the iron grip of retribution takes hold? So what really happened? How deeply was W. M. Carter involved in the murder? During my study of the crime, the trials, and the aftermath, I came to believe that except for risky behavior, poor decisions, and venial sins, he was a guiltless man on whom Ouida projected her own emotional moods and then blamed him for what she had done herself.

From the circumstantial evidence she stirred up, Laurel presumed Carter was guilty. His jury did the same. But a timetable from 1:30 a.m. to 5:30 a.m. on the date of the homicide raises doubt. He would have had no more than three and a half to four hours to enter Ouida's room, commit the murder, deal with Ouida's hysterics, load Mrs. Keeton's large body into his sedan, take it away and carve it up, discard the pieces somewhere in Jones County, return to Cross Street with the thighs and buttocks and demand that Ouida dispose of them, and then, after bundling the body parts in sugar sacks, stow them in her car without arousing the guard dog or the family next door. Gossips speculated that he dropped portions of Mrs. Keeton's corpse in woods or waterways along the highway to Mobile. The weakness in Carter's alibi for the crucial period is that it was supported mainly by family witnesses. Such testimonies can be questionable. Why was Mr. Price, an outsider, not brought to the stand? He could have testified whether the Pontiac was present or absent when he left the Carter home at 3:30 a.m. to deliver the Sunday morning newspaper.

I was acquainted with so many who had known and observed Ouida and Carter that I regret having begun this book too late to interview some of them. Most, like Mrs. Martin, were deceased or were too old to remember the story. Years ago, a favorite teacher, Ellen Steele Satterfield, did not care to answer my questions about the case. She had attended a Saturday session of Ouida's trial, and her only response to my query was quick and final: "I think Ouida was drugged." Bertie Belle Cook, another of my teachers, a Keeton neighbor, and a childhood friend of Ouida's, could have given a valuable interview, although I am aware that she, like most Laurelites, was reluctant to speak. But the horrible past would not stay buried. In its day and long thereafter as the legend grew, the evocative mystery of the Legs Murder case was heightened by jokes, hearsay, hushed reports, misinformation, and the delicious rumor of ax marks on the Keetons' bathtub. Thrilled by the butchery and by the wreckage of personal reputations, the public regarded the two trials as a Roman holiday.

And how should we interpret the strange events in this story? Perhaps in the manner of Chief Brown. Whether a mortal is a saint or a sinner, this sagacious lawman had learned that personal motives and human quirks are exposed in behavior. That those who judge and indict must be not only practical and efficient but also wise. That the mystery of life is unpredictable and uncontrollable. That a mass of data is not necessarily truth. That in criminal investigation things exist only in context. That facts cannot explain impulse, coincidence, and simultaneity. That the complicated story of Ouida Keeton and William Madison Carter, so highly charged by contradictions and by the ambiguities of love, crime, punishment, and vengeance, deserves fair examination, a just recounting of the murder, the enormity, and the shame. I hope I have told it that way.

(Photo by Jim Sentilles)

After Daisy Keeton's butchered remains were interred in the McNeill cemetery, a plain block of gray marble marked her grave. It identifies the deceased as "Daisy McKinstry Keeton." However, in chiseling her dates incorrectly as "1897–1935," the stonemason intensified the familial disorder as though to spite her recalcitrant children. He transposed the last two digits of Daisy's birth year (she was born in 1879) and made the mother, recalled by her family as "a stubborn woman," appear to be only two years older than the most phenomenal of her daughters.

No obituary announcing Ouida's death appeared in Laurel or Jackson. In fact, her funeral was so unceremonious that no newspaper noted that this star of the Grand Guignol crime story in Mississippi history had slipped quietly away. And where is she buried? It still is assumed that she lies in the patients' graveyard at the State Hospital. But this is not so. Except in the confidential files at Whitfield, in the state registry of deaths, and in the account books at McDonald Funeral Home in Pearl River County, Ouida's demise left a blank in the record. Her mystery and the vexing, unanswerable questions "Was Mr. Carter really the murderer?" and "What did Ouida do with the rest of her mother?" were left in quandary. Truly, this persecuted woman was laid to rest in troubled peace and eerie silence.

By 1973 a fresh generation of reporters were staffing Mississippi newspapers. Since to them Ouida Keeton, by and large, was unknown or forgotten, some newshound missed a once-in-a-lifetime thrill—the coup of penning the definitive headline marking the end of the enigmatic Ouida. Although belated, here's my attempt to redress that oversight:

Mad Murderess
Buried Beside Legs
Of Mutilated Mother

—Hunter Cole
Cole Ridge Farm, 2009

POSTSCRIPT

Lurid and macabre, the "Legs Murder Case" claimed the attention, not only of Mississippi but of the whole nation and beyond. Why would a beautiful young woman, well-to-do, and devotedly living with her mother, take up a poker one winter night and hit her over the head? The blow was not lethal, so Ouida Keeton shot her. What to do next but chop her up and burn her? Some remaining parts (legs) she dumped on a country road, where a rabbit hunter with dogs immediately found them. Was she insane? The trial proved nothing of the sort. She was clever enough to condemn W. M. Carter—her constant admirer, helper, father figure, possible lover—as the killer, though he was certainly elsewhere. Three doomed figures emerge—the mother, the girl, the admirer. All are ruined, for the time is 1935, and forensic evidence must wait decades to be of use. And speculation, small town gossip, theories without number emerge and still may circulate. Many accounts have been written, none accurate.

By careful research, leaving no detail unexplored, no stone unturned, Hunter Cole has reconstructed the entire sequence of the murder from start to finish. The reader becomes like the jury, hearing, seeing, judging. After this conclusive report, no guesses could remain as to what exactly took place.

But questions will still linger. We remember Fall River, Massachusetts, and another young spinster, named Lizzie Borden. The drive to freedom lives in the spirit, often hidden beneath respectable behavior, but powerful, seeking an outlet. And side by side, equally powerful, the sexual urge lives in the flesh. Another young woman might turn to art—writing, singing, painting. Another might run away, or marry an unlikely stranger. But with some the violent impulses explode and turn her into another person. Both Ouida and Lizzie claim innocence. Ouida puts the blame on Carter.

Another query: why do such cases fascinate us? The Borden case has been dramatized, written about, discussed, and explored in every way for all these years since 1892. In the same way, Hunter Cole's present book will both attract and draw the reader into its compelling whirlpool of horror.

—Elizabeth Spencer

CHRONOLOGY

1935

January 19 (Saturday) In the afternoon W. M. Carter converses with Ouida Keeton when he buys gasoline at McRae's Service Station. Around six o'clock, he closes his store, goes to his barber's for a shave and a haircut, visits family members, and heads home for the night. Although Ouida claims that he stopped by her house at 6:00 to deliver ice cream, he states that he did so on the day before.

January 19–20 (Saturday–Sunday) After midnight Daisy Keeton is murdered and mutilated.

January 20 (Sunday) Around dawn Carter leaves for Mobile secretly to see Harriet Adams.

January 21 (Monday) Soon after 8:00 a.m. Ouida abandons a swaddled bundle in the woods north of Laurel. Around noon Dan Evans Jr. discovers it. The temperature plummets, and a heavy snow covers Jones County. Carter drives from Mobile to Evergreen on family business.

January 23 (Wednesday) Carter, returning home, stops by to see Ouida. They sit in his car talking. When brought to light and debated in court, the topics of their conversation will help decide what may have happened the night of January 19–20.

January 25 (Friday) Ouida is arrested, and toward evening after lengthy interrogation she accuses Carter of murder. He is brought in for questioning and then released.

January 26 (Saturday) Ouida is locked in the Jones County jail. Fearful of Ouida's reckless brother and of mob violence after the story breaks, Carter flees back to Mobile.

January 27 (Sunday) In her cell Ouida gives the district attorney and the police chief a new statement about the murder. No stenographer is present to record it. Carter returns to Laurel.

January 28 (Monday) Carter is arrested and for his safety is incarcerated in Hinds County. Ouida is taken to Jackson to confront him and then is jailed again in Laurel.

January 30 (Wednesday) After suffering nervous collapse, Ouida is placed in Charity Hospital.

February 1 (Friday) In her hospital room Ouida willingly submits to another interrogation by Jack Deavours and signs her statement. The document will be used to prosecute her and Carter.

February 10 (Sunday) Ouida is returned to the Jones County jail, again falls ill, and becomes mute.

February 13 (Wednesday) Ouida is transferred to Laurel General Hospital under round-the-clock guard.

February 19–20 (Tuesday–Wednesday) Ouida and Carter are arraigned.

February 27–March 12 Ouida's trial.

May 21–June 6 Carter's trial.